Tony Piper

Cambridge International AS and A level

Computer Science

Revision Guide

CAMBRIDGE
UNIVERSITY PRESS

CAMBRIDGE
UNIVERSITY PRESS

University Printing House, Cambridge CB2 8BS, United Kingdom

One Liberty Plaza, 20th Floor, New York, NY 10006, USA

477 Williamstown Road, Port Melbourne, VIC 3207, Australia

4843/24, 2nd Floor, Ansari Road, Daryaganj, Delhi – 110002, India

79 Anson Road, #06–04/06, Singapore 079906

Cambridge University Press is part of the University of Cambridge.

It furthers the University's mission by disseminating knowledge in the pursuit of education, learning and research at the highest international levels of excellence.

www.cambridge.org
Information on this title: education.cambridge.org

First published 2016

20 19 18 17 16 15 14 13 12 11 10 9 8 7 6 5 4 3

Printed in the United Kingdom by Latimer Trend

A catalogue record for this publication is available from the British Library

ISBN 9781107547544 Paperback

Cambridge University Press has no responsibility for the persistence or accuracy of URLs for external or third-party internet websites referred to in this publication, and does not guarantee that any content on such websites is, or will remain, accurate or appropriate. Information regarding prices, travel timetables, and other factual information given in this work is correct at the time of first printing but Cambridge University Press does not guarantee the accuracy of such information thereafter.

....

The past paper questions used are reproduced with the permission of Cambridge International Examinations.

All other examination-style questions and comments that appear in this book were written by the author.

Cambridge International Examinations bears no responsibility for the example answers to questions taken from its past question papers which are contained in this publication.

Contents

Revision guidelines

Revision, by the nature of the word, implies re-visiting content and topics that you have studied throughout the year. What you already have in terms of resources to help you with your revision will largely determine the way in which you set about and plan your revision programme.

Key issues include:

- Have you got a copy of the textbook you have followed throughout your course?
- Did you use it as your course progressed to make your own notes?
- Has your teacher provided you with notes as each topic has been covered?
- Have you worked through worksheets prepared by your teacher?

All of these are a good starting point and your first revision task is to gather together all the materials you have produced and accumulated throughout the course. Organise them in the same way as the 9608 syllabus, that is, by section and subsection.

When should I start revising?

Start as early as possible. Examinations are generally a stressful time and so you need to do everything possible to make this a 'stress-free' experience.

A trawl through all the materials you have should establish:

- what topics you have clear notes for and where you do not
- topics where you can do lots of practice, for example, the number systems content in Part 1, 1.01
- topics about which you are definitely confident
- topics that you are not confident with – you probably 'put it off' when the content was covered in lessons.

Preparing for examination

You must not have large gaps in your understanding and you need the skills to apply your knowledge. Both are important. The trend generally for all advanced level examinations is away from questions which only ask you to reproduce basic knowledge, for example giving a basic definition. For a question about database design a knowledge question could be 'State what is meant by a primary key and a foreign key'. However, it is a much better assessment of your ability if you are able to apply this to a given simple practical scenario. The question style you are more likely to face is:

1 Which attribute would be the primary key for table X?

2 How is the relationship formed using a foreign key to table Y?

Computing is a practical subject – probably second only to engineering – and so it is reasonable that your computing examination papers should reflect this, with questions that require answers which apply your knowledge in the context of practical scenarios.

Past examination paper questions

Looking at as many previous questions as possible can be a very valuable part of revision. Many examples from Cambridge past papers have been carefully selected and included at the end of each section in the course textbook. (Cambridge International Examinations bears no responsibility for the example answers to questions taken from its past question papers which are contained in this publication.)

Your teacher will be able to supply you with further past papers and specimen papers and guide you to relevant questions for the topic you are revising.

So, you've trawled through and organised the materials you have produced throughout the course – what next?

Specific revision materials

Cambridge International AS and A Level Computing Revision Guide

This book should provide you with a helpful structure to plan your revision around. The organisation of this guide is similar to the course textbook and it has frequent 'test yourself' questions as you work through each chapter.

Revision cards

These are a favourite with students and have the obvious advantage that you can carry them around with you and dip into them in any odd five minutes you can find. Cards are available in different colours and so you could easily develop a system to code cards on the same general topic in the same colour.

The figures below are for Chapter 8, on databases:

> **Database design**   **Card 1 (of 10)**
>
> **Attribute** – Data item recorded as part of a database design.
> **Entity** – In database design, something about which we record data, for example, a Customer. Entities are implemented as tables.
> **Primary key** – An attribute (or combination of attributes) chosen to ensure that all the records in a table are unique.
> **Relationship** – A link between two tables, which can be:
> * One-to-one – uncommon
> * One-to-many – the most common
> * Many-to-many – cannot be implemented with relational database software

> **Database design**   **Card 2 (of 10)**
>
> **Foreign key** – An attribute in a table which links back to the same primary key attribute in a second table.
> **Candidate key** – Attribute(s) which are unique in a table and so are a 'candidate' to be used as the primary key.
> **Secondary key** – An attribute other than the primary key for which an index has been created.

How will you organise the cards?

* a separate set for each section
* a separate set for each topic

There are some clear links between content in, for example, Part 1 and Part 3. Assembly language is introduced in Section 1 and then studied in more depth in Part 3. Can you have a system with your revision cards which allows for this?

Mind maps

Mind maps provide an effective way to break the content down into manageable amounts and if you are a person who 'thinks visually' then you will probably take to mind-mapping. My experience is that students tend to be polarised into 'I like using them' or 'I hate them' but I have found that students do agree they are a useful revision tool. A simple example for (some of) the database content for Chapter 8 is shown below:

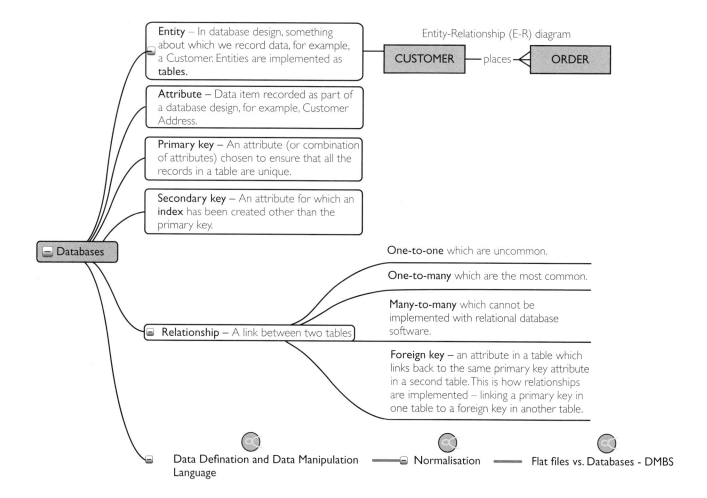

Also there is available on the World Wide Web free mind-mapping software and this usually has features which are very appropriate for revision:

- the expansion of branches (to see detail)
- the collapsing of branches (to see the 'big picture')
- the inclusion of graphics.

How do I revise?

What time of day?

There are all sorts of conflicting evidence about when your brain is at its most receptive! You will need to decide what time of day seems to work best for you and how long each session should be.

Shall I revise on my own?

Maybe, but it will be much less daunting if you team up with a fellow student – a 'revision buddy' – and revise together. This could include:

- sharing the work of producing the revision cards or mind maps
- testing each other on some basic definitions and the factual knowledge of a topic.

I do lots of past examination questions

Consider carefully what 'doing examination questions' actually means for you. It is tempting to look at a question then, talking to yourself, recite the answer you would give – then move on to another question. That might be sufficient but, remember, the examination is a written paper; why not spend the extra time in writing out the answer on rough paper? That way when you read it back it may be clear that there are some points which you have omitted or some points where the meaning is unclear.

Seek advice

You need to be confident with all the syllabus content (remember, there is no choice of questions) so don't try to bury problems and topic areas about which you are unsure. Your revision buddy may be confident about it and after five minutes of him or her talking it through, something about which you have been unclear for six months, may become clear for the first time. Failing that, be honest that you are unsure and seek help from your teacher. Problems do not go away and solve themselves – you must be pro-active in plugging the gaps in your knowledge and understanding.

On the day – examination technique

Reading the paper

It is sensible to read the entire paper before you start to attempt any of the questions. This will give you a good idea as to the questions you are confident about and those which may need more time spent on them. The number of marks is a good indicator of how long you should spend on each question. Get used to planning how you will divide your time for questions through an examination paper using the marks as a guide. It is a good idea to read back through your answers once you finish.

Layout of the paper

Where questions are displayed in an answer booklet, the amount of space provided is an indicator of the length of answer the examiner is expecting.

Is it important to answer the questions in a paper in order? No, you can answer the questions in any order. As a general rule questions which are considered less demanding will be at the start of the paper.

Understanding the question command words

Some questions will have a short introduction (called the 'stem' of the question) and this will apply to all parts of the questions which follow. Specific questions will each have a keyword which is the indicator as to the style of answer expected.

Questions starting 'Define ...', 'State ...','Give ...' or 'Name ...' all require an answer of only one or a few words giving a short and concise answer.

For example:

Give the attributes for the Loan table below, showing the primary key.

You should not create a `LoanID` for this table.

`Loan (.............., ............., .............., .............)` [2]

A question starting 'Describe ...' wants more detail. The indicator of precisely how much detail is the number of marks for the question: a three-mark question will usually require three different points to be made.

For example:

Describe how an assembly language program is translated into machine code. [2]

A question starting 'Explain ...' wants not only a description but an answer that contains some reasoning.

For example:

Explain why an interpreter has better diagnostics features than compiler software. [2]

A sample examination question is shown below:

(a) State what is meant by a real-time application.

There is no introductory statement.
The keyword is 'State' and what is wanted is the basic 'bookwork' definition of a real-time system. [1]

(b) An air conditioning system is a real-time application.
Explain how sensors and actuators are used to control an air-conditioning system in an apartment.

The introductory statement applies to part (b) only
The keyword is 'Explain' and there are four marks.
The answer must make at least four clear points describing how a temperature sensor sends data values to the processor and how they are processed when an actuator is involved. [4]

(c) Give **one other** example of a real-time application. Justify why your choice is a real-time application.
Example:

Justification:

The keyword is 'Give' but you are having to be more resourceful and come up with your own example of a real-time system.
The key requirements are the example and its justification. The paper makes it clear how you are to present them. You can assume there will be one mark for the example and one mark for the justification. [2]

Cambridge International AS and A Level Computing 9691 Paper 31 Q4, June 2011

PART I

THEORY FUNDAMENTALS

Chapter 1

Information representation

Revision objectives

By the end of the chapter you should be able to:

- [ ] show understanding of the basis of different number systems; use the binary, denary and hexadecimal number systems; and convert a number from one number system to another

- [ ] express a positive or negative integer in two's complement form

- [ ] show understanding of, and be able to represent, character data in its internal binary form

- [ ] express a denary number in binary coded decimal (BCD) and vice versa and describe practical applications where BCD is used

- [ ] show understanding of how data for a bitmapped image is encoded

- [ ] use the terminology associated with bitmaps: pixel, file header, image resolution, screen resolution

- [ ] perform calculations estimating the file size for bitmapped images of different resolutions

- [ ] show understanding of how data for a vector graphic is represented and encoded

- [ ] use the terminology associated with vector graphics: drawing object, property and drawing list

- [ ] show understanding of how typical features found in bitmapped and vector graphics software are used in practice and are therefore appropriate for a given task

- [ ] show understanding of how sound is represented and encoded

- [ ] use the associated terminology: sampling, sampling rate, sampling resolution

- [ ] show understanding of how file sizes depend on sampling rate and sampling resolution

- [ ] show understanding of how typical features found in sound-editing software are used in practice

- [ ] show understanding of the characteristics of video streams: frame rate (frames/second); interlaced and progressive encoding; video interframe compression algorithms and spatial and temporal redundancy; multimedia container formats

- [ ] show understanding of how digital data can be compressed, using 'lossless' (including run-length encoding, RLE) or 'lossy' techniques.

1.01 Number representation

We present any denary number with some combination of the digits 0, 1, 2, 3, 4, ..., 8 and 9.

Any number system is founded on the concepts of:

- a base

- that digits in certain positions each have a place value

- the number of possible digits used is the base.

Denary system

We were taught to use the **denary** (or **decimal**) numbering system – that is, using base 10 with possible digits 0, 1, 2, ..., 8 and 9.

> **TERMS**
>
> **denary (decimal):** numbering system using base 10 with possible digits 0, 1, 2, ..., 8 and 9
>
> **binary:** numbering system using base 2

Binary system

The base 2 numbering (**binary**) system has possible digits 0 and 1.

This can be summarised as shown in Table 1.01.

System	Base	Possible digits	Place values				
denary	10	0, 1, 2, 3, 4, 5, 6, 7, 8, 9	etc.	10^3	10^2	10^1	Units
				8	7	2	6
binary	2	0, 1	etc.	2^3	2^2	2^1	Unit
				1	0	1	1

Table 1.01 Denary and binary numbering systems

Intuitively we would read the denary number as "eight thousand, seven hundred and twenty six".

Appreciate that it is based on the place-value concept that we have:

$$(8 \times 1000) + (7 \times 100) + (2 \times 10) + 6 = 8726$$

Applying the same method to the binary pattern 10111, computes the pattern as binary number:

$$(1 \times 16) + (0 \times 8) + (1 \times 4) + (1 \times 2) + 1 = 23$$

Hexadecimal system

The base 16 numbering system can be summarised as shown in Table 1.02.

System	Base	Possible digits	Place values				
hexadecimal	16	0, 1, 2, 3, 4, 5, 6, 7, 8, 9, ~~10, 11, 12, 13, 14, 15~~ A, B, C, D, E, F	etc.	16^3	16^2	16^1	Units
					1	B	5

Table 1.02 Hexadecimal numbering system

The Hexadecimal numbering system follows our three basic rules.

Since the 'digits' allowed in base 16 extend past 9 then we need a way to represent 10, 11, 12, 13, 14 and 15. The solution in hexadecimal is to use the characters A to F as shown.

TIP

If we did not do this, then the hexadecimal representation 13, could either be interpreted as 13 denary or $(1 \times 16) + 3 = 19$ denary.

The number shown in Table 1.02 is:

$$(1 \times 256) + (B \times 16) + 5 = 256 + 176 + 5 = 437 \text{ denary}$$

Conversion between different number presentations

We can now convert from binary to denary and vice versa and also from hexadecimal to denary and vice versa. What about conversion between binary and hexadecimal?

One approach would be to convert into denary first – but there is a more direct way.

Example:

Convert   `0011110101010100` into hexadecimal

Divide the binary into groups of four binary digits:

        `0011`   `1101`   `0101`   `0100`

Write the denary for each group

        `0011`   `1101`   `0101`   `0100`

         3   13   5   4

We can then convert each denary number to its hexadecimal equivalent:

         3   D   5   4   = `3D54` hex

The method can be used in reverse to convert from hexadecimal to binary.

Example: Convert 4AE hex to a binary number stored as two bytes.

Hexadecimal:	4	A	E
Denary:	4	10	14
Binary:	0100	1010	1110

'Stored as two bytes' means this number will be stored as 16-bit binary pattern as shown in Figure 1.01.

0	0	0	0	0	1	0	0	1	0	1	0	1	1	1	0

Figure 1.01 A binary number stored as two bytes

Note the need to pack out the leftmost group of four bits with zero bits.

Numbers in the computer

All data in the computer must be represented in binary form.

Consider a single byte used to represent a positive integer.

- the most significant bit position has place value of 128
- the least significant position has place value of a 'unit', that is 0 or 1.

Progress check 1.01

1   What positive integer is this?

0	1	1	0	0	1	1	1

2   A positive integer is represented using a single byte. What is the denary value?

   a 0100 0001   **b** 1010 1010   **c** 1111 1111

3   What is the eight-bit binary representation for these integers?

   a 3   **b** 89   **c** 257

4   Convert these hexadecimal numbers to denary:

   a 1A   **b** 10B

5   Convert these hexadecimal numbers to 12-bit binary representations:

   a 7D   **b** 196   **c** AEC

Two's complement representation

We need to be able to represent both positive and negative integers.

One (simple) method would be to use the most significant bit to act as a 'sign' bit (1 for a negative integer and 0 for a positive integer) . This method is called 'sign and magnitude' but is not in our 9608 syllabus.

We shall use a representation – two's complement – which has a negative place value for the most significant

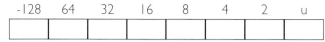

bit. For a two's complement presentation using a single byte the place values are as shown in Figure 1.02.

-128	64	32	16	8	4	2	u

Figure 1.02 Two's complement place values

Example:

Convert the following denary numbers to an eight-bit two's complement binary number.

1   56 = 32 + 16 + 8

-128	64	32	16	8	4	2	u
0	0	1	1	1	0	0	0

2   -125 = -128 + 3 = -128 + (2 + 1)

-128	64	32	16	8	4	2	u
1	0	0	0	0	0	1	1

3   -17 = -128 + 111 = -128 + (64 + 32 + 8 + 4 + 2 + 1)

-128	64	32	16	8	4	2	u
1	1	1	0	1	1	1	1

TIP

Note the method for a negative number. If its negative, we must have the '1 lot of -128' – we then need to work out what positive number to add to it.

Representing characters

All data – including characters – must be represented in main memory, saved in the backing store and processed by a program as a number value. A coding system such as ASCII or Unicode will be used.

LOOK FORWARD »

ASCII and Unicode are discussed in Chapter 10, section 10.01.

Binary-Coded Decimal (BCD)

Binary-coded decimal is a binary representation which can be used for a positive denary integer.

Each digit of the denary number is represented in sequence with a group of four binary digits.

Example: Represent the denary integer 859 in BCD.

8	5	9
1000	0101	1001

So, 859 denary is 100001011001 as a BCD representation.

Early computers stored date and time values in the BIOS of the operating system using BCD representation. Some later games consoles including Atari and Sony PlayStation did likewise. However in 2010, the PlayStation software interpreted the final two digits of the date '10' (stored in BCD) as the hexadecimal number 16. The resulting date of 2016 made the console inoperable!

1.02   Images

Bitmapped image

A bitmap graphic is a rectangular grid built up from a number of **pixels**. A pixel is the smallest addressable picture element which can be represented. The term bitmap comes from the concept that the bit patterns which make up the file are 'mapped' to an area in the main memory. Each pixel will be a particular colour. Each pixel's colour will be represented as a binary pattern. The contents of the bitmap file will be this sequence of binary colour codes.

TERMS

pixel: the smallest addressable picture element which can be represented.

There are several types of encoding and file formats for bitmap images:

* Monochrome: black and white pixels only

* 16 colour: 16 available colours for the pixels

* 256 colour: 256 possible colours

* 24-bit colour (or true colour) where millions of different colours are possible.

The encoding for each type can be worked out as shown in Table 1.03.

Bitmap encoding	Pixel representation	Explanation
Monochrome	1 bit	Only two colours needed (Black and white). One byte can store eight pixels.
16 colour	4 bits	Each byte can store two pixels.
256 colour	8 bits (1 byte)	Each byte stores one pixel.
24-bit colour	24 bits (3 bytes)	The number of different colours possible is 2^{24} (16, 777, 216).

Table 1.03 Encodings for bitmap images

TIP These calculations are an application of the study of number systems in Chapter 1, section 1.01.

In addition to the pixel data, the bitmap file will have other data stored in a file header. The header data will give the size of the bitmap (width and height measured in pixels) and the type of bitmap (encoding)

Bitmaps have the drawback that they have a large file size. If an attempt is made to over-enlarge the bitmap with -editing software the individual pixels may become visible. This is called the staircase effect. Figure 1.03 shows an image of a mouse on the left and the same image after it has been enlarged – the individual pixels can clearly be seen.

Figure 1.03 A bitmap and its enlarged version

The clarity with which a bitmap image is viewed on a monitor screen will depend on two factors:

- resolution of the image: the number of pixels per centimetre. A small image size made up from a large number of pixels will produce a sharper display.

- screen resolution: the number of pixels which can be viewed horizontally and vertically on the screen. A typical PC screen resolution is 1680 pixels × 1080 pixels. This is a key factor to consider when purchasing a monitor – what is the highest possible screen resolution?

Vector graphics

A vector graphic is made up from a number of drawing objects. A vector graphic program such as Microsoft Visio or Corel Draw comes with a vast number of different objects organised into groups or 'shape libraries'.

Objects are organised into groups of shapes – the creator has selected a straight line from the 'Connectors' group and an LCD monitor from the 'Computer' group.

Objects have properties. These properties determine the size and appearance of each object. If an object is re-sized its properties are simply recalculated.

An example could be a network topology diagram where a library of networking shapes exists containing objects for a computer, file server, printer, etc. The user could quickly construct a network topology diagram.

The advantage of vector graphics is that changing the size of any object will not affect the quantity of the drawing's appearance. That is, the objects are scalable.

Applications of bitmapped and vector graphics

Bitmapped graphics are used to:

- capture scanned images from a paper document.

- scan a photograph.

Vector graphics are used for:

- general line-drawing diagrams

- diagrams for specialist applications, such as flowcharting, object-oriented class diagrams, network topologies and any application where there is a specialist shapes library available.

A diagram using vector graphics software could be intended for inclusion in a word processor document. When completed it must be saved in one of the universally recognised file formats.

1.03 Sound

Sound is a key requirement for most software. Sound will be used for:

- sounding context-sensitive warning messages to the user

- the playback of music files, video and bit-streamed media content

- specialist applications, such as the reading of a text document to a visual impaired user.

A sound signal is an analogue signal. To be saved as data on the computer, the sound signal must be converted from an analogue to a digital signal. This will be done by some form of analogue-to-digital converter (ADC).

The sound will be sampled at a set time interval and these sample values form the binary values which form the sound file. The issues which affect the sound quality and the file size are:

- How many bits are used to encode each sampled value (the **sampling resolution**)

- How often the samples are taken, that is, how many values per second (the **sampling rate**)

The graph in Figure 1.04 illustrates the sampling rate. Samples are being taken every one millisecond; that is, 1000 samples will be taken every second.

This example used only eight bits to store each sample. Figure 1.05 shows the sampled data values stored in main memory from address 300 onwards.

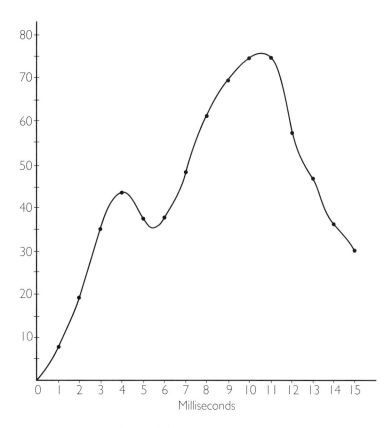

Figure 1.04 A graph of sound samples

300	301	302	303	304	305	306	307	308	309
8	20	35	44	38	38	48	61	69	75

					310	311	312	313	314
					75	57	45	36	29

Figure 1.05 Samples stored in memory

It should be apparent from Figure 1.05 that:

- If samples are taken more frequently, the quality of the sound wave will increase.

- If a larger number of bits is used to encode each sample, the sound resolution will increase.

Sound editing software is used for the recording of:

- Spoken word using a microphone

- The 'digitising' of an analogue sound source. An example could be the connection of a record turntable to the computer. The sound from a vinyl record is then recorded using the sound recording software

Editing features of the software would include:

- Cutting and pasting of sections of the recording

- Filtering out certain sounds. For example the 'clicks' on a scratched vinyl record

- Recording as a single (mono) channel or two channels (stereo)

- Normalising the recording level

- Export of the sound recording to a variety of file formats. For example MP3.

1.04 Video

Video is in widespread use on computers for recreational and educational use:

- YouTube is one of the most popular websites where users can post their own video content.

- Videos are an excellent medium for an explanation of the working of a piece of equipment or to provide a learning tutorial.

A video is a sequence of still photographic images which are displayed in sequence. The frequency with which they are displayed gives the appearance of continuous motion, and what is contained on individual frames is not apparent.

The frequency with which the frames are displayed is called the **frame rate**. A continuous effect to the human eye is achieved with a frame rate of 25 frames per second or higher.

TERMS

Frame rate: the frequency with which video frames are displayed

Progressive encoding

A system which stores the data for an entire frame and displays all the frame data at the same time is called 'progressive encoding'. This means the frame rate will be the number of pictures displayed per second. Traditional film uses progressive encoding.

Interlaced encoding

The problem is that some devices, such as a television, are not designed to display all the frame data at the same time. The data from a single frame is encoded as two separate fields; one containing the data for the even numbered rows and the second frame has the data for the odd numbered rows. The term interlaced comes from the concept that the image is rendered by switching between the even field and the odd field. It follows that the rate of picture display is twice the frame rate.

With increasing demand for the display of video content through DVD players, set-top boxes and other home electronic devices there is still a need for interlaced encoded video format files.

The picture frames that make up interlaced fields have a correct order relative to each other:

- The spatial order shows which should be the odd or even field.

- The temporal order refers to a field or frame and which field represents an earlier moment in time.

If either one or both of these orders is incorrect the result of the playback will appear as jerky motion or blurred edges to content.

1.05 Compression techniques

Both sound and video files tend to have large file size. Techniques used which encode the data in a way which results in less bytes for the file are highly desirable.

Compression is the technique of reducing the size of a file without a significant loss in the later quality in the use of the file.

Image compression techniques

Run-length encoding (RLE)

Consider a bitmapped file of a photograph where over half of the pixels are the same pixel value, representing the blue sky. An alternative to saving (say) the 300 consecutive pixel values on a row could be to save a single copy of the pixel value followed by the number of occurrences of the value (300). This way we have reduced the number of pixels used to store this portion of the graphic from 300 to a very small number.

This technique would be appropriate for a monochrome image consisting of a black line drawing on a white background. This will contain 'runs' when horizontal or vertical straight line are drawn.

Consider a 256-colour image that is 30 × 4 pixels as shown in Figure 1.06. The image has four different colours, coded as w, b, r and g.

w	w	w	w	w	w	w	w	w	b	b	w	w	b	b	b	b	g	g	g	g	w	w	w	w	w	w	w	w	w
w	w	w	w	g	g	g	g	g	b	b	b	b	b	r	r	r	r	r	r	r	w	w	w	w	w	w	w	w	w
w	w	w	w	w	w	w	w	w	w	w	w	w	w	w	w	w	r	r	r	r	r	r	r	r	w	w	w	w	w
w	w	w	w	w	w	w	w	w	w	w	w	w	w	w	w	w	w	w	w	w	w	w	w	w	w	w	w	w	w

Figure 1.06 Representation of a 30 × 4 image

The first row of pixels could be encoded: 9w2b2w4b4g9w.

Assuming each 'run number' is stored as a single byte, the first line will be stored using 14 bytes (compared to the original 30). This is a very effective compression.

Progress check 1.02
Calculate the encoded RLE for rows 2, 3, and 4 of Figure 1.06.

Lossless encoding
We now have two alternatives for encoding a bitmapped image:

- Save the colour code for every pixel.
- Use run-length encoding.

Both of these techniques mean that the original bitmap can be re-created when the data is read from the bitmap image file and displayed on the output device.

For bitmap files several of the universal file formats are lossless. These include .bmp and the Portable Network Graphics (.png) format, which was intended as a replacement for the older .gif format.

Lossy encoding
Using a 'lossy' technique for encoding bitmap data has the objective of compressing the file size.

Lossy techniques are based on two concepts which exploit the limitations of the human eye:

- An image which has a large background could encode the background pixels with a lower resolution.
- Colours such as blue, to which the human eye is less sensitive, could be encoded at a lower resolution.

The popular .jpeg file format is lossy.

Video compression techniques

Since a video is made up of a number of frames, we are interested in applying various compression techniques to a video frame or a frame sequence.

Spatial redundancy
This is the similar to the concern over 'redundancy' in a bitmap file. Is there a sequence of the same pixels within a single frame which could be encoded or effectively compressed?

Temporal redundancy
Is there a sequence of similar pixels in the same position in consecutive frames? In which case, we do not need to repeat them in each frame. It will depend entirely on the content. A room full of people disco-dancing will not compress as well as a panoramic view of a beauty spot.

Interframe coding addresses the issue of temporal redundancy. The encoding method is based on the idea of **key frames**, which store data for all the picture, and intermediary frames which store only the differences from the next intermediary frame or key frame.

File formats

Over the years standards in the computing industry have emerged for image files (we have already mentioned .BMP, .PNG, .GIF and .JPEG) and sound data. Popular sound formats include .WAV, .MPEG and .MP3.

Video – which is a combination of moving pictures and sound – requires its own industry standards. The detail about encoding methods used for this is outside the scope of our syllabus. The key issue is that there is correct synchronisation between the picture display and the accompanying sound commentary.

The current popular multimedia container formats include:

- AVI (standard Microsoft Windows container)
- MOV (standard QuickTime container)
- MP4 (standard container for MPEG-4 multimedia)
- Matroska (not standard for any codec or system, but it is an open standard).

The differences between container formats arise from issues such as:

- popularity: is the container format widely supported? This is the reason that the AVI format is still the most popular format.
- overheads: This refers to the difference in file size between two files with the same content in a different container. For a two-hour film, an AVI file may be up to 10 MB larger than a file in Matroska format.
- support for advanced codec functionality: Older formats, such as AVI, do not support new codec features, such as streaming media.

Summary

- ☐ Numbers can be written using a binary, denary or hexadecimal base.
- ☐ Two's complement is a representation which allows both positive and negative integers to be represented.
- ☐ Binary-coded decimal (BCD) is a coding system used for positive integers.
- ☐ Images can be encoded as a bitmap, made up of a rectangular grid of pixels. The file header will contain data about the image: its height, width and the type of bitmap. Bitmap resolutions are monochrome, 16 colour, 256 colour and true colour. From the resolution and the dimensions, the file size can be calculated.
- ☐ Vector graphics are constructed using drawing objects selected from shape libraries provided by the software. Each object has a set of properties which are stored as part of the vector file.
- ☐ Sound is encoded as samples taken from the analogue source with a set sampling rate. The number of bits used to encode each sample (the sampling resolution) determines the sound quality.
- ☐ Video is made up of a sequence of image frames with an accompanying sound track. The encoding can be interlaced or progressive. Various multimedia formats are used commercially. These formats may uses compression techniques to address spatial and temporal redundancy.
- ☐ Compression techniques use either 'lossy' or 'lossless'. One lossless technique is run-length encoding (RLE).

Exam-style questions

1   Binary representation is used for many different data values.

Consider the binary pattern   1010 0110

What is its value if it represents:

a   an 8-bit two's complement integer?   [1]

b   an 8-bit sign and magnitude integer?   [1]

c   a hexadecimal number?   [1]

Cambridge International AS and A Level Computing 9691 Paper 33, Q2 a Nov 2012

2   a   i   Convert the hexadecimal number 7A to denary.   [1]

ii   Convert the binary number 0101 1100 to hexadecimal.   [1]

iii Why do computer scientists often write binary numbers in hexadecimal?   [1]

b   The diagram shows a program loaded into main memory starting at memory address 7A Hex.

Address	Main memory (contents shown in Hex.)
7A	2150
7B	A351
7C	A552
7D	FFFF
90	003C

How many bits are used for each main memory location?   [1]

Cambridge International AS and A Level 9691 Paper 31, Q3 b & c (i) Nov 2013

Communications and Internet technologies

2.01　Networks

Most networks used for business applications are server based.

In a server-based network, a dedicated server provides for the administration of users, security and resources. There may be a single server which carries out all tasks.

The server is a computer which provides the administrative tools and resources which are shared by all computers on the network.

Client–server model

A client computer application will access various resources and services provide by a server.

There are many types of server, all named after the service they perform. For the most common network applications required by users, this will include:

- File server: All software and user data files could be stored on the server. Alternatively the application software can be installed on the client, then requests to the server are for data files only.

- Domain controller server: This server is used for the management of user accounts – IDs and passwords. The client computer software will send a log-on request to the server, which processes it and grants the request if the user ID and password are recognised.

- Email server: This server is used for sending, receiving and storing emails. A 'sent email' is sent to the server for processing and forwarding to the Internet Service Provider. When the client computer requests 'receiving email', the email server sends the request to the server of the email provider.

- Print server: This server manages print jobs from network client computers.

- Database server: This server manages a database management system such as mySQL or SQL Server.

- Web server: This server manages pages available from a website.

LOOK FORWARD »

Database management systems are discussed in Chapter 8.

The tasks done by a server are varied, but they all have in common:

- The client computer makes a request to the appropriate server.
- The processing of the request is carried out on the server.
- The server packages the results in a form which is displayed by the client computer's software.

The Internet and the World Wide Web

The Internet

The Internet is a global communication infrastructure which links together computers and networks.

It forms a collection of connected internets and is a packet-switched network. All network traffic is made up of packets of data with a source address and destination address. There will be a large number of available paths for the transmission of any data packet.

The communications methods used are various, including wired, radio and satellite communications.

The Internet is an open network. Access to it is provided by a company called an Internet Service Provider (ISP). The Internet protocol used is TCP/IP where all devices which connect to the Internet are identified by an IP address.

LOOK FORWARD »

IP addresses are discussed in Chapter 2, section 2.02.

The Internet is also a transit network that moves data. The Internet allows anyone to access, retrieve, process and store all manner of information (e.g. voice, video, documents, images) in a digital format.

The World Wide Web (WWW)

The World Wide Web consists of content organised as web pages made available across the Internet from web servers. The WWW was the invention of computer scientist Tim Berners-Lee in 1989 and uses three key concepts: **HyperText Markup Language (HTML)**, **Uniform Resource Identifier (URI)**, **Hypertext Transfer Protocol (HTTP)**.

TERMS

HyperText Markup Language (HTML): the publishing format for all web content; it provides for formatting documents and links to other documents or resources

Uniform Resource Identifier (URI): a unique address for a resource on the WWW

Hypertext Transfer Protocol (HTTP): a protocol to allow for the retrieval of linked resources from across the WWW

The WWW has changed the way we teach and learn, research information, buy and sell products and communicate globally with others.

TIP

The terms 'Internet' and 'World Wide Web' are loosely used and are often thought to be the same – they are not.

Hardware to support the Internet

Networks

A local area network (LAN) is made up of a set of computers which can communicate across the network. For example, a computer can communicate with a file server device, a print server or a user using email. Network users will want to use the Internet to access content available from the WWW.

Routers

A router is used on a packet-switched network. Data is organised into packets for sending between the various devices. The common protocol used is TCP/IP and the routing of packets is done by giving each packet a destination address.

LOOK FORWARD »

IP addresses are discussed in Chapter 2, section 2.02.

TCP/IP is discussed in Chapter 14.

Gateways

A gateway is the hardware device need to allow two networks which use different protocols to communicate. A network gateway can be implemented completely in software, completely in hardware, or as a combination of both.

Because a network gateway, by definition, appears at the edge of a network, related capabilities such as firewalls tend to be integrated with it. On home networks, a broadband router typically serves as the network gateway providing access to the Internet.

Servers

A list of the typical servers used by various computer systems were given earlier.

Progress check 2.01

Explain the difference between the World Wide Web and the Internet.

Communication systems to support the Internet

The Public Switched Telephone Network (PSTN)

The Public Switched Telephone Network (PSTN) was designed for two-way voice communication. The concept was to create a dedicated line or circuit between two end-points.

Over time, the telephone network has grown to support more users and end-points through a network of switches; thus the concept of circuit switching was born. This revolutionised voice communications and telephone network design, creating the PSTN architecture that is still in place today.

This established a system in which each usage of the network required a 'call setup' stage, in which a connection or circuit was established between the two end-points.

Dedicated lines

A business may prefer to use a communication line which is dedicated for use by its computers only. It will purchase a dedicated line from a telephone company under some leasing agreement. This contrasts with the shared resources of the PSTN and Internet.

Typical business uses include:

- linking corporate offices to the Internet.

- connecting the LANs of several corporate offices to form a wide area network (WAN) that allows offices to communicate and share IT resources.

Dedicated lines have major advantages which impact on the applications which are possible:

- consistent data transfer speeds.

- high and consistent bandwidth: the bandwidth available to most Internet users drops at peak times, when other customers of the same ISP are attempting to connect.

- high data throughput and fast upload speeds.

Dedicated lines offer major speed advantages compared to broadband. A UK broadband connection offers around only 12 Mb/s downstream and 1 Mb/s upstream. In contrast, a high-capacity dedicated line can provide a connection speeds of up to 10 000 Mb/s (10 Gb/s) for both uploads and downloads.

This enables a dedicated line to:

- carry phone calls

- allow lots of staff to connect simultaneously to their work computers from home

- carry video transmission without buffering and signal degradation.

Cell phone networks

The name come from the land mass being divided into areas called 'cells'. Each cell is served by at least one transceiver or base station. The cells are usually hexagonal in shape and the base station for each cell uses a different frequency range to that of any of its neighbouring cells.

The large capacity using a cellular network is made possible because the same frequency can be used:

- by multiple callers in any cell

- in non-adjacent cells.

The most common usage of a cell network is a mobile phone network which provides for communication from a portable mobile phone to the base station with radio waves. Since radio waves travel in straight lines a large land mass is divided into smaller cells, where necessary, to avoid a 'line-of-sight' signal interruption.

Radio waves have the longest wavelength and the lowest frequencies. The ability to focus a beam decreases with increasing wavelength. Radio waves broadcast in all directions and are least affected by obstacles.

Progress check 2.02

1 What do the initials PSTN stand for?

2 A business is based on a number of UK sites. List advantages to the company of using dedicated lines for all its digital communications.

Communication media

Copper cable

Copper cabling comes in different forms.

TERMS

Twisted-pair cable: a pair of copper cables, twisted together

Coaxial cable: a cable with a central single strand wire

Twisted-pair cable is a pair of copper cables, twisted together. This is designed to cancel out electromagnetic interference.

Twisted-pair cable is available in several specifications – the simplest is made up of two insulated copper wires surrounded by the external insulation. One of the Ethernet networking standards uses a cable with four twisted-pairs (called 'Cat-5') which supports a maximum cable segment length of 100 metres.

All forms of copper wiring suffer from a loss of signal strength proportional to the cable length. The shielding screen is used either as a return path for the signal or as a form of screening to eliminate forms of electro-magnetic interference.

Coaxial cable has a central single strand wire which is insulated from the outer multi-strand wire mesh braided around the central insulation. Coaxial cable is also available in a number of specifications.

The most widely used bus networking standard for the physical layer is called Ethernet. This has developed standards based on the transmission speeds called 10BASE-T (transmits at 10 Mb/s), 100BASE-TX (100 Mb/s) or 1000BASE-T (1000 Mb/s, i.e. 1 Gb/s).

LOOK FORWARD »

Protocols are discussed in Chapter 2, section 2.02.

Uses of coaxial cable include:

- connecting a radio or television receiver/sender and an aerial
- computer network connections
- cable television connections.

An advantage of coaxial cable is that the signals are unlikely to be affected by electro-magnetic interference from other metal objects in close proximity.

A bus network uses either twisted-pair or coaxial cabling.

Fibre-optic cable

Up to 24 glass strands are grouped into a single fibre-optic cable. Pulses of light are used to transmit a signal along a single strand as a modulated light beam. Because the medium for communication is light – rather than electrical signals – the data should be free of interference and also less susceptible to unauthorised access.

Fibre-optic cable has many advantages over copper wire:

- The signals will be free of any interference.
- Signals do not suffer from a loss of strength (attenuation).
- The cabling does not suffer from corrosion.

Typical applications include any form of long-distance communication including:

- telephone communication
- Internet communications
- networking.

Telecommunications and the electro-magnetic spectrum

All forms of telecommunications include some form of electro-magnetic wave, acting as the signal carrier, and a form of modulation for the signal when the carrier wave is made to change to represent different signals and hence different data.

If two humans communicate by talking, the carrier is a sound wave and the range of frequencies possible with a sound wave will limit the possible signals. The same is true for electro-magnetic communication. Each form will have a range of frequencies which are possible with corresponding benefits and drawbacks which make them suited to particular applications.

Radio waves

Radio waves have the largest range of wavelengths and include AM radio (around 400 m), television (40 m) and FM radio (around 4 m).

Radio waves are used for:

- domestic antennae receiving television signals sent from the TV broadcaster radio mast
- sending/receiving of mobile phone communications.

Microwaves

Microwaves have wavelengths measured in centimetres.

Unlike infrared and visible light, microwaves can penetrate haze, light rain and snow, clouds and smoke. For this reason, satellites which capture pictures of the earth use microwave communication.

Infrared waves

Infrared waves occupy the range of wavelengths between microwaves and visible light. The range of wavelengths varies from the size of a pin-head to the size of a cell; they are measured in a unit called a 'micron', which is one millionth of a metre.

The shorter infrared ranges are the wavelengths used for remote control signals between a controller and a device such as a television.

Satellite communication

Artificial satellites orbiting the earth provide telecommunications between the satellite and receiving/sending stations.

Applications are numerous and varied:

- satellite radio and television broadcasting
- photography of the earth
- satellite-based Internet
- satellite phones
- military communications.

Wireless

Communication can use any of the wavelengths: radio, microwave or infrared. The term 'wireless' has come to be used to describe any form of data communication which is 'without wires'.

Wi-Fi is the term for the industry standard IEEE.802.11. Wi-Fi hotspots are now popular, for example, as a way of attracting custom to a cafe.

The range of applications of wireless communication is now widespread and includes:

- communication for a local area network
- smartphones and other portable devices.

Progress check 2.03

State two advantages of using fibre-optic cabling rather than copper cable.

Bit streaming

A bitstream is a sequence of bits, representing a stream of data. The sequence of bits will be transmitted continuously over a single channel. The bits are transmitted serially, one after the other. The bits probably originated from software as a sequence of bytes and so the terms byte stream or octet are also used. The bytes could represent any form of digital data – a sequence of text characters, pixels from a picture or video clip, or a sound file.

TERMS

bitstream: a sequence of bits, representing a stream of data

Real-time bit streaming

The Sky satellite channel in the UK now has the facility to allow a subscriber to watch live television on a device such as a personal computer, tablet or smartphone.

The device needs the appropriate software or app. The communication channel will be a wireless connection for a PC, smartphone or tablet or a 3G or 4G connection for a smartphone or tablet.

The BBC in the UK provides a similar facility – called BBC iPlayer – for the viewing of (some) live television programmes and a service for listening live to its radio broadcasts.

On-demand bit streaming

Both Sky and the BBC offer the facility to 'catch up' on broadcasts that the user has missed. The user can select programmes which have already been broadcast.

The bitstream is saved to the device's secondary storage and can be watched by the user when convenient. Other providers, such as Netflix, offer a large selection of films which can be provided 'on demand'.

Issues with bit streaming

On-line forums are awash with queries about bit streaming. The most common problems are about the connectivity of various devices, the software to provide the service and the quality of the service.

The content may be subject to a pause in the delivery of the picture or sound before it resumes. The reasons for this is that the bitstream will be directed into a storage area on the device called a buffer. The data stream is processed by the viewing software and appears as a sequence of picture frames.

The factors which determine if this results in a satisfactory experience for the user are:

- Can the communication channel deliver the bitstream at a sufficiently high rate? Broadband providers suggest this requires a download speed of 3 Mb/s or higher.

- Can the software process and display the content of the buffer at a high enough speed? The two key factors here are the speed at which data is retrieved from the hard disk and the specification of the processor inside the device.

2.02 IP addressing

Using the Internet Protocol (IP), networks are joined into a network of networks through interconnected gateways or routers that use the standard protocol suite – Transmission Control Protocol/Internet Protocol (TCP/IP) for interworking.

Most Internet traffic is still using Internet Protocol version 4 for addresses. This uses 32 bits for an IP address – expressed as four numbers in the range 0–255, separated by full stops.

The original addressing for networks used the first byte for the Network ID and the other bytes for the host identifier. This quickly proved inadequate and lead to a system of defined **classes**, where a variable number of bits is used for the network identifier. The system defined five classes (A, B, C, D and E). Classes A, B and C use different bit lengths for network identification.

The Class formats impose some restrictions on the available addresses; for example, a Class C address is not allowed to use host numbers 0 or 255.

LOOK FORWARD »

The network class identifiers are discussed in Chapter 14.

The TCP/IP protocol suite is also studied in Chapter 14.

Internet traffic has no dedicated path; there is no single interconnection point or fixed network hierarchy as used by the PSTN. Individual data packets may take different routes over separate networks as they travel to their final destination to be reassembled and delivered to the requesting computer and application program. This is unlike circuit switching which relies on physical, point-to-point connections. On the Internet, data is placed in packets with an IP address for the packet's destination and an IP source address.

An IP address is a four-byte number usually written in denary, for example, 192.168.4.7. This is called the 'dotted decimal' notation. The address can also be written as 'dotted hexadecimal' or 'dotted binary'.

Internet Protocol Version 6

In 2011, the IP version 4 address space was finally exhausted – all 4 billion Version 4 IP addresses had been allocated. However, the ever-increasing number of Internet users had given concerns about 'address space exhaustion' earlier. This gave rise to a new standard, Internet Protocol Version 6 (IPv6), which was adopted for the first time in 2006.

IPv6 increases the address length to 128 bits, providing a vastly greater address space.

The immediate issue is that host devices which only recognise IPv4 addresses cannot directly communicate with IPv6-only hosts. Migration to IPv6 is in progress but completion is expected to take some considerable time.

LOOK BACK «

This is an application of the number systems studied in Chapter 1.

Progress check 2.04

1 How many bits are used to encode an IPv4 address?

2 Write the denary value for the following IP address: 11111111.10101000.00000100.00001101.

3 Explain why 259.168.7.8 cannot be a valid IP address.

Domain name service

A web browser requests a resource using the known URI. What is usually not known by the user is the matching IP address for this resource. Therefore, somewhere on the Internet, the IP address must be 'looked up' from the URL. This is the role of the Domain Name Service (DNS).

Once the IP address is known, it is the function of hardware called **routers** to route the data packets to the receiving device.

Because maintaining a central list of domain names and IP addresses mapping would be impractical, the lists of domain names and IP addresses are distributed throughout the Internet in a hierarchy of authority. The DNS database resides on a hierarchy of special database servers.

At the top level of the hierarchy, **root servers** store a complete database of Internet domain names and their corresponding IP addresses. The Internet employs 13 root servers that have become somewhat famous for their special role. Maintained by various independent agencies, the servers are aptly named A, B, C and so on up to M. Ten of these servers are sited in the United States, one in Japan, one in London and one in Stockholm.

Most lower-level DNS servers are owned by businesses or Internet Service Providers (ISPs). For example, Google maintains various DNS servers around the world for management of google.com, google.co.uk and other Google domains. Your ISP also maintains DNS servers as part of your Internet connection setup. There is probably a DNS server within close geographic proximity to your access provider that maps the domain names used in your Internet requests or forwards them to other servers in the Internet.

When a client web browser requests a resource with a URI, a piece of software called the DNS resolver (usually built into the network operating system) first contacts a DNS server to determine the server's IP address. If the DNS server does not contain the mapping, it will forward the request to a different DNS server at the next higher level in the hierarchy. Further forwarding of the request may be needed before the URI is resolved.

LOOK FORWARD »

If you are running the Windows operating system, key into a command prompt window 'ipconfig' to see all the settings on your computer for Internet access.

An IP address can be thought of as a private or public IP address. Any device on a Local Area Network will have a private (or non-routable) IP address allocated by the Network Administrator. This is sufficient if the only communication is between host devices on the LAN. If however a computer needs to access a resource using the Internet, the device needs to know the public address of the server holding the resource. Every resource on the Internet must have a globally known and unique IP address. As there is a shortage of IPv4 addresses, devices on the LAN are allocated a private IP address.

The three ranges used for private addresses are:

10.0.0.0/8
172.16.0.0/16 to 172.31.0.0/16
192.168.0.0/24 to 192.168.255.0/24

This will be a requirement for any of the devices on the LAN; they will communicate to the Internet through a proxy server and firewall which has a single public (or routable) IP address. All data packets whose destination in a device on the LAN will arrive using the LAN's public IP address. It is then the role of the proxy server to route the data to the appropriate device.

2.03 Client-side and server-side scripting

Before we start talking 'scripting' (that is 'programming'), let's get clear what the web server and the computer on which it is running must do.

The web server must be 'hosted' on a host computer. The web server uses the HTTP protocol to:

• receive request messages from client computers

• deal with each request

• send a response message back to the client.

The web server will continually listen for 'request messages' and then respond to the client computer with a 'response message'.

The host computer must have an operating system which supports the TCP/IP communications protocol. It deals with all the communications between the web server and the client.

−Requesting data from a database server

Users working with a database send requests to the server for information, as shown in Figure 2.01.

For example, a user will create and run a query which is held on the client computer. The query is turned into an SQL request which is sent to the server.

1 The client web browser application requests the page using the URI.

2 The DNS directs the request to the appropriate domain.

3 The server retrieves the page.

4 The server sends the page content, consisting of HTML tags and text content only, to the client.

5 The client web browser software 'renders' the page and displays it.

However, the content may need to change each time the page is requested; that is, the page has dynamic content. For example, a web page may display today's date or may be used for data entry.

The inclusion of dynamic content requires that the webpage contains a 'script', that is, program code, which determines some or all of the final content displayed on the page.

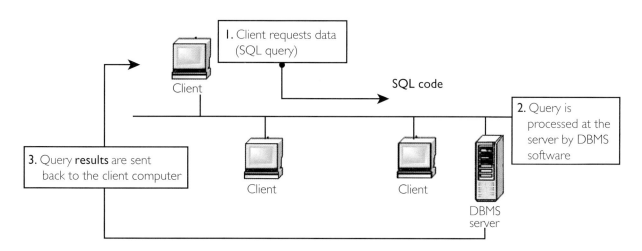

Figure 2.01 Request to a database server

The server processes the SQL request received and the results of the processing are then sent back to the client computer.

Note, all processing is done at the server.

−Requesting web pages from a web server

Web pages are constructed using the HTML markup language. This is not a programming language but – as it says – the HTML tags 'mark up' the text and graphics content to determine how it will appear to the user.

For many pages the content is only HTML tags, so the request sequence is:

Progress check 2.05

State the sequence of steps when a client web browser requests a page which contains no program code from a web server.

Client-side scripting

Using client-side scripting, the dynamic content is processed when the web page is received by the client web browser. The popular languages used for client-side programming are JavaScript (the Microsoft version is called JScript) and VBScript.

The use of client-side scripting assumes that the client web browser is configured to support this. The ability to interpret JavaScript code is a feature of all the popular web browsers – Internet Explorer, Chrome, Opera and Firefox.

JavaScript is a third-generation programming language. The code is embedded in a web page with all the HTML tags which determine the page's format and content.

All programming languages must be either compiled or interpreted. JavaScript program code statements are interpreted, either when the web page is loaded or later, in response to some event taking place (e.g. the user clicks on a button on the page).

Figure 2.02 shows an example of a web page containing JavaScript.

```
 1
 2 <html>
 3 <head>
 4 <title>LAB 1</title>
 5
 6 </head>
 7
 8 <body>
 9 This is some text
10
11 <Script Language = "JavaScript">
12 alert("First script block');
13 document.bgcolor = "RED';
14 alert("Second alert pop up');
15 </Script>
16
17 </body>
18 </html>
```

Figure 2.02 Simple JavaScript code

Study Figure 2.02 and you should be able to deduce:

• The JavaScript program statements are lines 12, 13 and 14.

• The **alert** keyword causes a dialogue box to appear to the user.

• This code uses no variables.

• This code does not contain any structures such as 'if' statements or a loop.

• The **alert** keyword causes a dialogue box to appear to the user.

TIP

You are not expected to learn JavaScript or any client-side scripting language or a server-side language such as PHP in preparation for the examination.

You should, however, be able to study a JavaScript program and understand its construction. You will need to use the skills you have learnt from Section 2 to understand some JavaScript and PHP program code: using variables, sequence, selection and iteration.

The JavaScript code in Figure 2.03 illustrates the dynamic nature of a web page. It includes the four basic high-level language constructs.

The program in Figure 2.03 produces the sequence of interactions with the user shown in Figure 2.04.

Progress check 2.06

State the sequence of steps when a client web browser requests a page which contains JavaScript program code from a web server.

JavaScript code is used for:

• interacting with the user

• accepting data input from the user

• validating data input and other actions: for example, if an important field has been left blank, we need to address this before 'posting' the data to the server for processing or storage

• manipulating images, for example, changing the image displayed when the mouse does a 'roll over' on an image.

The code in Figure 2.03 is a simple example of validation of a number entered by the user.

```
 1  <html>
 2  <head>
 3   <title> JavaScript sample</title>
 4  </head>
 5
 6  <body>
    Demonstrating a client-side JavaScript script
    Validate data entry from the user

10  <Script Language = "JavaScript">
11   alert("Get ready to input a number   ...") ;
12   var myNumber ;
13   var validNumber = "NO" ;
14   while (validNumber == "NO")
15     {
16      myNumber = prompt("Enter the number (40-50)", "") ;
17      if (isNaN(myNumber) == true)
        {
          alert("That's not a valid nu      enter
        }
       else
        {
23          validNumber = "YES" ;
24          alert("The valid number entered was " + myNumber) ;
25        }
26     }
27  </Script>
28
29  That's the JavaScript code finished ...
30  </body>
31  </html>
```

The <Script> tag marks the start of the program code at line 11

The var keyword is followed by variable identifier

The while loop starts here; there is no endwhile keyword – curly brackets are used to enclose the loop statements

The prompt keyword is used to get input from the user

The if selection statement also uses curly brackets to enclose statements

isNaN is a JavaScript built-in function which tests for 'is not a number'

The alert keyword is used to output to a dialogue box

Figure 2.03 Client-side JavaScript code

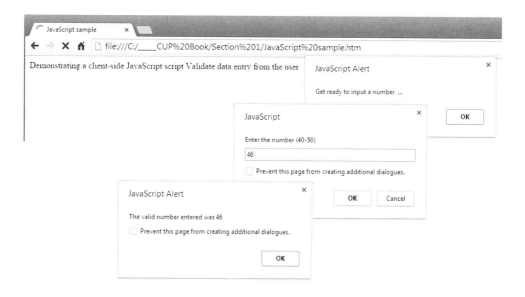

Figure 2.04 The dialogue from the code in Figure 2.03

Progress check 2.07

Study the script in Figure 2.05.

```
1   <html>
2   <head>
3    <title> JavaScript sample</title>
4   </head>
5
6   <body>
7
8   <Script Language = "JavaScript">
9
10   document.write("data entry for students exam results" + "<BR>") ;
11   document.write("Total on three papers must be > 120" + "<BR>")
12   document.write("Each paper must be > 40") ;
13   var totalMark = 0 ;
14
15   for (loopCounter = 0 ;  loopCounter < 3 ; loopCounter ++)
16     {
17      nextMark = prompt("next paper mark   ..." ) ;
18      totalMark = totalMark + parseInt(nextMark) ;
19     }
20     if (totalMark < 120)
21       {
22       alert("A resit will be required ...") ;
23       }
24     else
25       {
26       alert("You have passed") ;
27       }
28   </Script>
29
30   </body>
31   </html>
```

Figure 2.05 Sample JavaScript code

I What line number is the start of a count-controlled loop?

2 Explain how the syntax of the count-controlled loop works.

3 What line effectively marks the end of the loop?

4 What will be the output if the user keys in the sequence of numbers 39, 42, 38?

5 Which statement contains both the declaration and assignment of a value to a variable?

6 List the variables used in the script.

Server-side scripting

Contrast the following sequence of actions with the sequence given earlier for client-side scripting.

If the web page contains a script which is to be executed on the server:

1 The web browser requests the page.

2 The web server is aware it contains code.

3 The web server processes the code (on the server).

4 The web server renders the page content (as HTML tags and text only).

5 The web server delivers the page to the browser (as HTML tags and text only).

6 The client browser displays the page.

Figure 2.06 shows some PHP server-side code and its output in a browser. It is not really useful as the data values are hard coded within the PHP code.

```
1    <html>
2    <head>
3     <Title> First PHP sample </title>
4     </head>
5    <body>
6    <?php                                    The start of the PHP code
7     settype($studentName, 'string') ;
8     settype($mark, 'integer') ;
9     settype($grade, 'string') ;
10
11    $studentName = 'Ahmed' ;                 Variable identifiers start with $
12    $mark = 56 ;
13    $grade = 'C' ;
14    echo 'Exam performance summary' .'<BR>';
15    echo $studentName.' got mark of '.$mark.' which is grade '. $grade ;
16    ?>
17
18    </body>                                  The Echo keyword
19    </html>                                  outputs to the screen
```

(a)

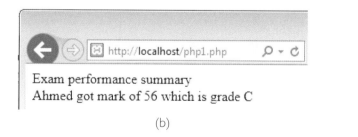

(b)

Figure 2.06 (a) PHP server-side code and (b) its output in a browser

---

TIP

When we access a web page with JavaScript, the web page is simply loaded or requested from the file system of the computer (Figure 2.04 shows the file path on drive C).

To display a web page which uses server-side scripting, the user's computer must retrieve the page from a web server. The usual development environment to do this is to set up a 'local server' on the computer. The author has installed the WAMPP application, which then has the Apache web server running, with a path to its root folder of 'localhost'. Note the path displayed in the address bar of the browser in Figure 2.06(b).

Progress check 2.08

1 State the essential difference between the use of JavaScript and PHP.

2 State the sequence of steps when a client web browser requests a page which contains PHP program code from a web server.

A database JOBS is created to store data for all current jobs at a company. The database has a table JobList with the structure shown in Figure 2.07.

Figure 2.07 Table attributes for JobList

The user will enter data for one job into a web data collection form (HTML only with form controls) as shown in Figure 2.08. When the Submit button is clicked, the data is sent for processing (Figure 2.09) by another form.

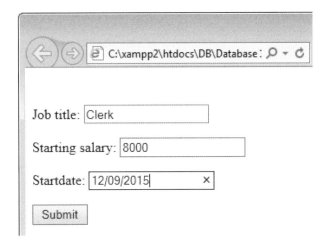

Figure 2.08 Web data collection form

The processing form (`Database 2.php`) contains a PHP script (Figure 2.10) that processes the data for the new job:

1 Data is collected from the first form and the three data items are stored in variables.

2 A connection is made to the database.

3 The server process a SQL command to insert the record to the database.

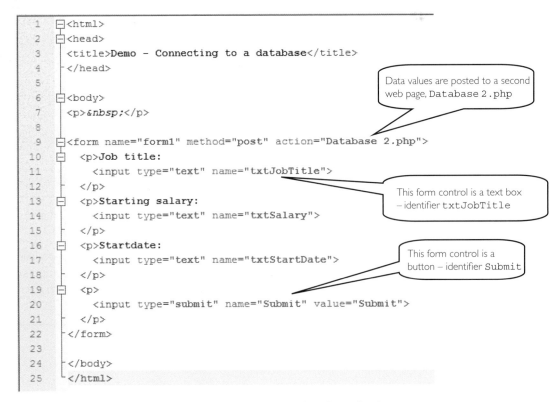

Figure 2.09 'Posting' data from the form

```
1   <body>
2   <?php
3   $connection = mysql_connect("localhost", "root", "password")
4                           or trigger_error(mysql_error, E_USER_ERROR) ;
5   if (!$connection)
6       echo "Sorry - Connection to the database could not be made" ;
7   else
8     {
9       $databaseSelected = myql_select_db("Jobs", $connection) ;
10      if (!$databaseSelected)
11        echo "Connection was made - but database could not be found" ;
12      else
13        {
14        $jobTitle = $_POST('txtJobTitle') ;
15        $startDate = $_POST('txtStartDate') ;
16        $startSalary = $_POST('txtSalary') ;
17
18        $myQuery - mysql_query("INSERT INTO JobList
19                 VALUES ('$jobTitle', '$startDate', '$startSalary')") ;
20        if (!myQuery)
21          {
22            echo ("new record was not added to the database") ;
23            die('Invalid query: ' . mysql_error() ) ;
24          }
25         else
26           echo "New job added to the database table" ;
27        }
28      }
29    ?>
30  </body>
```

Make a connection to the web and database server

Check for successful connection

Connect to the Jobs database

Assign data values from the data entry form to variables

Execute an SQL command to add the record to the JobsList table

Figure 2.10 Processing the PHP script

Summary

■ Most network applications use the client–server model. Applications include database, email, file transfer and web servers.

■ The Internet is the hardware infrastructure – consisting of routers, gateways and networks – which supports global communication. The World Wide Web is the content which is available from various web servers.

■ Various communications systems support the Internet including: the Public Service Telephone Network (PSTN), dedicated lines and the cell phone network.

■ Communication signals use copper and fibre-optic cabling, radio waves, microwaves and satellites.

■ Bit-streaming is used to access content from servers to provide video and sound to users either on-demand or in real time.

■ The packet-switching network on the Internet uses IP addressing. An IP address can be either private or public.

■ Resources available on the WWW are identified using a Uniform Resource Locator (URL). The Domain Name Service has the task of mapping all URLs to an actual IP address.

■ Web pages can contain program code in addition to HTML tags. This code is processed either by the client computer ('client-side scripting') or on the server ('server-side scripting'). JavaScript is used for client-side code; PHP is used for server-side code.

Exam-style questions

I The website www.checkyourwellbeing.com offers help and advice about personal well-being.

The website has a link – 'Calculate my BMI' – that users can click to work out their Body Mass Index.

When the 'Calculate my BMI' link is clicked on the client computer, this webpage is requested:

```
1    <html>
2    <head>
3    <title>Body  Mass   Index</title>
4
5    </head>
6
7    <body>
8    Calculate my body  mass   index
9
10   <Script  Language  =  "JavaScript">
11
12   var myWeight  =  prompt("Enter  your   weight  (in kg.)", "");
13
14   var  myHeight = prompt("Enter  your   height (in  m.)",   "");
15
16   var myBMI  =  myWeight  / (myHeight  *  myHeight);
17   myBMI  =  myBMI.toFixed(2)
18
19   alert("My  calculated BMI  is ..." +  myBMI)   ;
20
21   if (myBMI   <  18.5)
22   {
23     alert("UNDERWEIGHT")  ;
24   }
25
26   if (myBMI   >  25)
27   {
28     alert("OVERWEIGHT")  ;
29   }
30   if (myBMI   >=18.5  &&  myBMI<=25)
31   {
32     alert("WITHIN  RANGE")
33   }
34
35   </Script>
36
37   </body>
38   </html>
```

Loading the webpage produced this sequence of dialogue boxes:

a   Which lines in the webpage script are JavaScript code?   [1]

b   i   Give the identifiers of **two** variables which have been used by the programmer.

        1

        2   [2]

    ii What group of program statements are performing selection?

        line number   up to line number   [1]

c   By studying the web page script and its use, what is the use in JavaScript of:

    i   the `prompt` function?   [2]

    ii the `alert` function?   [2]

d   The diagram shows the client computer network with the connection to the Internet.

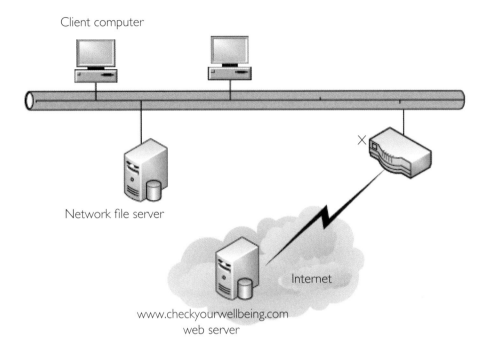

Client computer

Network file server

Internet

www.checkyourwellbeing.com
web server

What is the hardware device labelled X?   [1]

e   Put **five** of these statements in the correct sequence to describe how the content of the page shown is displayed by the client computer's browser software.

Two of the statements will **not** be used.

A   The client computer processes the JavaScript code.

B   The page content is transmitted to the client computer.

C   The page is displayed on the client computer.

D   The user clicks on the hyperlink and the web page is requested from the network file server.

E   The web server processes the JavaScript code.

F   The user clicks on the hyperlink and the web page is requested from the www.checkyourwellbeing.com web server.

G   The server finds the web page.

The sequence is: (fill in the letters)

f   How is this JavaScript code run?   [1]

g   The web developer tested the JavaScript code without involving the web server.

Explain how this is possible.   [1]

Cambridge International AS and A Level Computer Science 9608 Specimen Paper 1, Q4 2015

2 a   What does URL stand for?   [1]

b   Name the component parts of the URL shown:

http://www.w3schools.com/ tutorials/sql/index.htm   [4]

```
  (A)        (B)              (C)        (D)
```

Hardware

3.01 Input, output and storage devices

One of the fundamental diagrams (see Figure 3.01) to describe a computer system is to distinguish between the input devices, the output devices, the processing which various programs will carry out and the need for both primary and secondary storage.

On a typical PC computer, the following would be the various devices:

- Input: keyboard and mouse
- Output: the monitor
- Secondary storage: the hard disk or a solid-state drive
- Main memory: memory chips inside the box
- Processor: the microprocessor inside the box

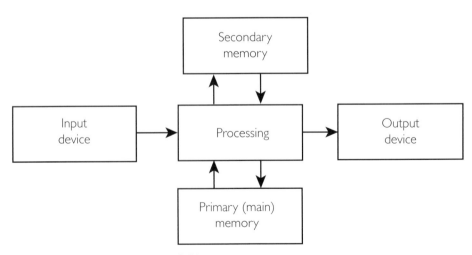

Figure 3.01 Typical computer system

The syllabus requires that we have some knowledge about the basic internal operation of a number of input and output devices.

Keyboard

A keyboard is an input device. Every key on the keyboard has a 'plunger' at the base of the key. When the key is depressed the plunger presses against two electrical contacts which completes a circuit. Each key on the keyboard will complete a separate electrical circuit. This grid of circuits is called a 'key matrix'.

The keyboard has its own processor and circuits. A large part of this circuitry makes up the key matrix. The processor continually scans the circuits to find a circuit that is closed, then it compares the location of that circuit on the key matrix to the character map in its read-only memory (ROM). The character map is essentially a lookup table. It will determine what character a particular key-press represents. For example, the character map lets the processor know that pressing the 'A' key by itself corresponds to a lower case 'a', but the Shift and 'A' keys pressed together correspond to upper case 'A'.

Trackerball

A **trackerball mouse** is like an upside-down mouse, using the original mouse design. The ball Is supported by a socket that contains sensors designed to detect a rotation of the ball about two axes. The user rolls the ball with their hand. The data from the sensors is processed by software to produce a movement of the pointer on the screen. The device has buttons similar to any mouse device.

Optical mouse

A mouse is an input device. The **optical (laser) mouse** uses a technology called 'laser tracking'. The technology uses irregularities on the work surface to track the direction and speed of the mouse movements.

A red light-emitting diode (LED) acts like a camera. This LED bounces light off the surface onto a complementary metal oxide semiconductor (CMOS). The light from the

LED is reflected back off the surface to the CMOS sensor. The CMOS sensor sends each image that is reflected back to a digital signal processor (DSP) for processing.

The DSP is able to detect patterns and images and can determine from analysis of the images if the mouse has moved, at what distance it has moved and at what speed. It is able to determine coordinates which are then sent to the computer's operating system. The system for image processing is called 'digital image correlation'. The DSP software calculates how much each successive image is offset from the previous one and translates this data into movement of the mouse. The operating system is updated with mouse coordinates around 1500 times per second.

Scanner

A scanner is an input device. A drawing or photograph can be digitised by a scanning device.

1 The scanner shines a light beam onto the document.

2 The scanner detects the level of reflected light from set positions on the document.

3 The light intensity is converted by software for each pixel position into a combination of 0s and 1s by sensing different intensities of light and dark from the document.

Inkjet printer

All printers are output devices. An inkjet printer is a 'non-impact' printer. It is also a 'line printer' that is, the head of the printer moves across the page printing a line at a time.

The print head of the printer contains a series of nozzles which are fed ink from a number of print cartridges. A belt connects the print head to a stepper motor which moves the print head horizontally across the paper. The head fires tiny droplets of ink onto the paper. Various coloured droplets are obtained by spraying various amounts of ink from the different ink cartridges.

There are two different technologies used to form the droplet of ink:

• Heat: Canon and Hewlett-Packard printers use resistors which vaporise ink to create a bubble. The print head has around 500 tiny nozzles each of which are capable of forming a bubble of ink at the same time. Hence the term 'bubble-jet printer'. When the bubble pops, the ink is dispensed to the paper. A vacuum is then created which attracts more ink from the cartridge.

- Vibration: Epson printers have a piezo crystal located at the back of the ink reservoir of each nozzle. When the crystal receives a tiny electric charge, it vibrates inwards and the vibration forces ink out of the nozzle. When it vibrates outwards, it pulls replacement ink into the reservoir.

Laser printer

Laser printers use the same technology as that used by photocopiers:

1 A laser beam and a rotating mirror are used to draw an image of the page on a photosensitive drum.

2 The image is converted on the drum into an electrostatic charge, which attracts and holds toner.

3 The electro-statically charged paper is rolled against the drum.

4 The charge pulls the toner away from the drum and onto the paper.

5 Heat is then applied to fuse the toner to the paper.

6 The electrical charge is removed from the drum and the excess toner is collected.

By omitting Step 6 and repeating only the toner-application and paper-handling steps, the printer can make multiple copies.

Microphone

A microphone is an input device. All microphones need to input a varying pressure wave and then convert this to an electrical reading.

There are many technologies which achieve this. One of the most common is a dynamic microphone. The sequence for the use of this microphone is:

- The sound vibration hits a diaphragm
- The movement of the diaphragm causes a coil to move
- The movement of the coil induces a current - through the electromagnetic effect
- The electrical current is digitised
- The digital content is played back using software

TIP

The microphone and loudspeaker use the same technologies but in reverse. A loudspeaker takes the digital content (the sound file) and has to convert this to an analogue signal (the sound wave).

A microphone takes the analogue sound wave and 'digitises' this to either digital software playback or is saved to a sound file.

3D printer

The first thing to do is forget printers with paper! 3D printing is also called additive printing and is the key to what the printer does.

A 3D printer will build up an object from adding more and more layers of material calculated from a digital 'blueprint' file.

- The process must start from a saved digital file of the blueprint
- Creation of a 3D printed object is then achieved using additive processes
  - o the object is created by laying down a sequence of layers of material until the complete object is created.
  - o Each of the layers can be visualised as a horizontal cross-section of the object.
  - o The final 3D object is built up from a large number of 2D (slices) images.

The required object will be either be a copy of an existing object or a design for some new object.

- A copy of an existing object is digitised using a 3D scanner.
- The design for a new object is produced using 3D modelling software.

The material used can vary. In common use is polymer resin which is built up layer-by-layer and then hardened with an ultra-violet light source.

Touchscreen

A touchscreen is both an input and output device. The display gives you the output in the form of the visual menu and then you input your choices by touching the screen. You should be familiar with two of the technologies used in touchscreen devices.

Resistive technology

'Resistive' because as the user presses with their finger the screen resists. If you press hard enough you can feel the screen bend. The 'touch' is designed to make two electrically conductive layers touch each other.

The construction of the screen consists of:

- a glass panel
- covered with:
  - o a conductive layer
  - o a resistive metallic layer - these two layers are held apart by spacers
  - o a scratch-resistant layer placed on top of the whole setup

When the device is switched on:

- An electric current runs through the two layers.
- When the user touches the screen, the two layers make contact at that exact location.
- The change in the electrical field is noted and the coordinates of the point of contact are calculated by software.
- Once the coordinates are known, driver software translates the touch into data that the operating system can understand.

Applications:

ATMs and supermarkets and any application which requires only a single touch at one time.

Capacitive technology

In physics, a capacitor is a device which stores electrical charge. Your skin is made up of millions of atoms which attract electrical charge.

The construction of the screen consists of:

- The glass panel.
- A layer that stores electrical charge placed on the glass panel.
- When a user touches the panel, some of the charge is attracted to and transferred to the user.
- This charge on the capacitive layer is less - causing a drop in voltage.
- This decrease in voltage is measured by circuits located at each corner of the screen.

- Software calculates, from the relative differences in charge at each corner, the exact coordinates of the touch.
- This data is sent to the touchscreen driver software.

Applications:

Modern smartphone applications such as a iPhone, include interactions such as a the 'two-finger zoom'. This can only be achieved using capacitive technology.

> **TIP**
>
> The final stage using both technologies is the same principle as would be used for a mouse input device.

The multiple layers will reduce the ambient light from the screen compares to a screen using capacitive technology.

Speakers

A speaker is an output device. Sound is an electro-magnetic wave. We hear different sounds due to the changes in the frequency and amplitude of these waves.

A loudspeaker (see Figure 3.02) takes an electrical signal and translates it into physical vibrations to create sound waves. The speaker is carrying out the exact reversal of what is done by a microphone. The task of a microphone is to receive as inputs the electro-magnetic wave signals, translate them into electrical signals and convert the signals to digital data.

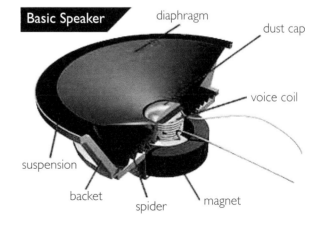

Figure 3.02 Loudspeaker

The key components of a loudspeaker are a diaphragm, a voice coil and a magnet. The diaphragm or cone is connected to a circular suspension at the wide end and to the voice coil at the narrow end.

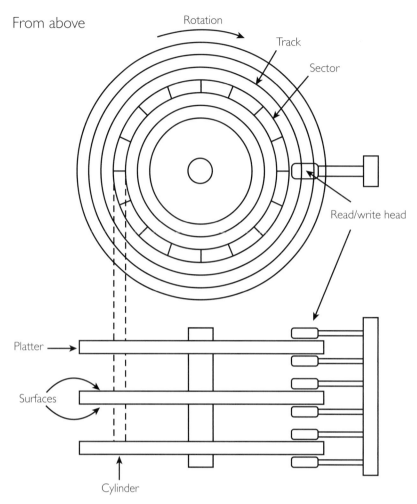

From above

Rotation

Track

Sector

Read/write head

Platter

Surfaces

Cylinder

Figure 3.03 Hard disk platters

There is a magnet on the end of the voice coil which interacts with an electro-magnet. Changing the polarity of the current sent to the electro-magnet will cause the permanent magnet on the coil to move. It is these very fast changes in the movement of the diaphragm or coil which produces sounds. The movement of the coil causes the air in front of the cone to vibrate. The amount of movement will determine the frequency and amplitude of the sound wave produced.

Hard disk

Hard disks are used for secondary storage or memory. Originally they were called 'hard' disks, since the disk platters were rigid and to distinguish them from 'floppy' disks.

A hard disk has one or more platters made of aluminium or glass (as shown in Figure 3.03). The surface of a platter is ferrous-oxide which is capable of being magnetised. The platters are mounted on a central spindle and the entire mechanism is contained inside a sealed aluminium box.

The disk is rotated at high speed. Each platter of the disk will have a read/write head which are mounted on an arm which is positioned just above the surface of each platter. The arm can move between the outer and inner tracks of each platter at very high speed. Electronic circuits control the movement of the arm (and hence the heads). The surface of the platter is divided into concentric tracks and each track will be divided into a basic unit of storage called a block. The data contained in a block – typically around 512 bytes – is the basic unit of storage which can be read/written with a single read/write operation of the hardware. The data is encoded as a magnetic flux pattern for each block.

TIP

Hard disks are spelt with a 'K'. All forms of optical discs spell 'disc' with a 'C'.

There are three factors which determine the performance of a hard disk:

- data transfer rate: the number of bytes per second which can be read from the disk and transferred to the processor

- seek time: the time the disk takes to:

  - position the head assembly onto the required track.

  - rotate until the required block is under the head (called the 'latency time').

  - capacity: desktop computers now commonly measure capacity in terabytes.

The capacity of a hard disk is a key factor when purchasing a computer or a replacement or external hard disk.

Optical disc

An optical disc is a secondary storage device. It is the general term given to all formats of CD and DVD storage. Unlike a hard disk with separate concentric tracks, an optical disc has a surface arranged in a long spiral. The spiral is a sequence of bumps and pits (lands) which encode the digital data.

The basic disc is made from plastic, coated with a layer of aluminium. The reading of the bumps and pits is done with a laser beam. Data is read from the disc as the laser beam passes through the CD's polycarbonate layer. The laser light is reflected from the aluminium layer and is received by an opto-electronic device that detects changes in light. The electronics in the player device then interprets the changes in light patterns as data bits.

Solid state (flash) memory

A solid-state memory (SSM) is constructed entirely from electronic components which are designed to perform traditional block input/output (I/O) similar to a hard disk.

SSM has many advantages over magnetic disk storage:

- There are no moving (mechanical) components.

- They are typically more resistant to physical shock.

- They run silently.

- They have lower access times and latency.

Currently most solid-state devices (SSD) use NAND-based flash memory, which retains data without power. This is done using floating gate transistors.

For applications requiring fast access, but not necessarily data persistence after power loss, SSDs may be

constructed from random-access memory (RAM). Such devices may use a separate power source, such as batteries, to maintain data after power loss.

Sensors

A sensor is an input device deigned to sense some physical characteristic of its surroundings, such as:

- pressure

- temperature

- wind speed or flow

- light intensity.

Other sensors are designed to detect the proximity of some thing or body to some point at which the device is placed.

A sensor is a transducer whose purpose is to sense (that is, to detect) some physical property of its environment. Data values are sent from the sensor to computer software which detects events or changes in quantities and provides a corresponding output, generally as an electrical or optical signal.

For example a temperature sensor will be a thermocouple, which sends an electrical signal through an analogue-to-digital converter to produce a digital value which is processed by computer software.

Sensors are now used in everyday objects such as touch-sensitive elevator buttons (tactile sensor) and lamps which dim or brighten by touching the base.

Progress check 3.01

Name an application for each of the sensor types listed above.

Actuators

An actuator is a motor that controls a piece of mechanical equipment. It is operated by a source of energy, typically:

- electric current

- hydraulic (fluid) pressure

- pneumatic (air) pressure.

The actuator converts the energy into motion of some component.

The energy which drives the actuator will originate as the output from computer software which is receiving data from one or more sensors.

TIP

Sensors and actuators have been removed from Paper 1 for the 2017 syllabus. They do still feature for Paper 3.

Progress check 3.02

Name an application for each of the actuator types listed above.

3.02 Main memory

The fundamental model of the Von Neumann computer is a set of program instructions and data stored in the 'primary' or 'main' memory of the computer.

Memory is conceptually a sequence of memory cells which each contain a number of bits. Personal computers use 'byte-addressable' memory, so each memory cell stores an eight-bit binary pattern. Each memory cell is referenced by a computer program using its unique memory address.

Random Access Memory (RAM)

The term 'random access' implies that the processor is able to directly access any individual memory location from knowing its address.

The memory will be formed from either SRAM or DRAM memory chips. The contents of RAM memory are retained as long as the power supply to the computer remains. The contents of RAM is lost when the computer is powered off. However, initiatives have been developed to retain the contents; the circuits used in flash memory is an example when the storage can be written to many times and the contents of memory retained.

Dynamic RAM (DRAM)

DRAM is the predominant form of main memory used in modern computers.

DRAM stores each bit of data in a memory cell using a single transistor and a capacitor. The capacitor holds a high or low charge (to represent 1 or 0). The transistor acts as a switch that lets the control circuitry on the chip read or

change the capacitor's state of charge. In comparison with SRAM, DRAM:

- is less expensive to produce
- provides slower access
- requires more power.

Static RAM (SRAM)

For SRAM circuits, each bit of data is stored using the state of a six-transistor memory cell. In comparison with DRAM, SRAM:

- is more expensive to produce
- provides faster access
- requires less power.

An application of SRAM is for cache memory for the CPU.

Read-only memory (ROM)

'Read only' implies that the contents of the memory is written to once, the contents are permanently retained and then read many times. There are variants of ROM however which contradict this: 'erasable programmable memory' (EPROM) chips exist.

ROM is typically used in:

- a PC for storage of the boot program code
- a device such as a washing machine for storage of the program code for the various washing programmes.

3.03 Logic gates and logic circuits

The second generation of computers followed the invention of the transistor in 1947. A logic gate is a unit made up from one or more transistors. There are no moving parts and one or more input signals produce an output signal. Because of the way in which a transistor works, the least complicated to produce are the NOT, NAND and NOR gates.

These assume the more fundamental gates of AND, OR, NOT and XOR.

AND gate

An AND gate has two or more inputs and a single output (as shown in Figure 3.04).

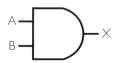

Figure 3.04 AND gate

Table 3.01 shows all the possible combinations of input and the output each produces. This is called a **truth table**.

Input		Output
A	**B**	**X**
0	0	0
0	1	0
1	0	0
1	1	1

Table 3.01 Truth table for the AND gate

The AND gate produces a 1 output only when input A is 1 and input B is 1.

OR gate

An OR gate has two or more inputs and a single output (as shown in Figure 3.05).

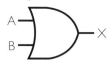

Figure 3.05 OR gate

Table 3.02 is the corresponding truth table.

Input		Output
A	**B**	**X**
0	0	0
0	1	1
1	0	1
1	1	1

Table 3.02 Truth table for the OR gate

TIP The syllabus does state that gates used will have, at most, two inputs.

NOT gate

Sometimes called an inverter, a NOT gate has a single input and single output (as shown in Figure 3.06).

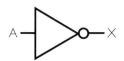

Figure 3.06 NOT gate

Table 3.03 is the corresponding truth table.

Input	Output
A	**X**
0	1
1	0

Table 3.03 Truth table for the NOT gate

Exclusive OR (XOR) gate

An XOR gate has two or more inputs and a single output (as shown in Figure 3.07).

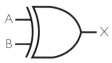

Figure 3.07 Exclusive OR gate

Table 3.04 is the corresponding truth table.

Input		Output
A	**B**	**X**
0	0	0
0	1	1
1	0	1
1	1	0

Table 3.04 Truth table for the XOR gate

NAND gate

A NAND gate follows the same logic as an AND gate followed by a NOT gate (as shown in Figure 3.08).

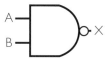

Figure 3.08 NAND gate

Table 3.05 is the corresponding truth table.

Input		Output
A	**B**	**X**
0	0	1
0	1	1
1	0	1
1	1	0

Table 3.05 Truth table for the NAND gate

NOR gate

A NOR gate follows the same logic as an OR gate followed by a NOT gate (as shown in Figure 3.09).

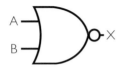

Figure 3.09 NOR gate

Table 3.06 is the corresponding truth table.

Input		Output
A	B	X
0	0	I
0	I	0
I	0	0
I	I	0

Table 3.06 Truth table for the NOR gate

Constructing a logic circuit

The starting point for constructing a circuit could be either:

- a logic expression (expressed in words)
- a logic expression which has used labels for any input and the logic operators (AND, OR, NOT, etc.)

The equivalent circuit for the following logic expression is shown in Figure 3.10:

X = NOT (A OR B) AND (B OR C)

Constructing a truth table

An expression with three inputs (such as the circuit in Figure 3.10) will need eight rows for the truth table. The corresponding truth table is used to show all possible combinations of input and the output each produces (see Table 3.07).

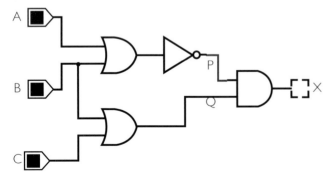

Figure 3.10 Logic circuit constructed from an expression

> **TIP**
>
> A good idea is to label some intermediate points in the logic circuit (here we have used P and Q) and calculate the bit values at these intermediate points.

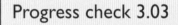

Input					Output
A	B	C	P	Q	X
0	0	0	I	0	0
0	0	I	I	I	I
0	I	0	0	I	0
0	I	I	0	I	0
I	0	0	0	0	0
I	0	I	0	I	0
I	I	0	0	I	0
I	I	I	0	I	0

Table 3.07 Truth table for the circuit in Figure 3.10

The final column shows the output X.

Progress check 3.03

1 Draw the logic circuit for the following logic expression:

X = (A AND B) AND NOT(A OR B)

2 Draw the truth table for the circuit:

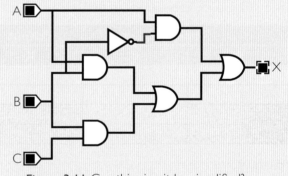

Figure 3.11 Can this circuit be simplified?

Before you draw up the truth table, will you show any intermediate points?

Efficient circuits

The electronics designer will be interesting in constructing a circuit from as few gates as possible. This will be an efficient circuit.

Consider the circuit shown in Figure 3.11.

The truth table for the circuit in Figure 3.11 is shown in Table 3.08.

Input			Output
A	**B**	**C**	**X**
0	0	0	0
0	0	1	0
0	1	0	0
0	1	1	1
1	0	0	1
1	0	1	1
1	1	0	1
1	1	1	1

Table 3.08 Truth table for the circuit in Figure 3.11

Consider now the circuit shown in Figure 3.12.

The truth table for the circuit in Figure 3.12 is shown in Table 3.09. As it is identical to Table 3.08, we conclude that the two circuits are equivalent.

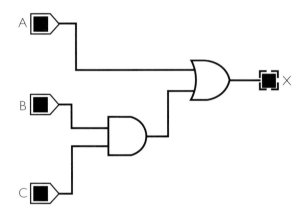

Figure 3.12 Simplified circuit

Input			Output
A	**B**	**C**	**X**
0	0	0	0
0	0	1	0
0	1	0	0
0	1	1	1
1	0	0	1
1	0	1	1
1	1	0	1
1	1	1	1

Table 3.09 Truth table for the circuit in Figure 3.12

The first circuit was constructed with six gates but the second circuit is constructed using only two gates.

LOOK FORWARD »

This raises the question: how do we take a given circuit and then attempt to find a circuit which is more efficient?

The question becomes: how do we start with a logic expression and then attempt to simplify it?

For the circuit in Figure 3.12, the question becomes, is it possible to simplify the following expression:

A.B + B.C + A.NOT B?

This will be covered in Chapter 15, with a study of Boolean algebra and the use of Karnaugh maps.

Progress check 3.04

1 Study the following circuit. Can this circuit be simplified? If so, draw the simplified circuit.

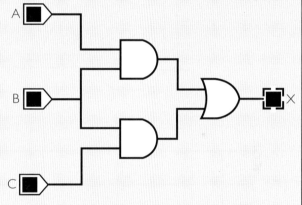

2 Study the following circuit. Can this circuit be simplified? If so, draw the simplified circuit.

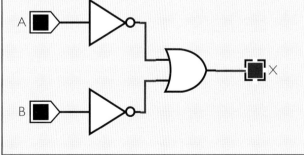

Summary

- [ ] There are a variety of devices available for input, output and secondary storage.

- [ ] You are familiar with the basic internal operation for a number of devices.

- [ ] There are different types of primary memory: RAM, ROM, SRAM and DRAM. There are differences between their construct and usage.

- [ ] You can construct a logic circuit using the basic logic gates of AND, OR, NOT, XOR, NAND and NOR.

- [ ] You can draw up a truth table.

- [ ] A logic circuit can be constructed from a given logic expression.

- [ ] Given a circuit, It may be possible to construct a more efficient circuit which produces the same logic.

Exam-style questions

1   **a**   Complete the table to show the outputs for the possible inputs to this circuit.

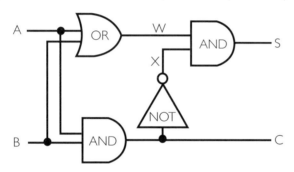

A	B	w	x	C	S
0	0				
0	1				
1	0				
1	1				

[5]

   b   State a possible use for this circuit in a processor.   [1]

Cambridge International AS and A Level Computer Science 9608 Specimen paper 1, Q7 2015

2   Describe the internal construction and working of a laser printer.   [5]

Processor fundamentals

Chapter 4

Revision objectives

By the end of the chapter you should be able to:

- [ ] show understanding of the basic Von Neumann model for a computer system and the stored program concept

- [ ] show understanding of the roles carried out by registers, including the difference between general-purpose and special-purpose registers

- [ ] show understanding of the roles carried out by the Arithmetic and Logic Unit (ALU), Control Unit and system clock

- [ ] show understanding of the use of the address, data and control buses and how the bus width and clock speed contribute to the performance of the computer system

- [ ] describe the stages of the fetch–execute cycle

- [ ] show understanding of the need for ports to provide the connection to peripheral devices

- [ ] show understanding of 'register transfer' notation

- [ ] describe how interrupts are handled

- [ ] show understanding that the set of instructions are grouped into different types of instruction

- [ ] show understanding of modes of addressing

- [ ] show understanding of the relationship between assembly language and machine code

- [ ] describe the different stages of the assembly process for a 'two-pass' assembler. Trace the translation of a given simple assembly language program by the assembler

4.01   Computer architecture

The Von Neumann model

Von Neumann in 1946 proposed the fundamental model for most modern computer systems.

> **TERMS**
>
> **Program:** a sequence of instructions stored in memory and the data the program will process
>
> **Arithmetic Logic Unit (ALU):** performs calculations on data
>
> **Control unit:** processes and executes instructions held in main memory

The computer system will have various input and output devices connected.

Registers

A register is the smallest unit of storage on the microprocessor. Transfer of a data value between registers, or between a register and a memory cell, is only electronic and so extremely fast. Registers can be classified as either:

- general-purpose registers
- special-purpose registers.

A typical modern microprocessor will have around eight general-purpose registers. These will be used to store data values which have been read from memory or the result of some processing. These registers can be used by the assembly language programmer.

The other registers are special-purpose registers. Some registers are accessible by assembly language program instructions – other registers are not and should be thought of as 'buried inside' the microprocessor circuits. All of the general-purpose registers and some of the special-purpose registers are accessible to the programmer.

Accumulator

We shall soon consider some simple assembly language instructions. We shall assume a single general-purpose register called the 'accumulator'.

Program Counter

If a **program** is thought of as a sequence of instructions stored in a consecutive block of memory cells, the processor must always be clear about the address at which the next program instruction to be executed is stored.

The Program Counter (PC) holds the address of the next instruction to be fetched.

Memory Data Register

When a data value is to be fetched from memory (it could be a 'data value' or a program instruction), its value will be temporarily stored in the Memory Data Register (MDR).

Memory Address Register

Whenever a memory cell is to be accessed its address must be known to the processor. The address about to be used by a program instruction is held in the Memory Address Register (MAR).

Index Register

The Index Register stores a number which will be used to change an address value.

Current Instruction Register

Once the next program instruction has been fetched, it will be stored in the Current Instruction Register (CIR). It will be the task of the processor to make sense of it and execute it.

Status Register

All of the above special-purpose registers deal with the entire byte.

The Status Register (also called the Flag Register) is different. The processor considers its individual bits, since each of the eight bits is used to 'flag' whether or not some event has occurred.

An individual bit position will flag outcomes such as the following for arithmetic operations:

- carry: there was a value to carry.
- zero: the result was zero.
- negative: the result was negative.
- overflow: the result (on a two's complement number) was out of range.

Arithmetic and logic unit (ALU), control unit and system clock

Figure 4.01 is a schematic diagram of what happens inside the processor.

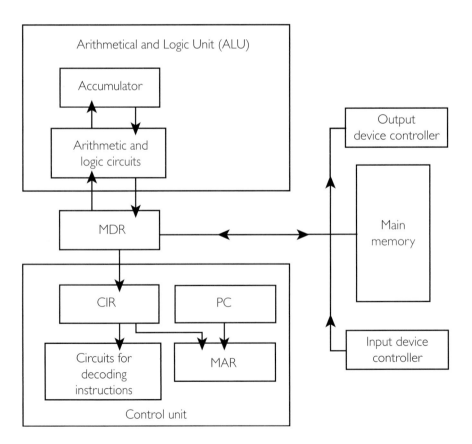

Figure 4.01 Inside the processor

Figure 4.01 will help to make sense of how the processor executes a sequence of instructions using the fetch–execute cycle.

- The memory data register (MDR) is connected directly to main memory – using the data bus – and is able to temporarily store a value when read or written.

- The **arithmetic and logical unit** is where Instructions which require some form of arithmetic or logical operation are processed.

- The 'processor' can be thought of as the **control unit** and the ALU working together.

Buses

Figure 4.02 shows the buses which connect the various components and how input and output devices would be connected to the computer system.

Address bus

The address bus carries address values. Typically when a value is to be read from memory, the address bus must first be loaded with the correct address. Then the program instruction to perform an operation, for example, read, at that address can be performed.

Data bus

When a read operation takes place, the data bus is used to transport the value from the memory location addressed to the processor. In fact the memory data register is involved in this transfer – more about this later.

The data bus is bi-directional: it will be used to perform both memory read and memory write operations.

Control bus

The control bus is made up of a number of lines which are each dedicated to sending or receiving a signal. In the data transfer example above, one of the control bus lines would be used to send a signal to the control unit in the processor to indicate that the 'read operation has now completed'.

Other control signals include:

- User presses the 'reset' button.

- A memory write operation has completed.

- An input/output operation has completed.

- An interrupt has been received.

TIP

For both the data bus and address bus, all the lines are used to represent a binary pattern when the bus is in action – unlike the control bus.

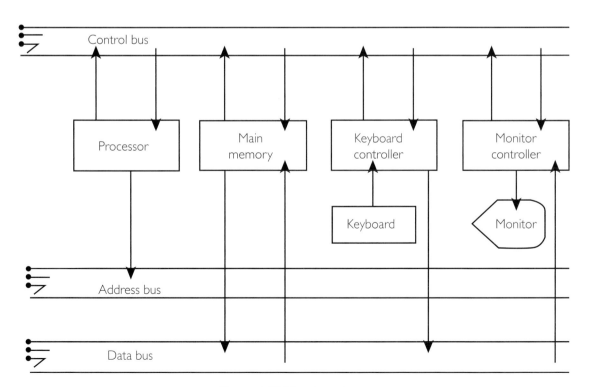

Figure 4.02 The three buses

Performance of the PC

Bus width

The number of lines in the address and data buses determine the size of the binary pattern which can be transmitted.

Binary arithmetic shows that a bus with eight lines would give numbers which range from 0000 0000 to 1111 1111, that is 256 different numbers.

Hence an address bus with eight lines would only be able to address 256 different memory locations.

Similarly, a data bus with eight lines would be able to transfer binary patterns ranging from 0000 0000 to 1111 1111.

> **TIP**
>
> Some values for processors in widespread use are:
>
> - Intel x86 processors: 16-bit data bus with 16-bit address bus
>
> - Motorola 68000: 16-bit data bus with 24-bit address bus

Clock speed

Each instruction in the processor's instruction has a stated number of clock cycles it takes to execute that instruction. A simple instruction – such as the incrementing of the value in the Accumulator – would take few clock cycles.

Compare this with an instruction which has to access a location in main memory and then copy the value to the Accumulator. Since this involves the setting up of a value on the address bus and the use of the data bus, this would take many more clock cycles.

The stated number of clock cycles for each instruction in the processor's instruction set never changes. What can change is the time taken for one clock cycle.

Table 4.01 gives a comparison of the performance of two processors.

The conclusion would be that Processor A is able to execute the same program around two and a half times faster than Processor B.

Ports

At least one input and output device must be connected to any computer system. They are connected through one of a number of ports found on the case of the computer. The term 'port' here is taken to mean the hardware port used to provide the physical interface between the computer and a device (including a second computer).

> **TIP**
>
>
>
> The term used in this section of the syllabus should not be confused with the use of the term 'port' to describe a virtual data connection between computer programs used in a client–server application.

Common ports on a PC and whether they can be used for input or output are shown in Table 4.02.

Port	Input	Output
Centronics ('Parallel')		✓
Universal Serial Port (USB)	✓	✓
RS232	✓	✓
FireWire	✓	✓
VGA		✓
HDMI		✓
Ethernet ('network')	✓	✓

Table 4.02 Ports on a PC

4.02 The fetch–execute cycle

The principle is that a program consists of a set of instructions which are stored in a set of continuous memory locations. Table 4.03 shows the stages and steps of the fetch–execute cycle.

	Time for one clock cycle (μs)	Instruction 1		Instruction 2	
		Clock cycles	Execution time	Clock cycles	Execution time
Processor A	2	3	6	12	24
Processor B	5		15		60

Table 4.01 Comparison of two processors

[PC] denotes 'the contents of the PC register'.

The 'assign' operator (similar to that used for assignment statements in pseudocode in Part 2) denotes that the register on the left is 'given the value which follows'.

Stage	Register transfer notation
Fetch the next instruction ...	
The program counter (PC) is loaded with the address of the next instruction to be fetched.	
The contents of the PC are copied to the memory address register (MAR).	MAR ← [PC]
The contents of the PC are incremented (ready for the next fetch).	PC ← [PC]+1
The address given by MAR is located and the contents of this address are copied to the memory data register (MDR).	MDR ← [[MAR]]
The contents of MDR are copied to the current instruction register (CIR).	CIR ← [MDR]
Decode the instruction ...	
The opcode and operand parts of the instruction are identified.	
Execute the instruction ...	
The instruction is executed.	

Table 4.03 The fetch–execute cycle

Interrupts

The kernel of the operating system is designed to recognise an **interrupt.**

LOOK FORWARD »

Interrupts and the operating system are discussed in more detail in Chapter 16.

Interrupt: a signal to the processor – generated by hardware or software – to flag that some event has occurred

Examples of interrupts include:

- a printer which sends a message that the device is out of paper.
- a program which causes an error when it attempts to divide by zero in a calculation.

When the processor receives an interrupt, it must:

1 Identify the source of the interrupt.

2 Run some appropriate program code to deal with the event (called the Interrupt Service Routine (ISR)).

3 Return to processing of the program at the point of the interrupt.

In order that the processor can return to the current program at a later stage, the data stored in all the registers must be stored. This is done on a special area of memory called the **stack**.

4.03 The processor's instruction set

The set of basic machine operations the processor can carry out are called the instruction set for that processor.

The syllabus lists a set of assembly language instructions for a fictitious processor. The processor is assumed to have:

- a general-purpose register, the Accumulator (ACC)
- an index register, IX.

Instructions by category

Instructions can be categorised as in the following tables.

Instruction			Explanation
Opcode (mnemonic)	Operand	Opcode (binary)	
LDM	#n	0000 0001	Immediate addressing: Load the number n to ACC
LDD	<address>	0000 0010	Direct addressing: Load the contents of <address> to ACC
LDI	<address>	0000 0101	Indirect addressing: <address> holds the address to be used; load the contents of this second address to ACC
LDX	<address>	0000 0110	Indexed addressing: Form the address for <address> plus the contents of IX; copy the contents of this calculated address to ACC
LDR	#n	0000 0111	Immediate addressing: Load number n to IX
STO	<address>	0000 1111	Store the contents of ACC at <address>

Table 4.04 Data movement assembly language instructions

Instruction			Explanation
Opcode (mnemonic)	Operand	Opcode (binary)	
OUTCH		0000 1000	Output the character corresponding to the ASCII character code in ACC
IN		1001 1001	Input a denary number from the keyboard and store in ACC

Table 4.05 I/O assembly language instructions

Instruction			Explanation
Opcode (mnemonic)	Operand	Opcode (binary)	
ADD	<address>	0000 1010	Add the contents of the given address to ACC
INC	<register>	0000 1011	Add 1 to the contents of the register (ACC or IX)
DEC	<register>	0000 1100	Increment the contents of the register (ACC or IX)

Table 4.06 Arithmetic assembly language instructions

Instruction			Explanation
Opcode (mnemonic)	Operand	Opcode (binary)	
JPE	<address>	1000 0000	Following a compare instruction, jump to <address> if the compare was True
JPN	<address>	1000 0001	Following a compare instruction, jump to <address> if the compare was False
JMP	<address>	1000 0010	Unconditionally, jump to <address>

Table 4.07 Jump assembly language instructions

Instruction		Opcode (binary)	Explanation
Opcode (mnemonic)	Operand		
CMP	`<address>`	1000 0011	Compare the contents of ACC with the contents of `<address>`
CMP	#n	1000 0100	Compare the contents of ACC with number n

Table 4.08 Comparison assembly language instructions

Finally, we have an instruction in a category of its own: END (with binary opcode 1111 1111) ends the program and returns to the operating system.

Note that – for the majority of instructions – there are two parts, the operation code (opcode) and the datum needed, the operand.

Consider the instruction:

LDM #39

It is decoded as:

Opcode: Load the number which follows to the Accumulator

Operand: (number) 39

Similarly, the following instruction:

ADD 67

is decoded as:

Opcode: Load the contents of the address which follows to the Accumulator

Operand: (address) 67

Progress check 4.01

Which instructions do not have an operand?

Modes of addressing

The different modes of addressing are illustrated with examples using the assembly language instructions in the previous section.

Immediate addressing does not use an 'address' value as such. The operand is the actual number to be used:

- LDM #13: Load number 13 to the accumulator (ACC)
- LDR #27: Load number 27 to the index register (IX)

In direct addressing, the address value in the operand is the actual address to be used:

- LDD 56: Copy the contents of address 56 to the accumulator
- STO 112: Store the contents of the accumulator at address 112

In indirect addressing, the operand contains the address of the value to be used.

LDI 56: Treat the value found at address 56 as an address and load its contents to the accumulator

For example, if the value found at address 56 is 71, the contents of address 71 are loaded to the accumulator.

In indexed addressing, the operand is added to the value of the index register. Assume the index register (IX) contains the value 3 (0000 0011):

LDX 56: Form the address as 56 + 3 = 59 and copy the contents of address 59 to the accumulator

Relative addressing

In the syllabus sample instructions, there is a no example of an instruction which uses relative addressing.

Relative addressing calculates the address to be used from some base address when the program is loaded into memory. The two base points which could be used are:

- the address of the first program instruction.
- the address of the current instruction.

With the first method, the instruction JMP +8 would mean 'jump to the address eight locations from the start address of the program'.

With the second method, the instruction JMP -9 would mean 'jump to the address nine locations before the address where this current instruction is loaded'.

Progress check 4.02

Describe what happens when the following sequence of assembly language instructions are executed.

1 LDM #14

   STO 156

2 LDI 105

Use the data values stored at the addresses in this diagram:

100	0
101	0
102	56
103	59
104	60
105	102

3   LDX 102

Use the data values stored at the addresses in this diagram:

IX	2

100	0
101	162
102	163
103	163
104	165
105	167

4.04 Assembly language

Relationship between assembly language and machine code

Every instruction in assembly language program code (the source code) translates into exactly one instruction in the machine code (the object code).

LOOK BACK «

The assembly language instructions we have introduced show the binary machine code which will be used for each operation code (opcode).

Progress check 4.03

Write the eight-bit or 16-bit machine code instructions for the following instructions:

1   LDM #102

2   LDX 29 (if the IX register currently contains 7)

3   OUTCH

2   STO 45

Symbolic and absolute addressing

Study the following assembly language program. It is a sequence of instructions with the first instruction loaded at address 300.

300	LDI 309
301	CMP 314
302	JPE 308
303	OUTCH
304	LDD 309
305	INC ACC
306	STO 309
307	JMP 300
308	END
309	500
310	65
311	74
312	65
313	90
314	32

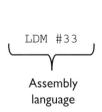

	Opcode	Operand
LDM #33	0000 0001	0010 0001

Assembly language

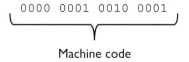

0000 0001 0010 0001

Machine code

Figure 4.03 Mapping assembly language to machine code

Absolute addressing

Note all the address values used by the program are shown as actual address numbers. This has implications later when the program is translated by the assembler. If the machine code similarly shows the absolute address values, then the program when executed must be loaded to start at address 300.

There is a simple solution: the assembler could calculate all the addresses as relative values. Then when the program is loaded and executed, it can occupy any area in the memory space.

Symbolic addressing

Simply, we use symbols to represent addresses. These will be shown in an additional 'label' column in the source code:

```
StartProg:   LDI Here
             CMP Value
             JPE EndProg
             OUTCH
             LDD Here
             INC ACC
             STO Here
             JMP StartProg
EndProg:     END
Here:        500
             65
             74
             65
             90
Value:       32
```

The programmer has used four labels: `StartProg`, `EndProg`, `Here` and `Value`.

LOOK FORWARD »

We shall use the same concept – using labels – in Chapter 9, when we write the steps in some algorithm and need to be able to refer to a particular step in the sequence.

Directives

A directive is a not a program instruction; that is, it is not one of the instructions in the actual program. It is information that the assembler translation software needs to be able to translate the source code.

Assembler directives are instructions that direct the assembler to do something, such as:

- set aside space for variables.
- include additional source files, e.g. `INCLUDE "File56.LIB"`
- state the start address for the program, e.g. `ORG 0300`.

Macros

A group of instructions may need to be executed several times within the same program. The statements would be written once and the block of statements given an identifier name. The statements can then be called using the name whenever they need to be executed.

The syntax within the source code would be:

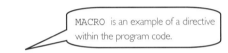

MACRO is an example of a directive within the program code.

```
MACRO MyMacro

    <Instruction list>

ENDMACRO
```

The code is then called or evoked whenever need with the call:

```
MyMacro
```

When the assembly starts it will look for macro calls and duplicate the macro code wherever it is called.

LOOK FORWARD »

We shall later use the same concept in our high-level programming. In a high-level language, the group of statements would be called a procedure or subroutine.

The assembly process for a 'two-pass' assembler

The processor cannot directly understand an assembly language source program. The source code must be translated by software, called the 'assembler'. The assembler software used must be for the appropriate processor instruction set.

LOOK BACK «

Every assembly language instruction has a machine code for the instruction:

Assembly language: `ADD <address>`

Machine code: `0000 1010`

To carry out the assembly, the software must have access to the opcode table showing each opcode and its machine code equivalent. If symbolic addressing has been used in the code, the assembler will add entries to a symbol table.

Most assemblers are two-pass assemblers, which means the source code will have to be scanned twice in order to complete the symbol table and produce the final machine code.

Consider now the translation of the program shown below.

```
StartProg:  LDI Here
            CMP Value
            JPE EndProg
            OUTCH
            LDD Here
            INC ACC
            STO Here
            JMP StartProg
  EndProg:  END
     Here:  500
            65
            74
            65
            90
    Value:  32
```

The instruction set table (some entries only) which will be used as a lookup table is shown in Table 4.09.

Opcode (mnemonic)	Operand	Opcode (binary)
LDD	<address>	0000 0010
LDI	<address>	0000 0101
STO	<address>	0000 1111
OUTCH		0000 1000
JPE	<address>	1000 0000
JPN	<address>	1000 0001
CMP	<address>	1000 0010
JMP	<address>	1000 0011
INC	<register>	0000 1011

Table 4.09 The opcode lookup table

The first task of the assembler is a 'pre-assembly' process to scan the code and look for the use of any macros. If present, the macro code will be inserted at each point in the code where the macro is evoked. Our program does not contain any macros.

The assembler then makes a first pass through the code to find symbolic addresses, enter them in the symbol table and (if known) enter the absolute addresses. We shall enter this address as a value relative to the address used for the first instruction.

For our program this will give the sequence of entries shown in Figure 4.04. Note that some addresses (e.g. `Value`) are first entered when the absolute address is not known; others (e.g. `StartProg`) will have the absolute address known the first time that address is found. The circles in Figure 4.04 show the sequence in which data is entered to the symbol table. At 1, the label `StartProg` is entered and its absolute address (0) is known. At 2, the label `Here` is entered but its absolute address is not yet known.

Figure 4.04 Entries to the symbol table during translation

The assembler then makes a second pass through the code. Now the addresses are known, the complete machine code program can be produced. Figure 4.05 shows the object code for our source code.

Assembly language		Machine code	

Label

StartProg:	LDI	Here	0000 0101	0000 1001	(+9)
	CMP	Value	1000 0010	0001 0000	(+14)
	JPE	EndProg	1000 0000	0000 1000	(+8)
	OUTCH		0000 1000		
	LDD	Here	0000 0010	0001 1001	(+9)
	INC	ACC	0000 1011		
	STO	Here	0000 1111	0001 1001	(+9)
	JMP	StartProg	1000 0010	0000 0000	
EndProg:	END		1111 1111		
Here:		50	0011 0010		
		65	0100 0001		
		74	0100 1010		
		65	0100 0001		
		90	0101 1010		
Value:		32	0010 0000		

Figure 4.05 The source code and its matching object code

Summary

- A processor's architecture is constructed with:

  - general-purpose and special-purpose registers

  - an address bus, data bus and control bus.

- A program is executed with the 'fetch–execute' cycle. The stages can be represented using register transfer notation.

- The processor has a set of basic machine operations called its instruction set. These can be grouped into categories: data movement, arithmetic, input and output, jump and compare instructions. Data movement instructions use various modes of addressing.

- An assembly language program is translated into machine code using a two-pass assembler software.

Exam-style questions

1 The table below gives a subset of the assembly language instructions for a computer with a single general-purpose register, the Accumulator (ACC), and an index register (IX).

Instruction		Opcode (binary)	Explanation
Opcode (mnemonic)	**Operand**		
LDD	<address>	0000 0100	Direct addressing: Load the contents of the given address to ACC
LDV	<number>	0000 0101	Load the given number to ACC
STO	<address>	0001 0000	Store the contents of ACC at the given address
LDI	<address>	0000 0110	Indirect addressing: At the given address is the address to be used. Load the contents of this second address to ACC
LDX	<address>	0000 0111	Indexed addressing: Form the address as <address> plus the contents of IX. Copy the contents of this address to ACC
INC	<register>	0000 0011	Add 1 to the contents of the register (ACC or IX)
OUTCH		1000 0001	Output to the monitor the character corresponding to the ASCII character code in ACC
IN		1001 0000	Input a denary number from the keyboard and store in ACC
JMP	<address>	1100 1000	Unconditional jump to the given address
END		1111 1111	End the program and return to the operating system

The diagram shows a program loaded in main memory starting at location 100.

Locations 200 onwards contain data which is used by the program.

100	LDI 150
101	OUTCH
102	LDD 150
103	INC ACC
104	STO 150
105	JP 150
106	END
107	

150	200

200	65
201	76
202	65
203	77
204	32
205	32

a i   The instruction at address 102 is fetched.

Show the contents of the registers after execution.

Write on the diagram to explain.

ACC

[   ]

IX

[   ]

[2]

ii The instruction at address 100 is fetched.

Show the contents of the registers after execution.

Write on the diagram to explain.

ACC

[   ]

IX

[   ]

[3]

b   The given table of instructions shows the binary number used for each instruction's opcode.

All instructions in machine code are stored as a 16-bit pattern, with the first 8 bits the opcode and the second 8 bits the operand.

i   What is the maximum number of different instructions this processor could have?   [1]

Consider the instruction:

0	0	0	1	0	0	0	0	0	1	0	0	0	0	0	1

ii Describe what this instruction does.   [2]

iii Programmers will prefer to write machine code instructions in hexadecimal.

Explain why.   [1]

iv What is the hexadecimal for this instruction shown in **part (b)(ii)**?   [1]

Show the machine code for the following instructions:

v   LDI 150

[2]

vi LDV 15

[2]

vii A programmer makes the statement:

"For this instruction set, some of the instructions do not require an operand"

State if this statement is true or false. Explain with reference to the instructions given.   [2]

c   Use the ASCII code table to trace the **first four iterations** of the given program.

ASCII code table (part)					
Character	**Decimal**	**Character**	**Decimal**	**Character**	**Decimal**
<Space>	32	I	73	R	82
A	65	J	74	S	83
B	66	K	75	T	84
C	67	L	76	U	85
D	68	M	77	V	86
E	69	N	78	W	87
F	70	O	79	X	88
G	71	P	80	Y	89
H	72	Q	81	Z	90

ACC	Location 150	OUTPUT

100	LDI	150
101	OUTCH	
102	LDD	150
103	INC	ACC
104	STO	150
105	JP	100
106	END	
107		
150	200	
200	65	
201	76	
202	65	
203	77	
204	32	
205	32	

[5]

Cambridge International AS and A Level Computing 9691 Paper 31, Q4, Nov 2014

System software

5.01   Operating system

Why does a computer need an operating system?

The computer hardware is completely unusable without an operating system (**OS**). The operating system provides the visual user interface which allows the user to communicate with the computer system.

Management tasks carried out by the operating system

The computer system has various resources which must be managed:

- Main memory: Do we have enough memory to load another program?

- Secondary storage: Is there sufficient hard disk space to save a file download?

- Processor: If a number of processes are concurrently loaded, how does the operating system decide which process gets the next use of the processor?

- Input/output devices: Are they working? Are they recognised by the various application programs in use?

Progress check 5.01

1   Is the operating system classified as system software or applications software?

2   Write a definition for operating system software.

5.02   Utility programs

Any PC computer system will need to use utility software. This section describes various utilities.

TIP The list of possible utility software is huge. For the examination, you are only expected to know about those covered in this section.

Disk formatter

LOOK BACK «

Chapter 3 described the construction of a hard disk.

Formatting a disk is the process of preparing the hard disk for use with the operating system's file storage system, such as Windows NTFS or FAT32. Formatting will delete any existing data on the disk.

Other types of storage, such as flash memory cards and flash drives, come pre-formatted.

The disk can be divided into partitions (or volumes) and this should be done before the formatting process. Each partition is then referred to with a different logical drive letter.

Virus checker

A virus is software which is designed to cause harm to a computer system. The term 'malware' is now commonly used to describe a vast range of threats. Malware is any software which is designed to cause some form of malfunction of a computer system.

> ### LOOK FORWARD »
>
> Malware is studied in detail in Chapter 17, section 17.04.

Defragmenter software

When data is written to a hard disk the operating system will decide which file allocation units are to be used. The net result is that the file – which requires 53 allocation units of storage, for example – may use storage units which are scattered across various tracks. A 'best case' is that the units are stored on as few tracks as possible. This requires the fewest number of movements of the read/write heads and so results in a faster overall speed in the writing or reading of the file.

Defragmentation is the software process that reduces the amount of fragmentation. It does this by physically re-organising the contents of the disk used to store files using the smallest number of contiguous regions (fragments). A secondary consequence should be to create larger contiguous regions of free space. Running the 'defragmentation' software should be a task which is done by the PC user around once a month.

Disk contents analysis/disk repair software

Loss of the data on a hard disk would be a worst-case scenario for a user! A disk could report that the computer is unable to read data from the disk. Software is available which will attempt to offer a solution in retrieving the data from the disk. The user could purchase software to perform this task. Alternatively 'disk recovery' is offered as a commercial service by various providers.

File compression

> ### LOOK BACK «
>
> Chapter 1 discussed compression techniques for use with image, sound and video files.

Compression software is designed to take an original file's contents and process the bytes in such a way as to produce a new version of the file that requires fewer bytes. Software must then be available which takes the compressed file and is able to recreate (or restore) the file to its original state.

Backup software

Regular backups should be taken for the data on any computer system. This will safeguard against computer failure – in particular, failure of the secondary storage. Backup software verifies the backup copy. That is, it compares, byte by byte, the data on the original medium and the copy on the backup device.

Backups are of no use unless there is software available to restore the backup if and when it is needed.

Commercial backup software often has many variants. The software can provide synchronisation between two devices, which can be either one way or two way. This could be implemented either at regular intervals or in real-time. The objective is to ensure that two file stores contain exactly the same files and file versions. One-way synchronisation is called 'file mirroring'.

> ## Progress check 5.02
>
> List the five resources which are managed by the operating system of the computer.

5.03 Library programs

Program libraries

When a programmer sets out to write programs in a particular high-level language they will choose the environment to use. The language will include all the essential keywords and other syntax which make up the language. However certain coding features will have been made available to the programmer using program libraries. The programmer will need to specify in their code that a particular library will be required. These libraries often take the form of classes which then make objects available to the programmer.

The libraries will be very varied, ranging from libraries which provide basic input/output to specialised applications such as interfacing to the controller of some piece of electronics.

With the arrival of Visual Basic .NET developers have access to a comprehensive program library that was not available to them with Visual Basic version 6 and earlier. Microsoft's substantial .NET framework class library (FCL) offers VB.NET developers thousands of reusable type classes, which encapsulate the functionality of core system and application services. The objective is to make program design and coding easier and faster for the developer.

Dynamic link library (DLL) files

A DLL file is executable code which is only loaded into main memory when required. Consider a user using a word processor. The spell-checker may first be required after 20 minutes of the session.

DLLs provide a mechanism for shared code and data, allowing a developer of shared code or data to upgrade functionality without requiring applications to be re-linked or re-compiled. From the application development point of view, Windows is a collection of DLLs that are upgraded, allowing applications for one version of the operating system to work in a later one.

The concept of code sharing is useful, as the same DLL (for example, spell-checker code) can be used by a word processor, presentation software and a spreadsheet application. The code in a DLL can be shared among all the processes that use the DLL. That is, the DLL file occupies a single place in physical memory.

5.04 Language translators

Assembler software

> **LOOK BACK «**
>
> The use of assembler software has already been covered in Chapter 4.

Compiler software

A compiler translates a source code program written in a high-level language into a machine code file. If there are syntax errors present in the source code these will be reported to the developer. The programmer will make changes to the source code using the text editor and re-compile the program. The cycle is repeated until the compiler finds no errors and the final executable machine code file is produced. The object file can now be executed as many times as required without any further use of the compiler software.

Interpreter software

Interpreter software also makes sense of a program written in a high-level language. The process is entirely different to a compiled program. The program can attempt to run the program at any stage. The interpreter will analyse the first statement and, if no syntax errors are found, the interpreter will execute the statement. It then analyses the next statement and again executes it if possible. There is a continual progress of analysis and execution until an error is found.

Benefits and drawbacks of compilers and interpreters

Benefits of a compiler

- A compiler creates object code – that is, an executable file.
- Compiled programs execute faster than interpreted code.
- The compiler software is not needed at runtime: once compiled, no further translation is needed.
- If a program contains loops, the compiler will need to translate this section of code once only.

Benefits of an interpreter

• Interpreted code makes for easier debugging.

• An interpreter allows an attempted execution of the program at any stage in its development.

• An interpreter allows for testing parts of a program before all the code is written.

Java – the odd one out!

Java is a platform-independent language, which means you can run a Java program on any platform – hardware and operating system – without any modification.

Java uses a two-step compilation process. Java source code is compiled (using the javac compiler) down to 'bytecode'. The bytecode is executed by the Java Virtual Machine (JVM) software. The current version of JVM uses a technique called just-in-time (JIT) compilation to compile the bytecode to the native instructions understood by the CPU 'on the fly', at run time.

Some implementations of JVM might interpret the bytecode instead of JIT compiling it to machine code and running it directly; this is still considered an 'interpreter'. It's significantly different from interpreters that read and execute the high-level source code (in this case, the Java source code is not interpreted directly; it's the output of the Java compiler – the bytecode – which is interpreted).

In fact, once the Java compiler has produced the bytecode, the bytecode can be:

• compiled ahead of time and executed as machine code (similar to the traditional compilation process)

• compiled 'just-in-time' and executed

• interpreted

• directly executed by a supported processor, as bytecode is the native instruction set of some processors.

Progress check 5.03

Draw a system flowchart showing the third option above for the creation and translation of a Java source program ProgA.jav. Show the files which are produced.

Summary

■ Any computer system needs an operating system to provide a user interface and manage the resources of main memory, the processor, secondary storage and the input/output devices.

■ A PC computer system needs utility software including a disk formatter, virus checker, defragmenter software, disk analysis/repair software, file compression and backup software.

■ New programming projects make use of existing code which is available from program libraries. This includes files made available as dynamic link library (DLL) files.

■ An assembler is the software used to translate a source program written in assembly language into an object file in machine code.

■ A program written in a high-level language can be translated by software called a compiler. The compilation process is similar to the assembly process.

■ An alternative to a compiler is to use interpreter software. The interpreter analyses and executes the program statements in sequence.

■ There are various benefits from using either a compiler or interpreter.

■ The Java programming language uses a process which is part compilation and part interpreted. The process produces intermediate code called bytecode.

Exam-style questions

1 The following are the first few lines of a source program written in a high-level language which is about to be translated by the language compiler.

```
// invoicing program
// program written 21 Oct 2014
DECLARE i : INTEGER;
DECLARE Customer(40) : STRING;
DECLARE Address: STRING;
CONSTANT DiscountRate = 5;
// start of main program
CALL InitialiseCustomerData
REPEAT
    ...
    ...
    ...
```

During the lexical analysis stage the compiler will use a keyword table and a symbol table.

a Describe what information is contained in the keyword table.   [2]

b List **three** entries which must be in the keyword table for this program.   [1]

c Describe what information is contained in the symbol table.   [2]

d List **three** entries which will be entered in the symbol table for this program.   [1]

Cambridge International AS and A Level Computing 9691 Paper 31, Q6 a Nov 2014

Chapter 6

Security, privacy and data integrity

Revision objectives

By the end of the chapter you should be able to:

- explain the difference between the terms 'security', 'privacy' and 'integrity' of data and appreciate the need for all three

- describe security measures designed to protect computer systems including user accounts, firewalls and general authentication techniques

- describe security measures designed to protect the security of data, including data backup, a disk-mirroring strategy, encryption, access rights to data (authorisation)

- show awareness of what kinds of error can occur and what can be done about them

- describe error detection and correction measures designed to protect the integrity of data, including data validation and data verification

6.01 Data security

TERMS

Security: the safeguarding of the data against accidental or malicious damage or loss

Data integrity: the safeguarding of the validity and 'correctness' of the data

Privacy: preventing access to personal data by persons other than the subject or a third party who has permission to do so

TIP

Care is needed here; the terms **'security'**, **'privacy'** and **'integrity'** are often confused.

The provision of access to the computer system and access to certain data only are quite separate issues.

Security of the computer system

User accounts

Access to the computer system is only possible with a User ID (that is a user 'account') and the required password.

Users must carefully follow company policy about the choosing and changing of passwords. For example:

- A password may have to consist of a mixture of upper case, lower case and digit characters.

- A password may have to be at least eight characters.

- A password cannot be a password which has previously been used.

- Users may be forced to change their password every 30 days.

- Users are encouraged not to use 'memorable data', such as your dog's name or birthday.

Access for certain users can be restricted to the use of certain terminals only. For example, call-centre staff are only authorised to log-on from terminals situated in certain rooms.

Firewalls

A firewall is a system designed to prevent unauthorised access to and from a private network. Firewalls can be implemented in hardware, software or a combination of both. Firewalls are frequently used to prevent unauthorised Internet access to a private network.

All messages entering or leaving the private network pass through the firewall. It examines each message and blocks those that do not meet some specified security checks.

A firewall is used to allow remote access to the private network through secure authentication certificates and logins.

- A hardware firewall is typically found in a broadband router.

- A software firewall is installed on the computer and can be customised to set up the protection features required. A software firewall will protect your computer from outside attempts to control or gain access the computer.

Techniques used by a firewall include:

- packet filtering: each packet entering or leaving the network is examined and accepted or rejected, based on rules.

- application gateway: security checking is applied to specific applications, such as data from file transfer protocol (FTP) and Telnet servers.

- proxy server: all messages entering and leaving the network are intercepted. The proxy server effectively hides the true network addresses.

Static packet filtering examines a packet based on the information in its header and (fixed) rules which have been set by the administrator.

Stateful (or dynamic) packet filtering works at the network layer. The firewall tracks each connection the packet has made and makes sure they are valid. The firewall:

- examines the header information.

- examines the contents of the packet up through the application layer in order to determine more about the packet than just information about its source and destination.

- monitors the state of the connection and compiles the information in a state table.

Because of this, filtering decisions are based not only on administrator-defined rules (as in static packet filtering) but also on the context that has been established by prior packets that have passed through the firewall.

Authentication techniques

Authentication is a technique or procedure designed to prove that an identity is indeed who the person is claiming to be.

- Passwords: A user who attempts to log on as user TonyP is insufficient for authentication as user IDs are generally public. If user TonyP is the only person with knowledge of the password then its use will establish that this log on attempt is from the authentic user.

- Biometric techniques: This includes fingerprint scanning and retina scanning. It can be used to access certain computers or rooms and establishes that this is the authentic user.

- Digital signatures: This technique can be used when sending an email. The addition of a digital signature to the email establishes that the email was indeed sent from the perceived sender.

LOOK FORWARD »

See Chapter 17, section 17.02 for a further discussion of digital signatures.

Security of data

LOOK BACK «

Data backup was discussed in Chapter 5, section 5.02 on utility software.

Disk-mirroring strategy

A file is 'on-line' if the file is held on some file server and is constantly available to some program.

For example, an airline reservation booking system must have the master bookings file constantly available to terminals 24 hours a day. A security strategy could be:

- having two complete copies of the master file held on different servers. If one disk fails then the processing could still be achieved with the second copy of the data files.

- taking a frequent backup of the data files (say every 30 minutes). A worst-case scenario would then be that we would lose only the last 30 minutes' transactions or bookings.

Encryption

Encryption is a safeguard to protect the security of the data.

The original data file has all the data bytes changed in some way by applying an 'encryption key'. The file is then transmitted to some receiver; the file is meaningless unless the receiver knows the decryption key (or cipher) needed to change the encrypted file back to its original state.

For example, a text file may have 6 added to the ASCII value for each character. A file starting with characters CPT2 would be encrypted as IVZ8. Unless the decryption key of 'take the ASCII value for each character and subtract 6' is known, it will be impossible to decrypt the file.

Access rights to data (authorisation)

The user is 'authorised' to use certain files or programs.

LOOK FORWARD »

Chapter 8, section 8.01 describes database management (DBMS) software. Figure 8.01 illustrates different groups of users having different access rights to certain files.

Individual files can be password protected. For example, Microsoft Office software can have a password set for access to a document, spreadsheet or database.

When working with database software, syntax and commands of SQL are used extensively for this. SQL is used to create groups of users. These user groups are then granted various permissions – read only, read and write, etc. – to certain objects created by the database designer, such as tables and views.

What errors can occur and what can be done about them?

The system should record repeated unsuccessful attempts at logging on by a user account. The user account or terminal could be disabled after, for example, three wrong passwords have been entered.

The Network Manager should be alerted by a message at the server if a number of wrong passwords have been entered in a short time, or a log file records logon attempts at unusual times of day.

The network operating system will generate a log of all user usage.

6.02   Data integrity

We already have a definition for integrity at the start of the chapter – it means checking that a data value is 'valid' or just 'sensible'.

We need to carefully avoid other descriptors such as 'correct'. For example, an employee workplace code could be stored as 'London' which is a valid code, but this employee's workplace is actually 'Paris'. So the integrity of the datum stored is fine, but the value is not correct.

Data validation

Validation checks are carried out on data values using software. The validation checks will be done with program code.

Check digit

An extra character is added to an important field, for example, an employee code, to ensure that it is transmitted as entered.

Assume an employee code is 3675C where 'C' represents a final calculated digit, the check digit. The check digit is calculated by multiplying the original digits by a standard number and then taking the modulus.

The method is illustrated in Figure 6.01. The complete employee code is, therefore, calculated as 3675X.

Employee code	Multiplier	Calculation
3	1	3
6	2	12
7	3	21
5	4	20
	Total	56

The total is divided by 11 to give a remainder of 1. The check digit is calculated as 11 minus the remainder (10, in this case, which is then encoded as 'X').

Figure 6.01 Calculating a check digit

The data entry software would know the calculation used for the check digit and so can check the integrity of any employee code entered.

Note: the checking software does not know what is wrong with the number, only that it must be in error.

Progress check 6.01

The code 94372 is invalid. What check digit would the software calculate for this employee code?

Select values from a list

Certain data values only are possible and are taken from the list of permitted values.

For example, the first two characters of a product code are always selected from the following list: EL (electrical), CO (consumables) or HA (hardware).

Range check

A number value must be within a certain range.

For example, suppose a main menu offers six choices: 1 2, 3, 4, 5 and finally 6 to exit. The number input by the user must be an integer in the range 1 to 6. Any other input from the user will be refused.

Format check

A product code must follow a certain format.

For example, all product codes must start with a two-character code followed by four digits. EL9623 is a valid product code; C8432 and CO268 are invalid product codes.

Length check

A value must be a certain length.

For example, all product codes must be exactly six characters.

Presence check

A field must contain a value (it cannot be left blank).

For example, when entering the data for a customer order, a product code must be present.

LOOK FORWARD »

The SQL data definition language uses the syntax NOT NULL as part of the attribute definition (see Chapter 8, section 8.03), to define that the field cannot be left blank.

Uniqueness check

The data value for an attribute cannot be repeated for other records.

For example, all product codes in the products file must be different.

Data verification for data entry

Manual data entry is done by the user typing in characters at the keyboard or making selections from a list provided. We would not use the term 'data entry' for a word-processed document. Data entry assumes this is a data set which will then be used for some form of processing: ordering a new coat from a website, registering your details on a forum, etc.

Web forms are constructed using standard controls:

- a text box for text entry.

- making a single selection from a group of radio buttons.

- making one or more selections from a group of check boxes.

- making a single selection from a drop-down list.

The choice of which control to use for which data value is an important design consideration for the form.

Data verification may take place on one or more of the data values entered – usually the user will have to enter the data value twice. If the two entries do not match, the user will be asked to re-enter the values.

Progress check 6.02

A gym is to design a web form for application for membership. These are some of the fields the applicant will complete:

- family name

- forenames

- date of birth (members must be over aged 18 and under 80)

- address

- email address

- membership type: A – Adult, J – Junior, S – Senior citizen

- type of membership required (F – Full, L – Limited to certain times of the day)

- number of times likely to visit the gym in any one week

- have you been a member of a gym before?

Consider validation checks which could be used on the web form for data capture.

Draw up a table as shown below and tick any appropriate checks for each attribute.

Attribute	Verification / Validation check							
	Verify	From a list	Range	Format	Length	Presence	Uniqueness	Check digit
Family Name								
Forenames								
DateOfBirth								
Address								
Email								
MemType								
NoOfVisits								
Before								

Data verification during data transfer

We used the term 'verification' when describing the process of take a backup copy of files in Chapter 5. The process may make a verification check between the original data and the copy made of the data.

Parity check

Parity is a check on the validity of the codes of individual characters within a file when it is read or written.

For example, all ASCII codes need a seven-digit code to represent a character. 'A' is coded as decimal value 65, that is, 1000001 in binary. All computers store data in eight bits, that is, a byte. An eighth bit is added to the code, which can then be used to check the validity of the byte.

The system works on either even or odd parity. Assume, for this example, odd parity is used. This requires that the parity bit for the letter 'A' is set to 1, and the complete code for character 'A' becomes 11000001. The inclusion of the '1' parity bit makes the total number of 1 bits in the byte an odd number (in this case, 3).

If the byte was read from the disk as 1100 1001, then the 'parity system' would know that this code must be in error.

Parity block check

A parity check can be made on a group of bytes which are transmitted in sequence. Data for an additional byte – called the parity byte – is calculated and added to the block sequence. The data bytes and the parity byte together are called the parity block.

A parity block is calculated from a rectangle made up of a row for each data byte. The parity byte is calculated from the vertical columns of the data bytes. A parity check is still made on individual data bytes by considering the bit value in the final column.

Each bit in the parity byte is calculated by using the normal parity calculation for each of the eight columns of the data bytes.

In Figure 6.02, each group of four data bytes is followed by a parity byte.

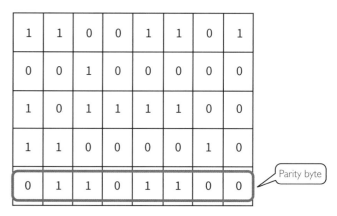

Figure 6.02 Data bytes and parity byte

Progress check 6.03

Study Figure 6.02 and check:

- the final column of parity bits
- the bit values in the parity byte

Case 1: Assume that there was an error in the bytes transmitted. The error is the bit marked in Figure 6.03.

1	1	0	0	1	1	0	1
0	0	1	0	0	0	0	0
1	0	0	1	1	1	0	0
1	1	0	0	0	0	1	0
0	1	1	0	1	1	0	0

Figure 6.03 Parity block with a single error

This error will mean the receiving software calculates the parity bit for this byte as 1 – but it was received as a zero. So, there must be an error. Also, the parity byte calculation will trigger there is an error in the third column. The software can therefore conclude that the error must be the highlighted bit and so will change this from the received 0 to a 1.

Case 2: Two of the bits received from one of the data bytes were in error as shown in Figure 6.04.

1	1	0	0	1	1	0	1
0	0	1	0	0	0	0	0
1	0	1	0	1	1	0	1
1	1	0	0	0	0	1	0
0	1	1	0	1	1	0	0

Figure 6.04 Parity block with two errors

Byte 3 passes the parity check for the byte, but the issue is that the parity bit itself is one of the errors. The parity byte will trigger that there is an error in columns 4 and 8.

It is claimed that the use of parity bits and a parity byte will identify 99% of all data transmission errors.

Progress check 6.04

A data transfer sends the following four data bytes followed by a parity byte. The system uses even parity.

0	0	0	0	1	1	1	1
1	1	1	0	0	0	0	0
1	0	1	1	0	0	0	1
0	1	1	1	1	0	0	0
0	0	1	0	0	1	0	0

1 Circle the bit errors which have occurred when the above five bytes are received.

2 Will the receiving software be able to identify where the error(s) occurred?

Checksum check

A checksum check is carried out on a complete block of data within the file, when is read or written.

LOOK BACK «

Chapter 3 discussed the construction of a hard disk. Data is read from or written to the disk in blocks.

The checksum figure is calculated from all the other bytes within the block and stored as part of the block. When the data block is read or written, the checksum figure can be calculated and compared with the stored value.

Progress check 6.05

Give a definition of the computing terms:

• Security

• Privacy

• integrity

Summary

■ Issues concerned with data include its security, privacy and integrity.

■ Security of data and the computer system itself should both be planned for.

■ Computer system security measures include user accounts, a firewall, general authentication techniques including the use of passwords and digital signatures.

■ Security of data is safeguarded using backups, a disk-mirroring strategy, encryption and the setting up of access rights to allow authorisation of a user or group of users to certain data.

■ Measures to ensure data integrity include:

• data validation: format, length, range, 'from a list', presence and uniqueness checks

• data verification both for data entry and during a data transfer process

• verification checks during data transfer include the use of parity and checksums.

Exam-style questions

1 When data is transmitted, it may become corrupted.

a Explain how a parity check can be used to detect a possible error in a transmitted byte. [3]

b Describe how parity can be used to identify and correct the single error in this transmitted data block.

```
0 1 1 0 1 1 0 1

1 0 0 1 0 1 1 1

0 1 0 1 0 1 0 0

1 0 0 0 1 0 0 1

0 1 1 0 0 0 1 1

1 0 0 0 0 1 1 0

0 1 1 0 1 1 0 1

0 1 0 0 0 0 0 0   Parity byte
```
[3]

Cambridge International AS and A Level Computer Science 9608 Specimen paper 1, Q2 2015

2 A database holds data for thousands of products. Each product code is a six-character code and two letters of the code indicate the type of product. For example, a product with EL is an electrical item.

a Suggest a format for the product codes. [1]

b Describe five validation checks which would be appropriate to use on the product code when a new product is entered into a web form. [5]

Ethics and ownership

Chapter 7

Revision objectives

By the end of the chapter you should be able to:

- [ ] show a basic understanding of ethics
- [ ] explain how ethics may impact on the job role of the computing professional
- [ ] show understanding of the eight principles listed in the ACM/IEEE Software Engineering Code of Ethics
- [ ] demonstrate the relevance of these principles to some typical software developer workplace scenarios

- [ ] show understanding of the need for a professional code of conduct for a computer system developer
- [ ] show understanding of the concept of ownership and copyright and describe the need for legislation to protect ownership, usage and copyright
- [ ] show understanding of the implications of different types of software licensing

7.01 Ethics and the computing professional

Ethics

The term **ethics** is not restricted to computing and the use of computers.

> **TERMS**
>
> **Ethics:** the moral principles that govern a person's behaviour or the conducting of an activity

In our context, we will look at ethics which apply to the computing workplace. Many employers will have drawn up a Code of Conduct about the behaviour expected of their employees. Some of these will have a moral dimension – others will amount to little more than common-sense guidelines about the way the employees conduct themselves in the workplace.

ACM/IEEE Software Engineering Code of Ethics

Computers have an all-pervading role in industry, government, medicine, education, entertainment and society at large. Software engineers contribute, by direct participation or by teaching, to the analysis, specification design, development, maintenance and testing of software systems.

Because of their roles in developing software systems, software engineers have significant opportunities to do good, to cause harm or to influence others. Software engineers must commit themselves to making software engineering a beneficial and respected profession. In accordance with that commitment, software engineers shall adhere to the following code of ethics and professional practice.

The ACM/IEEE Software Engineering Code of Ethics contains eight principles related to the behaviour of and decisions made by professional software engineers, including practitioners, educators, managers, supervisors and policy makers, as well as trainees and students of the profession. The principles identify the ethically responsible framework in which individuals, groups and organisations participate and their primary obligations.

Figure 7.01 shows the headers for the eight principles with the first-level boxes. The expansion boxes illustrate some specific actions/safeguards to be implemented.

Typical software developer workplace scenarios

Much of software design and coding is done with teamwork. Each member of the team has a collective

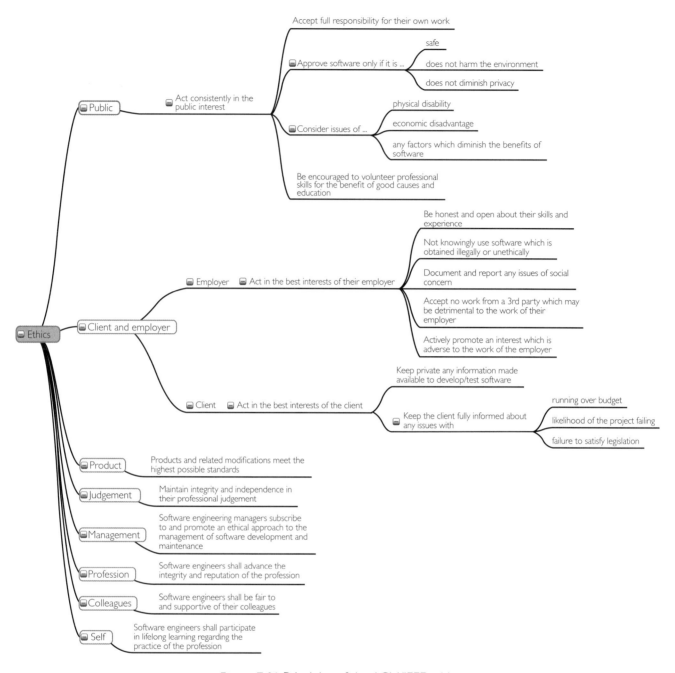

Figure 7.01 Principles of the ACM/IEEE ethics

responsibility to the other team members. This would extend to the sharing of expertise and general recognition of the contribution made by other team members to their work.

The analyst will need to spend a considerable amount of time in the client's workplace and should be respectful of rules and procedures which are in place for the client's employees.

The list of eight principle headings are clearly all-pervading both at individual and organisation level and would impact

on all aspects of the developer's work irrespective of their precise job role.

Professional code of conduct for a computer system developer

Becoming a member of a professional body or the employee of an organisation will require you to follow a code of conduct expected by the organisation. This may be summarised in a formal document which the individual must sign. For example the Chartered Institute of IT (formerly the British Computer Society) has a published code of conduct.

An employer's code of conduct would include:

- individual responsibilities in the workplace
- guidelines for the use of the Internet in the workplace
- guidelines for the use of use of internal and external email
- what is considered misuse of equipment and other resources
- what is considered unacceptable behaviour
- rules about the use of sensitive data.

An employee who does not adhere to these guidelines could expect disciplinary action. Some behaviour and actions could be the subject of legal action.

Progress check 7.01

Business A is a software house which is developing software for Business B which is expected to take six months to develop and install. List a number of ethical issues the manager at Business A should consider when communicating with Business B.

7.02 Ownership of software and data

Legislation to protect ownership, usage and copyright

The software developer has obligations regarding legal and regulatory considerations which they need to bear in mind when developing their products. These include:

- intellectual property rights and licenses
- consumer protection
- age ratings and classification
- advertising
- data protection and privacy.

Legislation will differ for various countries. In the UK, legislation includes: Copyright Law, the Data Protection Act (UK) and the Computer Misuse Act (UK).

Copyright Law

The use of material on the Internet is subject to similar copyright conditions as other types of media. It is recommended that only a single copy of material is downloaded and that this copy is erased when the purpose for which it has been made has ended. Consent of the copyright holder should be sought if any large-scale or systematic use of material is to be made. If it is proposed to incorporate material in a report, the permission of the copyright holder must first be sought and full attribution given.

In recent years, the software industry has taken determined action to protect its rights. The Federation Against Software Theft (FAST) has undertaken a number of successful legal actions.

The Data Protection Act (UK)

The Data Protection Act is concerned with information stored by an organisation about 'living individuals' which is processed both manually and automatically. It gives rights to those individuals (the data subjects) about whom information is recorded.

The law requires good practice in handling information by the organisation holding the personal data (the data controller). The applications for which the personal data is to be used must be registered.

Computer Misuse Act (UK)

The Computer Misuse Act introduced several criminal offences related to computers which were not covered by the earlier Data Protection Act.

It is an offence for a person knowingly to obtain unauthorised access to a computer system. A more serious offence is to gain such authorised access with the intention of modifying data or programs. This would include the deliberate installation of any form of malware software.

Progress check 7.02

A hacker has gained access to the computer system of Business B and left a message suggesting the Network Manager should tighten up on the network security.

1 Is this an offence?

2 What UK legislation would be broken here?

LOOK BACK «

Measures to restrict access to data made available through the Internet and World Wide Web were covered in Chapter 6, section 6.01.

Software licensing

A license defines the rights and obligations that a licensor (usually the author of the software) grants to a licensee (a user to whom the software is made available). The granting of a licence does not assume that a charge has been made for the software.

When you buy a proprietary software package you are not buying the software – you are buying the right to use the software in a specific way. The software company owns the software.

Free Software Foundation (FSF)

'Free' is not intended to mean 'free of charge'. The philosophy of the organisation is that 'free' means the user of the software is free to:

- run the software

- copy the software

- distribute the software to other users

- study the code and change and improve the software. The user is then encouraged to make their improvements available to other users. (This may be a condition of the license.)

The philosophy is designed to encourage a programmer/developer community.

Following some modifications, the user might re-distribute their modifications. They can impose some rules about its use, but none which conflict with the four central freedoms. This is called 'copyleft'.

The flagship software of the FSF is GNU, a collection of many programs: applications, libraries, developer tools and games. GNU is a Unix-like operating system that allocates machine resources. GNU is typically used with a kernel called Linux. This combination is the GNU/Linux operating system. GNU/Linux is used by millions, though many call it 'Linux' in error.

The name 'GNU' is a recursive acronym for 'GNU's Not Unix'. GNU is pronounced as one syllable: g'noo.

Open Source Initiative

The Open Source Software Institute is a membership-based, non-profit organisation established in 2001 that promotes the development and implementation of open source software solutions within US government agencies.

Open-source licenses grant the right to copy, modify and redistribute the source code. These licenses may also impose obligations. Modifications to the code that are distributed must be made available in source code form and author attribution must be included in a program or documentation using that open source code.

Some of the organisations involved in OSS development include the Open Office and Wordpress software, Apache Software Foundation (the Apache web server), the Linux Foundation (Linus OS) and the Mozilla Foundation (Firefox web browser).

Several open source programs have become defining entries in their application area including the GIMP image editing system, the Java programming language and environment, and the MySQL database management system.

Open source software is made available under a licence that allows you to make copies and pass them on to anyone. The software comes with the source code, which you can change to meet your needs.

Licences for open source software vary. Some licences require you to make any changes made to the source code publicly available, while others will allow you to keep those changes private.

The advantages of open source software include:

- Start-up costs of adopting the software are nil.

- There is no supplier lock-in.

- You have freedom to do what you want with the software.

- Open standards support and encourage collaborative development.

- Licencing for a large number of users of the software is simplified.

The disadvantages of open source software include:

- It may be difficult to get support.

- Some proprietary formats, such as Microsoft's .docx file format, are so widely used that other formats may be less acceptable for business.

Progress check 7.03

A software license from the Free Software Foundation gives the recipient liberty (or freedom) to do what?

Shareware

Shareware is software that is distributed free on a trial basis with the understanding that the user may need to pay for it later. Some software developers offer a shareware version of their program with a built-in expiration date. For example, after 30 days the user can no longer get access to the program.

Other shareware (sometimes called 'liteware') is offered with certain capabilities disabled as an enticement to buy the complete version of the program at a later date.

Commercial software

Proprietary software is made available to an individual user or business under an end-user licence agreement (EULA). EULAs are generally long and complex contracts. You effectively accept the conditions of the licence when the software is installed.

The licence sets out how the software can be used and usually prohibits certain things:

- making unauthorised copies of the software and passing them on
- selling your licence to someone else
- using it on more than a certain number of computers
- attempting to reverse engineer it.

Proprietary software will be sold without access to the source code. The intention is that – without this code – neither you nor any other software supplier can make changes to the software package.

Proprietary software is made available under a number of different types of licence:

- Shrink-wrap licences are usually for one installation of the software. This is the most common type of licence for 'off-the-shelf' software purchased either online or from a retail store. Some types of licence may require software activation. This allows the supplier to check that the software is installed on just one PC. Re-activation will be required if the software is installed on a different PC.

- Per-user licences are common where software may be in use by more than one user simultaneously. The licence is usually for a specified maximum number of users.

- Site licences are much less restrictive. They typically allow an unlimited number of users from the same organisation to use the software.

Summary

- [ ] A computing professional is expected to behave ethically at all times.

- [ ] The Software Engineering Code of Ethics lists eight guiding principles concerned with the public, the client and employer, the product, judgement, management, the profession, colleagues and oneself.

- [ ] These points would be formalised and made clear to employees by the employer introducing a professional code of conduct.

- [ ] Software and data in various countries is protected by legislation covering the issues of ownership, usage and copyright.

- [ ] There are different types of software licensing. These include the Free Software Foundation, Open Source initiatives, shareware and commercial software.

Exam-style questions

1 The ACM and IEEE set out eight principles for ethics and professional practice.

The categories, with a short explanation, are shown in this diagram.

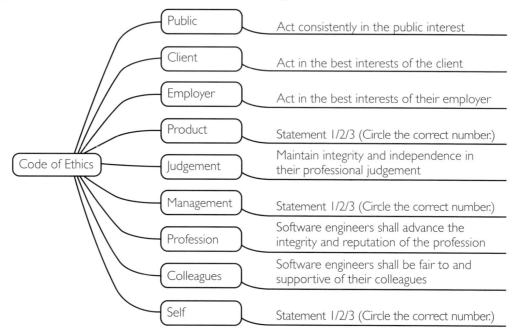

a These **three** statements need to be added to the diagram.

Statement 1: Team leaders should subscribe to and promote an ethical approach to the management of software development and maintenance.

Statement 2: Software engineers shall participate in lifelong learning regarding the practice of the profession.

Statement 3: Software and related modifications meet the highest possible standards.

Circle the correct numbers on the diagram to indicate the positions for Statement 1, Statement 2 and Statement 3. [2]

b For the following workplace scenario, unethical behaviour is demonstrated.

A large project is devolved to project teams, each led by a project leader. One project leader fails to inform his manager that he has major concerns that:

- their team's software contribution is taking much longer to write and test than anticipated

- they are consequently at risk of spending over their allocated budget.

Explain the principle(s) which are **not** being met. [3]

Cambridge International AS and A Level Computer Science 9608 Specimen paper 1, Q6 2015

2 Manjit works for a software house, CODEIT, writing programs. She also writes software in her spare time which she looks to market and sell for profit. For each activity/incident tick to indicate whether you consider this to be ethical or unethical behaviour.

	Ethical	Unethical
To save time, Manjit often makes up the test results for her CODEIT programs.		
Manjit has used many of the coding techniques she learnt from other employees at CODEIT in her own spare-time programs.		
Manjit has twice recently turned down the opportunity to leave CODEIT and work for another company for more pay.		
Manjit organises training courses in the writing of software in her spare time.		
Manjit has taken electronic copies of code from her CODEIT job and used it in her own programs.		
Other employees at CODEIT often ask Manjit for help and she always refuses, saying she is too busy.		

[5]

Database and data modelling

Revision objectives

By the end of the chapter you should be able to:

- [ ] show understanding of the limitations of using a file-based approach for the storage and retrieval of data

- [ ] describe the features of a relational database which address the limitations of a file-based approach

- [ ] show understanding of the features provided by a DBMS

- [ ] show understanding of how software tools found within a DBMS are used in practice

- [ ] show awareness that high-level languages provide access to data stored in a database

- [ ] show understanding of, and use, the terminology associated with a relational database model

- [ ] produce a relational design from a given description of a system including an entity–relationship diagram

- [ ] show understanding of the normalisation process

- [ ] explain why a given set of database tables are, or are not, in third normal form (3NF) and make changes to produce a solution in 3NF

- [ ] show understanding that DBMS software creates and modifies the database structure using its DDL queries and maintains data using its DML

- [ ] show understanding that the industry standard for DDL and DML is Structured Query Language (SQL)

- [ ] show understanding of a given SQL script

- [ ] write simple DDL commands

- [ ] write a SQL script for querying or modifying data (DML) in database tables

8.01 Database management systems (DBMS)

What is a database?

A database is a collection of related data. The data could relate to (for example) a firm's customers; each customer data is a record. Each record will store the same items of data, for example, customer name, address etc., and these are called attributes.

Database software has been commercially available for over 50 years and early software simply mirrored on the computer what a user would have done using a card index system. The cards would have a header line and the cards would then be filed in some determined order, for example, customer name. That was fine if we wanted to find a particular customer by name but what if we wanted to find the firm based at 13 The High St or the company with the contact person called Jamie Edwards? The major limitation of a manual card index is that the cards can only be held in one particular order and so can only be searched on one data item.

File-based approach

Before database software, a database application would have been programmed and constructed using one or more flat files.

The record structure would first be designed. For example, for our customer database, the fields would be:

- Customer name
- Contact person
- Address
- Town
- Account customer? (Yes/No)

LOOK FORWARD »

Different methods for file organisation and access will be studied in Chapter 13, section 13.02.

A major limitation of any solution based on files is that the record structure is fixed.

If after using the database for six months, we wanted to add a field, it would require a considerable amount of redesign of the files and program code.

Relational database approach

Program–data independence and changing data requirements

Database management system (DBMS) software stores not only the data itself but also the definition of the database in a data dictionary. Program–data independence is the separating out of the data definition (as accessed by application programs) and the programs which access the data. Changes to the structure of the data can be done quite independently of the programs which access the existing data.

For example, if an attribute is added to the Customer table, programs, queries and reports which access the existing attributes require no modification following the change to the data structure.

This ability to add and delete attributes easily avoids unproductive maintenance of the data.

Compare this to a file-based approach where the description of the data is held as 'data types' or class definitions within the program code. Once the new attribute is added, all program code must be re-written to take account of the new field.

Concurrent access to data

A feature of DBMS software is control over 'multi-user access' to the data with techniques such as record locking and file or table locking.

A lock may be applied to the entire database, preventing activity from all other users. Total locking like this is used when the entire database is involved in some activity such as rebuilding the indexes or deleting data marked as deleted.

A less severe lock is table-level locking, leaving other tables free for access by other users. However, as many transactions involve more than one table, table-level locking can also result in severe delays when one of the required tables is locked.

Locking individual records will cause the least delay. A single row of a table (i.e. record) is locked.

The scenario which must be considered is when two different users attempt to concurrently update the same record. What could happen is that one of the updates will be lost.

Queries are produced quickly

Since a DBMS has facilities such as a query generator (written in SQL or visually designed with QBE) and a report generator, the time taken to create a new query is minimal.

Compare this to the time it would take to create a new program.

Database management system (DBMS) software

A DBMS is software which enables the definition, creation and querying of a large collection of data. The software provides features for the maintenance of the data including:

- backup
- security
- interrogation of the data with SQL queries
- controlled access to the data with views which are only available to certain database users.

All aspects of the use of the DBMS software will be administered by a database administrator (DBA).

LOOK FORWARD »

This is studied in detail in Chapter 8, section 8.02.

Data dictionary

The data dictionary is a repository of all the information about the basic database design and all objects which have been created for its use, for example, queries, views and reports.

Progress check 8.01

Which of the following would be contained in the database's data dictionary?

- The lists of attributes for all tables
- The detail for all attributes (for example, data type and whether it has a secondary index)
- The customer data
- The results of all queries
- Query descriptions

Data integrity

Database management systems offer excellent validation support. The DBMS uses its data dictionary to perform validation checks on data entered into the database. Validation checks are set up at the table design stage and are effective every time a reference is made to that item of data including application programs which access data in that table.

Compare this to a 'file-based approach', where the validation checks have to be coded. Every time that data item is used, the validation-checking code must be present as part of the program code.

Data security

Backup is a centralised task administered by the database administrator (DBA). Since all data is centrally held within the DBMS, strategies for controlling the security are much easier to implement than with a file-based approach.

A database backup saves a database to a file on a hard disk or other storage medium. To protect a database from power failure, a disk crash or other potential data loss, the DBA will regularly back up the database. Backup and database maintenance is designed to:

- improve database performance by performing garbage collection of space occupied by deleted records and packing the remaining data; this often reduces database size

- give the option of changing the database page size or distributing the database among multiple files or disks

- enable backups to run concurrently while other users are using the database; the DBA does not have to shut down the database

- create a stable snapshot of the database for archiving purposes.

Access rights to particular tables or views can be created by the database designer. This allows particular individuals or groups of users access to only certain data.

Read again the points made about concurrent access to data. The various levels of locking are effectively a security feature.

Software tools found within a DBMS

A variety of software tools can use a DBMS, as shown in Figure 8.01.

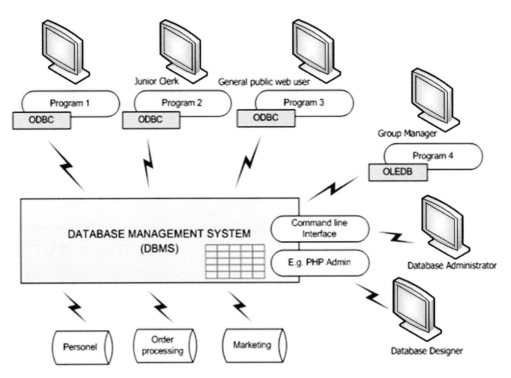

Figure 8.01 Typical DBMS usage

The database designer must have the ability to create all the basic objects, such as tables and queries, which make up the database. For software such as XAMPP, the developer interface is web-based software called PHPAdmin. Other features will be accessed from a command line interface.

Some users with competent computing skills would use a query processor to design their own SQL queries to extract information from the database.

Other users (such as the manager, junior clerk and others shown in Figure 8.01) will not have these skills and so applications programs must be written to perform tasks to carry out their job role. For example, the junior clerk has to enter the data for a new employee. This will be done using a program which displays a web form into which the data is entered. What the applications program must do is connect to the database and generate the appropriate SQL to save the data. Technologies, such as ODBC (Open Database Connectivity), have developed to do this. Other companies, such as Microsoft, have developed their own variants, such as OLEDB.

8.02   Relational database modelling

Relational database terminology

> **TERMS**
>
> **Entity:** some 'thing' about which data is recorded – a customer, a product, a customer order
>
> **Table:** the implementation of the data for an entity in relational database software
>
> **Tuple:** the data for one row in the table
>
> **Attribute:** one of the data items for an entity – a customer table could include the attributes customer name, address and town

Table notation

We use the following notation to describe the design for a **table**. The **attribute** underlined indicates the primary key.

```
CUSTOMER(CustomerName,
         CustomerAddress,
         CustomerTown,
         ContactPerson,
         AccountCustomer)
```

```
PRODUCT(ProductID,
        Description,
        TypeOfItem,
        RetailPrice,
        InStock)
```

```
ORDER(OrderNo,
      OrderDate,
      CustomerName,
      ProductID, Quantity)
```

Primary key

It is a fundamental rule of relational database design that every **tuple** in a table must be unique.

There may be an attribute which will 'do this job' for us. For the `CUSTOMER` table, this could be the customer name. Hence the designer could use `CustomerName` as the primary key for the `CUSTOMER`.

If there is no suitable attribute, we add a reference number attribute to ensure all the tuples are different. `ProductID` is the primary key for the `PRODUCT` table and `OrderNo` is the primary key for the `ORDER` table.

Candidate key

There could be more than one attribute which would act as the primary key, If so, each attribute is said to be a candidate key – that is, a contender for the primary key.

Secondary key and indexing

Part of the table design process will be to decide which attributes users are likely to use frequently for searching. For example in the `ORDER` table, we may frequently search on customer name, but not on quantity. Hence we would decide to index the `CustomerName` attribute. `OrderNo` is the primary key and so this attribute is already indexed.

The database software will update the list of indexes every time the data in the `ORDER` table is changed. Indexing is used to make data retrieval faster.

Any attribute which is indexed (and is not the primary key) is called a secondary key.

A table can have any number of secondary keys but every index has to be updated when the database data changes, so there is a trade-off between the processing time taken to keep the indexes up to date and the fast data retrieval times (for example, when running a query) which indexing provides.

Relationship

A link between two tables is called a relationship.

A relationship is one of three kinds:

- 1-to-1: rare and probably only occur because the two tables were created at different times

- 1-to-many: the most common type of relationship; the two relationships for the order processing scenario are both 1-to-many (see Figure 8.02)

- many-to-many: in the order processing scenario, we have a third relationship – 'Many customers will receive many products' (see Figure 8.03).

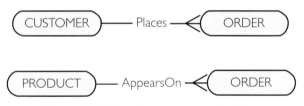

Figure 8.02 Two 1-to-many relationships

Figure 8.03 A many-to-many relationship

It is not possible to implement a many-to-many relationship with relational database software. Had the designer started with this many-to-many relationship, the strategy must be to re-design by introducing the ORDER table with two 1-to-many relationships (as shown in Figure 8.02).

Foreign key

How are relationships formed? The primary key attribute in the table on the 'one' side will link to (the same) attribute in the table on the 'many' side. This attribute in the 'many' side table is called the foreign key.

Consider the relationship: One customer (over a period of time) will place many orders.

Primary key `CustomerName` (in the `CUSTOMER` table) will link to foreign key `CustomerName` (in the `ORDER` table).

Consider the relationship: One product is present on many orders.

Primary key `ProductID` (in the `PRODUCT` table) links to foreign key `ProductID` (in the `ORDER` table).

Referential integrity

The data stored in the tables must obey the relationships which exist. For example, referential integrity would be violated if there was a customer name which appeared in one of the `ORDER` table tuples, but which was not present in the `CUSTOMER` table.

A relational design

The entities and the relationships are shown on an **entity–relationship (ER) diagram** (see Figure 8.04).

- The entities each have a name.

- The relationship line shows the degree of the relationship.

- The relationship can be labelled to indicate its purpose.

TIP

Some designers will show each relationship as a separate ER diagram (not all on one diagram, as shown in Figure 8.02).

Each relationship in Figure 8.04 has been given a description:

- Places

- AppearsOn

- Purchases

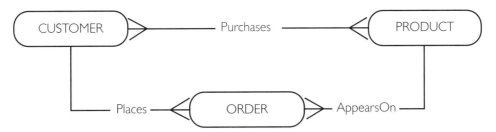

Figure 8.04 ER diagram with all relationships

Progress check 8.04

Consider this scenario:

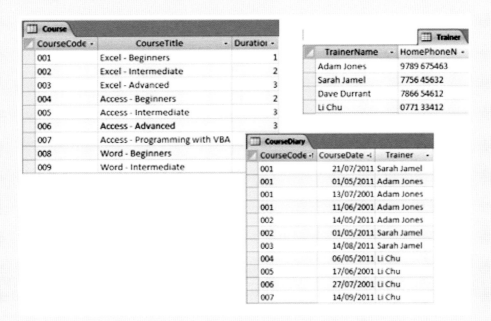

A training agency offers courses in software skills for popular PC software. Courses run for 1 to 5 days. Each course is delivered by one trainer. Courses offered are shown in the **COURSE** table. Each course is available many times throughout the year and this course schedule data is stored in table **COURSEDIARY**.

1   What attribute is used for the primary key of the **COURSE** table?

2   What data type was used for the `Duration` attribute?

3   Suggest two other attributes which the company might store about each trainer.

4   What will be a suitable primary key for the **TRAINER** table?

5   What will be a suitable primary key for the **COURSEDIARY** table?

6   Describe two relationships which exist between the tables **TRAINER**, **COURSE** and **COURSEDIARY**.

7   The **COURSEDIARY** table has two foreign keys. What are they?

8   Draw the entity–relationship diagram for this scenario.

Duplicated data

Note, we did not have the course name in the COURSEDIARY table – the CourseCode is sufficient for us to be clear what course is referred to. Similarly, the COURSEDIARY table did not store any other data about the trainer – the trainer name is sufficient.

A golden rule of relational database design is to avoid unnecessary duplicated data. If data does become duplicated then some of it will be redundant.

The normalisation process

If we return to the original task of designing the database, we must ask the question: How do we know we have a design which will not result in duplicated data?

There are three formal rules called first, second and third normal form (1NF, 2NF and 3NF), which we must use to check the final design.

Normalisation is the process – using the formal set of rules – which has to be followed to ensure that the data model produced (i.e. the table designs) are such that they will not give rise to duplicated (hence 'redundant') data. A fully normalised set of tables will contain no redundant data.

Consider this scenario: A firm encourages its staff to attend training courses. Each course has a unique course

title and duration from 1 to 5 days. Some courses are offered more than once on different dates. Employees have a StaffID and their name is recorded. Data is recorded showing all courses attended by each employee.

First Normal Form (1NF)

First normal form states that there should be no repeated groups of attributes.

```
STAFF(StaffID,
       StaffName,
       CourseTitle1,
       Date1,
       Duration1,
       CourseTitle2,
       Date2,
       Duration2,
       CourseTitle3,
       Date3,
       Duration3, ...)
```

This table design repeats the group of attributes CourseTitle, Date and Duration, and so the table is not in 1NF.

Table 8.01 illustrates this with data which shows the course attendance information being repeated for a single employee.

StaffID	StaffName	CourseTitle	SessionDate	Duration
037	Polly Searle	Managing People	12/03/2015	2
		Health and Safety 1	19/04/2015	1
		Health and Safety 2	23/12/2015	2
067	Will Harris	Health and Safety 1	19/04/2015	1
		Excel Stage 1	03/03/2015	2
184	Neal King	Marketing Stage 1	05/06/2015	2
		Excel Stage 1	03/03/2015	2
		Customer Care	10/05/2015	1

Table 8.01 Course data for staff members

The solution is to create a second table to store the course attendances separately for each employee, with a foreign key to link back to the original STAFF table.

The table design becomes:

STAFF(StaffID, StaffName)

STAFF-RECORD(StaffID, CourseTitle, CourseDate, Duration)

We assume that:

- The course title is unique.

- A particular course can be offered on more than one date.

- A member of staff never attends the same course more than once.

Second normal form (2NF)

Second normal form states that the non-key attributes in the table must be dependent on knowing all of the primary key.

For tables which have a single value primary key, the table must be in 2NF. The STAFF table, therefore, must be in 2NF.

But consider the STAFF-RECORD table:

```
STAFF-RECORD(StaffID,
             CourseTitle,
             CourseDate,
             Duration)
```

The primary key (is a composite key) of StaffID and CourseTitle. There are two non-key attributes: CourseDate and Duration, which can be known from knowing only the CourseTitle (i.e. only part of the primary key).

Hence the STAFF-RECORD table is not 2NF.

The solution is to move Duration and CourseDate into a new table, COURSE-SESSION.

```
STAFF(StaffID, StaffName)
```

```
STAFF-RECORD(StaffID,
             CourseTitle, Date)
```

```
COURSE-SESSION(CourseTitle,
               CourseDate,
               Duration)
```

But there is an issue with the COURSE-SESSION table: there is a composite primary key and the duration is known from knowing only the course title. Hence table COURSE-SESSION is NOT in 2NF.

The solution is to create a new table, COURSE.

```
STAFF(StaffID, StaffName)
```

```
STAFF-RECORD(StaffID,
             CourseTitle, Date)
```

```
COURSE(CourseTitle, Duration)
```

```
COURSE-SESSION(CourseTitle,
               CourseDate)
```

Third Normal Form (3NF)

Like 2NF, third normal form is concerned with non-key attributes: there must not be a dependency between any non-key attributes.

All four tables in our design have only one or no non-key attributes, therefore there cannot be non-key attributes which are dependent and, so we conclude, all four tables are in 3NF.

Consider if we had stored more data items in the STAFF table because the company has a single location in each of a number of different cities.

```
STAFF(StaffID,
      StaffName, City,
      CityAddress, Country)
```

But, if we know the city, we know the country and the address,. so we can create a new table, LOCATION. We must retain a foreign key of City in the STAFF table to give:

```
STAFF(StaffID, StaffName, City)
```

```
LOCATION(City, CityAddress, Country)
```

You should now check these final table designs to confirm all four tables are in 1NF, 2NF and 3NF.

```
STAFF(StaffID, StaffName, City)
```

```
LOCATION(City, CityAddress, Country)
```

```
STAFF-RECORD(StaffID,
             CourseTitle, Date)
```

```
COURSE(CourseTitle, Duration)
```

```
COURSE-SESSION(CourseTitle,
               CourseDate)
```

Progress check 8.05

1 Compete the table below to summarise the foreign keys in this design and state the table each foreign keys links to.

Foreign key Table.Attribute	Links to
STAFF.City	LOCATION.City

2 Draw the ER diagram.

Progress check 8.06

1 Which of these are true statements?

   a 'There must be no repeated group of attributes' – this is second normal form.

   b Non-key attributes means those which are not part of the primary key.

   c Both 2NF and 3NF are concerned with non-key attributes.

   d A table with a composite primary key using two attributes must be in 2NF.

   e A table with a single attribute primary key must be in 2NF.

2 Consider this scenario:

   All students have a tutor. Tutors are referred to by the three initials of their name, which are unique. For example, tutor Will Smythe has initials WSM. All tutors have their own separate tutor room.

```
STUDENT(StudentID,
        StudentName,
        TutorName,
        TutorInitials,
        TutorRoom)
```

   Which of these are true statements?

   a The primary key of student is `StudentID`.

   b The table is not in 3NF since `TutorName` is dependent on `TutorInitials`.

   c The table is not in 3NF since `TutorRoom` is dependent on `TutorInitials`.

   d The table is not in 3NF because it has a single-attribute primary key.

3 Consider this new design:

```
STUDENT(StudentiD,
        StudentName,
        TutorInitials)

TUTOR(TutorInitials,
      TutorName,
      TutorRoom)
```

   a What attribute in `STUDENT` acts as a foreign key?

   b Describe the relationship between these two tables.

8.03 Data definition language (DDL) and data manipulation language (DML)

Data definition language

The industry standard for both the data definition language (DDL) and the data manipulation language (DML) is Structured Query Language (SQL).

Modern database software provide features for the user to carry out much of the database design and the writing of queries using 'point-and-click' features. What happens behind the scenes is that the actions of the user are processed by forming SQL scripts.

DDL is used for the creation of the database, table design, creation of relationships and any changes to the table designs.

DML is used for the creation of queries and basic maintenance of the data (add, delete and amend data records).

We illustrate the following commands using the training records database – TRAINING. The data model for this database was:

```
STAFF(StaffID, StaffName, City,
Department)

LOCATION(City, CityAddress, Country)

STAFF-RECORD(StaffID,
             CourseTitle,
             Date)

COURSE(CourseTitle, Duration)

COURSE-SESSION(CourseTitle,
               CourseDate)
```

Creating a database
```
CREATE DATABASE TRAINING ;
```

The command could have additional parameters which give a user name and password required to access the database.

Creating a table definition
```
CREATE TABLE STAFF
 (
 StaffID : VARCHAR(6),
 StaffName : VARCHAR(40),
 City : VARCHAR(30),
 Department : VARCHAR(10)
 ) ;
```

Changing a table definition

Add an attribute: The number of years' service for each member of staff is to be recorded.

```
ALTER TABLE STAFF

ADD YearsService INTEGER ;
```

TIP

The syntax used for data types in SQL is different in some cases to the syntax we shall use in Part 2 for pseudocode and program code. For example:

	Pseudocode	SQL
String data	STRING	VARCHAR (<number>)
Integer	INTEGER	INT

You are not expected to know the detail of the syntax for the various SQL data types. In the exam, use the syntax we shall introduce in pseudocode from Chapter 9.

Delete an attribute (column): The department is to be deleted from the staff data.

```
ALTER TABLE STAFF

DELETE Department ;
```

Change the data type for an attribute: The `StaffID` is to be stored as an integer (not a string).

```
ALTER TABLE STAFF

MODIFY StaffID INTEGER ;
```

Adding a primary key to a table

This is done when the table is created.

```
CREATE TABLE LOCATION
(
City NOT NULL,
City : VARCHAR(30),
CityAddress : VARCHAR(40),
Country : VARCHAR(30),
PRIMARY KEY (City);
```

> NOT NULL says the attribute cannot be left blank

Or, if the primary key is added at a later stage:

```
ALTER TABLE LOCATION

ADD PRIMARY KEY (City) ;
```

Adding a foreign key to a table

Again this can be done at the table design stage:

> NOT NULL can be included with the data type

```
CREATE TABLE COURSE-SESSION
(
CourseTitle : VARCHAR(50) NOT NULL,
CourseDate : DATE NOT NULL,
PRIMARY KEY (CourseTitle, Date),
FOREIGN KEY (CourseTitle) REFERENCES
COURSE(CourseTitle)
);
```

Data Manipulation Language (DML)

Queries – using data from a single table

The keywords used in a query are:

- SELECT
- FROM
- WHERE
- ORDER BY
- GROUP BY
- INNER JOIN

Example: Display all attributes for cities in India.

```
SELECT *

FROM LOCATION

WHERE Country = 'India' ;
```

Example: Display only the city names for cities in the UK.

```
SELECT City

FROM LOCATION

WHERE Country = 'UK' ;
```

Example: Display the Staff Ids for all staff who attended the Excel Stage 1 course on 13th May 2015.

```
SELECT StaffID
FROM STAFF-RECORD
WHERE CourseTitle = 'Excel Stage 1'
  AND CourseDate = #13/05/2015#;
```

> # is used to enclose a date

> The logic of the query requires the AND operator

Example: Display the cities where the company has offices, alphabetically by city.

```
SELECT City

FROM Location

ORDER BY City
```

Example: Display the cities where the company has offices, grouped by country.

```
SELECT City

FROM Location

GROUP BY Country
```

Queries – needing data from two tables

Above, we wrote a query to display the Staff Ids for staff who attended a course. What if we also require the staff name to be displayed?

The name is stored in the `STAFF` table and there is a relationship between `STAFF-RECORD` and `STAFF`.

The `INNER JOIN` keyword selects all tuples from both tables where there is a match between the columns in both tables.

```
SELECT STAFF.StaffID, Staff.StaffName

FROM STAFF-RECORD INNER JOIN STAFF

WHERE STAFF-RECORD.CourseTitle =
  'Excel Stage 1'

AND STAFF-RECORD.CourseDate =
  #13/05/2015# ;
```

Note: the table name is now added to the attribute name.

Data maintenance

Add a record: Add a new staff record.

```
INSERT INTO STAFF

  (StaffID, StaffName, City)

VALUES ('050091', 'Rankin', 'London');
```

Delete a record: Staff member 060078 has left the company.

```
DELETE FROM STAFF
WHERE StaffID = '060078' ;
```

> Take care! This may cause referential integrity problems: records in the STAFF-RECORD table may also require deleting

Amend a record: The Excel Stage 1 course has been changed from a one-day to a two-day course.

```
UPDATE COURSE

SET Duration = 2

WHERE CourseTitle = 'Excel Stage 1';
```

Progress check 8.07

Study the following scenario:

Bands are registered with an agency. An agency will have several artists and bands on its books. A band or artist never has more than one agent.

Bands go 'on tour'. Concerts which are 'one offs' are rare and the band will indicate the maximum number of gigs which they intend performing on any tour. A tour therefore consists of one or more gigs.

The promoter tends to use the same set of venues. Each venue has recorded:

- venue name

- location (e.g. London)

- capacity.

Each band's tour gigs are booked into a venue. The same venue may be booked for a number of tour dates if the promoter is anticipating a high demand for tickets.

The following data model is produced:

```
BAND(BandName, AgentName)

AGENT(AgentName, AgentAddress,
AgentContactName)

BAND-TOUR(BandName, TourName,
StartDate, FinalDate, MaxNoOfGigs)

BAND-TOUR-GIGS(BandName, TourName,
GigDate, VenueName)
```

```
VENUE(VenueName, Capacity, Loca-
tion)
```

1 Complete the table showing the primary key and any foreign keys) for each table.

The first entry is done for you.

Table	Primary key	Foreign Key(s)
BAND	BandName	None
AGENT		
BAND-TOUR		
BAND-TOUR-GIGS		
VENUE		

2 Draw the ER diagram for the data model.

3 Write the SQL queries for the following:

a Display a list of all band names who use agent Maximum Exposure.

b Display a list of all the band names who go on tour on or after 01/01/2015.

c Display a list of tour names which start after 01/06/2015 and have more than ten tour gigs.

d Display a list showing band name, tour name and venue for all tours which have a concert in Paris.

e Display a list of all gig dates and venues for the 'Back to the future' tour in ascending date order.

Summary

- ■ A relational database is used to model some real-world data-processing application. Terminology used includes entity, table, tuple, attribute and relationship.

- ■ There are number of attribute keys which can be set: primary key, foreign key and candidate key. Secondary keys are used for indexing the data.

- ■ Relationships can be shown using an entity–relationship diagram.

- ■ A final data model design must satisfy the rules of first normal form, second normal form and third normal form. If the design does not satisfy these rules, then duplication of data will result; that is, there will be redundant data.

- ■ The database structure is created and modified using the data definition language (DDL). The data manipulation language (DML) is used for queries and maintenance tasks such as adding, deleting and amending data.

- ■ The industry standard for DDL and DML is structured query language (SQL).

- ■ Commands for DDL include `CREATE DATABASE`, `CREATE TABLE` and `ALTER TABLE`.

- ■ Key syntax for queries is: `SELECT`, `FROM`, `WHERE`, `ORDER BY`, `GROUP BY` and `INNER JOIN`.

- ■ Key commands for data maintenance are: `INSERT INTO`, `DELETE FROM` and `UPDATE`.

Exam-style questions

1   A country has a number of cross-country running clubs. Clubs each organise races which attract runners from other clubs. A database is to be created storing data about races and runners. The clubs have agreed to stage one race only on any date.

A number of attempts have been made at the database design.

a   Consider Design 1:

```
Runner(RunnerID, RunnerName, ClubName)

Race(RaceDate, RaceDistance, ClubName)

RaceRunner(RaceDate, RunnerID)
```

   i   Circle the two foreign keys in this database design.   [2]

   ii   Draw the entity–relationship diagram for these three entities.

[2]

b   More data is to be stored. Consider Design 2:

```
Runner(RunnerID, RunnerName, ClubName)

Race(RaceDate, RaceDistance, ClubName, ClubTown,
        ClubSecretaryName)

RaceRunner(RaceDate, RunnerID, RunnerName, FinishingPosition)
```

   i   Name the table which is not in second normal form (2NF) and explain why.   [1]

   ii   Re-design this table.   [2]

   iii   Name the table which is not in third normal form (3NF) and explain why.   [1]

   iv   Re-design this table and add a new table to make these two tables fully normalised.   [4]

c   Records have been created for all the runners entered for the race on the 26/11/2014.

   i   Write a data manipulation language query to display a list of the IDs of all the runners entered for this race.   [3]

   ii   Following the race, the record for runner 8816 must now be updated to show she finished in 2nd place.

    Write a data manipulation language command to update this record.   [3]

Cambridge International AS and A Level Computing 9691 Paper 31, Q3, Nov 2014 (adapted)

PART II

FUNDAMENTAL PROBLEM-SOLVING AND PROGRAMMING SKILLS

Algorithm design and problem-solving

9.01   Algorithms

An algorithm is a sequence of steps designed to perform some task which:

- has been done manually

- has been done manually with the aid of a device, such as a calculator

- has been done using a computer program, but for which we are now seeking a better computer-based solution.

The 'sequence of steps' could be implemented as a computer program. The program will be designed to solve a problem and the computer system is used to provide a solution. Consider a variety of applications which are done by a computer program:

- the printout of utility bills

- the issuing of reminders for utility bills which have not been paid on the due date

- the control or simulation of an industrial process

- stock control and management

- order processing and tracking

- accounting

- resource management.

For all of these common data-processing applications there is a clear problem to be solved for which the computer system is used to provide a solution.

What are the underlying algorithms? The algorithms to solve the problem will be designed from a detailed knowledge of the operation of the application. For example:

- We know that bills are sent out every three months.

- A payment reminder is sent when the payment becomes 30 days overdue.

Consider the task of repairing a puncture on a bicycle. A computer solution will not be used to solve the problem but the underlying steps for the task can be called an algorithm. To complete the task, we work through a sequence of steps:

1   Check all tools and materials are available

2   IF 'no' then delay the task

3   IF 'yes' then

3.1   Remove the wheel

3.2   Remove the inner-tube

4   Check – is there major damage?

4.1   IF 'yes' then buy a new inner tube

4.2   IF 'No' then

4.2.1   Inflate the tube to locate the leak

4.2.2   Apply glue and a patch

4.2.3   Inflate the tube to re-test

5   IF 'still leaking' then

5.1   Purchase new inner tube

6   Re-assemble.

Structured English

Structured English provides a more formal way of documenting the stages of the algorithm:

```
PROCESS RepairPuncture
Start:  JobDone ← "NO"
        IF 'all tools are not available'
          THEN
              Delay the task
              GOTO End
          ELSE
              Remove the wheel
              Remove the inner-tube
        ENDIF
        IF 'there is  major damage'
            THEN
                Buy a new inner tube
                GOTO Delay
            ELSE
                Inflate the tube to locate the leak
                Apply glue and a patch
                Inflate the tube to re-test
        ENDIF
        IF 'still leaking'
            THEN
                Purchase new inner tube
                GOTO Delay
            ELSE
                Re-assemble
                JobDone ← "YES"
        ENDIF
Delay:  Purchase new inner-tube
        IF JobDone ← "NO"
            THEN
                GOTO Start
        ENDIF
End:
ENDPROCESS
```

> **TIP**
>
> An algorithm design may be shown using a consistent font which is different to the main text. The syllabus states that the Courier New font will be used.

In the structured English:

- Three labels (`Start`, `Delay` and `End`) have been used to mark particular steps in the algorithm.

- When a decision has to be made the keywords `IF – THEN – ELSE – ENDIF` have been used.

- Indentation and the use of blank lines ('whitespace') has been used to indicate which steps belong together.

- The complete process has been given an identifier name, `RepairPuncture`.

- The process is marked with clear `PROCESS` and `ENDPROCESS` statements.

> **TIP**
>
> The algorithm has used a `GOTO` keyword to jump to a particular step in the algorithm.
>
> For a high-level language, the use of `GOTO` is considered bad programming practice as it encourages 'spaghetti-like' algorithm design.
>
> For assembly language (see Chapter 4.04), a GOTO structure is used: the `JMP <address>` instruction is the equivalent of a pseudocode `GOTO` statement.

Identifier names

We have used several identifier names:

- for the whole process – `RepairPuncture`

- to indicate whether or not the process has been completed – `JobDone`

- to label steps – `Start`, `Delay` and `End`.

Four basic constructs

All problems which can be documented as a sequence of steps can be shown using the four basic constructs: assignment, sequence, selection and repetition (iteration).

Sequence

Traditional high-level programming languages are designed for problems which can be designed as a sequence of steps. It is a feature of a text editor or IDE for program development that the lines of code can be numbered to show the sequence.

Assignment

In our algorithm, `JobDone` is initially assigned the value 'NO' and later assigned a value of 'YES'.

Note that the symbol ← has been used to mean 'the value on the right of the statement is assigned to the identifier on the left'.

Selection

In our algorithm, a question is asked: 'are all the tools available?'

This is called a condition. The result of the condition is always either TRUE or FALSE. The algorithm carries out a different set of steps for the TRUE and FALSE results.

Iteration

Iteration will occur in an algorithm design when a block of steps is repeated. This is done in a program with the use of a loop structure.

> **TERMS**
>
> **Sequence:** the order of steps which make up the design of the algorithm
>
> **Assignment:** setting an identifier to a data value
>
> **Selection:** a decision has to be made
>
> **Iteration:** steps that are repeated

Stepwise refinement

In the design, one of the steps is stated as `Re-assemble`.

This may not convey to a reader of the design precisely what this involves, so the step could be expanded; that is, we could use stepwise refinement.

`Re-assemble` consists of:

```
Replace the inner tube
Replace the tyre
Replace the wheel
Inflate the inner tube
```

Program flowcharts

A flowchart can be used as an alternative to a structured-English description of the algorithm design.

A program flowchart uses the following symbols:

- start and Stop

- assignment or action

- decision box

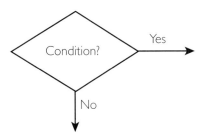

- flow lines to show sequence

- input and output

Figure 9.01 shows a flowchart for the `RepairPuncture` problem. It does not require any input from the user and did not produce outputs. Most tasks – and so, most programs – will perform both input and output.

Note the following features of the flowchart in Figure 9.01:

- Every flow-line has an arrow.
- The main 'flow' of the flowchart should be from top to bottom.
- There is only one start point and one end point.
- The left-hand vertical flow-line is effectively causing iteration.
- The two decision boxes are performing selection.

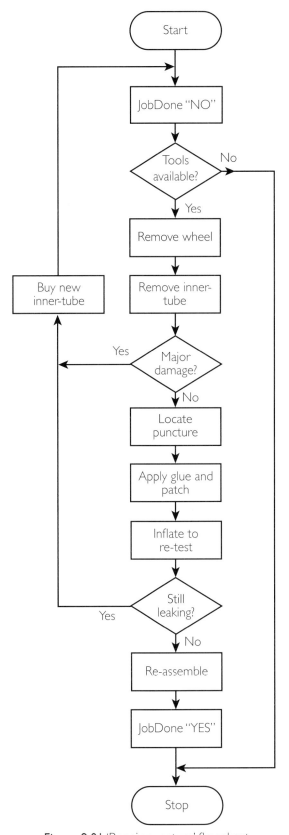

Figure 9.01 'Repair puncture' flowchart

Input – Processing – Output

A garage buys in used cars and aims to sell the vehicles at a profit. The garage has to decide on the selling price. The garage will record data for:

- the price paid

- the date the vehicle was first registered (i.e. when it was new)

- the mileage.

A program is to be written to calculate the selling price.

The design for this task has three clearly defined stages:

- The input is the three data items about the car.

- The processing will calculate the selling price as follows:

  o The price will drop by 5% for every month in age.

  o The calculated price is called the 'Provisional Sell Price'.

  o An adjustment may be made to this figure based on the mileage of the vehicle.

  o Normal mileage is 1000 km for every one month. This normal mileage is calculated for the vehicle. If the actual mileage is less than this figure, the Provisional Sell Price is increased by 5%. This Provisional Sell Price is then set to be the advertised price, called 'Sell Price'.

- The output from the program is the Sell Price and Profit.

An identifier table

The task requires the input, processing and output of data items. We shall use the identifier names summarised in Table 9.01.

Identifier name	Description
PricePaid	Original price paid
RegDate	Registration date
Mileage	Car mileage when purchased
NormalMileage	The expected car mileage based on the age of the car
ProvSellPrice	The calculated selling price
SellPrice	The adjusted selling price
Profit	Sell Price – Price Paid

Table 9.01 The identifier table for the garage application

Later, when we attempt to write pseudocode or program code for the problem, the programmer will need to specify the type of data which will be stored by each identifier.

LOOK FORWARD »

Chapter 10, section 10.01 discusses data types.

9.02 Structure charts

A first description of the problem could be in structured English:

1 INPUT the price paid, registration date, mileage

2 CALCULATE Selling price

3 CALCULATE Profit

4 OUTPUT Selling price, Profit

These processes will have data inputs, called parameters. We shall make up an identifier name for each process and use the identifiers in Table 9.01 for the parameters.

This gives a high-level description of the problem:

```
InputCarData(PricePaid, RegDate, Mileage)
CalculateSellingPrice(RegDate, PricePaid, Mileage)
OutputSellPrice(SellPrice, Profit)
```

These stages are designed as 'modules'. Later they will be implemented with program code as 'procedures'.

The breaking down of the problem into modules and the passing of data values into each module can be shown using a structure chart (see Figure 9.02).

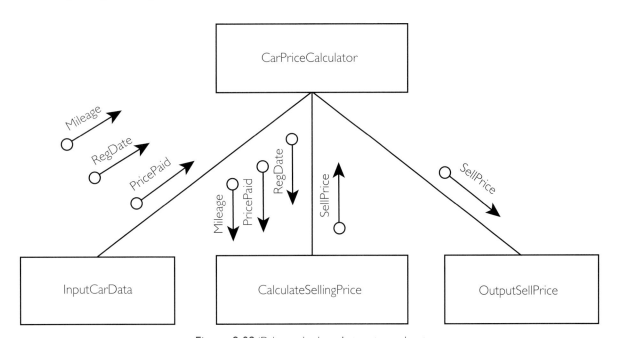

Figure 9.02 'Price calculator' structure chart

9.03   Corrective maintenance

The name implies that something is wrong! All program code needs to be extensively tested. This will involve:

• choosing appropriate test data

• using a trace table to check carefully how the data values change as each step of the program is executed.

Before we can complete a trace table, we need to formalise the algorithm required. We shall write this using pseudocode with the identifier names from Table 9.01.

The // symbol denotes a 'comment'.

```
01  // InputCarData module
02  INPUT PricePaid
03  INPUT RegDate
04  INPUT Mileage
05  // CalculateSellingPrice module
06  Months ← TodaysDate - RegDate
07  NormalMileage ← Months * 1000
08  ProvSellPrice ← PricePaid * (100 - 5 * Months) / 100
09  IF Mileage < NormalMileage
10      THEN
11          SellPrice ← ProvSellPrice * 105 / 100
```

```
12      ELSE
13          SellPrice ← ProvSellPrice
14   ENDIF
15   Profit ← PricePaid - SellPrice
16   // OutputSellprice  module
17   OUTPUT SellPrice, Profit
```

TIP

- As this is pseudocode it is displayed using the Courier New font.

- The lines of pseudocode have been numbered (for easy reference only).

- The stages in the pseudocode follow exactly the three stages in the structure chart.

- The pseudocode has used a number of 'keywords':

  o INPUT

  o OUTPUT

  o IF – THEN – ELSE – ENDIF

- The symbol ← has been used for 'assignment': Line 6 is read as 'The Months value is calculated by subtracting the RegDate value from the TodaysDate value.

Completing the trace table

We now have everything we need to complete a trace of the algorithm for selected data.

What test data would be appropriate for our car price calculator program? The data items are the original price paid for the car, the mileage and the registration date.

Take today's date as August 2016.

Case 1 : A car registered in June 2015 is purchased for $5000. It has done 12 000 miles. The values of the data items are shown in Table 9.02.

PricePaid	RegDate	Mileage	Months	NormalMileage	ProvSellPrice	SellPrice
5000	06/2015	12 000	15	15000	1250	1250

Table 9.02 Trace of data values for Case 1

Case 2: A car registered in October 2015 is purchased for 5000. It has done 8000 miles. These figures mean the vehicle has the 'low mileage' price adjustment. The values of the data items are shown in Table 9.03.

PricePaid	RegDate	Mileage	Months	NormalMileage	ProvSellPrice	SellPrice
5000	10/2015	8000	10	10 000	2500	
					2625	2625

Table 9.03 Trace of data values for Case 2

As the provisional selling price has changed, this new value is shown on the next row. In any trace table, as more values are calculated the numbers will occupy more rows.

Progress check 9.02

1   Draw the program flowchart for this savings calculator algorithm.

2   A program calculates the interest earned on $100. The value of the investment increases by 20% each year. Stop the process when the amount reaches $150. Draw a up a trace table to complete the execution of this algorithm:

```
01   YearNumber ← 1

02   Amount ← 100

03   Amount ← Amount * 1.20

04   IF Amount >= 150

05      THEN

06         OUTPUT YearNumber

07         STOP

08      ELSE

09         YearNumber ← YearNumber + 1

10         GOTO Step 03

11   ENDIF
```

> This reads: The new value for `Amount` is assigned its current value * 1.20

> This reads: The value for `YearNumber` is incremented by 1

Complete this trace table, adding blank rows as required:

YearNumber	Amount	OUTPUT

9.04   Adaptive maintenance

An existing program may need to be 'adapted' or changed. This could be for a variety of reasons. The most likely is that the user now has slightly different requirements and so the specification of the program needs to be changed. If the program design needs to be changed. so will the program code.

For our car purchase program, the garage might decide the following:

• Car users are now traveling on average a greater distance in a month. It's now on average 1200 miles per month (not 1000).

• Cars seem to be holding their price better. We need to calculate that the value goes down by only 3% per month (not 5%).

These changes to the specification, and possible other specification changes, will require that the program code is amended and re-tested.

Progress check 9.03

A program is to developed to calculate the tax paid by employees each month. The program has been written and successfully used for a year. Why might adaptive maintenance be required at some future date?

Summary

- An algorithm is a solution to a problem expressed as a sequence of defined steps. The algorithm may involve logic statements.

- In programming, identifier names are used for the various data items used in the problem and are documented in an identifier table showing the identifier name, data type and a description.

- Many algorithms use the four basic constructs: assignment, sequence, selection and repetition.

- Some steps may be expanded into more detail. This processing is called stepwise refinement. Individual steps are often coded in the program using procedures and functions.

- Many problems consist of the three stages: input, processing and output.

- An algorithm can be expressed in structured English, pseudocode or a program flowchart.

- A structure chart is used to document the parameters passed in and out of modules which make up the program design.

- Corrective maintenance is carried out using white-box testing. This involves drawing up suitable test cases with appropriate data and then – using a trace table – tracing various routes through the code.

- Adaptive maintenance takes place when the user makes a change to the program specification.

Exam-style questions

I Ali uses a sequential file of records to store the user IDs and encrypted passwords.

When a user types in their User ID, the program calls a function, `FindPassword`, with parameter `ThisUserID`.

The function searches each record in the file for `ThisUserID` and returns the encrypted password.

If `ThisUserID` is not stored in the file, the function returns an error code.

Complete the pseudocode:

```
FUNCTION FindPassword(ThisUserID   STRING) RETURNS ....................
    DECLARE Found : BOOLEAN
    OPENFILE FOR INPUT                              // for reading
    Found ← FALSE
    WHILE ............................................................
       FILEREAD next record
       IF ...........................................................
          THEN
             ......................................................
          ENDIF
    ENDWHILE
    IF ...............................................................
       THEN
          ............................................................
       ELSE
          ............................................................
    ENDIF
    CLOSEFILE "PASSWORDS"
ENDFUNCTION
```

[8]

Cambridge International AS and A Level Computing 9691 Paper 23, Q2b, Nov 2014

Data representation

Revision objectives

By the end of the chapter you should be able to:

- ☐ select appropriate data types for a problem solution

- ☐ use in practical programming the data types that are common to procedural high-level languages: integer, real, char, string, Boolean, date

- ☐ show understanding of how character and string data are represented by software

- ☐ use the technical terms associated with arrays

- ☐ select a suitable data structure (1D or 2D array) to use for a given task

- ☐ use pseudocode and write program code for 1D and 2D arrays

- ☐ write algorithms/program code to process array data including sorting and searching

- ☐ show understanding of why files are needed

- ☐ use pseudocode for file handling

- ☐ write program code for handling of a text file, consisting of several lines of text

10.01 Data types

The computer system – or, more precisely, the programming language or applications software, such as a spreadsheet – will distinguish between different types of data. When writing pseudocode, the algorithm will need to make clear the data type intended for all identifiers used.

This is done by:

- including the data type in the identifier table

- using a `DECLARE` pseudocode statement.

Integer

In pseudocode, the data type is `INTEGER`. In math, this is any positive or negative whole number. Table 10.01 shows Table 9.01 amended to include the data type of the identifier.

In pseudocode, we write:

```
DECLARE Mileage : INTEGER
```

Boolean

In pseudocode, the data type is `BOOLEAN`.

Some data only have a TRUE or FALSE value:

- Is a customer allowed credit?

- Is the car taxed?

In pseudocode, we write:

```
DECLARE CreditAllowed : BOOLEAN
DECLARE CurrentTax : BOOLEAN
```

Identifier name	Data type	Description
Mileage	INTEGER	Car mileage when purchased

Table 10.01 The identifier table with the data type

Date and time

In pseudocode, the data type is DATE.

We write:

`DECLARE RegDate : DATE`

> **TIP**
>
> There are considerable variations across programming languages for how the language stores and processes date values. Visual Basic .NET and SQL use the format YYYY/MM/DD and enclose the characters inside the hash character.
>
> The representation for 13 April 2016 is #2010/04/13#.

Numbers

The programming language must be able to distinguish between different types of number.

Real

Numbers which have a fraction part are called (in math) real numbers.

In pseudocode, the data type is REAL.

> **TIP**
>
> Visual Basic .NET has two data types for real numbers:
>
> - single
> - long (for a greater range)
>
> Pascal has data type Real.

Currency

In pseudocode, the data type is CURRENCY.

We write:

`DECLARE PricePaid : CURRENCY`

> **TIP**
>
> A currency type is available in Visual Basic .NET and software applications such as MS Access and Excel. The data type is used for money values which have two digits after the decimal point.

Character

In pseudocode, the data type is CHAR.

Some data values will be a single character only:

- gender – with possible values 'M' and 'F' only
- fuel type – 'P' for petrol, 'D' for diesel

In pseudocode, we write:

`DECLARE Gender : CHAR`

`DECLARE FuelType : CHAR`

String

In pseudocode, the data type is STRING.

A string is a sequence of characters from the character set. Most program applications will need to store string data.

For example, a name and address could be stored by a program as three separate strings:

`Ali Harris`

`14 The High Street`

`01925758565`

- A data value containing digit and letter characters (line 2) would have to be data type STRING.
- Digits only (line 4) could also be treated as a string value.
- A string may have no characters – called the 'empty string'.
- The programming language used may have an upper limit on the maximum length of a string.
- The programming language will have built-in functions for the manipulation of string data.

> **LOOK FORWARD »**
>
> We introduce two other data types later in Chapter 10, sections 10.02 and 10.03: ARRAY and FILE.
>
> Built-in functions are discussed in Chapter 11, section 11.05.

Progress check 10.01

Explain why 8, "8" and '8' will be treated differently by a computer program.

Character sets

Computers store and process numeric and character data. A digital computer stores all data as binary digits – hence all characters must be stored in main memory as numbers.

The character set will use a different number representation for each character.

The character set must include upper case letters, lower case letters, the number digits and all the punctuation and other characters found on the standard QWERTY keyboard.

This suggests that we must have a standard set of character codes which is used by all computers.

ASCII (American Standard Code for Information Interchange)

The ASCII coding system uses a 7-bit code to represent each of the characters. Any programming text book should include this table of codes. A selection of the codes is shown in Table 10.02.

Character	Denary	Character	Denary	Character	Denary
<Space>	32	I	73	R	82
A	65	J	74	S	83
B	66	K	75	T	84
C	67	L	76	U	85
D	68	M	77	V	86
E	69	N	78	W	87
F	70	O	79	X	88
G	71	P	80	Y	89
H	72	Q	81	Z	90

Table 10.02 Part of the ASCII character set

The characters with codes 0 to 31 are called control characters. Their use in a program will cause such things as:

- a 'bleep' (ASCII code 7)
- the paper in the printer to be ejected (ASCII code 12).

The math tells us that seven bits makes possible 128 different codes (with binary codes 0000000, 00000001, ..., 1111111).

The computer stores all ASCII codes as a byte (eight bits).

Extended ASCII character set

Consider if all eight bits of the byte were to be used. The number of different characters which can be now represented increases to 256. This is called the extended character set.

Agreement was reached with a standard called ANSI as to what all the character codes below 128 would represent (including the control characters). Standards then started to emerge as to how the codes 128–255 would be used and these tables were called code pages. Different countries had, over time, used the character codes from 128–255 to represent different characters. Typically, codes were used for accented characters and line drawing. The result could be that a computer user in the UK reading a document produced in a different country might find some of the characters unreadable.

This was the basis for the introduction of a new universally recognised character set called Unicode.

Unicode

Unicode provides a unique number for every character which will be recognised as the same character on different platforms, programs and spoken languages.

Most, but not all, Unicode characters are stored as a 16-bit representation; a code may use up to six bytes. The range of characters is extensive including characters used in a particular spoken language.

Unicode codes are written as U+0041. U+ indicates 'Unicode' and the digits are the hexadecimal code to be used. U+0041 is the code used for 'A'. Note, there is some reference back to ASCII, as this code is the denary value 65. Hence the same code – denary 65 – is used in both ASCII and Unicode.

The most popular Unicode standard, UTF-8 is one of the standards for encoding characters. Any data which is to be read by other programs – for example, an email message or web page – must specify the encoding method used.

For a typical webpage the HTML tag would be:

```
<meta http-equiv="Content-Type"
content="text/html; charset =utf-8">
```

10.02 Arrays

When we store three team names with the identifier names, `Team1`, `Team2` and `Team3`, the identifiers will be declared in the program. This is the trigger for the interpreter or compiler to reserve three storage locations in memory ready to store the values assigned in the program.

You should appreciate that the data items have no relation to each other; the identifier names `Team1`, `Team2` and `Team3` are as different as A, B and C.

Why do we use arrays?

An array allows program code to use the same identifier name for several related data values.

We should assume for this syllabus that the items will be of the same data type. Hence a set of data values stored as an array would be described as "an array of string values" or "an array of integer values".

A garage sells cars and stores data for the number of cars sold in each month of the year. The array will have identifier `MonthlySales`. We need to store 12 values. The array can be visualised as shown in Figure 10.01. It has exactly the same meaning whether drawn horizontally or vertically.

The number alongside each value is called the index or subscript number of the array.

Typical values are `MonthlySales[1]` is 12 and `MonthlySales[4]` is 7.

MonthlySales

1	12
2	3
3	4
4	7
5	8
6	12
7	14
8	6
9	6
10	8
11	9
12	2

MonthlySales

1	2	3	4	5	6	7	8	9	10	11	12
12	3	4	7	8	12	14	6	6	8	9	2

Figure 10.01 The MonthlySales array

One-dimensional arrays

`MonthlySales` is a one-dimensional (ID) array. Each position in the array is called a cell.

The `MonthlySales` array stores integer values. We can have arrays that store values of any of the recognised data types, for example, `CHAR`, `STRING` and `BOOLEAN`.

Declaring a ID array

Table 10.03 shows how to declare a one-dimensional array.

Identifier name	Data type	Description
MonthlySales	ARRAY[1:12] OF INTEGER	The sales figure for each month of the year

Table 10.03 The identifier table showing a ID array.

In pseudocode, we write:

```
DECLARE MonthlySales[1:12] OF INTEGER
```

The terminology to use here would be:

- the lower bound of the array is I
- the upper bound of the array is 12.

> **TIP**
> Visual Basic .NET uses parentheses – that is, (and) – to enclose the array subscript.
> PASCAL and Python use square brackets.

Throughout the text we shall use square brackets for arrays in our pseudocode.

Initialising an array

'Initialising' means declaring the array (its identifier name, subscript range and data type) and also populating each array cell with a value.

Assume all array elements are given an initial value of zero. We can use a loop to initialise `MonthlySales`:

```
FOR MonthNumber ← 1 TO 12

    MonthlySales[MonthNumber] ← 0

ENDFOR
```

> **LOOK FORWARD »**
> Loop structures are discussed in detail in Chapter 11, section 11.04.

Two-Dimensional (2D) arrays

A data set can be visualised as a two-dimensional table.

Six employees of a company are sales staff. We are to store the number of sales made by each employee over 12 months. Figure 10.02 shows the sales in a grid:

- Each row represents a salesperson.
- Each column represents a month.

Sales

	1	2	3	4	5	6	7	8	9	10	11	12
1	0	0	0	3	4	0	0					
2	1	12	12	6	7	8	9	18	8	12	11	6
3	2	4	5	1	2	3	11	6	7	2	3	1
4	11	12	3	4	6	7	1	2	6	7	11	4
5	1	0	0	8	8	0	1	1	2	3	4	
6	0	0	1	2	3	4						

Figure 10.02 Sales data grid

This dataset will be represented as a two-dimensional (2D) array.

Declaring a 2D array

In pseudocode, we write:

```
DECLARE Sales[1:6,1:12] OF INTEGER
```

The array has two subscript numbers. The convention is to denote the row number using the first subscript.

Initialising a 2D array

As with a 1D array, 'initialising' means declaring the array (its identifier name, subscript ranges and data type) and also populating each array cell with a value.

Assume all array elements are given an initial value of zero. We can use a loop to initialise Sales:

```
FOR SalesPersonNumber ← 1 TO 6
    FOR MonthNumber ← 1 TO 12
        Sales[SalesPersonNumber,MonthNumber] ← 0
    ENDFOR
ENDFOR
```

LOOK FORWARD »

This pseudocode uses a nested loop – the inner loop is for the 12 months and the outer loop for each of the six salespersons. Loops are discussed in detail in Chapter 11, section 11.04.

Assigning values to an array

We can assign values to each array element individually:

```
Sales[3,7] ← 11
Sales[6,4] ← 2
```

And similarly for all other values in the grid.

Progress check 10.02

1 How many sales were made by salesperson 4 in April?

2 What array cell stores the 18 sales figure made by person 2 in August?

3 Data is to be recorded and stored as follows:

- the surname of 203 employees
- the date they joined.

   a What data structure(s) would be appropriate for this data?

   b Write the pseudocode declaration statements for each data structure.

LOOK FORWARD »

Searching the array data

Once the data is stored in the array it can be searched. This needs some programming techniques which we cover in detail in Chapter 11, section 11.04.

Sorting the array data – A bubble sort

Our monthly sales figures were in the array in 'month' order. The user might want to see a list of the sales figures in ascending order, which requires sorting the sales figures.

Sorting requires programming techniques which we cover in Chapter 11, section 11.04.

10.03 Files

Why do we need files?

Data stored in main memory, including data in arrays, will be lost when the program is ended. Most applications will require some data to be permanently saved so that the data is available to the program the next time it is run.

A company which processes, for example, employee and product data must have this data permanently stored on some form of secondary or backing storage.

Section 2 of the syllabus is restricted to the use of a text file. The file will have an identifier name and text files are usually given the file extension .txt. A text file consists of one or more lines each consisting of one or more characters. Each line of text will be terminated with `<Carriage Return><Line Feed>` characters.

The files shown in Figure 10.03 are storing data for four employees: the name, date of birth, salary grade and number of years' service. The data is in a different format in each file:

- For `File1.txt`, the programmer has decided to store the data for each employee as a single line of text. Each of the data items is separated by a Space character.

- For `File2.txt`, each data item is stored on a new line in the file.

Any program which is to use one of these data files must be clear about the organisation of the data within the file.

Number digits, such as the years' service values, will be treated when they are read from the file as a string value. The program must then convert this string to an integer or real number.

```
        File1.txt                    File2.txt
Adam Smith 12/04/1998 A 3       Adam Smith
Jules Ahmed 04/12/1987 A 4      12/04/1998
Mary Simmons 09/11/1996 B 1     A
Adam Jones 09/07/1976 C 11      3
                                Jules Ahmed
                                04/12/1987
                                A
                                4
                                Mary Simmons
                                09/11/1996
                                B
                                1
                                Adam Jones
                                09/07/1976
                                C
                                11
```

Figure 10.03 Alternative text file structures

Pseudocode for text files

Opening a file

When we create or read data from an existing file it must be 'opened'. Its use must be made clear by stating the file mode:

- READ: for reading a line of text from a file

- WRITE: to write a line of text to the file

- APPEND: to add a line of text to an existing file

Writing to a file

The programmer uses the `File1.txt` structure to write the first employee line to the file.

The employee data is assigned to an identifier `EmployeeString` and then written to a file in Figure 10.04.

- The file must be opened at the start of the session and closed at the end.

- The file name is included in the `WRITEFILE` statement since a program may be using more than one text file.

- The program code for this design would create a new file `File1.txt` with one line of text.

```
EmployeeString ← "Adam Smith 12/04/1998 A 3"

OPENFILE "File1.txt" FOR WRITE

WRITEFILE "File1.txt", EmployeeString

CLOSEFILE "File1.txt"
```

Writes the string stored in `EmployeeString` to the file `File1.txt`

Figure 10.04 Writing to a text file

TIP

If this program was run a second time the original file `File1.txt` would be overwritten.

Progress check 10.03

1 What would be the final result after running this as program code?

```
OPENFILE "Products.txt" FOR WRITE

WRITEFILE "Products.txt",
   "Screwdriver"

WRITEFILE "Products.txt", "Hammer"

WRITEFILE "Products.txt", "Saw"

CLOSEFILE "Products.txt"
```

2 What would be the final result after running this as program code?

```
OPENFILE "Products.txt" FOR WRITE

WRITEFILE "Products.txt",
   "Screwdriver"

OPENFILE "Products.txt" FOR WRITE

WRITEFILE "Products.txt", "Hammer"

OPENFILE "Products.txt" FOR WRITE

WRITEFILE "Products.txt", "Saw"

CLOSEFILE "Products.txt"
```

LOOK FORWARD ≫

In Progress check 10.03, we attempted to write only three lines of text into the file. Each write action had its own `WRITEFILE` statement. In Chapter 11, section 11.04, we use a loop to write several lines of text within the same `OPENFILE–CLOSEFILE` session.

Reading data from a file

This is very similar sequence of steps to writing to the files. The file must be opened at the start of the session – but this time the file mode is READ. The file should be closed when no longer in use.

We shall assume we ran the program code for writing the Adam Smith employee data. `File1.txt` contains one line of text. Figure 10.05 shows some code that reads the file.

```
DECLARE EmployeeString : STRING
OPEN "File1.txt" FOR READ
READFILE "File1.txt", EmployeeString
CLOSE "File1.txt"
OUTPUT EmployeeString
```

Reads one line of text (a string) from the `File1.txt` and assigns it to `EmployeeString`

Figure 10.05 Reading from a text file

This code would display:

```
Adam Smith 12/04/1998 A 3
```

LOOK FORWARD ≫

We shall use a loop to write and read several lines of text to and from a text file.

Summary

- In program code, identifiers are declared to be of a certain data type. Data types include: INTEGER, REAL, CHAR, STRING, BOOLEAN, DATE

- Single character and string data uses a standard coding system such as ASCII or Unicode to code each character as a number.

- A common data structure is a one-dimensional (1D) or two-dimensional (2D) array. An array has a single identifier name and data items are identified by their index in the array.

- Pseudocode and program code can be written to store data in a file.

- A text file is made up of one or more lines of text.

Exam-style questions

1 Meena wants to develop a program to keep a record of her coursework assignments.
  She will want to enter, sort and print out data.
  She decides to modularise the solution.

  a State **two** reasons why using modules is a sensible way for her to proceed.   [2]

  One way of storing her data will be to use a file of records.

  Each record will contain at least the following data:

Data	Identifier	Description of input data
subject	Subject	Name of the subject, for example Physics
title	Title	Title of assignment
date set	DateSet	Format DDMMYYYY
hand-in date	HandInDate	Format DDMMYYYY
marked?	IsMarked	Y or N
date returned	DateReturned	Format DDMMYYYY
mark	Mark	Range 0 to 100

  b i Each record needs another field to uniquely identify that record.

        State an appropriate identifier for this field and state a suitable data type for it.   [2]

     ii In a programming language write the declaration for the record structure, giving it the identifier
        `Assignment`.

        Programming language

        Declaration   [4]

     iii State the number of bytes needed to store a value in the field `IsMarked`.   [1]

  c Describe what the function `EOF ()` does when used in a program.   [2]

  d Meena creates a sequential file, `MyAssignments`, of `Assignment` records.

     Using pseudocode write the algorithm to search this file for the first Physics assignment.

     `OPENFILE MyAssignments FOR OUTPUT`

     `CLOSEFILE MyAssignments`   [4]

Cambridge International AS and A Level Computing 9691 Paper 22, Q1, June 2013

Programming

11.01 Programming basics

We already have some of the fundamentals required for writing program code.

We have used in our pseudocode the DECLARE, INPUT and OUTPUT keywords. Also, the IF–THEN–ENDIF statement and its variations for dealing with selection.

Identifier names

In both pseudocode and program code, use meaningful identifier names – this is common sense. Meaningful variable names will make the code easier to follow and understand. The particular language used will place some restrictions on the identifier names which can be used.

We have already written a declaration statement or drawn up an identifier table for documenting the identifiers we shall use in a problem.

In Visual Basic .NET, identifier names must comply with the following rules:

- maximum of 64 characters

- cannot start with a digit character

- no punctuation characters allowed.

The choice of an identifier name by the programmer will be a compromise between names which are meaningful but without being too long, and may follow some style adopted by the programmer. For example, we have consistently used Camel Caps.

Variables and constants

A variable is the representation of a data value which is required by the problem. A memory location is used to store the data value. The variable name or identifier – decided by the programmer – is the label for this memory location.

If a data value will change during the execution of a program, it is a variable with a chosen identifier name and data type.

If the value does not change, then it can be declared as a constant with a chosen name and stated value:

```
CONSTANT Pi = 3.142
```

The scope of variables and constants

The scope of a variable or constant refers to the parts of the program code within which the identifier is recognised.

Global scope describes a variable which is recognised throughout all the program code. If we are programming in console mode with the code organised within a module, then 'global' is taken to mean anywhere within the module.

Local scope means the code where the variable is recognised is restricted. It could be restricted to:

- a procedure (including `Sub Main`)
- a function
- an 'event procedure' when using a forms-based environment.

Declaring variables and constants

Most programming languages insist that all variables and constants are declared before they are used within the program code. Such languages are said to be strongly typed languages.

The variable may also be initialised with a value.

TIP

Visual Basic .NET and Pascal are strongly typed languages.

Python is not.

11.02 Transferable skills

When we learn to drive a car we practise in the same car leading up to the driving test. When we pass, it is a short step to have to the skills needed to drive a different car. The basics are the same. The car will have three pedals – accelerator, brake and clutch. Other basic features will be the steering wheel and a handbrake. Almost all these features would be found in any car. There will be details the driver must be familiar with, such as whether the lights and indicator controls are on the left or right of the steering wheel column.

Programming in a high-level language is a transferrable skill. A programmer who is confident in writing code in a language they have learnt should be able to study code in a second language and identify the key components. The programmer will be able to recognise:

- IF and CASE structures for selection
- loops
- identifiers used for variables, constants, procedures and functions.

LOOK BACK «

In Chapter 2, section 2.03, we studied some program code written in both JavaScript and PHP. The key task here when making sense of the code was to be able to identify the points listed above.

Programming languages have several basic features which would suggest the skill of writing code should be transferrable from one programming language to another. Chapter 9, Section 9.01 summarised that any high-level language will have structures and syntax to implement assignment, sequence, selection and iteration.

What will be different for different languages is the precise syntax which is used. Table 11.01 shows a count-controlled loop and Table 11.02 shows a simple selection statement in each of Basic .NET, Python and Pascal, compared to pseudocode.

	Count-controlled loop	Explanation

Pseudocode	`FOR i ← 1 TO n`
	`    <statement(s)>`
	`ENDFOR`
		Statements to be executed are terminated with the `ENDFOR` keyword.

Visual Basic .NET	`For i = 1 To n`
	`    <statement(s)>`
	`Next i`
		The end of the statements inside the loop is marked with the `Next` keyword.

Python	`For i in range (1, n)` `    <statement(s)>`	The statements inside the loop are indicated with the indent.
Pascal	`For i := 1 To n Do` `    <statement(s)> ;`	The end of the statements inside the loop is marked with the semi-colon.

Table 11.01 Loops in the three languages

	IF selection	Explanation

Pseudocode	`IF x >= 40`
	`    <statement(s)>`
	`ENDIF`
		Statements to be executed are terminated with the `ENDIF` keyword.

Visual Basic .NET	`If x >= 40 Then`
	`    <statement(s)>`
	`End If`
		Statements to be executed are terminated with the `End If` keywords.

Python	`If x >= 40:` `    <statement(s)>`	The statements following the `If` line are indicated with the indent.

Pascal	`If x >= 40 Then`
	`Begin`
	`    <statement(s)>`
	`End;`
		The block of statements is enclosed by the keywords `Begin` and `End`.

Table 11.02 Selection in the three languages

The expectation is that although there are slight differences in the syntax for each language, the meaning for all languages should be understood by a competent programmer.

11.03   Selection

LOOK BACK «

We have already used the keywords `IF-THEN-ELSE-ENDIF` in our pseudocode.

A statement in the code could ask a question. A different route is taken through the code depending on whether the condition is TRUE or FALSE. The question is called a condition.

There are many variations of the IF structure.

IF–THEN–ENDIF

```
IF <condition>

    THEN

        <statement(s)>

ENDIF
```

For example, in an examination, the grade is a PASS for a mark of 40 and above.

```
INPUT Mark

IF Mark >= 40

    THEN

        OUTPUT "PASS"

ENDIF
```

IF–THEN–ELSE–ENDIF

```
IF <condition>

    THEN

        <statement(s)>

    ELSE

        <statement(s)>

ENDIF
```

For example, the grade is a PASS for a mark over 40, otherwise the program reports a FAIL.

```
INPUT Mark

IF Mark >= 40

    THEN

        OUTPUT "PASS"

    ELSE

        OUTPUT "FAIL"

ENDIF
```

Nested IFs

Assume that a grade is now awarded as shown in Table 11.03.

Mark	Grade Awarded
Under 40	FAIL
40 and under 75	MERIT
75 and over	DISTINCTION

Table 11.03 Marks and grades

The logic could be structured with a sequence of three separate IF statements, as in Figure 11.01.

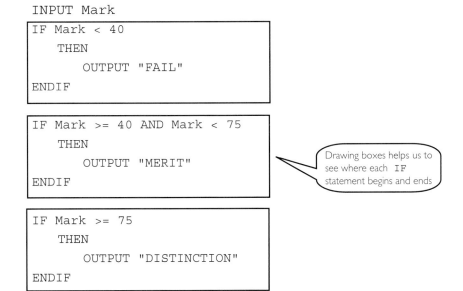

```
INPUT Mark

IF Mark < 40
    THEN
        OUTPUT "FAIL"
ENDIF


IF Mark >= 40 AND Mark < 75
    THEN
        OUTPUT "MERIT"
ENDIF


IF Mark >= 75
    THEN
        OUTPUT "DISTINCTION"
ENDIF
```

Drawing boxes helps us to see where each IF statement begins and ends

Figure 11.01 Separate IF statements implementing logic

An alternative is to use **nested IF statements**, as in Figure 11.02.

```
INPUT Mark
IF Mark <40
    THEN
        OUTPUT "FAIL"
    ELSE
        IF Mark >= 40 AND Mark < 75
            THEN
                OUTPUT "MERIT"
            ELSE
                OUTPUT "DISTINCTION"
        ENDIF
ENDIF
```

Figure 11.02 Nested IF statements implementing logic

TERMS

Nested IF statement: one IF statement sitting inside another

TIP

Read carefully through the IF structures shown in the pseudocode above. Note the indentation which has been used.

This raises the question – what if there are many more alternatives?

CASE structure

The answer is to use a CASE structure.

A grade is awarded as shown in Table 11.04.

Mark	Grade Awarded
Under 40	FAIL
40 and under 50	E
50 and under 60	D
60 and under 70	C
70 and under 80	B
80 and over	A

Table 11.04 Marks and grades

We can implement this with a CASE structure:

```
INPUT Mark
CASE OF Mark
    <40                 : OUTPUT "FAIL"
    >=40 AND <50        : OUTPUT "E"
    >=50 AND <60        : OUTPUT "D"
    >=60 AND <70        : OUTPUT "C"
    >=70 AND <80        : OUTPUT "B"
    >=80                : OUTPUT "A"
ENDCASE
```

TIP

The CASE structure can have a final CASE:

```
OTHERWISE :  <statement>
```

The CASE structure is available in Visual Basic .NET and Pascal.

Python does not have a CASE structure. The programmer would use several ELIF statements as part of an IF statement.

Figure 11.03 shows a CASE statement using a flowchart.

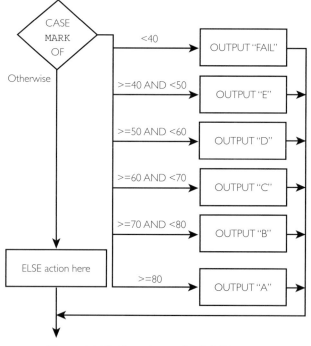

Figure 11.03 Flowchart of a CASE structure

11.04 Iteration

If something is 'iterated', it is repeated. If a program has a loop, the code inside the loop will be iterated or repeated. In most high-level programming languages, there are three alternative structures available for implementing a loop.

> **TERMS**
>
> **Loop:** code that is iterated or repeated
>
> **Repeat–Until:** a post-condition loop
>
> **While–EndWhile:** a pre-condition loop

For–EndFor

This is the loop structure to use if we know, by the nature of the problem, the number of iterations to be made.

For example, we need to process the exam marks for seven students.

The code requires an integer variable to act as the loop counter. After each iteration, the value of variable `Student` is incremented.

```
DECLARE Student : INTEGER

FOR Student ← 1 TO 7

   <statement(s)>

ENDFOR
```

On the first iteration `Student` has the value 1

On the second iteration it has the value 2, and so on

Figure 11.04 Implementing a For–EndFor loop

The For–EndFor structure is called a 'count-controlled' loop.

The loop can include text which specifies the increment to be made each time. The statement `FOR Student ← 1 TO 7` assumes that the `Student` loop counter will increment in steps of 1. If a different increment is required, then the `STEP` keyword is added which can either increment (the most common) or decrement the loop counter:

```
FOR TemperatureValue ← 100 TO 0 STEP -1

FOR TemperatureValue ← 0 TO 200 STEP
0.5
```

> **TIP**
>
> It is good practice to indent the statements inside the loop – it makes the start and end of the loop stand out and improves the readability of the code.

Repeat–Until

Use this loop structure when the number of iterations cannot be predicted. A condition will test for more iterations at the end of the loop. This is called a 'post-condition' loop.

```
REPEAT

   <statement(s)>

UNTIL <condition>
```

Note, with the condition at the end, the statements inside the loop are executed at least once.

For example, student marks are to be keyed in and stored in array `Mark`. The program terminates when a mark of –1 is entered.

```
i  ← 1
REPEAT
   OUTPUT "Mark ..? "
   INPUT NextMark
   IF NextMark <> -1
      THEN
         Mark[i] ← NextMark
         i ← i + 1
   ENDIF
UNTIL NextMark = -1
```

While–EndWhile

This structure is similar to a **Repeat–Until** loop but here the condition comes at the start of the loop. This is called a 'pre-condition' loop.

```
WHILE <condition>
   <statement(s)>
ENDWHILE
```

Note, if the condition is false the first time, then the statements inside the loop are never executed.

Pseudocode for processing student marks using a **While–EndWhile** structure is as follows:

```
OUTPUT ("Mark ..? ")
INPUT Mark
WHILE Mark <> -1
   IF Mark < 40
      THEN
         OUTPUT "FAIL"
      ELSE
         OUTPUT "PASS"
   ENDIF
   OUTPUT Mark ...? ")
   INPUT Mark
ENDWHILE
```

TIP

When the problem design requires a loop, the first consideration is whether we know how many iterations.

Searching: a linear search

Now we have studied arrays and loops, we shall use both structures in a problem:

- A program stores 20 surnames in a 1D array.

- The user inputs the surname to be found.

- The program will output one of:

  o the array position at which the item is found

  o the message 'Item NOT FOUND'.

The algorithm required is a linear search. We consider the first item in the array, then the second, etc. We stop searching when the item is found or we reach the end of the array.

The variables needed are shown in Table 11.05.

```
INPUT SearchName
IsFound ← FALSE
Index ← 1
REPEAT
    IF Surname[Index] = SearchName
        THEN
            IsFound ← TRUE
            OUTPUT "Surname was FOUND –
at position ", Index
        ELSE
            Index ← Index + 1
        ENDI
UNTIL (IsFound = TRUE) OR (Index = 21)
IF IsFound = FALSE
    THEN
        OUTPUT  "Surname was NOT FOUND"
ENDIF
```

TIP

- The loop chosen to process the surnames was a Repeat–Until loop, as we may not need to consider all items in the array.

- The algorithm will only find and report the first occurrence of the requested surname.

Identifier	Data type	Description
SearchName	STRING	The surname input by the user
Surname	ARRAY[1:20] OF STRING	The surname data
Index	INTEGER	Index position in the surname array
IsFound	BOOLEAN	Flags whether or not the requested surname has been found

Table 11.05 Identifier table

How many comparisons?

When carrying out a linear search, if there are N values in the dataset, on average the program will have to compare N/2 values in the array before the required item is found.

Progress check 11.02

1 Rewrite the pseudocode for the problem to process the surnames using a While–EndWhile loop structure.

2 Ten car registrations are to be entered by the user and stored in a 1D array `Registration`.

  a Draw and complete the identifier table.

  b Write the pseudocode.

3 An unknown number of email addresses are to be entered by the user and stored in a 1D array `EMailAddress`.

  a Write the declaration statements.

  b Write the pseudocode using a Repeat–Until loop structure.

Sorting: a bubble sort

The method requires that the data values are stored in an array. The algorithm we shall develop could be used to sort string, integer or real number values.

Consider the array, `MyArray`, in Figure 11.05.

MyArray

1	2	3	4	5	6	7	8	9	10
23	12	4	11	56	2	51	17	8	20

Figure 11.05 The contents of `MyArray`

The method is as follows:

1 Compare adjacent items starting with cells 1 and 2.

2 If the first item is larger then,

   swap the items in the array

3 Repeat comparing adjacent items until we reach the last two.

Using the array in Figure 11.05, we first compare `MyArray[1]` with `MyArray[2]`, that is, we compare 23 with 12. 23 is larger, so we swap the items in the array. `MyArray[1]` now stores 12 and `MyArray[2]` stores 23.

We repeat comparing adjacent items until finally we compare `MyArray[9]` with `MyArray[10]`. Figure 11.06 shows the result of this first pass through the data items.

MyArray

1	2	3	4	5	6	7	8	9	10
12	4	11	23	2	51	17	8	20	56

Figure 11.06 `MyArray` after one pass

At this point we are certain that the largest value is in the final array position. We now start a second pass. This time the final comparison made will be items with subscripts 8 and 9. The third pass will do a final comparison between items 7 and 8. The ninth pass will compare items 1 and 2 only.

This suggests that if the array has an upper bound of N (N data items) then the total number of passes required is (N − 1).

Swapping two items

This needs some thought. If we carry out these statements, both array cells will contain the same value:

`MyArray[1]  ← MyArray[2]`

`MyArray[2]  ← MyArray[1]`

The solution is to use a temporary variable to store one of the values:

`Temp  ← MyArray[1]`

`MyArray[1]  ← MyArray[2]`

`MyArray[2]  ← Temp`

Writing the sort code

The variables needed are shown in Table 11.06.

Identifier	Data type	Description
MyArray	ARRAY[1:10] OF INTEGER	The array storing the data items
Temp	INTEGER	Stores one of the data values when a swap is made
Pass	INTEGER	Loop counter for the outer loop
UBound	INTEGER	The upper bound of the array
i	INTEGER	Index value for the array
Swapped	BOOLEAN	Set to FALSE at the start of each pass. Flags to TRUE when a swap occurs.

Table 11.06 Identifier table

The code is in Figure 11.07.

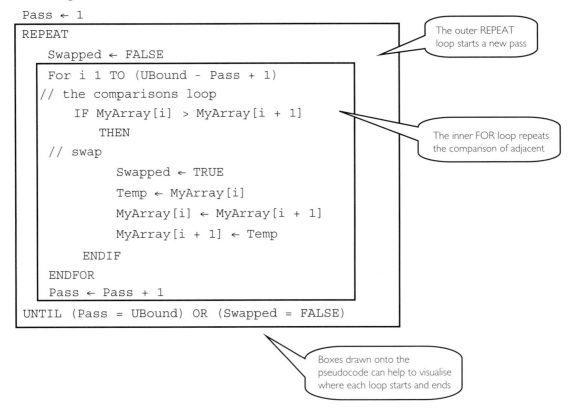

```
Pass ← 1
REPEAT
    Swapped ← FALSE
    For i 1 TO (UBound - Pass + 1)
    // the comparisons loop
        IF MyArray[i] > MyArray[i + 1]
            THEN
    // swap
                Swapped ← TRUE
                Temp ← MyArray[i]
                MyArray[i] ← MyArray[i + 1]
                MyArray[i + 1] ← Temp
        ENDIF
    ENDFOR
    Pass ← Pass + 1
UNTIL (Pass = UBound) OR (Swapped = FALSE)
```

The outer REPEAT loop starts a new pass

The inner FOR loop repeats the comparison of adjacent

Boxes drawn onto the pseudocode can help to visualise where each loop starts and ends

Figure 11.07 The sorting algorithm

TIP

The first iteration of the outer loop (`Pass = 1`) uses i values 1 to (UBound – Pass), that is, 9 for the inner loop.

The Boolean variable is used to check after each pass whether any values were swapped on that pass. If there were no swaps, the list must already be in order and so no more passes are required.

Progress check 11.03

Use the bubble sort algorithm to sort the array `Animal`.

1 Draw up and complete a trace table with the following headings. Add as many rows as necessary. You will need around 10 blank rows for the trace table.

Pass	i	UBound	Animal				
			1	2	3	4	5
1	1	5	CAT	ANT	COW	RAT	BEE

2 Were the items sorted before all possible iterations of the outer loop?

11.05 Built-in functions

There are two kinds of function: those written by the programmer (user-defined functions) and those provided by the language. Each programming language will have hundreds of 'built-in' functions.

String and character manipulation functions

We have already introduced the `STRING` and `CHAR` data types. The following is a selection of functions in pseudocode.

The function shown in Figure 11.08 returns the number of characters in `ThisString`. For example, `CHARACTERCOUNT("New York")` returns 8.

```
CHARACTERCOUNT(ThisString : STRING) RETURNS INTEGER
```

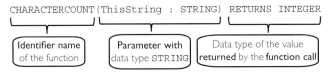

- Identifier name of the function
- Parameter with data type STRING
- Data type of the value returned by the function call

Figure 11.08 A string manipulation function

The function would be used in a statement to assign the value 7 to the variable `Length` as follows:

```
DECLARE Length : INTEGER

Length ← CHARACTERCOUNT("Cycling")
```

The `ONECHAR` function returns the single character at position `Position` (counting from 1 at the start of the string) from the string `ThisString`:

```
ONECHAR(ThisString : STRING, Position
: INTEGER) RETURNS CHAR
```

For example, `ONECHAR("Chicken curry", 9)` returns 'c'.

The `CONCAT` function (Figure 11.09) returns the string value formed by concatenating (joining together) the parameter strings.

```
CONCAT(String1 : STRING, String2 : STRING [, String3 : STRING])
RETURNS STRING
```

> Use of square brackets in a function definition indicates that the parameter is optional

Figure 11.09 A function with optional parameters

For example, `CONCAT("Game", "Of")` returns 'GameOf' and `CONCAT("Game", "Of", "Thrones")` returns 'GameOfThrones'.

The `SUBSTR` function returns a sub-string from `ThisString`:

```
SUBSTR(ThisString : STRING, Value1 :
INTEGER, Value2 : INTEGER) RETURNS
STRING
```

`Value1` is the start index position (counting from the left, starting with 1).

`Value2` is the final index position.

For example, `SUBSTR("rap artist", 5, 10)` returns 'artist'.

Progress check 11.04

The '&' operator is used to join together two strings. Evaluate the following expressions.

1 `CONCAT("George", " ", "Clooney")`

2 `CONCAT(CONCAT("Crystal", "Palace"), "FC")`

3 `ONECHAR("Best", 1) & ONECHAR("in", 1) & ONECHAR("town", 4)`

4 `CHARACTERCOUNT("Sydney Opera House") - 6`

5 `MyString ← "Be good at all times"`.

Using the SUBSTR function, write expressions to return the following strings from `MyString`:

a 'good'

b 'times'

c 'at times'

Functions for changing data types

Typically a value input to a program is entered as a string. If it is to be treated as a number then a built-in function could be used to convert it.

The TONUM function returns the integer or real number equivalent of `ThisString`:

`TONUM(ThisString : STRING) RETURNS INTEGER or REAL`

For example, `TONUM("193")` returns the integer 193 and `TONUM("0.843")` returns the real number 0.843.

The INT function returns the integer part of `ThisNumber`:

`INT(ThisNumber : REAL) RETURNS INTEGER`

For example, `INT(12.79)` returns 12.

Progress check 11.05

Evaluate the following expressions:

1 `TONUM("8") + TONUM("9")`

2 `TONUM("12" & "55")`

3 `MyNumber ← 3.852`

`INT(MyNumber)`

ASCII codes

LOOK BACK «

The ASCII coding system was covered in Chapter 10, section 10.01.

The following two functions return the ASCII code for a given character and character for a given ASCII code number.

The ASC function returns an integer which is the ASCII character code for character `ThisCharacter`:

`ASC(ThisCharacter : CHAR) RETURNS INTEGER`

For example, `ASC('A')` returns integer 65.

The CHR function returns the character represented by ASCII code `Value`:

`CHR(Value : INTEGER) RETURNS CHAR`

For example, `CHR(65)` returns 'A'.

Progress check 11.06

Use the ASCII code table in Section 10.01.

1 Evaluate these expressions:

  a ASC('P')

  b ASC('Z') - ASC('H')

2 What is produced by the following expressions?

  a CHR(72) & CHR(65) & CHR(80) &
    CHR(80) & CHR(89)

  b ThisString ← SUBSTR(CHR(69) &
    CHR(88) & CHR(67) & CHR(73),
    2, 1)

    ASC(ThisString)

Random number generator

The RND function returns a random number in the range 0 to 0.99999:

```
RND() RETURNS REAL
```

For example, RND() may return 0.67351.

There can be variations on this. The function might instead generate a random integer in the range Lower to Upper inclusive:

```
RND(Lower : INTEGER, Upper : INTEGER)
RETURNS INTEGER
```

For example, RND(10, 25) will return an integer between 10 and 25.

Random numbers can be used to generate a dataset.

For example, two players play a game by guessing a word. If Player A thinks of the word first, she scores one point. If Player B guesses the word first, she scores one point. Assume A and B are of the same standard at playing the game.

Figure 11.10 is a program that simulates the playing of the game for 20 words and outputs the total scores for Player A and Player B.

Progress check 11.07

Draw up the identifier table for the pseudocode in Figure 11.10.

```
PlayerAScore ← 0
PlayerBScore ← 0
FOR Words ← 1 TO 20
    NextNum ← RND()
    IF NextNum < 0.5
        THEN
            PlayerAScore ← PlayerAScore + 1
        ELSE
            PlayerBScore ← PlayerBScore + 1
    ENDIF
ENDFOR
OUTPUT PlayerAScore, PlayerBScore
```

> There is an even chance of A or B being first to guess each word.

Figure 11.10 A program uses random numbers

Technical documentation

Function descriptions are a good example of the need as a computer scientist and programmer to be able to read and understand technical documentation.

Key points when reading the above function descriptions are to identify:

- the function name
- the number of parameters, noting that a parameter can be optional
- the data type for each parameter
- the data type of the value returned by the function.

Built-in functions are just one example of technical documentation needed for programming. We have already used code tables. There will be documentation about installing the programming environment and much, much more.

Progress check 11.08

Find technical documentation for the functions which are available for your chosen programming language. The best source will be online. Are there equivalent functions in your programming language for all the pseudocode examples we have introduced?

11.06 Structured programming

Procedures

We have already stated that it is good practice to design an algorithm using the idea of sub-tasks which are designed and later coded separately. We used the term **procedure** when considering a structure chart.

Procedures (and functions) are called subprograms or subroutines and fit with the idea of using a modular approach to both the problem design and coding.

TERMS

Procedure: a block of code that can be repeatedly executed

Defining and calling procedures

The new pseudocode syntax we shall use is:

```
PROCEDURE <identifier>
    <statement(s)>
ENDPROCEDURE
```

The procedure code is called with the statement:

```
CALL <identifier>
```

Consider an application where the user is continually presented with a main menu with three menu choices available.

If the user selects Option 1, the program runs the `MyProcedure1` code. Similarly, Option 2 calls `MyProcedure2`. Figure 11.11 is a program that does this.

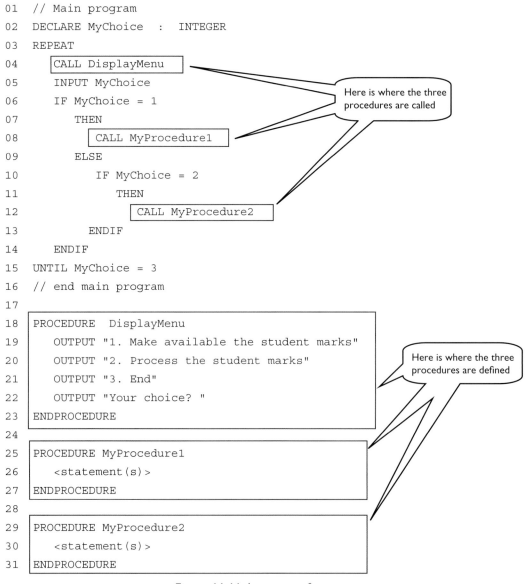

```
01   // Main program
02   DECLARE MyChoice   :   INTEGER
03   REPEAT
04       CALL DisplayMenu
05       INPUT MyChoice
06       IF MyChoice = 1
07          THEN
08               CALL MyProcedure1
09          ELSE
10              IF MyChoice = 2
11                 THEN
12                     CALL MyProcedure2
13              ENDIF
14       ENDIF
15   UNTIL MyChoice = 3
16   // end main program
17
18   PROCEDURE   DisplayMenu
19       OUTPUT "1. Make available the student marks"
20       OUTPUT "2. Process the student marks"
21       OUTPUT "3. End"
22       OUTPUT "Your choice? "
23   ENDPROCEDURE
24
25   PROCEDURE MyProcedure1
26       <statement(s)>
27   ENDPROCEDURE
28
29   PROCEDURE MyProcedure2
30       <statement(s)>
31   ENDPROCEDURE
```

Here is where the three procedures are called

Here is where the three procedures are defined

Figure 11.11 A program for a menu

TIP

- Each procedure must have an identifier name.

- The procedure code is a block of program statements.

- The block of statements inside the procedure are indented in pseudocode.

- The `DisplayMenu` procedure header has no parameters – there are no brackets after the identifier name. Remember: almost all the built-in functions we studied earlier had at least one parameter.

Progress check 11.09

1 List the statement numbers in Figure 11.11 where a procedure has been defined.

2 Give the line number where procedure `DisplayMenu` is called.

3 How many times will procedure `DisplayMenu` be called when the program is executed?

Procedures with parameters

Consider a dataset of 200 kitchen stock item prices. The values are stored in a 1D array `KitchenPrices`. A program is to display all product prices with a 15% increase.

The code is straightforward:

```
FOR Item ← 1 TO 200
    KitchenPrices[Item] ←
        KitchenPrices[Item] * 1.15
    OUTPUT KitchenPrices[i]
ENDFOR
```

This could be wrapped up inside a procedure `IncreasePrice`, as shown in Figure 11.12. We pass the name of the array and its upper bound to the procedure through the procedure header.

There are several things to note here:

- The procedure header/interface has two parameters.

- Variable `Item` is only used inside the procedure so it is declared as a local variable. That means its scope is only inside procedure `IncreasePrice`.

- `PriceArray` and `UBound` in the procedure code are the identifiers shown as parameters.

```
01  // Main program
02  // KitchenPrices array has the 200 prices stored
03
04  CALL IncreasePrice(KitchenPrices, 200)
                       └─────── Arguments ───────┘

                    Procedure header/interface

10  PROCEDURE IncreasePrice(PriceArray : ARRAY OF REAL, UBound :INTEGER)
11      DECLARE Item : INTEGER
12      FOR Item ← 1 TO UBound
13          PriceArray[Item] ← PriceArray[Item] * 1.15
14          OUTPUT PriceArray[Item]
15      ENDFOR
16  ENDPROCEDURE
```

Figure 11.12 A program using a procedure with parameters

What is the benefit of a procedure having parameters?

Consider a second array of 550 prices for electrical goods stored in array `Electricals`.

The 15% price increase could be done on those items using the same `IncreasePrice` procedure. The procedure call to do this is:

```
CALL IncreasePrice(Electricals, 550)
```

The use of procedures – with parameter passing – are a tool to produce re-usable program code.

Progress check 11.10

What changes would need to be made to the pseudocode if the percentage price increase could be varied?

Passing values by reference or by value

When the procedure code is run and the increased prices are calculated, will these increases change the price values in the array back in the main program?

When values are passed to a procedure by 'value', a copy of the values of the data items is passed as a parameter. Following the call to the procedure, when control passes back to the main program, the values of the data items used as arguments are unchanged.

When values are passed to a procedure 'by reference' and the values change as a result of running the procedure code, their value is still changed when control returns to the main program. This happens because the arguments in the procedure header are passed as a reference to the memory location where each of the arguments is stored.

Which mechanism is to be used is made clear by adding the syntax `BYVALUE` or `BYREF` before each parameter.

Consider that a permanent price increase is required. The function header would now become:

```
PROCEDURE IncreasePrice(BYREF PriceArray : ARRAY OF REAL, BYVALUE UBound :
INTEGER)
```

`UBound` is passed by value as we know its value will not be changed by the procedure code.

User-defined functions

We have studied the built-in functions which are provided as part of a high-level programming language. The programmer can also code their own 'user-defined' functions. This is a misleading term as it really means 'programmer-defined' functions.

We already have all the terminology; functions use the same terms as we have used for procedures.

The syntax for function design is:

```
FUNCTION <identifier>(<parameter> : <data type>[, <parameter> : <data type>])
RETURNS <data type>

    <statement(s)>

    RETURN <identifier>

ENDFUNCTION
```

The key difference between a procedure and a function is that a function always calculates and returns a single data value.

Consider a trivial example of a function to accept two integers and return their sum. The steps in designing the function are:

1 Decide on its identifier name – `AddTwoIntegers`.

2 Decide on the parameters – `Num1` and `Num2`, both of data type `INTEGER`.

3 The data type for the return value is `INTEGER`.

```
FUNCTION AddTwoIntegers(Num1 : INTEGER, Num2 : INTEGER) RETURNS INTEGER
    DECLARE Answer : INTEGER
    Answer ← Num1 + Num2
    RETURN Answer
ENDFUNCTION
```

The function would then be used in a program as follows:

```
// declaration statements not shown
INPUT FirstNum
INPUT SecondNum
MyAnswer ← AddTwoIntegers(FirstNum, SecondNum)
OUTPUT MyAnswer
```

Let's design a function to calculate how many words are in a string input by the user. The method is to count the number of Space characters in the string.

We shall avoid any special CASEs where the string could start or end with a Space. Figure 11.13 shows the output from the program code that follows.

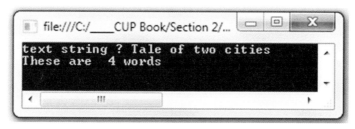

Figure 11.13 Output from the program

```
// declaration statements not shown for main program
OUTPUT "Text string? "
INPUT MyString
WordCount ← CountWords(MyString)
OUTPUT WordCount
FUNCTION CountWords(ThisString : STRING) : INTEGER
    DECLARE i            : INTEGER
    DECLARE SpacesCount : INTEGER
    DECLARE WordCount    : INTEGER
    SpacesCount ← 0
    FOR i ← 2 TO (CHARACTERCOUNT(ThisString) - 1)
    // the first and last characters are ignored
        IF SUBSTR(ThisString, i, i) = " "
            THEN
                SpacesCount ← SpacesCount + 1
        ENDIF
    ENDFOR
    WordCount ← SpacesCount + 1
    RETURN WordCount
ENDFUNCTION
```

There are several ideas here from earlier work:

- the use of the two built-in functions: CHARACTERCOUNT and SUBSTR
- the For–EndFor loop structure
- local variables i and WordCount
- calculating a running total.

In pseudocode, we use a built-in function, EOF, to test for the end of a file when it is open for reading.

The EOF function

Note that EOF follows the rules for any function:

- identifier name: EOF
- parameters: one parameter, the file name
- return value: TRUE or FALSE

```
OPEN "MyFile" FOR READ
REPEAT
    <statement(s)>
UNTIL EOF("MyFile")
CLOSEFILE "MyFile"
```

Progress check 11.11

Write the equivalent pseudocode to test for the end of a file using a While–EndWhile loop.

Writing program code

We now have most of the techniques, we need to write program code. Let's return to the bubble sort problem and see how the three high-level languages each implement the algorithm.

The code will illustrate how each language codes arrays, selection and loops. Table 11.07 repeats the bubble-sort identifier table (Table 11.06).

Identifier	Data type	Description
MyArray	ARRAY[1:10] OF INTEGER	The array storing the data items
Temp	INTEGER	Stores one of the data values when a swap is made
Pass	INTEGER	Loop counter for the outer loop
UBound	INTEGER	The upper bound of the array
i	INTEGER	Index value for the array
Swapped	BOOLEAN	Set to FALSE at the start of each pass. Flags to TRUE when a swap occurs.

Table 11.07 Identifier table for bubble sort algorithm

Visual Basic .NET Python and Pascal bubble sorts	
Visual Basic	<pre>Module Module1
    Dim Admissions(20) As Integer

    Sub Main()
      Admissions(1) = 13 : Admissions(2) = 26
      Admissions(3) = 11 : Admissions(4) = 33
      Admissions(5) = 1 : Admissions(6) = 145
      Admissions(7) = 4 : Admissions(8) = 18
      Admissions(9) = 22 : Admissions(10) = 21
      Admissions(11) = 5 : Admissions(12) = 19

      Call Output(Admissions, 12)
      Call BubbleSort(Admissions, 12)
      Call Output(Admissions, 12)
      Console.ReadLine()
    End Sub</pre> |

```
    Sub BubbleSort(ByRef List() As Integer, UBound As Integer)
      Dim NoSwaps As Boolean : Dim Posn As Integer : Dim Temp As
Integer
      NoSwaps = False
      While NoSwaps = False
        NoSwaps = True
        For Posn = 1 To UBound - 1
          If List(Posn) > List(Posn + 1) Then
            ' swap
            NoSwaps = False
            Temp = List(Posn)
            List(Posn) = List(Posn + 1)
            List(Posn + 1) = Temp
          End If
        Next
      End While
    End Sub

    Sub Output(List() As Integer, UBound As Integer)
      Console.WriteLine()
      For i = 1 To UBound
        Console.Write(List(i) &    )
      Next
      Console.WriteLine()
    End Sub

End Module
```

Python	
| | ```
def BubbleSort(List, UBound) :
    # NoSwaps - Boolean - Posn As Integer  - Temp Integer
    NoSwaps = False
    while NoSwaps == False :
        NoSwaps = True
        for Posn in range (0, UBound -1 ) :
            if List[Posn] > List[Posn + 1] :
                # swap
                NoSwaps = False
                Temp = List[Posn]
                List[Posn] = List[Posn + 1]
                List[Posn + 1] = Temp

Admissions = [13, 26, 11, 33, 1, 145, 4, 18, 22, 21, 5, 19]

print(Admissions)
BubbleSort(Admissions, 12)
print(Admissions)
``` |

Pascal	
| | ```
Program BubbleSort;
  Var Admissions : array [1..20] of Integer ;

  Procedure BubbleSort(Var List : Array Of Integer; UBound :
Integer) ;
    Var NoSwaps : Boolean ; Posn : Integer; Temp : Integer ;
    Begin
``` |

```
      NoSwaps := False ;
      While NoSwaps = False Do
        Begin
        NoSwaps := True ;
        For Posn := 1 To UBound - 1  Do
          If List[Posn] > List[Posn + 1]
               Then
                  Begin
                  {swap}
                  NoSwaps := False ;
                  Temp := List[Posn] ;
                  List[Posn] :- List[Posn + 1] ;
                  List[Posn + 1] := Temp ;
                  End;
        End;
  End;
Procedure Output(List : Array Of Integer; UBound : Integer);
  Var i : integer ;
  Begin
  For i := 0 To UBound-1 Do
    Write(List[i], ' ') ;
  Writeln;
  End;
Begin
  Admissions[1]  := 13   ; Admissions[2]  := 26 ;
  Admissions[3]  := 11   ; Admissions[4]  := 33 ;
  Admissions[5]  := 1    ; Admissions[6]  := 145 ;
  Admissions[7]  := 4    ; Admissions[8]  := 18 ;
  Admissions[9]  := 22   ; Admissions[10] := 21 ;
  Admissions[11] := 5    ; Admissions[12] := 19 ;

  Output(Admissions, 12) ;
  BubbleSort(Admissions, 12) ;
  Output(Admissions, 12) ;
  Readln;
  End.
End.
```

Progress check 11.12

Study the program code for each for the three languages shown. Identify and describe similarities and differences for the syntax used for:

- declaration of variables
- assignment of variables
- selection
- loops.

Summary

- Write pseudocode and program code for programming language basics:
  - o declaration and assignment of variables and constants
  - o input of data from the user
  - o output from the program.
- Appreciate that programming in a high-level language is a transferrable skill.
- Implement as pseudocode and program code, the basic constructs for:
  - o Selection – using variations of the IF statement and the CASE structure
  - o Iteration – using the three control structures: For–EndFor, Repeat–Until and While–EndWhile.
- Use a selection of the built-in functions available in the chosen programming language.
- Understand a given built-in function definition expressed in pseudocode.
- Use procedures and decide when it is appropriate to pass parameters by value or by reference.
- Design and code a user-defined function in the chosen programming language.

Exam-style questions

1   Sheena has inherited a recipe book from her grandmother.

Sheena wants to write a function to return the number of boxes of eggs that she needs to buy. The function takes, as a parameter, the number of eggs required for a recipe. There are 6 eggs in a box. Sheena needs to buy enough eggs, but does not want any full boxes of eggs left over.

She knows that she can use the operators DIV and MOD to calculate the required number of boxes.

a   Show the results for the following expressions:

  i   20 DIV 6 =

  ii   20 MOD 6 =   [2]

b   Complete the pseudocode:

```
FUNCTION CalculateNumberOfBoxes(NumberOfEggs : ....................)
                          RETURNS ...............................
    DECLARE .................. : INTEGER
    NumberOfBoxes ← .................... // how many full boxes?
    IF NumberOfEggs MOD ....................    // need part of a box?
        THEN  // increment number of boxes
            ...............................................................
    ENDIF
    RETURN NumberOfBoxes
ENDFUNCTION                                                                    [5]
```

c   Sheena could have written the algorithm in **part b** as a procedure.

What is the difference between a function and a procedure?   [1]

Cambridge International AS and A Level Computing 9691 Paper 23, Q1 b & c June 2014

Software development

12.01 Programming

The term 'program life cycle' is used in the syllabus. Do not confuse this term with 'system life cycle'. The system life cycle includes the analysis of a computer system and its subsequent development, installation and maintenance. These activities are not in the new 9608 syllabus.

The program life cycle involves:

- design of the program

- the coding stage

- testing of the program code.

Requirements specification

The starting point for the design of any code will be the requirements specification document produced by the systems analyst. This is the summary of the analysis stage, containing a number of objectives and criteria. On completion of the project, what has been produced and the performance of the new system will be matched to these objectives.

Design specification

The analyst and the programming team will work closely together to produce the design specification.

The design specification is a reference point for all members of the programming team as different parts of the system are developed and programs are produced by different programmers. The system will have been divided up into sub-tasks and the design of each sub-task will take a top-down approach to program specification.

Once the design and specification for the programs has been agreed then the programmer must follow these stages: design, coding and testing.

Historically, different software would have been used for code creation (a text editor) and program translation (a compiler).

Program specifications

The design of the programs is part of the overall design process. Note that 'program design' does not mean the writing of the code – we are not yet ready for this. Approaches such as the use of existing program libraries and object-oriented programming mean that it is even more important to delay the writing of new program code.

The specifications will include detailed algorithm designs showing the method of solution for parts of the problem. These algorithms could be documented using pseudocode, program flowcharts and structure charts. The data structures to be used must be clear; for example, what files are needed to store the application data? Do we already have program code which has been tested in program libraries which could be used?

From these specifications, writing the program code can be started.

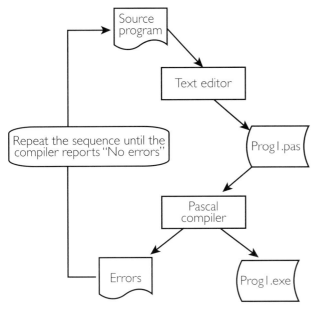

Figure 12.01 Development cycle using a compiler

Program testing

We have already used a trace table to check the working of pseudocode.

In Figure 12.03, the editor is highlighting matching blocks.

LOOK FORWARD »

The various types of testing are not discussed in detail until Chapter 22.

Features of an IDE: Text editor

Creating the code

The editor is trying to be helpful. Figure 12.02 shows it reporting issues it can detect.

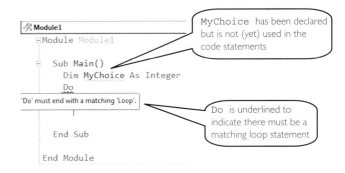

Figure 12.02 Matching syntax

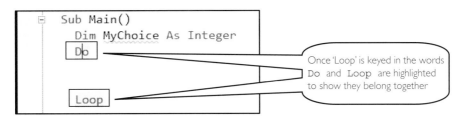

Figure 12.03 Matching blocks

In Figure 12.04, the editor offers additional information. These features are called 'context-sensitive prompts'.

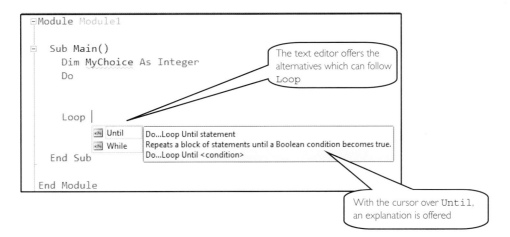

Figure 12.04 Context-sensitive prompts

In Figure 12.05, the editor highlights an error: the entire statement is underlined because the keyword 'Then' has been misspelt.

```
Module Module1

  Sub Main()
    Dim MyChoice As Integer
    Do
      Call DisplayMenu()
      Console.Write("Choice ? ")
      MyChoice = Console.ReadLine
      If MyChoice = 1 Then Call MyProcedure1()
      If MyChoice = 2 the call MyProcedure2
    Loop Until MyChoice = 3
  End Sub
```

Figure 12.05 Misspelt keyword

Viewing the code

The editor is using several prettyprint features:

- The structure keywords are shown in blue.

- Different colours are used to distinguish the variable names and keywords

- Text to be displayed as part of a `Console.Writeline` statement is shown in a different colour.

In Figure 12.06 the entire main program code (the `Sub Main()` part) has been collapsed to help with reading the remainder of the code. This does not affect the execution of the code.

```
Module Module1

  Sub Main() ...

  Sub Displaymenu()
    Console.WriteLine("")
    Console.WriteLine("+++++++++++++++++++++++++++++++++++++")
    Console.WriteLine("1. Make available the student marks")
    Console.WriteLine("2. Process the student marks")
    Console.WriteLine("3 End")
    Console.WriteLine("+++++++++++++++++++++++++++++++++++++")
  End Sub

  Sub MyProcedure1()
    Console.WriteLine("run code for menu option 1...")
  End Sub

  Sub MyProcedure2()
    Console.WriteLine("run code for menu option 2...")
  End Sub
End Module
```

Figure 12.06 Collapsing blocks of code

An alternative to collapsing blocks of code is to 'Comment Out' a selection of the code (see Figure 12.07). This way the code will not execute, as the selected statements are treated as comments (only).

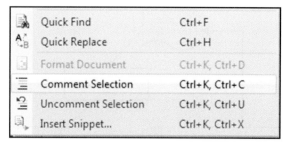

Figure 12.07 'Commenting out' statements

Running the program

For the examples which follow we have coded the 'Count the words' user-defined function which was used in Section 11.06.

Figure 12.08, the user has attempted to run the program and it has been refused. The compiler is being helpful and has suggested that the return value has been omitted from the function code.

```
      If Mid(ThisString, i, 1) = " " Then
        SpacesCount = SpacesCount + 1
      End If
    Next
    WordCount = SpacesCount - 1
  End Function()
```
Function 'CountWords' doesn't return a value on all code paths. Are you missing a 'Return' statement?
```
End Module
```
100 %

Error List		
🔴 1 Error	⚠ 1 Warning	ⓘ 0 Messages
Description		
🔴 2 End of statement expected.		

Figure 12.08 Execution refused

Debugging features

The programmer is able to single-step through the execution of the program.

Figure 12.09 shows the program part-way through its execution. The highlighted line is the statement which has just been executed.

The 'Locals' window (in Visual Basic .NET) is displaying the current value for all variables used by the code. It reports that currently one Space character has been found and it is now considering the fifth character.

This IDE debug feature is a visual way to see the program control moving from the main program code to the function code and vice versa.

```
Module1
        End Sub

    Function CountWords(ThisString As String) As Integer
        Dim i As Integer
        Dim SpacesCount As Integer
        Dim WordCount As Integer
        SpacesCount = 0
        For i = 2 To Len(ThisString) - 1
            ' the first and last characters are ignored
            If Mid(ThisString, i, 1) = " " Then
                SpacesCount = SpacesCount + 1
            End If
        Next
        WordCount = SpacesCount + 1
        Return WordCount
    End Function

    End Module
100 %
Locals
Name                Value               Type
  CountWords        0                   Integer
  i                 5                   Integer
  SpacesCount       1                   Integer
  ThisString        "the royal family"  String
  WordCount         0                   Integer
```

Figure 12.09 Reporting the value of variables

Setting a breakpoint (see Figure 12.10) will cause execution of the program to halt at this statement. When the breakpoint is reached, you could run the program in the normal way or single-step through it. Either way, the program execution will be halted at the breakpoint.

```
Module1
    Function CountWords(ThisString As String) As Integer
        Dim i As Integer
        Dim SpacesCount As Integer
        Dim WordCount As Integer
        SpacesCount = 0
        For i = 2 To Len(ThisString) - 1
            ' the first and last characters are ignored
            If Mid(ThisString, i, 1) = " " Then
                SpacesCount = SpacesCount + 1
            End If
        Next
        WordCount = SpacesCount + 1
        Return WordCount
    End Function

    End Module
```

Figure 12.10 Use of a breakpoint

In Figure 12.11, the user has set a breakpoint and is checking that the correct value for the expression `len(ThisString) - 1` is calculated (as 13). This is the 'expressions report window' (Visual Basic .NET calls it the 'Immediate Window').

```
    Function CountWords(ThisString As String) As Integer
        Dim i As Integer
        Dim SpacesCount As Integer
        Dim WordCount As Integer
        SpacesCount = 0
        For i = 2 To Len(ThisString) - 1
            ' the first and last characters are ignored
            If Mid(ThisString, i, 1) = " " Then
                SpacesCount = SpacesCount + 1
        End If
100 %
Immediate Window
? len(ThisString) - 1
13
```

```
file:///C:/___CUP Book/Section ...
text string ? united nations
```

Figure 12.11 Reporting the value of an expression

12.02 Program testing

There is a fundamental difference between the way the three programming languages, Visual Basic .NET, Python and Pascal, translate the source program code.

LOOK BACK «

Chapter 5, section 5.04 discusses language translators.

Python interprets the code. This means the programmer can attempt to run the code at any stage in writing the code.

Pascal and all versions of Visual Basic .NET translate the source code with a compiler which is part of the IDE.

Whether the code is interpreted or compiled has implications for testing the code.

12.03 Testing strategies

The use of the word 'strategy' implies there should be a formal and systematic approach to the testing of any program code produced. Program code which has been produced from some algorithm design should be executed with the wide range of all possible inputs anticipated by the programmer. It is possible that inputs which are not anticipated for the program are used after the formal sign-off is done. These inputs may produce incorrect outputs which are observed or could even go unnoticed by the user.

After any syntax errors are eliminated, the most likely cause of the failure of the program code is logical errors. These can be identified by careful checking (for example, using a trace table) or may become apparent when the program is run. Section 12.01 shows screenshots of various syntax errors which are present in the programmer's code.

Typical logic errors include:

- a loop which iterates five times (when the intention of the algorithm is that it should be four iterations)

- a selection structure which displays incorrect logic.

An analogy is that logical errors are like the yeti – the fact that we have not found any does not conclusively prove they do not exist!

Formal approaches for a testing strategy include white-box and black-box testing.

White-box testing

The tester must be familiar with the program code, so the tester is likely to be the programmer. The tester must then draw up a list of possible input data values which is carefully chosen to test every possible route through the code.

For example, a program inputs a single student exam mark and outputs the corresponding grade. If the grades Fail, C, B and A are possible, then the code must contain at least four selection statements (using either an IF or CASE structure). Consider, that a C grade is awarded for a mark of 'greater than or equal to 40 and less than 55'. Input data would be chosen to calculate each of the four possible grade results and within each grade:

- a data value (such as, 47) which is within this grade boundary

- data values which are on the boundary for the grade.

It is important that each of the boundary values of 40 and 54 are used for separate tests.

Black-box testing

In Chapter 11 we were introduced to the concept of a program subroutine. Functions and procedures (once coded and thoroughly tested) can be considered by programmers as a 'black box'. Programmers use this code by calling its identifier name. They need only a knowledge of the inputs and outputs of the subroutine. A programmer need have no knowledge of the code contained within the subroutine.

This is the thinking for the testing strategy called 'black-box testing'. The tester is concerned only with the inputs used and matching each of these inputs to the output they are expected to produce.

This strategy is appropriate for the testing of modules developed by a programmer who intends that they will be used repeatedly in several large projects under development. The actual program code will not be apparent to the tester. The tester is concerned with designing the range of inputs and monitoring the output produced. If the modules are coded as procedures or functions, then black-box testing is concerned with testing the procedure/function interface. The tester needs no knowledge of the underlying code contained in the subroutine, only of the number and data types of parameters used in the interface.

Stub testing

A main menu displays five possible option choices to the user and each option has a procedure which is called when that user choice is made. Consider menu options as follows:

- Create a produce file, which calls procedure `CreateFile`.

- Search for product by product code, which calls procedure `SearchByCode`.

- Search for products by type, which calls procedure `SearchByType`.

The use of stub testing enables the programmer to produce an executable program before all aspects of the design have been coded. The programmer would first write the menu code, then the `CreateFile` code. Without writing any further code, the programmer can check that the program successfully runs when the user selects option 1.

If the user did input any other response following the display of the menu, we would not want the program to crash. The strategy is to write the `SearchByCode` and `SearchByType` procedures as **stubs.** If either of these procedures is called, the action – for the moment – is only to display a message to the user telling them that the program is still under development and that this feature has not yet been implemented.

Summary

■ The programming development life cycle consists of: program design, coding and testing.

■ Most modern coding software provides an integrated development environment (IDE) which includes:

- help in writing source code, with context-sensitive prompts and dynamic syntax checking

- features for presentation, including prettyprint and the expansion/collapsing of code blocks

- debugging features including single-stepping, setting of breakpoints and reporting windows

- the identification of syntax errors before the code is executed.

■ Different types of error are: syntax errors, logic errors and run-time errors.

■ Data can be designed for both black-box and white-box testing.

■ A program may be written in stages using stub testing.

Exam-style questions

1 **a** Describe what is meant by an Integrated Development Environment (IDE) [3]

   b The programmer write the code for a new program.

   Name the feature of the IDE that allows the programmer to do this. [1]

   c During the keying in of the program there are several useful features which help the programmer before an attempt is made to translate the code.

   Describe **three** such features. [3]

PART III

ADVANCED THEORY

Data representation

13.01 User-defined data types

Non-composite types

An enumeration is a complete, ordered listing of all the items in a collection. The term applies to several data types which can be created in Visual Basic. The most general data set is a collection, which can store items of any data type including objects. Other types of collection in Visual Basic are a List or an ArrayList.

In pseudocode, we give the type an identifier name and list the data values which form the type

```
TYPE

    DECLARE Days : (Sunday, Monday,
                    Tuesday, Wednesday,
                    Thursday, Friday,
                    Saturday)

ENDTYPE
```

A variable of this type is then declared:

```
        DECLARE DayOfTheWeek : Days
```

We can then process the `DayOfTheWeek` variable:

```
DayOfTheWeek ← Thursday

IF DayOfTheWeek = Saturday OR
DayOfTheWeek = Sunday

    THEN

        OUTPUT "It is not a work day"

    ELSE

        OUTPUT "It's a work day"

ENDIF
```

The Visual Basic syntax for this is shown in Figure 13.01.

```
1  ⊟Module Module1
2  ⊟  Enum Days
3        Sunday
4        Monday
5        Tuesday
6        Wednesday
7        Thursday
8        Friday
9        Saturday
10     End Enum
11
12 ⊟  Sub main()
13       Dim DayOfTheWeek As Days
14       DayOfTheWeek = Days.Sunday
15       If DayOfTheWeek = Days.Saturday Or DayOfTheWeek = Days.Sunday Then
16          Console.WriteLine("It is not a work day")
17       Else
18          Console.WriteLine("It's a work day")
19       End If
20       Console.ReadLine()
21     End Sub
```

Figure 13.01 Code using an enumerated data type

TIP

Pascal uses the keyword TYPE (as for our pseudocode).

Python has Enums available from version 3.4.

Pointer

The purpose of an array declaration statement is to reserve memory for the storage of the data which will be used by the program. This is potentially wasteful. The statement on line 12 in Figure 13.02 code reserves 1000 storage spaces. Each one of the 1000 spaces reserves memory for the seven data items. The choice of 1000 by the programmer could be wasteful or, conversely, not enough.

Pointers are designed to overcome the need to reserve memory in advance. Main memory will be allocated as and when required, for example, when the data for a new transaction is saved to the array. The pointer data type allows for dynamic memory allocation.

A pointer is a variable which stores the address of a variable. Instead of the data, the pointer contains the address

of the data. Pointers are used to access data which is dynamically created at run-time. We implement this for the ATMTransaction data using the following declaration:

```
DECLARE TransactionPointer :
^ATMTransaction
```

The notation for the data type is read as:

^ATMTransaction is a pointer data type which provides a pointer to data of type ATMTransaction.

TIP

Of the three supported programming languages, only Pascal supports the pointer data type.

Pascal has a procedure New which creates a new pointer variable.

Composite data types

Set

Assume we wish to create a set of integers which are the choice values for a menu-driven program.

The set of valid values can be given an identifier name:

```
DECLARE ValidChoices : SET OF
        (1,2,3,4,5,6,7)
```

This then suggests a long-winded IF statement:

```
IF Ch=1 OR Ch=2 OR Ch=3 OR Ch=4 OR
   Ch=5 OR Ch=6 OR Ch=7
```

Using the set data type, this can be condensed to:

```
IF Ch IN ValidChoices
```

Here are another two examples:

```
DECLARE SweaterSizes : SET OF
(XXLarge, XLarge, Large, Medium,
Small)
```

```
DECLARE Title : SET OF (Mr, Mrs, Ms,
Miss, Dr)
```

TIP

Of the three supported programming languages, Pascal and Python support the set data type.

The following Python code illustrates that the set data type has operators – union and intersection – which can be used on two sets:

```
>>> full_time = Set(['Aayu', 'Jane', 'Poya', 'Paksha'])
>>> programmers = Set(['Poya', 'Sam', 'Susan', 'Paksha'])
>>> team_leaders = Set(['Jane', 'Poya', 'Susan', 'Zoe'])

# employees is a union of three sets
>>> employees = full_time | programmers | team_leaders
# full_time_team_leaders is an intersection of two sets
>>> full_time_team_leaders = full_time & team_leaders
# add an item to a set
>>> full_time.add('Marvin')
```

Record

The data for many applications consists – not of a single data value – but several data values of different types.

For example, a banking ATM transactions application would need to store:

- bank ID
- account number
- date of the transaction
- time of the transaction
- type of transaction – withdrawal or PIN services
- amount withdrawn
- identifier of the ATM where the transaction was made.

These seven data values together form the 'transaction data' for a single transaction.

The following record is used for our ATM transaction:

```
TYPE ATMTransaction

    Bank_ID         : STRING
    AccountNumber   : INTEGER
    TransactionDate : DATE
    TransactionTime : INTEGER
    TransactionType : CHAR
    Amount          : REAL
    ATM_ID          : INTEGER
ENDTYPE
```

The application will have to process the data for several transactions, so we use an array `Transaction` of data type `ATMTransaction` as shown in Table 13.01.

Identifier	Data type	Description
Transaction	ARRAY[1..1000] OF ATMTransaction	Array storing the data for many ATM transactions

Table 13.01 Identifier table for an ATM transaction system

This is implemented in Visual Basic .NET as a Structure (see Figure 13.02).

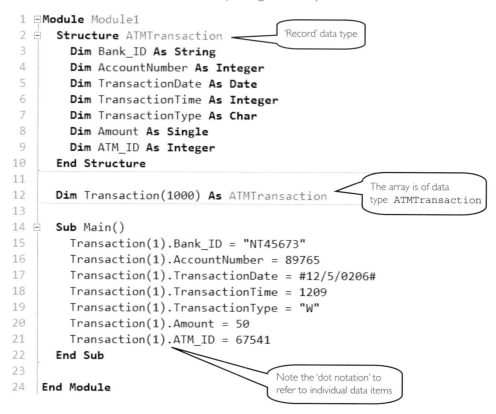

Figure 13.02 Code using a 'record' user-defined data type

LOOK FORWARD »

We re-visit 'user-defined' data types when we use the record structure in Chapter 21, Section 21.02.

Class/object

The use of classes and objects is the basis of the object-oriented programming paradigm. This is discussed extensively in Chapter 19, Section 19.01. A class is the blueprint from which actual objects (called 'instances') will be created.

Progress check 13.01

Data is to be stored for nurses who work in a hospital:

- nurse ID – a five-digit code
- family name
- first names
- date the nurse first registered with the Nursing Council
- whether or not the basic health and safety course has been completed,

Design a user-defined data type for the nurse data.

13.02 File organisation and access

Methods of file organisation

LOOK BACK «

In Chapter 10, section 10.03, we used a 'text file' which consisted of several lines of text. Our processing of the file included reading the lines of text in sequence and outputting the text or searching for a particular value.

We now need to consider, when a file is used to store data:

- how the data in the file will be organised
- the implications of a particular type of organisation for accessing the data in the file.

Serial file organisation

Records are written into the file in no particular order. The file is said to have **serial organisation**. When the file is opened for reading, the records can only be read from the file in order.

TERMS

Serial file organisation: the records are in no particular order

Sequentially organised file: the records are ordered in some way

A file stores a list of animals and the words used for their young, the female and the male. Figure 13.03 shows typical contents with 14 animal records, organised serially.

```
"nightingale", "chick", "hen", "cock"
"bear", "cub", "sow", "boar"
"goat", "kid", "nanny", "billy"
"octopus", "fry", "hen", "NA"
"camel", "calf", "cow", "bull"
"aardvark", "cub", "sow", "boar"
"dog", "puppy", "bitch", "dog"
"elephant", "calf", "cow", "bull"
"red deer", "calf", "hind", "stag"
"ant", "larva", "queen", "drone"
"goose", "gosling", "goose", "gander"
"alligator", "chick", "NA", "NA"
"zebra", "foal", "mare", "stallion"
"tiger", "cub", "tigress", "tiger"
```

Figure 13.03 Serial file organisation (with delimiters)

Sequential file organisation

A possible improvement is to have the records ordered in some way – e.g. stored in animal name order.

The file is then said to be a **sequentially organised** file, with animal name chosen as the key field. Figure 13.04 shows the same 14 records, organised sequentially.

```
aardvark, cub, sow, boar
alligator, chick, NA, NA
ant, larva, queen, drone
bear, cub, sow, boar
camel, calf, cow, bull
dog, puppy, bitch, dog
elephant, calf, cow, bull
goat, kid, nanny, billy
goose, gosling, goose, gander
nightingale, chick, hen, cock
octopus, fry, hen, NA
red deer, calf, hind, stag
tiger, cub, tigress, tiger
zebra, foal, mare, stallion
```

Figure 13.04 Sequential file organisation (without delimiters)

There are many variations on the precise encoding use for the file contents.

- The file in Figure 13.03 has 'delimiters' (speech marks) for each data item and a 'comma separator' between data values

- The file in Figure 13.04 has no text delimiters.

- The files could have stored just one data item per line.

When you are developing a file handling program – for a serial or sequentially organised file – you could create a test file – like the ones shown in Figure 13.03 and Figure 13.04 with text editor software.

Sequential access for serial and sequential files

Study Figure 13.03 and Figure 13.04. A major limitation of both serial and sequential organisation is that the data values can only be read from the file in sequence (i.e. 'sequentially').

- In the serial file, the 'goose' data can only be read after the preceding animals have been read.

- In the sequential file, the 'zebra' data can only be after all the other 13 animals have been read.

This is a major drawback when using data files with serial or sequential organisation.

Fixed-length data values

An alternative method for file organisation is to store each data item with a fixed length as shown in Figure 13.05.

```
aardvark    cub      sow      boar
alligator   chick    NA       NA
ant         larva    queen    drone
bear        cub      sow      boar
camel       calf     cow      bull
dog         puppy    bitch    dog
elephant    calf     cow      bull
goat        kid      nanny    billy
goose       gosling  goose    gander
nightingale chick    hen      cock
octopus     fry      hen      NA
red deer    calf     hind     stag
tiger       cub      tigress  tiger
zebra       foal     mare     stallion
```

Figure 13.05 Fixed-length records

Each animal's data in Figure 13.05 takes up 37 bytes. This has the benefit that the fourth data line in the file starts with byte number $4 \times 37 = 148$. There may be file access methods provided by certain programming languages which make use of this. This would involve positioning a file pointer to a certain byte position in the file.

Random access (using a record key)

The term 'random access' can be misleading as there is nothing random about the way a particular record is accessed. An alternative term is 'direct access' file. This suggests that using a random file organisation method, this allows us direct access to any particular record. Remember, a major disadvantage of serial files and certain sequentially organised files is that direct access to a particular record in the file was not possible.

For a random file each record is given an 'address' at which it is to be written. For the programmer, this will be some form of key number or record key which can be allocated as an integer (1, 2, 3 etc. as new records are created) or the key number can be hashed in some way.

The file will be opened in 'random' mode. The major advantage of this is that data can be both read and written in the same session. There will be file-handling statements to:

- open the file in 'random' mode
- write a single record to the file using its record key
- read a record back from the file, using its known record key.

LOOK FORWARD »

Chapter 21, section 21.02 contains code in which the key number is hashed from the band name and the hashing algorithm generates a key number in the range 1 to 26. It also gives the pseudocode keywords to use with a random file.

Methods of file access

Direct access to a random access file

A single record is retrieved (directly) from the file by using its known record key.

LOOK FORWARD »

Chapter 21, section 21.02 shows the program code to do this using Visual Basic .NET.

Direct access to a sequentially organised file

This is only possible if the file has been created with fixed-length records. The data will then work in conjunction with an index file.

The index file contents (see Figure 13.06) would be stored in main memory so there would be fast access to the value 'goat' and its index position in the ANIMALS file. The software will then effectively set up a file pointer positioned at byte number 37 × 8 = byte 296 in the file.

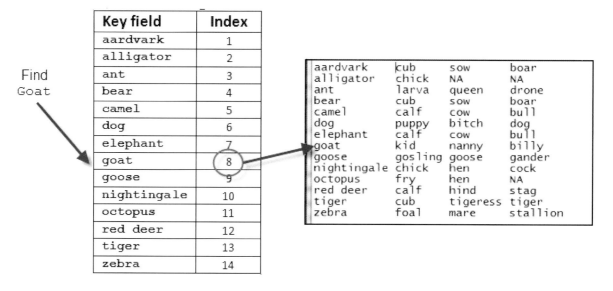

Figure 13.06 Direct access to a sequentially organised file

Choosing a file organisation and access method

A summary of possible file organisation and access methods is shown in Table 13.02.

	Sequential access	Direct access
Serial organisation	✓	✗
Sequential organisation	✓	✗
Sequential organisation with index file	✓	✓
Random organisation	✓	✓

Table 13.02 File organisation and access summary

The key issue in deciding what organisation method to use is the question – do we need fast access to individual records?

Consider the following problems and the choice of file organisation:

• A product file with 2000 items is to have each price stored increased by 5%.

Since all records have to be accessed, we can process them in sequence. So choose serial or sequential organisation with sequential access.

• An orders file has thousands of new orders added each day. Customer Services are always receiving queries from customers about a particular order.
We need fast access to individual orders. Therefore choose a random file organisation with the order number as the record key.

13.03 Real numbers and normalised floating-point representation

The format of binary floating-point real numbers

Computer programs will use, not only integer numbers, but numbers which may have a fractional part i.e. real numbers.

From math, we know that a number can be represented in 'standard form'. Consider 1987.381.

This can be expressed as 1.987381×10^3

or 0.1987381×10^4

For our floating-point format, we express the first part – called the mantissa – as a fraction and then calculate the appropriate exponent.

Very small numbers are also possible: 0.000876 is expressed as 0.876×10^{-3}.

Hence for the range of numbers we want to represent, any number can be expressed as:

$$\text{fraction} \times 10^{\text{Exponent}}$$

where both the fraction and the exponent can be positive or negative.

But, we store numbers in a computer system using base 2 (binary). The same principle can be followed and we conclude:

$$\text{number} = \text{fraction} \times 2^{\text{Exponent}}$$

This is called 'floating-point format':

$$\text{Number} = \text{Mantissa} \times 2^{\text{Exponent}}$$

Hence we can express any real number in floating-point form by stating:

- the mantissa (usually in two's complement)
- the exponent (usually in two's complement).

The only issue then is the number of bits available for the mantissa and exponent.

Convert binary floating-point real numbers into denary

A floating point number uses eight bits for the mantissa and a four-bit exponent (both in two's complement).

The place values for the mantissa and exponent are shown below. Note carefully the place values for the mantissa.

mantissa								exponent			
-1	$1/2$	$1/4$	$1/8$	$1/16$	$1/32$	$1/64$	$1/128$	-8	4	2	1

Consider these examples of calculating values for the mantissa and exponent:

mantissa									exponent			
-1	$1/2$	$1/4$	$1/8$	$1/16$	$1/32$	$1/64$	$1/128$		-8	4	2	1
0	1	0	1	1	1	0	0		0	1	0	0

Mantissa: $1/2 + 1/8 + 1/16 + 1/32 = +23/32$

Exponent: $+4$

Denary number: $23/32 \times 2^4 = 11.5$

mantissa									exponent			
-1	$1/2$	$1/4$	$1/8$	$1/16$	$1/32$	$1/64$	$1/128$		-8	4	2	1
1	1	0	1	1	1	0	0		1	1	1	0

Mantissa: $-1 + 1/2 + 1/8 + 1/16 + 1/32 = -25/32$

Exponent: -2

Denary number: $-25/32 \times 2^{-2} = -25/128$

Convert denary real numbers into floating-point representation

Positive numbers

Using an eight-bit mantissa and exponent, what is the representation for 11.5?

$$11\tfrac{1}{2} = 23/2$$
$$= 23/2 \times 16/16$$
$$= 23/32 \times 16$$
$$= (16/32 + 4/32 + 2/32 + 1/32) \times 2^{+4}$$
$$= (1/2 + 1/8 + 1/16 + 1/32) \times 2^{+4}$$

mantissa = 01011100

exponent = 00000100

Negative numbers

Using an eight-bit mantissa and exponent, what is the representation for −5.5?

$$-5\tfrac{1}{2} = -11/2$$
$$= -11/2 \times 8/8$$
$$= -11/16 \times 8$$
$$= (-1 + 5/16) \times 2^{+3}$$
$$= (-1 + 4/16 + 1/16) \times 2^{+3}$$
$$= (-1 + 1/4 + 1/16) \times 2^{+3}$$

mantissa = 10101000

exponent = 00000011

Progress check 13.03

Using an eight-bit mantissa and exponent, write the representation for:

1   17¾

2   3³⁄₁₆

3   −11½

Normalised floating-point format

There is more than one possible representation for a number using floating-point representation. These examples use an eight-bit mantissa and four-bit exponent.

Pattern 1

−1	½	¼	⅛	¹⁄₁₆	¹⁄₃₂	¹⁄₆₄	¹⁄₁₂₈		−8	4	2	1
0	1	0	0	1	0	0	0		0	0	1	1

Denary number: $^9/_{16} \times 2^{+3} = 4.5$

Pattern 2

−1	½	¼	⅛	¹⁄₁₆	¹⁄₃₂	¹⁄₆₄	¹⁄₁₂₈		−8	4	2	1
0	0	1	0	0	1	0	0		0	1	0	0

Denary number: $^9/_{32} \times 2^{+4} = 4.5$

Hence, both Pattern 1 and Pattern 2 are correct representations for the number 4.5. In Pattern 2, we have made the mantissa smaller by a factor of two, but then doubled the exponent.

This raises the question – how do we decide which representation to use?

The reasons for normalisation

The form to use is called the 'normalised representation'.

Pattern 1 is in normalised form and is the one which will ensure the maximum accuracy of the number is preserved.

For a bit pattern in its normal form:

* for all positive numbers, the mantissa must start with the digits 01

* for all negative numbers, the mantissa must start with the digits 10

TIP Do not confuse the term 'normalised' used here for floating-point format with the normal forms used in database table design.

If a real number is not represented by its normalised form then there is a risk that a loss of accuracy may result. The section on underflow and overflow illustrate this.

Changing the allocation of bits in a floating-point representation

Consider the scenario where 20 bits are available to store a floating-point number and the software designer must decide how many bits to allocate to the mantissa and to the exponent.

We shall discuss first the possible range of numbers for our eight-bit mantissa and four-bit exponent used earlier.

Table 13.03 shows the four extreme values.

Mantissa	Exponent	Denary number
01111111 = +1/2	0111 = +7	+127
01111111 = +1/2	1000 = −8	+1/512
10000000 = −1	0111 = +7	−128
10111111 = −65/128	1000 = −8	−65/32768

Table 13.03 Extreme values for mantissa and exponent

These examples should suggest that:

- More bits given to the mantissa allow for more accuracy.
- More bits given to the exponent allow a greater range of numbers to be represented.

Underflow and overflow

Underflow will occur if the number is too small to be represented by the bits available.

Assume a real number is represented with a five-bit mantissa and five-bit exponent. The place values are:

Consider attempting to represent the small number $+1/2^{21}$

The smallest exponent we can represent is −16.

$$+1/2^{21} = 1/2^5 \times 1/2^{16} \quad \text{Which is represented by:}$$

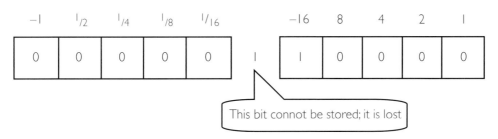

This bit connot be stored; it is lost

So the conclusion is, that using a five-bit mantissa and five-bit exponent, the number is too small to be represented – we have underflow.

Consider the largest positive number which can be represented.

−1	1/2	1/4	1/8	1/16		−16	8	4	2	1
0	1	1	1	1		0	1	1	1	1

This is the denary number +3720. Any attempt to represent a larger number than this will fail.

Progress check 13.05

Show working for the calculated largest value of +3720 using a five-bit mantissa and a five-bit exponent.

A binary representation may be an approximation

The representation of +4½ we considered earlier would be:

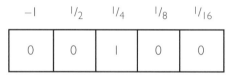

−1	1/2	1/4	1/8	1/16		−16	8	4	2	1
0	1	0	0	1		0	0	0	1	1

This calculates correctly as +4½ and is in its normalised form. An alternative attempt could have been:

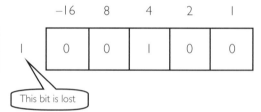

−1	1/2	1/4	1/8	1/16		−16	8	4	2	1
0	0	1	0	0	1	0	0	1	0	0

This bit is lost

We have made the mantissa smaller by a factor of two, but increased the exponent.

The least significant 1 bit in the mantissa is now lost. The bit pattern calculates to: $1/4 \times 2^{+4} = 4$.

The conclusion is that there has been a loss of accuracy with this alternative (un-normalised) representation. If this representation was given to represent the number +4½ then we have introduced a rounding error.

Summary

- User-defined data type are formed from the primitive data types of the language.
- Non-composite types are enumerated types and pointers.
- Composite data types include sets, a record and class.
- The methods of file organisation are serial sequential and random.
- File access methods depend of the organisation and are sequential access or direct access.
- Real numbers are stored using a mantissa and exponent.
- More than one possible bit pattern can be written for a given number. The representation which preserves the maximum accuracy is called the normalised representation.
- A number can be too small to be represented (underflow) or too large to be represented (overflow).
- The bit pattern may be a close approximation to the real number to be represented.
- This approximation will result in a rounding error.

Exam-style questions

1   Many computer systems need to store and process real numbers.

   A computer uses two bytes to store a real number. The first (Byte 7) stores the mantissa and the second (Byte 8), the exponent. Both mantissa and exponent use two's complement.

   a   **i**   What denary number is represented by Byte 7 and Byte 8?

			Byte 7									Byte 8			
0	1	1	0	1	0	0	0	0	0	0	0	0	0	1	1

   Show your working.   [3]

   ii   Without any working out, how can you recognise this 16-bit pattern (Byte 7 and Byte 8) is a positive number?   [1]

   b   **i**   Without any working out, how can you recognise that this 16-bit pattern (Byte 7 and Byte 8) is normalised? [1]

   ii   Both of the representations shown below are not normalised.

   Write in the empty rows the binary for the normalised form for the same value.

			Mantissa									Exponent			
0	0	1	1	0	0	0	0	0	0	0	0	1	0	1	1

			Mantissa									Exponent			
1	1	1	0	0	0	1	1	0	0	1	1	0	0	1	1

   [3]

   c   A change is made to use the two bytes as a 12-bit mantissa with a 4-bit exponent. Describe the effect of this change on the values that can be represented, compared compared with the old use of the two bytes.   [2]

   Cambridge International AS and A Level Computing 9691 Paper 31, Q5 d, e & f June 2014

Communication and Internet technologies

14.01 Protocols

A protocol for communication between computers

Protocol is not a term specific to computing. Its everyday use means 'a way of doing things'. In its computing context, it is set of rules about the format of messages that are exchanged between computers.

When an online purchase is made, there is a protocol to be followed by the seller. At the warehouse, the items will be picked. Are they packaged with other items for the same delivery area? Are there rules about which vehicles can carry which types of parcel? There will be rules about the way orders are packaged and delivered. The final result will be that the goods (the 'core data') are delivered to the customer.

Most forms of communication between, for example, a computer and a device, require some form of connection to be made. A computer about to send data to a printer sends a signal to the printer asking 'is it ready?' and the printer is required to send back an 'acknowledgement signal'. This is a 'connection required' form of communication. We shall soon meet other protocols which are 'connectionless' – that is they do not require a connection to be established before communication can start.

The TCP/IP protocol suite

Applications which use the Internet for communication are client–server applications. The communication requires a connection to be made between the two 'end-points'. The client will initiate some form of communication to or from the server. The server is simply waiting for requests from client applications.

In the example above, the computer and printer communicate using a wired connection and the data enters the computer or device through a particular input or output port.

The nature of communications across the Internet requires that the two end-points or 'hosts' use the Transmission Control Protocol (TCP). This transport layer is one of the four layers of the TCP/IP protocol stack (Figure 14.01). Each layer on the stack has its own role in ensuring successful communication.

Layer

Application	Software: web browser; e-mail client; FTP for file transfer
Transport	TCP
Network/IP layer	IP
Link	At the network cable — Ethernet

Figure 14.01 TCP/IP protocol stack

Application layer

The application software will package up the 'core data' which is to be transmitted:

- for an email client, it is the email text content

- for a web browser, it is the text content, the tags and, if present, JavaScript code

- for file-transfer client software, it is the downloaded file bytes.

Each application will have its own 'application protocol' for the way the core data is packaged.

These application layer protocols can be summarised as shown in Table 14.01.

Transport Layer

The TCP (Transport Communication Protocol) layer is responsible for setting up a bi-directional connection between the two hosts and maintaining this connection. There will be a software process (the TCP software) running on each host. The TCP software will need to detect when errors occur or when data packets are not received and instigate their re-transmission.

When data is sent from the server to the client, it is the role of TCP to re-organise the data packets received into a format that the client application is expecting.

When data is sent in the other direction – from the client application to the server – it is TCP's role to organise the data packets into a format the network layer is expecting.

The TCP layer may be dealing with several simultaneous connections between the client host and several server hosts. Consider, several files simultaneously downloading on a PC. Each one will be running its own TCP process.

When TCP is in receipt of packets from a server it must know to which running process these packets should be directed. This is done by associating each process with a **port number**. Be clear this is a 'software-generated port' – not a hardware port. Port numbers are allocated dynamically from 1046 onwards. Port numbers before this are universally used for particular server applications; some of these are shown in Table 14.01.

Progress check 14.01

1 What do the initials TCP and IP stand for in the TCP/IP protocol suite?

2 Write – in order – the four layers of the TCP/IP protocol suite.

3 State three different protocols which would be used at the application layer.

IP addresses

Since the client and the server are identified using an IP address, the port number is effectively added to the IP address. The two together are called a 'socket'.

TCP is not the only available transport protocol. An earlier protocol, User Datagram Protocol (UDP) was also a 'connectionless' protocol but considered less reliable than TCP.

Application	Application protocol	Name origin	Port number
Email – receiving	POP3	Post Office Protocol version 3	110
Email – sending	SMTP	Simple Mail Transfer Protocol	25
File transfer (e.g. for downloads)	FTP	File Transfer Protocol	20
Web browser	HTTP	Hypertext Transfer Protocol	80

Table 14.01 Application protocols

Network (or Internet Protocol) layer

An IP packet consists of a header section and a data section. The header section has 14 data items. These include:

- the version – an IPv4 packet will store the value 4

- source IP address

- destination IP address

- the 'time to live' value – this is designed to stop a packet being continually passed from one router to another without ever reaching its destination. It behaves as a 'hop count' – the value in the header is decremented every time it is passed to a new router. The packet is 'killed' and a message sent to the source IP address when the count reaches zero

- checksum – to check the integrity of the header data

- total packet length – the data section (and so the length of the packet) can be a variable size.

Link layer

The link layer receives packets from the network layer and adds hardware addresses. for a local area network using Ethernet, this hardware address is called a 'MAC address'. Manufacturers of devices are allocated their own range of numbers from which individual hardware devices are each given a unique MAC address. Using Ethernet, the final packaging of packets for sending across the cable is called an **Ethernet frame**. Figure 14.02 shows a typical Ethernet frame contents as data is sent from a client web browser to a web server.

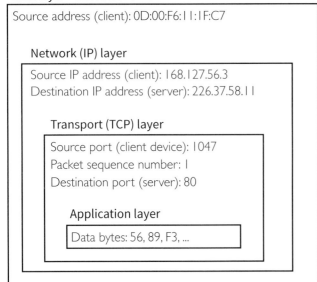

Link layer – Ethernet frame

Source address (client): 0D:00:F6:11:1F:C7

Network (IP) layer

Source IP address (client): 168.127.56.3
Destination IP address (server): 226.37.58.11

Transport (TCP) layer

Source port (client device): 1047
Packet sequence number: 1
Destination port (server): 80

Application layer

Data bytes: 56, 89, F3, ...

Figure 14.02 Makeup of an Ethernet frame

The BitTorrent protocol

BitTorrent is a communications protocol for peer-to-peer networking. Its basic philosophy is that it should be faster to copy files from one client computer to another rather than retrieving data files from some form of cloud storage. The BitTorrent protocol is now estimated to account for over 50% of all file-sharing Internet traffic.

Traditional peer-to-peer file sharing was done where a single source was able to provide copies of files to many recipients, known as 'single source – multiple mirrors'. Using this traditional file-sharing model, the client computer downloads the file following a request to a single server. BitTorrent does things differently.

The BitTorrent client software allows a user to join a 'swarm' of hosts to upload or download files from each other simultaneously. This way the final download is made up of file segments which have originated from a number of different sources who are all members of the swarm.

A user who wants to make a file available for upload will create an identification file called a torrent descriptor and will distribute this by email or give notification on a web page. The descriptor file contains meta data about the file to be made available. The user will have the BitTorrent client software on their computer and it acts as the initial 'seeder' by making the torrent descriptor file available to other users. The descriptor file is given to other BitTorrent nodes which act as peers or 'leeches'. A download can then be instigated at any peer by connecting with the seed and other peers which are in possession of the descriptor file.

A file to be made available is divided into segments or pieces. When a peer receives a piece of the file it can act as a distributor of this piece of the file to others in the swarm. This is the fundamental idea of BitTorrent: the task of distributing the file is shared by a number of peers.

In comparison with traditional peer-to-peer downloading:

- With BitTorrent the nature of the receipt of pieces is not sequential.

- The requests to peers is for pieces or files which have a relatively small file size.

- BitTorrent will make IP connections to many peer computers. (Traditional downloading makes a single IP connection to the host computer or server.)

Integrity of the file transfer is implemented by adding hashing function data to each piece. The hashing function is contained in the Torrent descriptor file. This way when any piece is received by a peer, its integrity can be verified.

The BitTorrent client software must keep a log of:

- which pieces it has successfully received and so can be made available to other peers

- which pieces are outstanding.

The download can be paused at any time, which makes the approach well suited to the transfer of large files.

Once a peer has received all the pieces of the file, it then becomes a seeder.

What files are available to download?

Torrent files are advertised for download on websites. A peer can download the descriptor file and open it with the BitTorrent client software. The descriptor file contains data about the tracker. This is a computer that monitors the identity of peers who are currently members of the swarm for this torrent file. The list initially shows only the seeder. With this information the potential peer can start the download.

Progress check 14.03

Explain the following terms when using the BitTorrent protocol:

- tracker computer

- seed

- swarm.

Other popular protocols

Some popular protocols were summarised in Table 14.01. The following general points apply to all these application protocols:

- They all use the client–server model.

- The client application must know of the existence of and address for the server.

- The server is not aware of any particular client applications. It is simply continually 'listening' for requests from clients.

- The client and the server communicate once a socket is established at each end of the two-point communication channel.

LOOK BACK «

We have already studied this. A client–server socket on the Internet consists of its IP address and a port number.

HyperText Transfer Protocol (HTTP)

HTTP is an application-level protocol used on the World Wide Web. It assumes a transport layer protocol such as TCP will make the connection between the client and the web server. The HTTP protocol will consist of request messages from the client and response messages from the web server. An HTTP server listening on the port receives the client request message. The server then responds with a typical message.

Two examples of response lines are:

- `HTTP/1.1 200 OK` followed by the body of the message – the requested resource, such as, the web page text and other content

- `HTTP/1.0 404 Not Found` – the requested resource does not exist, which I expect you have seen on occasions!

In general, the response message returned by the server will be a resource of some kind. The most common resource is a file. Appreciate – from our coverage of server-side scripting in Section 2.03 – that the 'resource' could be the results from running a server-side script, such as the results from a database query.

All the popular high-level languages support the use of HTTP. Popular commands will be for the basic request and response statements to establish the connection or report errors. `GET` is the most commonly used HTTP method. The format is:

```
GET /path/directory/filename.html
            HTTP/1.0
```

Other statements are used for the maintenance of data using a database server which is accessed through web pages. The latest HTTP 1.1 defines over 40 header methods, at least one of which is required when making a server request.

It is considered good practice to include the email address of the user making the request and the web browser from which the request has originated. This then allows the web-master for the server to troubleshoot any problems.

A typical sequence of the use of HTTP is shown by the following sequence. The task is to display a web page, `MyFile.html`, which is stored at domain `MyDomain.com` in folder `MyFolder`.

1   User keys into the address bar of the browser:
    `http://www.MyDomain.com/MyFolder/MyFile.html`.

2   This will open a socket on the client and connect to port 80 of the `MyDomain` host web server.

3   A text string is sent to the server:

    ```
    GET  /MyFolder/MyFile.html HTTP/1.0

    From: tonypiper@hostname.com

    User-agent: Internet Explorer 12
    ```

4   The server will respond with a text stream which is rendered by the client web browser and displayed:

    ```
    HTTP/1.0 200 OK

    Date: Friday 13 April 2016 12:00 GMT

    Content-Type: text/html

    Content-length: 1208

    <html>

    <body>

    <h1>It has to be – hello world</h1>
    ```

File Transfer Protocol (FTP)

The File Transfer Protocol (FTP) is a network protocol used to transfer files from one host to another host over a TCP-based network, such as the Internet. All of the file to be downloaded is obtained from a single source – an FTP server. There are many free or shareware FTP client software programs available.

Typical applications of FTP include:

• the provision of software and other files to download from a remote FTP site

• the updating of web site pages.

A strategy could be that a complete mirror copy of the web site is held on a client computer with the files viewed using a local server. When changes are made to any web pages or content, this is first done on the local site so that the links, etc. can be thoroughly tested. The amended files are then uploaded to the 'live' website using ftp client software which makes a connection from the client to the ftp server.

Post Office Version 3 (POP3) and Simple Mail Transfer Protocol (SMTP)

The popular email protocols are:

• SMTP – for the sending of a mail message

• POP3 – for receiving email.

A client computer will send the email message to one or more intended recipients. The client will have given its client software settings the address of the server and the port number to which it must be directed. The email server continually listens for incoming mail messages. When transferred, the message is saved on the server in one or more mailboxes marked for the recipients.

When the recipient next loads their email client software, the mail server will be contacted and the messages delivered from the server. The recipient client software will have settings (see Figure 14.03) which specify the server to be contacted and the protocol to be used – POP3, in this case.

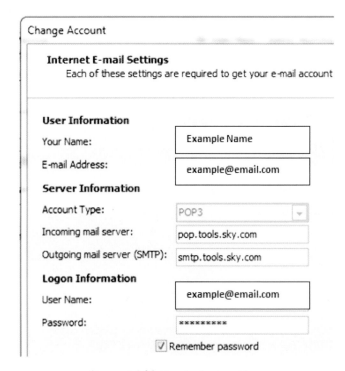

Figure 14.03 Email client settings

14.02 Circuit switching, packet switching and routers

Circuit switching

To enable communication between two network nodes or end-points, a dedicated communications channel or circuit has to be established. The link then guarantees communication at a constant bit-rate.

The earliest example of circuit switching was the analogue telephone network. A connection from the calling telephone established a connection to the telephone exchange – dialling the number instigated the connection request. In the early days, the connection to the receiver of the call was then established by a telephone operator plugging a copper cable into a patch panel to make the connection between caller and recipient via the exchange. The connection was retained for the duration of the call and then released when the telephone call hung up. Even if no data exchange is taking place, the connection remains until released. This suggests circuit switching could be relatively inefficient. The connection remains protected from other potential users of the networks, even though no communication may be taking place.

Packet switching

Data to be transmitted is divided into blocks of a fixed size called 'packets' or 'datagrams'. These packets are then transported through the network independently of each other and may well take different routes between the two end-points and arrive in a non-sequential order. Each network link will transport packets from many different communication sessions between many different hosts.

> **LOOK BACK ≪**
>
> The Internet Protocol (IP) layer of the TCP/IP stack is a packet-switched protocol (see Figure 14.02).

On the Internet it is the task of routers which support the Domain Name Service to decide the route taken by packets. Each packet consists of 'header data' and the 'payload'. The header will be the information shown in Figure 14.02 at the Network (IP) layer.

The IP protocol and Ethernet are both examples of a 'connectionless communication'. Each packet must contain the header data for its source and destination address. At the destination, the packets must be re-assembled using each packet's sequence number.

Another form of packet-switching is a 'connection-orientated' strategy called 'virtual circuit switching' or a 'virtual connection'.

Here the connection has to be established first before any form of communication can take place between the end-points. A setup phase takes place to establish the parameters for communication of the packets. The setup phase will also generate a routing table which establishes the route to be taken by all packets. This is all summarised with a communication ID to which the sending host will refer. In the TCP/IP protocol, the TCP transport layer is responsible for this 'connection-orientated' virtual connection or virtual circuit.

> **TIP**
>
> Do not confuse 'circuit switching' and 'virtual circuit packet switching'.

Routers

The task of a hardware router is to receive data packets from a packet-switched network and then route each packet towards its destination address. The router will maintain routing tables which suggest a best possible path for the packet's destination IP address. The packet may need to be re-directed many times before it reaches its destination.

Routers are a key component of the provision of the Domain Name Service for the World Wide Web. A router can also be used to monitor data packets on a segmented Local Area Network.

> **LOOK BACK ≪**
>
> IP addressing and the Domain Name Service was covered in Chapter 2.

> **LOOK FORWARD ≫**
>
> Figure 14.07 shows a router used to connect segments of a LAN.

For the home computer user, the router is the hardware supplied when the user signs up for their Internet connection to be provided by a particular Internet Service Provider (ISP). The router is constantly passing data between the home PC and the Internet.

14.03 Local Area Networks (LAN)

Bus and **star** are terms which describe the **topology** of a network. This is the physical layout of the cabling and the connection of the devices or nodes to the cable.

> **TERMS**
>
> **Topology:** the physical layout of the cabling and the connection of the devices or nodes to the cable
>
> **Bus topology network:** a single cable segment with several computers connected onto the cable
>
> **Star topology network:** a separate communications link from each computer to a centralised computer

In a star network, the connection from each computer will be to a separate port of the central hub and the types of communication link may be different.

Bus topology network

Early LANs used a bus topology, which was a single cable segment with several computers connected onto the cable. In the early days this was done using a T-connector into the network interface card of the computer. Modern buildings are now wired with a cabling infrastructure and the connections are made from each device into a patch panel/hub on the wall. Figure 14.04 shows a typical bus

network – four computers with a shared file server and printer.

The traditional single cable bus network is a shared access network where many nodes are connected on the same physical link. A bus network is a 'broadcast' system where data packets are sent along the network cable with the address of the receiving device. A node will send a data packet in both directions along the cable. A transmission sent by any node is received by all other nodes, but only retained by the node which recognises the destination address of the packet.

If the signal reaches the end of the cable it could bounce back and then collide with another signal on the cable. The terminators on the cable are there to stop this happening. The cable segment will be fitted with two terminators.

The file server will have the network operating system installed. Each client computer must have the client network operating system software.

Network Interface Card (NIC)

Each computer must be fitted with a network interface card (NIC).

Ethernet

The most widely used bus networking standard for the physical layer (see the discussion of protocols which follows) is called 'Ethernet'. This has developed standards based on the transmission speeds called 10Base-T (transmits at 10 Mb/sec), 100Base-TX (100 Mb/sec) or 1000Base-T (1000 Mb/sec i.e. 1 Gb/sec).

Nodes contend equally for available bandwidth and there must be a strategy for dealing with packet collisions when they occur. Note this is the opposite of a strategy which would partition the available bandwidth into several channels such as CDMA (Code Division Multiple Access) used on cellular and wireless environments.

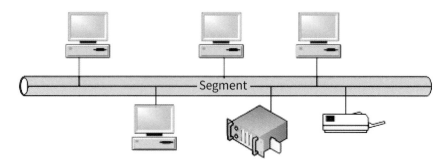

Figure 14.04 Single-segment bus network

Ethernet has evolved through various IEEE 802.3 standards, shown in Table 14.02.

Electrical signals weaken as they travel an increased distance. The distances in the table can be increased with the use of a hardware device called a repeater. This could increase the LAN length to 1500m.

The electrical signal is broadcast along the cable and will be received by the destination device. Each message is sent from one device to another as a data packet called an 'Ethernet frame'. Each Ethernet frame is made up of the source MAC address, destination MAC address and the 'payload' data. Frames can vary in size with up to 1500 bytes of data.

LOOK BACK «

Figure 14.02 shows an Ethernet frame at the Link layer in the TCP/IP protocol stack.

CSMA/CD Policy

CSMA/CD is Ethernet's 'media access control' policy to try to avoid collisions. The letters describe the key points of the policy:

- CS (carrier sense): the strategy is to attempt to send a data packet if the medium is idle.

- MA (multiple access): each node is competing for the communications line.

- CD (collision detection): if a collision is detected do not attempt to send more packets.

Figure 14.05 shows how the CSMA/CD process works:

- A device 'listens' to the communications line before attempting to transmit.

- If the line is in use ('Carrier sensed'), the device waits until the line is later sensed as idle.

- If the line is not in use ('No carrier sensed'), then the device transmits immediately – more packets are transmitted with a short time delay between each transmission.

- The device listens on the line to check for no collision of the packet. If a collision is detected then it stops sending and jams the line (to make other devices aware they are unable to use the line).

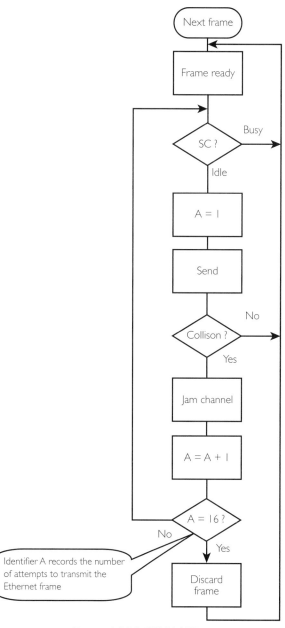

Figure 14.05 CSMA/CD

Name	Transmission speed	Cabling	Comment
10BaseT	Up to 2 Mbps	Thin coaxial	Maximum cable length 200 m.
			Uses CSMA/CD
100BaseT and many variants	Up to 100 Mbps	CAT 5 – Twisted pair	Wired using a hub. Maximum distance of a node from the hub is 100 m.
1000BaseT and many variants	1000 Mbps	CAT5, CAT6 and CAT7 – twisted pair	
1000BaseSX		Optical fibre	Maximum distance 500 m.

Table 14.02 Ethernet standards

Collisions

Collisions are detected by a voltage change at a node. Some figures should help our understanding. Assume the time taken from the start of the transmission of a frame and its receipt at the destination is 50 μs.

Node X starts transmitting; 40 μs later, device Y attempts to transmit and detects a collision. It is important that device Y notifies that the frame transmission was unsuccessful. This will take Y a further 40 μs to notify X and this must happen whilst X is still transmitting. (These timings depend on the IEEE standard in use and the maximum distance of the LAN.) The math for the bit-rates and the distance concludes that an Ethernet frame must be at least 46 bytes in length.

When a collision is detected, the jamming signal will effectively notify all nodes of the collision. All nodes should delay before attempting a new transmission. There is some complex math which will calculate what is an optimum wait time.

Hubs

Early LAN networks used a hub device into which a connection from each device was made. Although the 'plug-in' appearance of the device gave a star appearance, it was behaving as a bus network. The single communication line was shared between all the competing nodes.

A hub has the drawback that it has to share its available bandwidth amongst all the transmitting nodes.

Switched Ethernet

Hubs have now been replaced by an Ethernet switch. With a switch, the full bandwidth is available to all communications between sender node and receiver node. The connection is a full-duplex one allowing the sending and receiving of frames simultaneously.

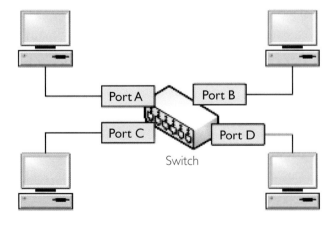

Figure 14.06 A four-port Ethernet switch

A 16-port switch would be able to support eight simultaneous sender–receiver sessions.

A switch completely eliminates collisions. The switch will filter and forward frames based on the link layer MAC address.

IP addresses and networks

If a local area network is using the TCP/IP protocol, the network administrator will allocate each device on the network a unique IP address.

A typical topology is shown in Figure 14.07: it has three segments which are connected using two routers. There is a third router which provides the connection to the Internet. This can be summarised as shown in Table 14.03.

Segment	Devices	Network ID starts with
A	Computer X	168.13.11
B	Intranet server and Computer Y	168.13.13
C	Computer Z	168.13.12

Table 14.03 LAN segments and IP addresses for the network in Figure 14.07

All Version 4 IP addresses are 32 bits, so stored as four bytes. This address is written as four numbers (usually written in dotted decimal notation).

There are three ranges of IP addresses – Class A, Class B or Class C – which have been reserved for use on a private networks. Each network class has a different capacity to address networks and hosts, as shown in Table 14.04.

Private and public IP addresses

Blocks of IP addresses have been reserved for private network use. These are the groups with the first denary numbers 10, 172 and 192.68.

Any IP address from these ranges is ignored by a public router. Two branch offices which are to communicate must have these private IP addresses encapsulated within a packet which uses a public IP address which is recognised across the Internet. When the packet is received its TCP protocol layer is removed.

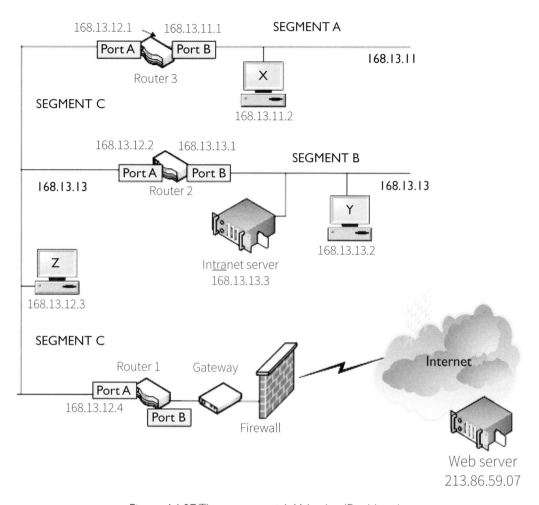

Figure 14.07 Three-segment LAN using IP addressing

Address type	IP address					Description
	Network ID		Host ID			
	Bytes used	No of bits	Bytes used	No of bits		
Class A	Byte 1	8	Byte 2, byte 3, byte 4	24		Starts with a 0 bit
Class B	Byte 1 and byte 2	16	Byte 3 and byte 4	16		Starts with the bits 10
Class C	Byte 1, byte 2 and byte 3	24	Byte 4	8		Starts with bits 110

Table 14.04 IP address classes

This means that several devices on a LAN which use different private IP addresses will communicate across the Internet using a single public address. This technique is called 'Network address translation (NAT)'.

One of the IP address structures used for a segmented network is as follows:

- the first two bytes identify the network
- the third byte identifies the segment
- the fourth byte identifies the device.

Values 0 and 255 are not used for device numbering, so the implication is that a maximum of 254 devices can be connected to any segment of the LAN.

Progress check 14.04

1 What is the network identifier for the LAN in Figure 14.07?

2 What is the identifier for the segment containing the intranet server?

Use of subnet masks

When a device sends a data packet it will be received by a router. If the packet is for a destination device on the same segment – for example Computer Y sending data to the Intranet server – then the router will work out that this IP address is on the same segment.

This is done using a subnet mask, which uses an AND bitwise operator. The AND operation is done on pairs of bits in the two bit patterns.

The following AND operation isolates the network ID:

The intranet server has IP address 168.13.13.3.

In binary, the IP address is:

　　　　10101000 00001100 00001100 00000011

The AND mask for the network ID is 255.255.255.0 or, in binary:

　　　　11111111 11111111 11111111 00000000

The result of the AND operation between those two binary numbers is:

　　　　10101000 00001100 00001100 00000000

In dotted decimal notation, that is 168.13.13.0.

The conclusion is that using the AND mask 255.255.255.0 on the destination IP address establishes the network ID. The router will know the destination of the packet is in the segment from which it was sent.

The following AND operation isolates the device number:

The intranet server has IP address 168.13.13.3.

In binary, the IP address is:

　　　　10101000 00001100 00001100 00000011

The AND mask for the device is 0.0.0.255 or, in binary:

　　　　00000000 00000000 00000000 11111111

The result of the AND operation between those two binary numbers is:

　　　　00000000 00000000 00000000 00000011

This gives the destination device number of 3.

LOOK FORWARD »

You might want to look ahead to Chapter 18, where an AND mask is used in a control application. The application is different but the use of the Boolean AND operator is the same.

A user, at Computer Z on a LAN sited in London, is loading data to a web server situated in the United States. The web server has known IP address 213.86.69.07. A packet of the data is routed from Computer Z to the web server in the following manner:

1　At computer Z, use subnet mask 255.255.255.0 on the address of the web server. This establishes that the destination address is not on this segment.

2　Packet is sent to Router 1 and Router 2.

3　Router 1 identifies – using the subnet mask 0.0.0.255 – that the IP address is outside this LAN so forwards the packet to the gateway.

4　The gateway calculates the network ID of the packet and decide to which router it should be directed. The router is part of a hierarchy of routing paths. At each 'hop' the router decrements the 'time to live' value of the packet.

5　The packet is directed to several routers using the routing tables stored at each router. The next router's MAC address must be used at each 'hop'.

Star topology network

A star network (Figure 14.08) has a separate communications link from each computer to a centralised computer. The connection from each computer will be into a separate port of the central hub and the types of communication link may be different.

A star topology is used for WANs where the communications link may be already in place e.g. the telephone network. The benefits of a star topology are obvious – if one of the communication links fails then the other computers are not affected.

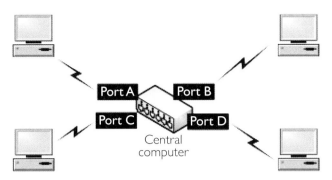

Figure 14.08 Star topology network

Progress check 14.05

A company has its computer system for offices, warehouse and the call centre on different sites.

The OFFICE site has a local area network (LAN) consisting of:

- four computers
- file server X, which contains all the administration and order processing data for all shops
- file server Y , which acts as a domain controller and authenticates all logons.

The CALL-CENTRE and WAREHOUSE sites each have a single computer which connects to the OFFICE network.

The computer systems are connected over a wide area network (WAN) using a star topology. Complete the diagram in Figure 14.09 showing any additional hardware needed for this computer system.

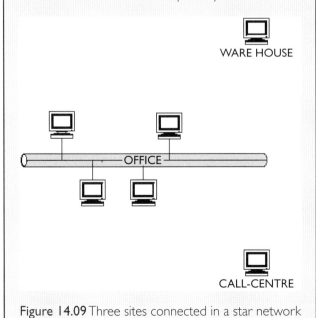

Figure 14.09 Three sites connected in a star network

Wireless network

'Wireless' means 'without wires'. This includes all forms of communication which use electro-magnetic waves: radio, infra-red and microwaves.

LOOK BACK «

Chapter 2, section 2.01 discussed communication systems used to support the Internet.

All forms of wireless communication are based on the IEEE standard 802.11. The term 'wireless' has become in widespread use to describe a Wi-Fi network which is found in a small business, a home or for the connection of mobile devices to some network in a business or public place.

For home or small-business computing, some form of wireless network has obvious advantages:

- It is a proven technology for the sharing of printers and other devices.
- It saves the cost of installation of some form of cabling (compared to an Ethernet LAN).
- It allows mobility for devices connected to the network and so more flexible work practices.
- The hardware infrastructure is simple: a single wireless access point connected to a router to provide the Internet connection

A widespread use of radio communications is for the cellular telephone network. 3G communications across the cellular networks is now widespread and 4G technology is also available in certain areas in the UK.

LOOK BACK «

Cellular communications was covered in Chapter 2, section 2.01.

Wireless access points

The signal is provided by a wireless access point. Receiving devices must be within range to connect to the wireless network. There were concerns over security when wireless networks were introduced as there is the potential to intercept the radio signal between the wireless access point and a device. The encryption standard WEP (Wired Equivalent Privacy) was hacked and proved vulnerable and has now been superseded by the WPA standard (Wi-Fi Protected Access).

Routers

As more devices are connected, to the cable the network traffic increases. This could cause a degradation in the performance of the network. One solution is to split the network into two or more segments (see Figure 14.07). Devices on one segment, however, need to communicate with devices on the others. The hardware device needed to provide a connection between the devices is a router. The router will maintain a routing table showing which MAC addresses are on each cable segment.

Servers

These can be many and varied. The two essential servers will be:

- a file server – to store all the user's data and the application programs

- domain controller authentication – to validate all user logons to the network.

It could well be the same piece of hardware which provides both of these services.

Depending on the nature of the workplace and the tasks carried out by its users, other servers could include any of those we described earlier: web server, mail server and ftp server.

Summary

- ☐ Computers communicate with each using an agreed protocol.

- ☐ The protocol used by the Internet is TCP/IP.

- ☐ The Internet is a packet-switching network with packets directed by routers.

- ☐ TCP/IP is a protocol stack with four layers.

- ☐ Application layer protocols include: HTTP, FTP, POP3 and SMTP.

- ☐ The BitTorrent protocol is used for peer-to-peer file sharing.

- ☐ The alternative to packet-switching is a communication line which uses circuit switching.

- ☐ A local area network using the Ethernet standard will connect nodes using a single line, a hub or switched Ethernet.

- ☐ If the topology is a single line or hub, signal collisions can occur.

- ☐ The Ethernet strategy for collision avoidance and detection is CSMA/CD.

- ☐ An alternative to a cabled LAN is a wireless network.

Exam-style questions

1   a   Complete the diagram to show how the layers of the TCP/IP protocol are related.

Choose from the terms: Internet Layer, Presentation Layer, Data Link Layer, Application Layer, Transport Layer.

Network Access Layer

[3]

   b   Give the names of **two** LAN network technologies that the Network Access Layer has to interface with.

Network technology 1:

Network technology 2:

[2]

c One layer of the protocol makes use of IP addresses. An IP address is a 32-bit number; for example, 205.123.4.192 is an IP address. Part of the IP address is used for the network ID and part of the address is used for the host ID.

    i Explain the terms:

    network ID:

    host ID: [2]

    Most IP addresses fall into one of three classes:

- If the 32-bit address starts with a 0 bit, the address is a Class A address.

- If the 32-bit address starts with the bits 10, the address is a Class B address.

- If the 32-bit address starts with the bits 110, the address is a Class C address.

    ii Show how to determine whether 205.123.4.192 is a Class A, Class B or Class C address. [2]

    iii In a Class A address, the first byte represents the network ID and the remaining three bytes represent the host ID.

    In a Class B address, the first two bytes represent the network ID and the remaining two bytes represent the host ID.

    In a Class C address, the first three bytes represent the network ID and the remaining byte represents the host ID.

    For the address 205.123.4.192 state the:

    network ID:

    host ID: [2]

Cambridge International AS and A Level Computer Science 9608 Specimen Paper 3, Q2 2015

Hardware

15.01 Logic gates and circuit design

Truth table for a given logic circuit

You should be familiar with drawing the truth table for a given logic circuit from the coverage in Section 3.03. In a typical problem, you are given a logic circuit or logic expression and then complete the truth table.

Simple guidelines are:

- Understand that the number of inputs will determine the number of rows in the truth table (two inputs needs four rows, three inputs needs eight rows, four inputs needs 16 rows, etc.).

- Write the row values in a logical order (see the example which follows).

Construct the truth table for the logic circuit in Figure 15.01.

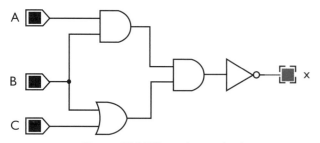

Figure 15.01 Three-input circuit

Three inputs (A, B and C) means the truth table has eight rows as shown in Table 15.01. Tracing through the eight combination of inputs for A, B and C gives the output X values shown.

Input			Output
A	**B**	**C**	**X**
0	0	0	1
0	0	1	1
0	1	0	1
0	1	1	1
1	0	0	1
1	0	1	1
1	1	0	0
1	1	1	0

Table 15.01 Truth table for logic circuit in Figure 15.01

The half adder

An 'adder' is any electronic circuit which performs the addition of bit patterns. Adder circuits are a component of the Arithmetic and Logical Unit in the processor.

A half adder is a circuit which behaves as follows:

- The two inputs are each a binary digit to be added together.

- The two outputs show the value of the addition (Sum) and the carry bit (Carry).

A half adder circuit is constructed using an XOR gate and an AND gate as shown in Figure 15.02.

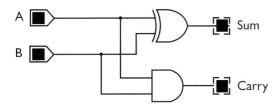

Figure 15.02 Half adder circuit

The truth table will show the results for these four additions:

$$
\begin{array}{cccc}
0 & 0 & 1 & 1 \\
\underline{0}+ & \underline{1}+ & \underline{0}+ & \underline{1}+ \\
\end{array}
$$

Sum > 0   1   1   1

Carry > 0   0   0   1

Progress check 15.01

Draw the truth table for the half adder circuit.

Note, this addition was for two bits only. Consider the task of adding together the contents of two bytes. The addition of the two bits in bit position zero will produce a carry value which must then be considered when adding the bits in position 1. The carry value produced at each bit position must always be part of the addition in the next (to the left) bit position. This gives rise to a circuit called a full adder.

The full adder

This is the circuit for a half adder – the addition of two bits – but with the further addition of a carry bit from the previous two-bit addition.

The full adder circuit will have:

- three inputs – A and B (as before) and a previous carry (PC)

- two outputs – the Sum and Carry

Input			Output	
PC	A	B	Sum	Carry
0	0	0	0	0
0	0	1	1	0
0	1	0	1	0
0	1	1	0	1
1	0	0	1	0
1	0	1	0	1
1	1	0	0	1
1	1	1	1	1

Table 15.02 Full adder truth table

The full adder circuit is constructed from five gates as shown in Figure 15.03.

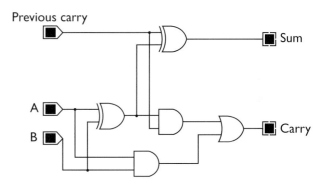

Figure 15.03 Full adder circuit

Figure 15.04 shows how four full adder circuits joined together are used to add bit pattern ABCD to bit pattern EFGH.

The same principle would apply if a circuit was required to add together the contents of two bytes. This would have eight full-adder circuits.

15.02 Boolean algebra

You are familiar with the sight of a Boolean expression from Chapter 3.

If A and B are the inputs to a circuit and X is the single output:

- X = NOT(A OR B) means 'X is 1 when (A OR B) is not 1'.

- X = (A OR B) OR (A AND C) means 'X is 1 when either (A OR B) is 1 or (A AND C) is 1'.

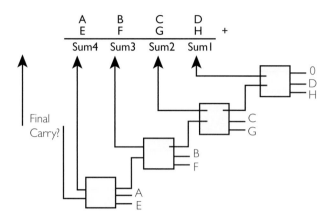

Figure 15.04 Adding two 4-bit numbers

Notation

Boolean algebra provides a tool for representing a logic expression or circuit using algebraic notation (see Table 15.03).

Boolean operator	Algebraic notation	Example	Meaning
OR	+	X + Y	X OR Y
AND	. (period or full stop)	X.Y	X AND Y
NOT	'bar' on top	$\overline{X}$	NOT X

Table 15.03 Boolean algebra notation

Progress check 15.02

Rewrite the following logic expressions as a Boolean algebra expression:

1 A AND NOT B

2 NOT(C AND D) OR NOT D

3 NOT(P OR Q OR R) AND R

Forming a Boolean expression from a truth table

Consider the truth table in Table 15.04. To create a Boolean expression from it, look for the combinations which produce a 1 output.

Input			Output
A	B	C	X
0	0	0	0
0	0	1	0
0	1	0	0
0	1	1	0
1	0	0	1
1	0	1	1
1	1	0	0
1	1	1	0

Table 15.04 Truth table

There are two rows:

• A AND NOT B AND NOT C

• A AND NOT B AND C

The output X is 1 if either the first combination occurs or the second combination. So the Boolean algebra expression is:

$$X = (A.\overline{B}.\overline{C}) + (A.\overline{B}.C)$$

Forming the Boolean expression from a circuit

There is nothing new here. We write on the diagram the output expression from each gate, until we have the expression for the final output.

The Boolean expression is $X = A.\overline{B}+C$

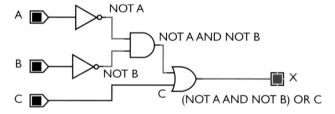

Figure 15.05 Logic circuit

Progress check 15.03

Write the Boolean expression for the following circuit:

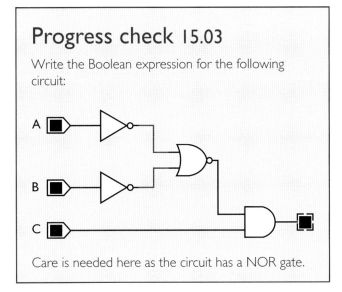

Care is needed here as the circuit has a NOR gate.

Simplification of Boolean expressions

The term 'algebra' reminds us of the algebra we met in math class. One of the first uses of algebra was for the simplification of expressions. The approach was to look for common elements and then to add brackets where required to make the order of precedence clear.

Given expression	Simplification
2X + 6Y	2(X+3Y)
PQ + PQR	PQ(1+R)
AC + BC + AD + BD	C(A+B) + D(A+B) = (C+D)(A+B)

Table 15.05 Example of simplifying algebraic expressions

The approach we shall take to simplify Boolean algebra expressions is the same. But first we need to study some identities which we shall use in the simplification process.

Boolean identities

The identities which follow can all be confirmed by considering the appropriate logic gate where one of the inputs is either 0 or 1.

Figure 15.06 shows an AND gate, with one input and 0, and its truth table. The truth table tells us that, whatever the value of A, the output from the AND gate is always 0. The equivalent Boolean algebra identity is:

$A.0 = 0$

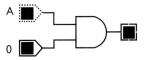

Input		Output
A	0	
I	0	0
0	0	0

Figure 15.06 AND gate, with one input and 0

Figure 15.07 shows an AND gate, with one input and 1, and its truth table. The equivalent Boolean algebra identity is:

$A.1 = A$

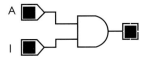

Input		Output
A	I	
I	I	I
0	I	0

Figure 15.07 AND gate, with one input and 1

Figure 15.08 shows an AND gate, with inputs A and NOT A, and its truth table. The equivalent Boolean algebra identity is:

$A.\overline{A} = 0$

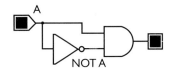

Input		Output
A	NOT A	
I	0	0
0	I	0

Figure 15.08 AND gate, with inputs A and NOT A

Progress check 15.04

1 Draw the truth table for an OR gate with inputs A and 1.

2 Deduce the identity for A + 1

To summarise, here is a list of the identities:

$A.A = A$

$A + A = A$

$A + \overline{A} = 0$

$A + \overline{A} = 1$

$A.1 = A$

$A + 1 = 1$

$A.0 = 0$

$A + 0 = A$

If you have studied Venn diagrams in mathematics, the same principles can be used for Boolean expressions containing zero and one. Think of a 1 value as 'everything' and zero as the set of 'nothing'. We shall use this Venn diagram analogy again later when we study Karnaugh maps.

We need some more identities before we start using them to simplify an expression. Table 15.06 introduces some laws that apply to Boolean expressions.

Identity name	Expression	Comment
Commutative law	$A + B = A + B$	The order can be changed – for a logic circuit the inputs could be reversed.
	$A . B = A . B$	
Associative law	$A + (B + C) = (A + B) + C$	The brackets could have been omitted.
	$A . (B . C) = (A . B) . C$	
Distributive law	$A . (B + C) = A . B + A . C$	This is just like the expansion of the brackets in algebra.
	$A + (B . C) = (A + B) . (A + C)$	

Table 15.06 Additional Boolean identities

TIP

You will not be expected to reproduce these law descriptions in the examination – only to apply the law to a given Boolean expression.

The second distributive law identity is less obvious. It can be proved by expansion of the right hand side:

$(A + B) . (A + C) = A . A + A . C + B . A + B . C$

$= A + A . C + A . B + B . C$

$= A . (1 + C) + A . B + B . C$

$= A + A . B + B . C$

$= A . (1 + B) + B . C$

$= A + B . C$

We have in fact simplified our first expression, using the identities involving 0 and 1.

Progress check 15.05

Simplify these Boolean expressions.

1 $A . B . C + A . B$

2 $A . B . (\bar{B} + D)$

3 $A . (B . C + 1) . C$

4 $P . (Q + \bar{P})$

5 $A . B . \bar{C} + A . B . C + A . \bar{B}$

6 $B . (A + C) + A + A . (\bar{A} + B)$

De Morgan's Laws

De Morgan's Laws are used with the logic functions NAND and NOR.

• A NAND gate behaves as two inputs to an AND gate, followed by the output into NOT gate.

• A NOR gates behaves as two inputs to an OR gate, followed by the output into a NOT gate.

Table 15.07 illustrates the NAND logic

A	B	NOT A	NOT B	NOT (A AND B) = A NAND B	NOT A OR NOT B
0	0	1	1	1	1
0	1	1	0	1	1
1	0	0	1	1	1
1	1	0	0	0	0

Table 15.07 NAND logic

The fifth column is A NAND B and the final column has the same outputs.

This suggests we have an identity for NAND:

$\overline{(A . B)} = \bar{A} + \bar{B}$

Progress check 15.06

1 Construct a similar truth table showing the result of A NOR B.

2 What operation between NOT A and NOT B gives the same outputs?

To summarise, here are De Morgan's laws:

$$(\overline{A.B}) = \overline{A} + \overline{B}$$

$$(\overline{A+B}) = \overline{A}.\overline{B}$$

We can use De Morgan's laws to simplify the following expression:

$$(\overline{\overline{A}.\overline{B}}) . (A+C) = (A.B).(A+C)$$

$$= A.B.A + A.B.C$$

$$= (A.A.B) + A.B.C$$

$$= (A.B) + A.B.C$$

$$= A.B(1+C)$$

$$= 1$$

Progress check 15.07

Use De Morgan's laws to simplify these expressions:

1 $\overline{A+B}$

2 $\overline{A.\overline{B}}$

3 $\overline{A+\overline{B}}$

15.03 Karnaugh maps

Drawing a grid – called a 'Karnaugh map' – is a tool that can be used to simplify certain expressions.

Consider a logic expression involving the values A and B (see Figure 15.09). The headings for the rows and columns represent A and B with a 1 and $\overline{A}$ and $\overline{B}$ with a 0. Each of the four cells in the Karnaugh map shows the relevant expression.

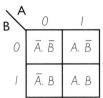

Figure 15.09 Two-variable Karnaugh map

We can extend this to a map designed for four variables, as shown in Figure 15.10.

CD \ AB	00	01	11	10
00	$\overline{A}.\overline{B}.\overline{C}.\overline{D}$	$\overline{A}.B.\overline{C}.\overline{D}$	$A.B.\overline{C}.\overline{D}$	$A.\overline{B}.\overline{C}.\overline{D}$
01	$\overline{A}.\overline{B}.\overline{C}.D$	$\overline{A}.B.\overline{C}.D$	$A.B.\overline{C}.D$	$A.\overline{B}.\overline{C}.D$
11	$\overline{A}.\overline{B}.C.D$	$\overline{A}.B.C.D$	$A.B.C.D$	$A.\overline{B}.C.D$
10	$\overline{A}.\overline{B}.C.\overline{D}$	$\overline{A}.B.C.\overline{D}$	$A.B.C.\overline{D}$	$A.\overline{B}.C.\overline{D}$

Figure 15.10 Four-variable Karnaugh map

The order of the bit pairs for the columns and rows is important. They use a system called 'Gray Code' – each bit pair differs by only one bit change from the previous pair.

Using a Karnaugh map: Example 1

Consider the following expression:

$$\overline{C}.D.\overline{A}.\overline{B} + \overline{C}.D.\overline{A}.B + \overline{C}.D.A.B + \overline{C}.D.A.\overline{B}$$

Figure 15.10 gives the expressions for each cell. Apply the following process:

1 Put 1 bits in the cells corresponding to each of the four terms.

2 Put 0 bits in all other cells.

3 Put a sausage – called a 'minterm' – around any complete rows or columns.

Figure 15.11 shows the result of the process.

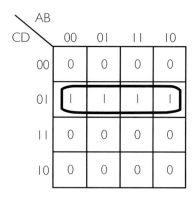

Figure 15.11 Karnaugh map resulting in one minterm

For the given expression, the conclusion is that the 1 bit positions do not depend on A or B.

The expression therefore simplifies to $\bar{C}.D$.

Using a Karnaugh map: Example 2

There can be more than one minterm. Consider the following expression, for which the result is in Figure 15.12:

$\bar{A}.\bar{B}.\bar{C}.\bar{D} + \bar{A}.\bar{B}.C.D + A.\bar{B}.\bar{C}.D + \bar{A}.B.\bar{C}.D +$
$\bar{A}.\bar{B}.C.\bar{D} + A.B.\bar{C}.D + \bar{A}.\bar{B}.\bar{C}.D$

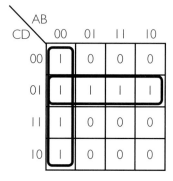

Figure 15.12 Karnaugh map resulting in two minterms

The vertical minterm is $\bar{A}.\bar{B}$.

The horizontal minterm is $\bar{C}.D$.

So the simplified expression is $\bar{A}.\bar{B}. + \bar{C}.D$

Using a Karnaugh map: Example 3

Consider the expression $\bar{A}.\bar{B}.\bar{C} + \bar{A}.B + A.B.\bar{C} + A.C$.

This is different as it only uses three variables and so the Karnaugh map has a different dimension, as shown in Figure 15.13.

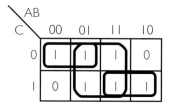

Figure 15.13 Karnaugh map resulting in three minterms

- We need not group an entire row or column.
- A group will have a 'power of 2' number of minterms (i.e. 2, 4, 8).

Working from the left, in Figure 15.13:

- The first minterm is: $\bar{A}.\bar{C}$
- The second minterm is: B
- The third minterm is: A . C

This gives the logic expression $\bar{A}.\bar{C} + B + A.C$

Progress check 15.08

1 Draw the Karnaugh map and simplify the following expression:

$\bar{A}.B + B.\bar{C} + B.C + A.\bar{B}.\bar{C}$

2 Given the following expression:

$\bar{A}.\bar{B}.C.D + \bar{A}.B.\bar{C}.D + \bar{A}.B.C.D + A.\bar{B}.C.D + A.B.\bar{C}.D + A.B.C.D$

a Draw the Karnaugh map.

b Deduce the simplified expression from the map.

c Use NAND and NOR gates to draw the logic circuit for the simplified expression.

15.04 Flip-flops

The logic circuits we have studied in Chapter 3 and this chapter are **combinational circuits**. This means their output is dependent only on the inputs being applied at that time.

A flip-flop is an example of a **sequential logic circuit**. This means output is dependent on the current inputs and a further input which is the result remembered from some previous input combination. This implies that a sequential circuit must have some form of memory built in. A sequential logic circuit will stay in its current state until the next clock cycle signal changes one of the states.

combinational circuit: output is dependent only on the inputs being applied at that time

sequential logic circuit: output is dependent on inputs and a the result remembered from a previous input combination

A sequential logic circuit is said to be a 'bistable' or 'two-state' device. This means the output will be set in one of two basic states (represented by a 1 or 0 value). The device is said to be 'latched' in this state and will remain so until a signal is applied which causes the state to change.

Sequential logic circuits are the basic building blocks for storage registers, shift registers and other memory devices.

A flip-flop is an example of a sequential logic bistable circuit. A sequential logic circuit can be made to change state by the application of some event in an asynchronous way. Alternatively the change can be a synchronous clock-driven signal that causes the change of state.

The SR flip-flop

The SR flip-flop is a one-bit memory device with two inputs. The S input (SET) causes the output to be set to 1. The R input (RESET) produces an output of 0.

The SR flip-flop is constructed from two cross-coupled NAND gates as shown on the left in Figure 15.14. In a circuit diagram containing an SR flip-flop, the detail of the gates would not be shown and the flip-flop would be shown as on the right of Figure 15.14.

It is conventional in electronics that, if it is the 'low' (zero) state which is significant, then the inputs are labelled $\overline{R}$ and $\overline{S}$.

We have labelled the 'SET' state as when $Q = 1$ and the 'RESET' state when $Q = 0$.

The combinations of R and S in Table 15.08 shows the changes to the output.

State	Input		Output		Action
	S	R	Original Q	Final Q	
SET	1	0	0	1	Sets Q to 1
	1	1	0	1	No change
RESET	0	1	1	0	Resets Q to 0
	1	1	1	0	No change

Table 15.08 SR flip-flop state changes

Things to note are:

- When $S = 1$ and $R = 1$, output Q can be either 0 or 1 depending on the state of R and S before this current state existed. Therefore $S = 1$ and $R = 1$ does not change the Q output.

- $S = 0$ and $R = 0$ is an undesirable state and must be avoided. It will cause both Q and NOT Q to be set high at 1 and the flip-flop to become unstable. If this state is reached, the future behaviours of the flip-flop become unpredictable.

A sequence of signal changes is shown in Figure 15.15. You should trace the changing values of R and S and how they determine the changed state of the output.

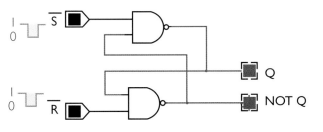
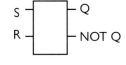

Figure 15.14 An SR flip-flop

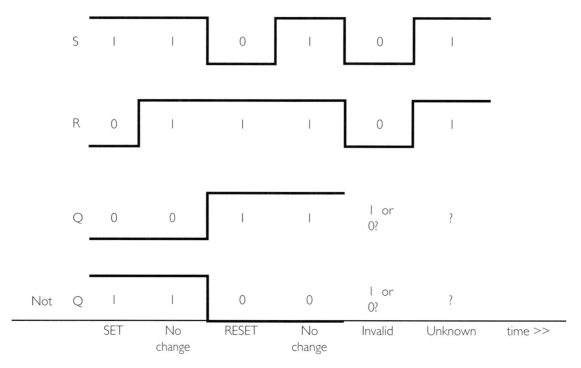

Figure 15.15 Signal change sequence

SR flip-flop using NOR gates

An SR flip-flop can be constructed using two cross-coupled NOR gates. The differences are that:

- the inputs are active HIGH

- the invalid state exists when both inputs (S and R) are at 1.

SR flip-flop for storage

When the circuit is retaining some binary value, it will have R = 1 and S = 1. The circuit can behave as a store for a single bit. The above discussion says there is one signal (R = 1) which will cause the bit stored (Q) to be set to 1. The signal (S = 1) causes the bit stored to be set to 0.

Several flip-flops together can be used to store a single byte value.

The JK flip-flop

The JK flip-flop is the most widely used flip-flop design. The JK flip-flop solves the issue of the condition of the SR NAND gate flip-flop when R and S are both 0. The invalid condition is now avoided by the addition of an input clock signal to the SR flip-flop circuit.

Two additional three-input NAND gates are added to the SR flip-flop. The clock signal acts as an input to each of the additional NAND gates, as shown in Figure 15.16.

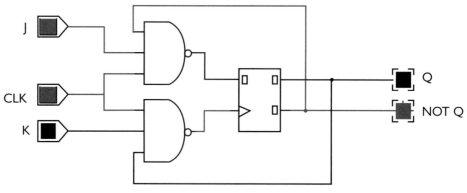

Figure 15.16 A JK flip-flop

State	Input		Output	Final Q	Action
	J	K	Original Q		
These combinations are as for the SR flip-flop (with inputs labelled J and K)	0	0	0	0	Memory no change
	0	0	0	1	
	0	1	1	0	Resets Q to 0
	0	1	0	1	
	1	0	0	1	Set Q to 1
	1	0	1	0	
Toggle	1	1	0	1	Toggles Q setting

Table 15.09 JK flip-flop states

Assume the starting point is that J = 1 and K = 1.

- A clock pulse then causes output Q to change state.

- If a sequence of clock pulses is sent, the output on Q will toggle: 1, 0, 1, 0, 1, 0, 1, 0, etc. This circuit construction could be used for a simple 'Toggle switch' in electronics.

- If J = 1, K = 0 and a clock signal is sent, Q is SET to 1.

- If J = 0, K = 1 and a clock signal is sent, Q is RESET to 0.

- If J = 1, K = 1, the Q output is toggled

Tracing these actions and monitoring the settings of the S and R input to the SR flip-flop within the circuit will confirm that only one of either SET or RESET can set active at the same time. This solves the SR flip-flop issue of the invalid state.

15.05 RISC processors

Background to RISC

RISC processors were first developed in the early 1980s. Their development however has been slowed by:

- the lack of software which is written to run on a RISC processor

- Intel's dominance in the PC computer market using the family of Intel x86 processors.

The home is likely to have many devices with RISC-based processors. These include the Nintendo Wii, Microsoft Xbox 360, Sony PlayStation3, Nintendo DS and many televisions and smartphones. However, the desktop PC is likely to have a non-RISC processor. The reason for this is that moving to a new RISC instruction set in the processor would mean that all the existing software would no longer work.

The assembly language we studied in Chapter 4 assumed that the processor architecture had only one general-purpose register, the Accumulator. This is a simplified scenario as PC processors generally have around eight general-purpose registers. The number of basic machine instructions would be several hundred. These computers were known as Complex Instruction Set Computers (CISC). The large number of instructions were matched closely to the hardware of the processor and the structures used in high-level language program code.

The different modes of addressing available in a CISC instruction set means that instructions can be of different lengths. For example LOAD A, B means 'copy the contents of general-purpose register B to register A' and may take only a single byte.

An instruction such as LOAD A, 019C ('copy the contents of address 019C to register A') will occupy at least two bytes. We already have examples of this from the simplified instruction set used in Section 4.03. Instructions such as OUT have no operand and would need only a single byte. Most other instructions have an operand and will occupy at least two bytes.

Depending on the nature of the instruction, a different number of clock cycles would be used to execute instructions. An instruction such as DEC ACC may require only two clock cycles. An instruction multiplying two numbers could require 20 clock cycles.

Chapter 4 covered the concept of the system clock and a different number of clock cycles for different instructions.

A Reduced Instruction Set Computer (RISC) uses only one clock cycle for all instructions.

Comparison of CISC and RISC

Assume the CISC instruction set has a 'multiply' instruction. An instruction in assembly language could have the format: `MULT NUM1,NUM2`. Where `NUM1` and `NUM2` are the address labels used for two memory locations.

The required processing would be:

1 Load the value of `NUM1` to a register.

2 Multiply the register contents by the contents of address `NUM2` (the answer is now in the register).

3 Copy the contents of register back to address `NUM1`.

The approach taken with a RISC processor is different. There will be separate instructions for the 'load' part, the 'calculation' part and the final 'store' part. Each stage is done with just one instruction, which each use exactly one clock cycle to execute. This 'one cycle per instruction' is the basis for a technique called 'pipelining'.

The differences between CISC and RISC are summarised in Table 15.10.

CISC	RISC
Limited number of general-purpose registers	Large number of general-purpose registers
The number of clock cycles taken by instructions vary	Each instruction takes exactly one clock cycle
Instructions are a variable length (e.g. they occupy 1, 2, 3 or more bytes)	All instructions are a fixed byte size
Instructions are in the hundreds and include specialised instructions hard-wired into the control unit	Very reduced number of instructions
Extensive use made of cache memory	Instructions and data held in RAM

Table 15.10 CISC v. RISC

A comparison of two processors is shown in Table 15.11.

	Intel 80486 (CISC)	Sun SPARC (RISC)
Number of instructions	235	69
Instruction size (bytes)	Between 1 and 11	4
Addressing modes	11	1
General-purpose registers	8	520

Table 15.11 Processor comparison

Pipelining

The term 'pipeline' is in everyday use. If you had three pieces of homework to complete you would say 'I have three pieces of homework in the pipeline'. You can only work on one homework task at any time but you might keep switching between the different tasks. This analogy holds for our computing definition of pipelining.

We are familiar from our study of the fetch–execute cycle in Section 4.02 that, for a CISC computer, the instructions are executed in sequence. The typical execution of three instructions is shown in Figure 15.17.

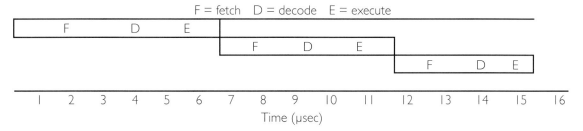

F = fetch   D = decode   E = execute

Time (µsec)

Figure 15.17 CISC sequential fetch–decode–execute

Because of the sequential nature of the execution, Instruction 2 is not fetched until Instruction 1 has completed its execution.

The instructions each take a different time for their fetch, decode and execution stages: Instruction 1 takes 6 µsec, Instruction 2 takes 5 µsec and Instruction 3 takes 4 µsec.

This is similar to many everyday tasks. Cleaning all the rooms in a house would involve sweeping the floor, washing the floor and waiting for the floor to dry. We could then start on the second room, except it might be possible to start on room 2 immediately after the room 1 floor has been washed (and not wait for floor 1 to dry).

This is the basis of the computer architecture technique called 'pipelining'. We are able to start on the execution of an instruction before some previous instruction has completed. All RISC processors will use some variation of the five basic steps in Table 15.12.

Step	Action
1	Fetch the instructions from memory
2	Decode the instruction
3	Execute the instruction or calculate an address
4	Access an operand in memory – memory read/write
5	Write the result to a register

Table 15.12 Typical RISC instruction sequence

Problems with pipelining

Two issues will cause the pipeline to stall: dealing with a data dependency between instructions and a branch instruction.

Data dependency

> # Progress check 15.09
>
> A program contains the following sequence of instructions:
>
> ```
> // add the contents of R1 and R2;
> store the result in R3
>
> ADD R3,R1,R2
>
> ADD R5,R4,R3
> ```
>
> Explain the data dependency here.

The detail for the pipelining of the two instructions is as follows:

- When Instruction 2 is at its second step (read the registers, as in Table 15.12), the processor will read the value of R3 and R4.

- Instruction 1 is one step ahead, so at this time the contents of R1 and R2 are being added, but will not yet have been written to R3.

- Therefore the second instruction is unable to read the R3 value it needs.

- The pipeline is stalled and loaded with a number of empty instructions called 'bubbles'.

One technique for dealing with data-dependent instructions is for them to be identified by the compiler which will then attempt to re-order the instructions.

Branch instructions

Consider the following sequence of instructions:

```
LOOP: ADD R3,R2,R1    // add R1 to R2 and store in R3

      ADD R6,R5,R4    // add R4 to R5 and store in R6

      JPE R3,R6,LOOP  // compare R3 and R6 - if equal jump to address LOOP
```

The issue is the same here as in Progress check 15.09: the third instruction has to know the values in registers R3 and R6. These are not known as neither instruction 1 or instruction 2 has yet written the value to the register. This can cause the pipeline to stall.

One strategy that pipelining can use to deal with this is branch prediction. The processor makes a guess at the outcome of the condition. Research has shown that if the branch instruction is at the bottom of a loop, the execution will go back to the start of the loop in around 90% of cases. Conditions at the start of the loop are true in 50% of cases. Therefore the strategy is to assume the condition is true in the first case and not true in the second case. If the guess proves to be wrong then the processor must re-instate the register contents and start the pipeline again with the correct instruction.

Interrupt handling on CISC and RISC processors

LOOK BACK «

Interrupts were covered in Chapter 4, section 4.02 and will be discussed again in Chapter 16.

The use of interrupts on a RISC processor is no different. The same definition for an interrupt holds: 'a signal sent to the processor from a hardware device to indicate that the device needs attention'.

The use of interrupts avoids the processor having to regularly check to see if a hardware device needs its attention. This strategy (called 'polling') was in use before interrupts.

The system uses vectored interrupts. Every device is assigned a device number that corresponds to bits sent to an interrupt register. Hence from the number, the processor knows the source of the interrupt.

Once the interrupt is received, the state of all registers must be saved and the appropriate interrupt service routine (ISR) code executed.

15.06 Parallel processing

Parallel processing means that the architecture has more than one processor. Different processors are responsible for different parts of a task. The programmer must design the code so that specific code is used for processing of the task's component parts. Each task is then processed by a different processor. The software will integrate the data produced to provide the final software solution.

The syllabus lists four variants of parallel processing.

Single instruction, single data (SISD)

The computer system has one processor with one data source which works on a single algorithm.

The overall task is coded as a sequence of tasks and so SISD is described as sequential processing.

Single instruction, multiple data (SIMD)

There are several programs which are all executing the same program code. Each processor is processing data from a different source.

This is an appropriate architecture for problems which need to do an analysis of a large dataset using the same criteria. The several processors each has its own local cache memory. This makes possible a single program instruction which performs the same action simultaneously on several data items.

A task where this would be appropriate is the inverting of an RGB bitmap image. The algorithm must iterate through each pixel integer value and perform the inversion calculation. This fits exactly with the SIMD definition: a single operation on many data values.

SIMD has been adopted for the processing of data in multimedia applications and data encryption problems.

SIMD is sometimes called 'array processing' or 'vector processing'.

SIMD was implemented on the Intel Pentium processor by adding eight 128-bit registers which were used for SIMD instructions.

The MISD architecture is in effect a collection of SISD units. This approach is called 'systolic arrays' and is an example of a massively parallel computer system.

A benefit of this approach is that all the data and intermediate results are contained within the processor array. There is no use of data transfers along buses or access to main memory. Systolic arrays are well suited to applications such as artificial intelligence, pattern matching and image processing.

Multiple instruction, single data (MISD)

Many processors perform operations on the same data value. The data may be one value from an array. One strategy for MISD is the parallel input of data values through a network of processor nodes. The nodes (whose behaviour is programmable with software) will merge or sort the data values into a final result.

Multiple instruction, multiple data (MIMD)

MIMD architecture will have a number of processors which function independently and simultaneously for different data values.

Summary

- ☐ A truth table can be produced for a given logic circuit.
- ☐ Two special circuits are a half adder and a full adder.
- ☐ Boolean algebra is used to simplify a logic expressions.
- ☐ There are a number of identities which are used for the simplification.
- ☐ A logic circuit can be expressed in Boolean algebra; if the expression can be simplified this suggests the circuit could be simplified.

- ☐ A Karnaugh map is used to simplify a Boolean expression.
- ☐ Two types of flip-flop are the SR and JK flip-flops.
- ☐ Different approaches are taken by traditional CISC processors and RISC processors.
- ☐ Pipelining and a large number of registers are used by the RISC approach.
- ☐ There are four different approaches to parallel processing: SISD, SIMD, MISD and MIMD.

Exam-style questions

1 **a** Write the Boolean expression that corresponds to the logic circuit.

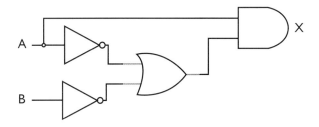

[3]

b Use Boolean algebra to simplify the expression. [3]

c Draw the logic circuit that corresponds to your simplified expression. [3]

d Complete the truth table for the logic circuit:

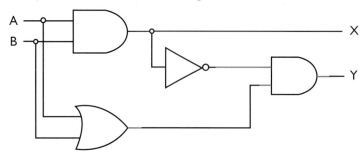

A	B	Work space	X	Y
0	0			
0	1			
1	0			
1	1			

[4]

e What is the name given to a logic circuit that has this truth table? [1]

Cambridge International AS and A Level Computer Science 9608 Specimen Paper 3, Q5 2015

System software

16.01 Purposes of an operating system (OS)

LOOK BACK «

We were introduced to the operating system in Chapter 5, which listed the key resources of any computer system which will need to be managed. The software which does this management is the operating system.

Maximising operating system resources

The file system

When the power to the PC is turned on, the computer goes through a process called booting-up. Switching on the power triggers the running of a small program stored in ROM called the BIOS (Basic Input Output System). The BIOS will identify all the peripheral input and output devices and then run the boot loader software. This program will contain the start address of the operating system stored on the hard disk, so the boot process will effectively load the operating system from secondary storage.

This secondary storage space must be managed. On a PC, it will usually be the hard disk space. The disk may be divided into logical drive areas called partitions. A new PC may already come with partitions. These could include:

- Drive C: for all the operating system and application program files.

- Drive B: intended for the user's application program data files.

- additional devices – CD/DVD drive, flash memory stick, etc. – will each be allocated a logical drive letter.

The file directory

The file directory is predominantly information for the user. The directory will show a list of all the files stored – their name, date and time last saved, file size and other information.

File allocation table (FAT)

We are already familiar with the idea of the surface of a magnetic disk divided into tracks and sectors from Chapter 3. A block (some books use the term 'cluster') is the amount of data which can be read/written in a single write/read operation and a block will consist typically of four contiguous sectors. A block forms the basic 'file allocation unit' which is allocated to files. A typical allocation unit size is 2048, 4096 or 8192 bytes. Earlier versions of Windows used a system called 'FAT32', meaning the size of each file allocation unit is 32 bits. This has now been replaced by a filing system called NTFS.

When the user gives the instruction to save a file, the operating system has to decide which file allocation units are to be used to store this file. The OS will manage this by:

- maintaining a linked list of all the unused file allocation units.
- recording which allocation units store each file on the hard disk, using a linked list of the allocation units.

When the user deletes a file, the allocation units for that file are returned to the list of available allocation units. The FAT is effectively forming a map of the usage of all the file allocation units. Note, on the hard disk, allocation units will not be in contiguous blocks

A large video file may well use blocks which are scattered all over the surface of the disk. The result will be that the file takes a long time to load, as many read operations are required. The file is fragmented across the disk. Hence the need to periodically run a utility program called 'the defragmenter', which will attempt to re-organise the allocation units used so that they occupy more contiguous blocks.

The boot sector, the FAT and the directory form the three important reserved areas on the hard disk which the operating system will use. If the hard disk has been set up with more than one partition, each partition will have its own FAT.

Main memory

LOOK BACK «

In Chapter 4 we were introduced to the Von Neumann model of the computer system and the concept of the program and its data stored in memory.

The processor must have a strategy for management of the available memory space. For example, what happens when a program finishes its execution?

When a program is compiled, the memory addresses will be expressed relative to the address used for the first instruction in the program. It will be a task of the loader software to allocate memory for each program. A key role of the memory manager software will be to track where in main memory the program and its data are currently stored. This is all the more important, as we suggest later

that all parts of a program could be moved in memory during the course of its execution. The memory manager must continually map all relative addresses in a program to their physical memory addresses.

One program loaded in main memory is the simplest possible scenario. Remember, the operating system is itself a set of program modules and so main memory will be needed for the operating system. If we load the application program at the first available memory location after the OS modules then the physical address for the process is easily calculated as 'start address' plus 'relative address' in the application program.

A key role of the memory manager will be to ensure the security of any process. That is, the process must not reference any memory locations used by other programs.

This strategy (of operating system and one process only) is wasteful on memory; on a modern PC we have sufficient memory available to load several processes into memory at the same time, called multiprogramming.

Various strategies can be used for the allocation of the available main memory.

Partitioned memory

TERMS

partition: divides up the available memory space, similarly to a partition in a room

The **partitions** could be fixed. They could be of different sizes but are set when the operating system boots up. The operating system must keep a table showing the start address of each partition and its size. Processes – depending on their size – are then loaded into a partition which is of an appropriate size.

Dynamic partitions are created to best fit the needs of the programs which are about to be loaded to memory.

Initially, after the operating system is loaded, the memory can be thought of as one large partition. As further processes are loaded, new partitions are created. The operating system must carefully manage these partitions – i.e. their start address and size, and which processes are resident in each partition. Since the partitions are created dynamically and are constantly changing, so the partition data changes.

Dynamic partitions can be changed whenever a process finishes execution.

High-level scheduling

Since there is only a finite amount of main memory there are likely to be processes waiting to be loaded. The operating system module that decides which process will be loaded next is called the 'high-level scheduler'.

Possible algorithms the memory manager could use are:

- 'first fit' – load the process into the first partition which is sufficiently large.

- 'best fit' – load the process into the partition which minimises wasted space.

- 'worse fit' – load the process into the largest available free partition.

The arguments for and against each strategy should be considered for both fixed and dynamic partitions.

Paged memory management

Paged memory management is also called 'paging'. Programs are divided into fixed-sized units called 'pages'. The main memory is divided into units of the same size, called 'page frames'. The implication of this is that:

- A program's pages may be scattered throughout the available page frames.

- The operating system must manage which page frames are allocated to which pages of a process. This is done by maintaining a page-map (or page-frame) table.

- The logical address of a program instruction is expressed as (PageNumber, Offset); for example, the address (2, 518) represents the 518th byte from the start address of page 2.

The basic idea of paging is that not all the pages of the program need to be loaded to start execution. There may be insufficient page frames available for the whole of the program to be loaded. This strategy is called 'demand paging'. This is a fundamental difference from the earlier technique of using partitions, where all of the program was loaded into memory before execution. It gives rise to the idea of virtual memory, in which there is no restriction on the size of a process which can be scheduled and start execution.

The process will continue to execute until an instruction is referenced which is in a page which is not currently loaded. The page must then be swapped into memory (at the expense of another page). This is called 'page swapping'. Too much page swapping will lead to degradation in performance, called 'thrashing'.

User interface

The user interface hides the complexities of the hardware from the user.

Consider the end of a word-processing session. The user:

1 Presses File, then Save.

2 Keys in the file name.

The operating system:

1 Checks there is sufficient secondary storage space available to save the file.

2 Looks at the file allocation table and decides which file allocation units are to be used for the file.

3 Makes a new entry in the file directory for this logical drive and records the file name, date and time the file was saved. The directory must also record the first allocation unit which has been used for this file.

The appearance and the interaction for the user will be very different for different types of interface. A command line interface will need the user to action events by keying in one-line commands. This will require the user to have a detailed knowledge of the available commands.

A graphical user interface (GUI) will be very different. The user must use a pointing device, such as a mouse, a stylus or finger to point to icons or text on the screen.

Progress check 16.01

Name three different strategies that could be used by the memory manager of the operating system.

Multitasking and processes

Modern PC computers have sufficient main memory to allow several programs to be loaded into memory and simultaneously available for execution. An instance of a program executing is called a 'process'.

Consider a session where four simultaneous file downloads are taking place. This involves four processes running, each using the (same) file download software. The operating system is said to be 'multitasking'. Its role is to decide how to make the most efficient use of the computer system in managing these four processes and any others which are running.

Processor management

Process states

All processes which are loaded in main memory will be in one of three states:

- running – the process which has current use of the processor

- ready (or 'runnable') – a process which is capable of using the processor but is having to wait

- suspended – a process which is not capable of using the processor for some reason:

  o It does not have the resources available to continue.

  o It could be waiting for a signal from some other process before it can move to the ready state.

  o In a paging system, It could be waiting for new pages to be loaded from secondary storage.

Progress check 16.02

During its execution a process will change state many times. Consider each of the following statements and determine the original and new state of the process:

1 A process is interrupted as its time slice has expired.

2 A process completes a sequence of disk read operations.

3 A process is given the use of the processor.

4 A process is executing but has to wait for some input from the keyboard.

Low-level scheduling means the management of processor usage by processes. This is a major task for the operating system and is done by storing data about the current state of each process in a process control block (PCB). The state of all loaded processes must be managed by the operating system. If there are one or more processes waiting in a runnable state, an algorithm is used by the low-level scheduler to decide which process will get the next use of the processor.

Strategies for low-level scheduling

- Round-robin scheduling: All the runnable processes are given a time-slice, i.e. a fixed amount of time after which the next runnable process will get its time slice and use of the processor.

- 'First in ready state, first served' scheduling: The processor is given to the process which is at the head of the 'ready' list. It keeps the processor until it moves to the suspended state. All processes in the ready state form a queue.

- Priority scheduling: When a process is loaded, the operating system takes note of the priority associated with that process. Priorities can be allocated on the basis of the user, the estimated run-time, the estimated run-time remaining (this priority changes as the process runs) or the resources the process will require.

If the operating system is implementing any system based on priorities then the starting and suspension of processes will be controlled using interrupt signals.

Progress check 16.03

If the scheduling algorithm is based on allocating a priority to each process, state three different criteria from which this priority could be calculated.

Interrupts and the kernel

An interrupt is a signal to the processor that some event has occurred. If processor time is to be allocated to various processes, then the starting of one process and the suspension of another will be controlled by the sending and receiving of interrupts. The operating-system module which does this is called 'the kernel'. Its prime role to act as a low-level interrupt handler.

The operating system may be capable of 'masking out' certain interrupts. For example, if a process has just been allocated the processor, it would not then want to be interrupted by a process with a lower priority.

LOOK FORWARD »

This can be achieved by setting certain bit positions in a register and is covered in Chapter 18.

Interrupts from a process

We shall consider the case where a process, PROCESS-LOW, is currently executing. An interrupt is then sent by PROCESS-HIGH. The sequence of steps taken by the interrupt handler is:

1 Save the contents of all general-purpose and special-purpose registers (including the Program Counter contents) for PROCESS-LOW in its PCB.

2 Load from PROCESS-HIGH's PCB the contents of all registers.

3 Mask out interrupts of a lower priority.

4 Execute PROCESS-HIGH, until an interrupt is received and PROCESS-HIGH has to move to the runnable or suspended state.

5 Restore the contents of the PCB for PROCESS-LOW and enable interrupts.

6 Continue execution of PROCESS-LOW.

If the low-level CPU allocation is a round-robin with a time-slice for each process, the above algorithm is simplified. The scheduler will recognise that the next process to be given the processor is the process at the head of the runnable queue.

Interrupts from a device

Consider a process, PROCESS-PRINT, which at some point sends output to a printer which is off-line.

This will require the process to be interrupted and some appropriate software run to deal with the unavailability of the printer. A software program written to deal with an interrupt of this kind is called an 'interrupt service routine' (ISR). Interrupts of this kind will have a priority. For example, the user pressing the Reset button will have a higher priority than any other interrupt request!

The sequence of steps for handling the device interrupt is:

1 Receive the interrupt and identify its source as the printer.

2 Mask out interrupts of a lower priority.

3 Save the register contents for PROCESS-PRINT to the PCB.

4 Load the ISR program for the 'printer off-line' event.

5 Execute the ISR code.

6 Restore the registers from the PCB for PROCESS-PRINT.

7 Enable all interrupts.

8 Continue with the execution of PROCESS-PRINT.

16.02 Virtual machine

> **TERMS**
>
> **Virtual machine (VM):** the emulation of a computer system using software

The role of a virtual machine

Virtual machines can be classified depending on the degree to which the target machine is copied.

System virtual machines

System virtual machines – full virtualisation – emulates a complete computer system by replicating the functioning of a different target operating system (the 'guest' operating system). The virtual machine provides an emulated hardware platform which is different from the host computer's instruction set.

Consider a PC computer running operating system X (the 'host' operating system). A number of application programs (including A and B) have been purchased to run under X. The user is keen to find out about a new beta version release of X but is also keen to have experience of using a different operating system, Y. Applications C and D are only available to run under Y. Figure 16.01 shows a software configuration for these user needs. The user has installed the VM software labelled V1.

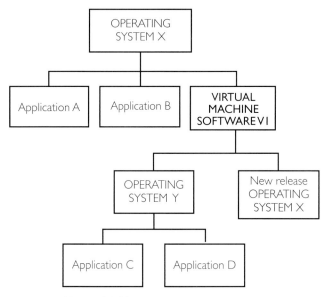

Figure 16.01 A system virtual machine

Process virtual machines

Process virtual machines (or application virtual machines) execute as a single application process under the host operating system software. A program can be run under the VM, which is platform-independent. Process virtual machines are implemented using an interpreter.

This type of VM is used by:

• the Java Virtual Machine: Once the Java software is installed on a computer, application programs designed to run in the VM environment are runnable.

- the Microsoft virtual machine, called the 'Common Language Runtime'. This is the basis of the Microsoft .NET framework which is the common software used to support program code written in several high-level languages, such as Visual Basic .NET, C# and many others.

LOOK BACK «

The use of the Java environment was covered in Chapter 5, section 5.04.

The software configuration in Figure 16.02 shows:

- two application programs, A and B, running under the host OS that make no reference to VM software

- virtual machine V3 supporting the Microsoft .NET framework, which allows application programs E and F to be run

- virtual machine V4, the Java Virtual Machine which allows applications G and H to be executed.

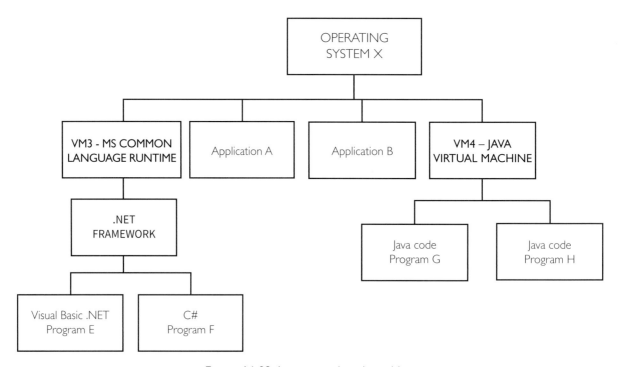

Figure 16.02 A process virtual machine

Benefits and limitations of virtual machines

Windows Virtual PC is virtual machine software available from Microsoft. It will emulate earlier versions of Windows. A programmer may have to be sure that an application under development will run perfectly on computers using an earlier version of Windows, such as XP or Vista.

Conversely when a new version of an operating system is released, the user may be anxious about performing a complete installation of the new software. One strategy could be to run the operating system upgrade under the virtual machine software, before 'ditching' the current operating system and moving entirely to the new version. The benefit to the user is obvious. They are experiencing the use of the emulated operating system, as if they were working on a computer that only has this OS installed.

16.03 Translation software

Compiler software

> **LOOK BACK «**
>
> We studied assembly language in Chapter 4; this code needed translating to machine code by software called the assembler.
>
> There are many similarities between assembler software and compilers.

Fig 16.03 summarises how a program written in assembly language is translated to machine code which can be executed.

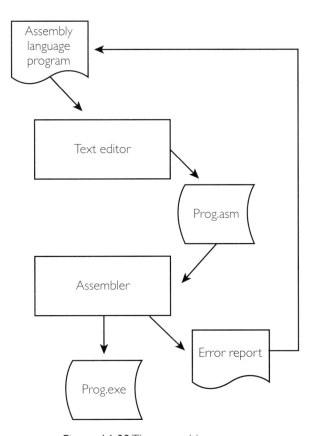

Figure 16.03 The assembly process

A compiler is the translator software required to translate a program written in a particular high-level language into machine code. A program written in Pascal would require the use of a Pascal compiler. Figure 16.03 could simply be reproduced for the compilation process by replacing the 'Assembler' process with 'Compiler'.

The compiler software considers all the source code statements, finds errors and only produces the executable version when all the errors have been found and fixed. Compilation can therefore be a repetitive process, until all errors are eliminated (as shown on the right hand-side of Figure 16.03 and Figure 16.04). Traditionally the source code would have been produced using text editor software and the compiler was a separate software program.

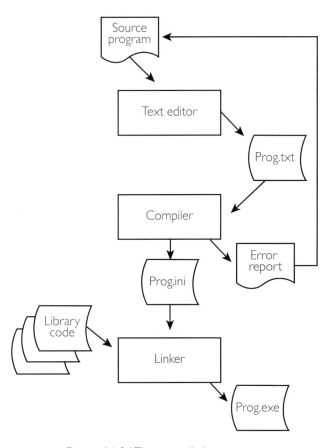

Figure 16.04 The compilation process

Key points about the use of a compiler are:

- The compiler used must match with the source code programming language.

- The program can only be executed once all errors have been found – this final compilation will reports 'No errors found'.

- The compiler might produce some form of 'intermediate code' that can be merged with existing compiled code from library files to produce the final executable.

- Once the final executable file has been created, neither the source code nor the compiler software is needed.

The issue of translation becomes clouded by the features provided by a modern programming language Integrated Development Environment (IDE).

LOOK BACK «

IDE software has features for all aspects of the program development cycle – writing the source code, eliminating syntax errors and compiling the program. Using an IDE was studied in Chapter 12, section 12.01.

Stages in the compilation process

Lexical analysis

Lexical analysis is the first stage of the compilation process. The lexical analyser will:

- remove any whitespace from the source file.

- remove any comment statements.

- check for obvious errors in the use of identifier names, for example that they do not exceed 64 characters.

- replace all language keywords with a token which is looked up from a keyword table and simplifies the code.

- replace all identifier names in the source code by a pointer value which links to an entry in the symbol table.

Identifying language keywords is very complex. For example, the sequence of characters 'P', 'R', 'I', 'N' and 'T' are identified as the keyword 'PRINT' and are replaced by a single token to represent PRINT.

Symbol table

The lexical analyser builds up a symbol table which contains all the identifiers found in the source code and – if applicable – their data type. Constants have their value stored. An array has its lower and upper bound recorded.

Most compilers must make two passes through the source code in order to complete the symbol table entries. The first pass inserts each new variable or constant name. A second pass through the source code can establish the actual memory address to be used for that identifier.

For a large program, the symbol table will contain hundreds of entries and it is important that fast access is possible to any identifier entry. This can be done by constructing the symbol table as a hash table with a hash key generated for each entry.

LOOK FORWARD »

Program code using hashing and hash tables is studied in Chapter 19, section 19.02.

Consider the following program statement:

```
// Calculate discount rate
IF Discount = True THEN
    DiscountRate = 5
ELSE
    DiscountRate = 0
END IF
```

What will the lexical analyser produce from this statement using the keyword table in Table 16.01?

Keyword	Token
REPEAT	Δ
UNTIL	ΔΔ
IF	□
THEN	□Δ
ELSE	□ΔΔ
END IF	□ΔΔΔ
True	▲
False	▲▲

Table 16.01 Keyword table used by the lexical analyser

The source code is scanned:

- The comment statement is removed.

- All 'whitespace' is removed.

- The two variables are added to the symbol table.

- The output string contains pointers to each of these variables.

- The keywords are looked up in the keyword table and replaced by their matching tokens.

The lexical analyser produces the following output string and symbol table (Table 16.02):

□Pointer to 01CD=▲□Δ^01CF=5□ΔΔ^01CF=0□ΔΔΔ

Note that ^01CF means 'pointer to 01CF'.

Identifier	Data type	Memory address
Discount	BOOLEAN	01CD
DiscountRate	INTEGER	01CF

Table 16.02 Symbol table produced by the lexical analyser

Source-code errors which are identified at the lexical analysis stage include the use of invalid identifier names. A keyword may have been spelt incorrectly, for example, `Cnsole`. The lexical analyser will fail to find this as an entry in the keyword table. The analyser could interpret it as an identifier and (wrongly) insert it as an identifier entry in the symbol table. However, for a strongly typed language, the compiler would then realise that there was not a matching declaration statement for this identifier.

Syntax analysis

Most syntax errors will be identified in the IDE by careful checking by the developer and using the various aids which the IDE provides. However some syntax errors may not be identified; then it is the task of the compiler's syntax analyser to identify any remaining errors.

LOOK BACK «

The IDE features were covered in detail in Chapter 12, section 12.04.

Syntax checking establishes whether a sequence of input characters matches the rules of the language. The language grammar rules must be available to the compiler and these would be in the form of a large number of Backus–Naur Form (BNF) sentences or rules. Alternatively, the rules can be shown visually using a syntax diagram.

LOOK FORWARD »

Backus–Naur Form (BNF) and syntax diagrams are covered later in this chapter.

For example the compiler will check the following statement and report that it is missing the closing bracket:

```
Console.Writeline("My best score was
... " & MyScore
```

At the syntax analysis stage, statements which are incorrectly formed will be identified. These statements do not conform to the rules of the language.

When an error is found the compiler will continue – unlike an interpreter – and all errors will be reported either on-screen or in a listing file. The programmer must then return to the source code, make the changes and re-compile the code. See Figure 16.04.

Code generation and code optimisation

Once the source code is compiled and no errors are found, the compiler will generate the object file or 'executable' file. This is the third stage of the compilation process called the 'code generation' stage.

Consider the following statement in a high-level program:

```
TriangleArea = Base * Height / 2
```

Lexical analysis creates the entries in the symbol table in Table 16.03.

Identifier	Data type	Memory address
Base	SINGLE	0F03
Height	SINGLE	0F04
TriangleArea	SINGLE	0F05

Table 16.03 Identifier table

The code translation process then produces the corresponding machine code. It is shown here as assembly language instructions for readability:

```
LOAD    0F03
MULT    0F04
DIV     2
STORE   0F05
```

This code illustrates that any one high-level language statement will be translated into several machine code instructions.

The code generation process will need to make reference to:

- the information stored in the symbol table.
- code contained in various program libraries, for example, when a source code statement uses a built-in function of the language.

Interpreter software

Using a programming language interpreter, the programmer writes the source code and can attempt to execute the code at any stage. The interpreter software will translate each statement in the program in sequence and execute these program statements until an error is found. When the first error is found, execution of the program terminates and the programmer will immediately try to fix the error by changing the source code.

Compiler or interpreter – benefits and drawbacks

Using a compiler, the programmer can only attempt to execute the program when all syntax errors have been fixed. If interpreted, the program can be run at any time without any prior translation taking place. This is the key difference between a compiler and an interpreter.

Compiler

The compiler produces an error report and the final executable object file. Successfully compiling the source program means the executable file produced by the compiler can be executed without reference to the compiler software.

Once translated the compiler software does not need to be used with the final executable file. Code which has been compiled should execute faster than code which is interpreted. The final executable file produced by a compiler can be widely distributed without the user having sight of the source code.

So, using a compiler makes the source code more secure: the user will be unable to make changes to the final executable file.

Interpreter

Using an interpreter, the interpreter software must be loaded in main memory whenever we attempt to execute our source program. Therefore, it uses up more main memory and every user of the software must have the interpreter software and the source code available.

Interpreters usually provide better diagnostics. Using an interpreter will allow some parts of the program to be tested and run, without all the program code being available. This generally fits with the strategy of a modular approach to program design and coding.

Progress check 16.04

1 Which of these are true statements?

   a A compiler generally will produced better diagnostic facilities than an interpreter.

   b A compiler must be present in main memory every time we run a program.

   c An interpreter produces an object file.

   d Using an interpreter will use more main memory at run time.

   e A compiler attempts to find all errors in the source code.

   f An interpreter attempts to find all errors in the source code.

   g An interpreter runs the program until the first error is found.

   h The same compiler can be used to translate a Pascal program and a Java program.

2 Consider this program statement:

```
FOR Index = 1 To 20
    Product = Index * Index
NEXT
```

Keyword	Token
REPEAT	Δ
UNTIL	ΔΔ
FOR	■
TO	■ ■
NEXT	■ ■ ■
IF	□
THEN	□Δ
ELSE	□ΔΔ
END IF	□ΔΔΔ
True	▲
False	▲ ▲

It is run through the lexical analyser using the keyword table. Show:

   a the contents of the symbol table.

   b the output character string produced.

Syntax diagrams

Syntax diagrams were used extensively in early textbooks for high-level programming languages. The following examples illustrate the diagrams needed to define the syntax allowed for an identifier.

Figure 16.05 defines a 'digit' character. The syntax diagram is always read from left to right and is designed to show here that a digit is always exactly one of the ten characters shown.

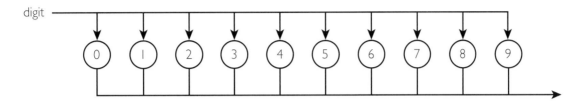

Figure 16.05 Defining a 'digit'

Figure 16.06 defines a 'letter'. We conclude that a letter is always exactly one of the upper or lower case letters.

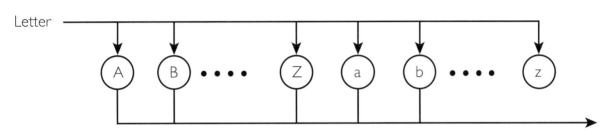

Figure 16.06 Defining a 'letter'

The previous two definitions can be used to define an 'identifier', as shown in Figure 16.07.

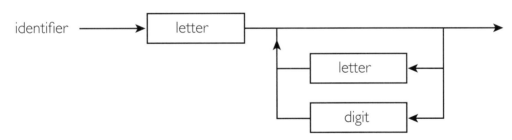

Figure 16.07 Defining an 'identifier'

Figure 16.07 explains why the identifiers in Table 16.04 are VALID or INVALID.

Suggested identifier	Valid?	Explanation
P	VALID	
MyObject	VALID	
8index	INVALID	Must start with at least one letter character
Count	VALID	
My_Object	INVALID	Contains the underscore character, which has not been defined
Loop5times	VALID	

Table 16.04 Identifier table

Backus–Naur Form (BNF) notation

Backus–Naur Form (BNF) is a special language, called a 'meta-language', which is used to describe the syntax and composition of statements which make up a high-level programming language.

A syntax element is enclosed between the < > characters and a typical statement would be:

```
<digit> ::= 0|1|2|3|4|5|6|7|8|9
<binarydigit> ::= 0|1
```

This first statement reads as `<digit>` 'is defined as 0 or 1 or 2 or ... or 8 or 9'.

Since each of the terms on the right-hand side of each rule cannot be broken down further 0, 1, 2, etc. are called 'terminal symbols'.

A rule definition may be recursive. Consider this definition to describe identifier names for a programming language:

```
<letter> ::= A|B|C|...|Z|a|b|c|...|z

<digit> ::= 0|1|2|3|4|5|6|7|8|9

<identifier> ::= <letter>|
                 <identifier><letter>|
                 <identifier><digit>
```

The third rule states that a valid identifier name can be any of:

- a single letter
- a letter followed by one or more letter or digit characters.

The process of analysing whether or not a given identifier is valid (following the given rules) is called 'parsing' the expression.

Consider the identifier name `She1`. Is it valid?

Figure 16.08 demonstrates that the expression is a valid identifier name.

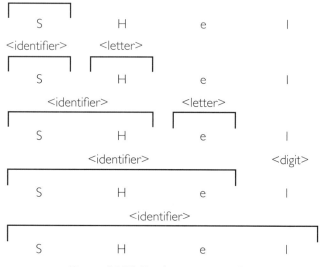

Figure 16.08 Parsing an expression

Consider the identifier name `1he`. Is it valid?

Figure 16.09 demonstrates that the expression is not a valid identifier name.

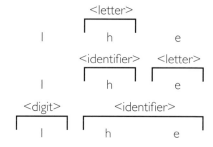

Figure 16.09 Parsing an expression

2 The following set of rules define the format for a list of letters.

```
<comma> ::= ,
<cap_letter> ::= A|B|C|D|E|...|X|Y|Z
<lower_letter> ::= a|b|c|d|e|...|x|y|z
<valid_character> ::= <cap_letter>|<lower_letter>
<list> ::= <valid_character>|<valid_character><comma><list>
```

Which of the following are valid lists ?

a S   **b** p   **c** s,y,u,   **d** s,h,y,4,6

Reverse Polish notation (RPN)

Infix notation

When we were taught the fundamentals of math, we wrote expressions using infix notation, for example:

$$\text{Area} = \text{Length} \times \text{Width}$$

The operator – the multiplication sign – is positioned between the two operands (Length and Width). The meaning of this expression is clear. However some expressions require the use of brackets to convey the order in which the component parts must be evaluated:

$$z = (x + y) / 5$$

The brackets are needed here to make it clear that the sum of x and y must be worked out first.

Reverse Polish (or postfix) notation

In Reverse Polish notation, the operand for the expression is written following the two operands:

$$\text{Area} = \text{Length} \times \text{Width}$$

$$z = x \; y + 5 \; /$$

Reverse Polish notation has the major advantage over infix in that the meaning for any expression is clear without the use of brackets.

Study carefully the examples in Table 16.05.

Infix expression	Postfix expression
(8 − 4) × 5	8 4 − 5 ×
(3p + 5) / (p − z)	3 p × 5 + p z − /
2 × 7 − 8 / 4	2 7 × 8 4 / −
7^4 − 9 / 3	7 4 ^ 9 3 / −

Table 16.05 Infix and reverse Polish (postfix) expressions

Converting between reverse Polish notation and infix form

A binary tree can be used to represent expressions both in infix and reverse Polish notation.

Consider the expression:

$$(3p + 5) / (p − z)$$

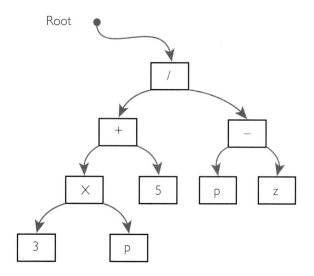

Root

Figure 16.10 Expression as a binary tree

LOOK FORWARD »

In Chapter 19, section 19.01, we develop a recursive algorithm for traversing a binary tree. If we use an in-order traversal algorithm, the values in the expression are output in the order which gives the infix expression.

Progress check 16.07

Here is the in-order traversal algorithm. Check that it outputs the infix expression.

```
InOrderTraversal (Root)
    IF Root.LeftPointer <> Null
        THEN
            // move left
            InOrderTraversal(Root.LeftPointer)
    ENDIF
    OUTPUT Root.Data
    IF Root.RightPointer <> Null
        THEN
            // move right
            InOrderTraversal(Root.RightPointer)
    ENDIF
ENDPROCEDURE
```

If we simply change the order of doing things for the traversal algorithm we shall traverse the tree in a different order.

```
PostOrderTraversal (Root)
    IF Root.LeftPointer <> Null
        THEN
            InOrderTraversal(Root.LeftPointer)
    ENDIF
    IF Root.RightPointer <> Null
        THEN
            InOrderTraversal(Root.RightPointer)
    ENDIF
        OUTPUT Root.Data
ENDPROCEDURE
```

We have effectively changed the order to 'left – right – root'. The traversal of the given tree will produce the traversal and output shown in Figure 16.11.

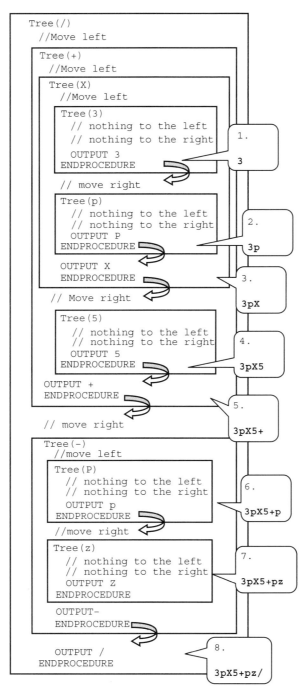

Figure 16.11 Traversing the expression tree

The trace confirms that, for the `PostOrderTraversal` algorithm, the expression is output in reverse Polish.

Progress check 16.08

1 Evaluate the following reverse Polish expressions:

a 11 6 - 5 *

b 3 4 ^ 9 / 3 + 4 /

c 14 6 - 8 *

2 Write these expressions in reverse Polish:

a $(a + b) / 6$

b $(2a + b)^3$

Evaluating a reverse Polish expression

This will demonstrate another advantage of the use of reverse Polish. The elements which make up the expression can be processed using a stack data structure.

Consider the evaluation of the expression:

$$(9 * 7 + 2) / 5$$

In reverse Polish this becomes:

$$9 \ 7 \ * \ 2 \ + \ 5 \ /$$

The method is:

1 Push operands onto the stack in sequence.

2 When an operator is met:
- Pop two values.
- Evaluate the expression.
- Push the result onto the stack.

Progress check 16.09

Trace the changing contents of a stack when it is used to evaluate the reverse Polish expression:

$$2 \ 4 \ ^ \ 5 \ - \ 2 \ /$$

Figure 16.12 shows a stack for the evaluation of:

$$9 \ 7 \ * \ 2 \ + \ 5 \ /$$

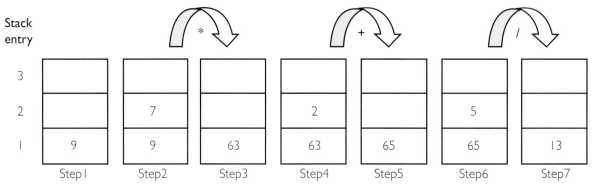

Figure 16.12 Stack used for evaluating reverse Polish expression

Summary

- The operating system is the software which maximises the resources of the computer – the processor, main memory, secondary storage, I/O devices and the user interface.

- Multitasking involves the idea of a process which can be in one of three states: running, ready or suspended.

- The kernel of the operating system carries out all interrupts to manage low-level scheduling.

- Paging is one strategy used for main memory management.

- A virtual machine is made possible using virtual machine software.

- High-level language program code is translated by either compiler or interpreter software.

- A language grammar can be documented with a set of syntax diagrams or Backus–Naur Form rules.

- Reverse Polish Notation is used – with a stack data structure – to evaluate expressions.

Exam-style questions

1 Two types of software which are used to translate high-level programs are a compiler and an interpreter.

   a Name **two** outputs produced by the compiler. [2]

   b Describe **two** advantages of using an interpreter rather than a compiler. [2]

   c Describe what happens during the syntax analysis stage of translation. [3]

   d Explain why linkers and loaders may be required to produce the final executable program file. [2]

   Cambridge International AS and A level Computer Science 9691 Paper 33, Q4, Nov 2012

2 Modern operating systems use a memory management technique called paging.

   Explain how paging works by using the terms:

   - Page

   - Page frame

   - Page table [3]

   Cambridge International AS and A Level Computer Science 9691 Paper 31, Q2(a), Nov 2014

Chapter 17

Security

Revision objectives

By the end of the chapter you should be able to:

- show understanding of the terms public key, private key, plain text, cipher text, encryption and asymmetric key cryptography

- show understanding of how keys can be used to send a private message from the public to an individual/organisation and to send a verified message to the public

- show understanding of how a digital certificate is acquired and used to produce digital signatures

- show awareness of the purpose of Secure Socket Layer/Transport Layer Security (SSL/TLS)

- show awareness of the use of SSL/TLS in client–server communication and situations where SSL/TLS would be appropriate

- show understanding of malware and vulnerabilities that the various types of malware can exploit

- describe methods that can be used to restrict the effect of malware

17.01 Keys and encryption methods

Encryption is not specific to computing. It has been used for thousands of years for the sending and receiving of messages. Encryption is not designed to stop a third party having access to data but to ensure that they are unable to understand the data if it is intercepted.

Data which is sent over a communication link is susceptible to interception. Emails and other data pass through many computers, routers and networks before they reach their destination, therefore the data could be read by a third party. After the message is delivered to the recipient's mail server, it could be days before the message is read.

Risks to the security of the communication are that there can be operator tampering or the data is electronically intercepted. If the data is scrambled in some way, it can still be intercepted, but the third party cannot make sense of it.

The encryption process requires the application of an encryption algorithm using an encryption key.

Consider a message which is to be sent and received. The user writes the message, for example, into a 5 × 5 grid (see Figure 17.01) and then sends the message in encrypted form: not each row in sequence but the columns in sequence.

I	L	L	Δ	M
M	E	E	T	Δ
U	Δ	A	T	Δ
6	Δ	O	C	L
O	C	K	Δ	Δ

Δ represents a space

Figure 17.01 A message in a grid

- The **plain text** is the message: ILLΔMEETΔUΔATΔ6ΔOCLOCKΔΔ.

- The encryption algorithm is 'Write the message into a grid starting with the first row'.

- The encryption key is 5 (the number of characters on each row).

- The **cipher text** is: IMU6OLEΔΔCLEAOKΔTTCΔMΔΔLΔ.

A recipient of the cipher text would be able to **decrypt** this message if they know the algorithm and the key.

Encryption: a process whereby a message can be securely stored and transmitted so that it is only understood by the sender and receiver

Plain text: describes the message before it is encrypted

Cipher text: the message after it has been encrypted

Decryption: the process of converting the cipher text back to plain text

Symmetric encryption

The example above uses symmetric encryption: the same algorithm and key is used for both the encryption and the decryption process.

The Data Encryption Standard (DES) is a cipher that was selected by the National Bureau of Standards in the US as an official standard in 1976; it has subsequently enjoyed widespread international use. It is based on a symmetric-key algorithm that uses a 56-bit key. The algorithm was initially controversial with classified design elements, a relatively short key length and suspicions about a National Security Agency (NSA) backdoor.

This raises an issue of public concern: if data is encrypted, who should hold the decryption key? This is a hot topic at the present, with terrorist groups using encrypted communications.

The Advanced Encryption Standard (AES) was adopted in 2001, intended as a replacement for DES.

Encryption in action: the mobile phone network

The standard for mobile phone encryption is part of the global system for mobile (GSM) communications standard. Most operators use encryption to hide the contents of the voice call in case of interception, but this usually only applies over the radio waves between the handset and the base station. Once the call is transmitted over fixed networks, call privacy relies upon standard security measures and so are as vulnerable to attack as any other data in an information technology infrastructure.

In 2009, a team of German computer scientists claimed to have cracked the encryption.

Many companies advertise to provide an additional layer of security for mobile communications.

Asymmetric encryption (Public key cryptography)

A much more secure technique is to use asymmetric encryption. Two keys are used, called the public key and private key.

The plain text is encrypted with the sender's private key and is then decrypted by the recipient who is in possession of the sender's public key.

The golden rule is that the public key can be widely known, but the private key will only ever be in the possession of its owner.

Asymmetric keys are typically 1024 or 2048 bits – keys smaller than 2048 bits are no longer considered safe. 2048-bit keys have more than enough unique encryption codes: it's a 617-digit denary number! Though larger keys can be created, the increased computational burden is such an overhead that keys larger than 2048 bits are rarely used. It would take an average computer more than 14 billion years to crack a 2048-bit key!

Asymmetric encryption uses encryption algorithms, such as RSA and elliptic curve cryptography (ECC), to create the public and private keys. These algorithms are based on the intractability of certain mathematical problems. This means the problem can be solved, in theory, given infinite time; however, in practice, it will take too long for the solution to be useful (in this case, for the private key to be derived from the known public key).

With asymmetric encryption, it is computationally easy to generate public and private keys, encrypt messages with the public key and decrypt messages with the private key. However, it is impossible for anyone to derive the private key based only on the public key.

Three computer scientists – Ron Rivest, Adi Shamir and Leonard Adleman – devised the RSA algorithm in 1977. The RSA algorithm is based on the presumed difficulty of factoring large integers. Full decryption of an RSA cipher text is thought to be infeasible on the assumption that no efficient algorithm exists for integer factorisation. A user of RSA creates and then publishes the product of two large prime numbers, along with an auxiliary value, as their public key. The prime factors must be kept secret. Anyone can use the public key to encrypt a message, but only someone with knowledge of the prime factors can feasibly decode the message.

17.02 Digital signatures and digital certificates

Digital certificates

To send and receive encrypted messages you must have a digital certificate from a Certification Authority (CA) such as Symantec (formally VeriSign). The most important part of a certificate is that it is digitally signed by a trusted CA. Anyone can create a certificate, but browsers only trust certificates that come from an organisation on their list of trusted CAs. Browser software will come with a pre-installed list of trusted CAs, known as the 'trusted root CA store'.

Some clients you communicate with may insist that all email communication, for example, is encrypted and so you must purchase a digital certificate and install it on the computer used for sending and receiving messages. Figure 17.02 shows a certificate. Note the text that says 'You have a private key that corresponds to this certificate'.

Encrypted email

Once a user has a digital certificate they must give their public key to the intended correspondent. The ownership and knowledge about keys is illustrated in Figure 17.03, which shows the keys used to encrypt and decrypt a message when A sends an encrypted email to B.

TIP

You will find information about sending encrypted communications in the help files of your email client software, as in Figure 17.04.

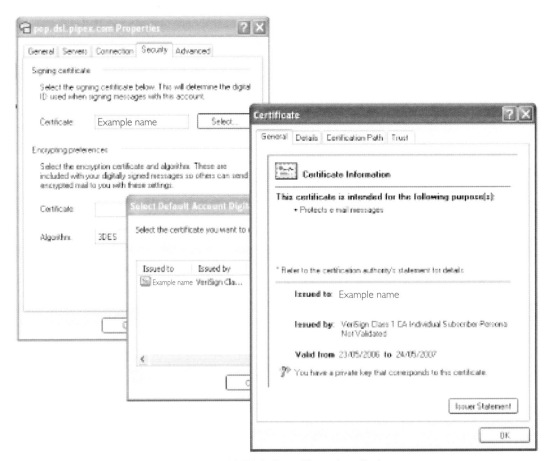

Figure 17.02 Digital certificate installed

Adding a digital signature

Figure 17.05 shows a digital signature added to the message sent in Figure 17.03. In the encryption stage, the first step is to produce the cipher text in an identical way to Figure 17.03. That is, as if no digital signature was to be added.

A hashing algorithm is provided as part of the digital certificate purchased. When recipient B receives A's public key, they are also provided with the hashing function of A's certificate. The hashing function is used on the plain text to produce a message digest, which is encrypted with A's private key. The cipher text and the digital signature are communicated to recipient B.

In the decryption stage, the cipher text is decrypted using A's public key exactly as in Figure 17.03. The hashing algorithm is applied to the decrypted text to produce the message digest. A second copy of the message digest is produced using A's public key on the digital signature received. A match between the two message digests confirms that neither the cipher text or digital signature were changed in transit.

17.03 Encryption protocols

Secure Socket Layer/Transport Layer Security (SSL/TLS)

Secure Socket Layer (SSL) is used when a user needs to be assured that communication over the Internet is secure. Customers want assurances that a company they do business with take security seriously and have in place systems necessary to protect their information. More and more customers are becoming savvy online shoppers and are likely to do repeat business with a company they trust with their data. SSL secures a communication using the Internet's TCP.

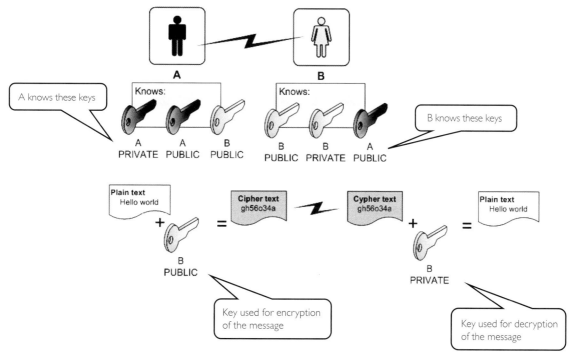

Figure 17.03 Sending an encrypted email from A to B

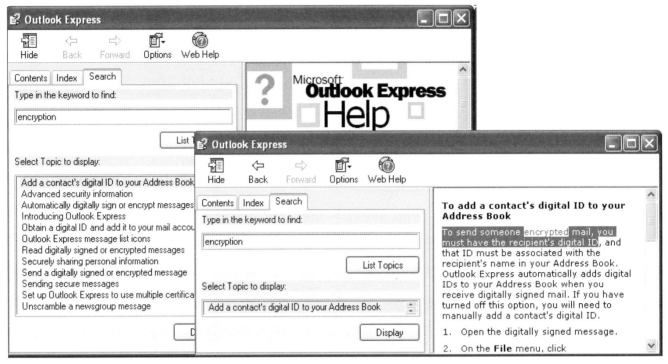

Figure 17.04 Microsoft Outlook Express encryption

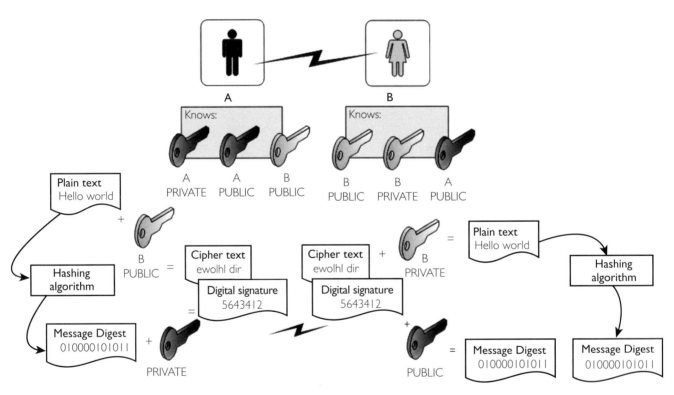

Figure 17.05 Adding a digital signature

SSL is a standard security protocol for establishing an encrypted link between a server and a client, typically between a web server (a website) and a browser or between a mail server and an email client. The SSL protocol defines variables for both the link and the data being transmitted.

The Secure Socket Layer protocol has three objectives:

- privacy – through the use of encryption
- identity authentication – through the use of a certificate
- reliability – using message integrity checking during the lifetime of the connection.

SSL allows sensitive information such as credit card numbers and login information to be transmitted securely. Normally, data sent between browsers and web servers is sent in plain text, leaving you vulnerable to eavesdropping. If an attacker is able to intercept data being sent between a browser and a web server, they can see and use that information.

Internet users can identify the use of SSL in their browser by:

- https (rather than http) as part of the URL
- the lock icon that displays for an SSL-secured website
- the green address bar that comes with an extended validation SSL-secured website.

How is an SSL connection established?

The client browser must connect to a web server secured with SSL as shown in Figure 17.06.

1   The browser requests that the server identify itself.

2   The server sends a copy of its SSL Certificate, including the server's public key.

3   The browser checks the certificate root against a list of trusted CAs stored by the browser. It must check that the certificate is unexpired, unrevoked and that its name is valid for the website to which it is connecting.

4   If the browser trusts the certificate, it creates, encrypts and sends back a symmetric session key using the server's public key.

5   The server decrypts the symmetric session key using the server's private key

6   The server sends back an acknowledgement encrypted with the session key to start the encrypted session.

7   The server and browser now encrypt all transmitted data with the session key.

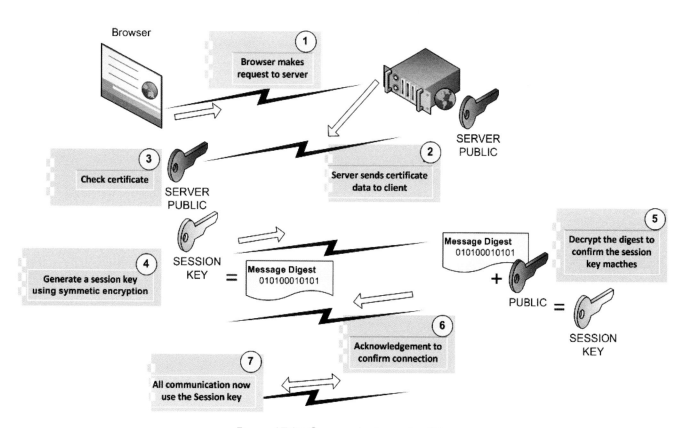

Figure 17.06 Communication using SSL

- SSL is an example of a handshaking protocol – each end-point exchanges messages until they agree they are ready to communicate.

- There is no requirement for the client to be in possession of a certificate.

- SSL requires a large amount of processing due to the various communication exchanges. Many servers are fitted with hardware called an 'SSL accelerator'.

- SSL uses a combination of symmetric and asymmetric encryption.

The current version of SSL was released in 1999. The Internet Engineering Task Force created the similar **Transport Layer Security (TLS)** protocol in an attempt to standardise the use of SSL. It is the intention to rebrand future releases of SSL as TLS.

17.04 Malware: viruses, worms, phishing, pharming

Malware is the term used to describe any form of software which is designed to cause malfunction/harm to a computer system. The range of threats is now widespread and varied:

- Browser hijackers: when the browser is loaded, malware code, such as code designed to log the user's key strokes, becomes active.

- Ransomware threatens the user with avoidance of the loss of data in return for a money ransom.

- Backdoor access is designed to bypass the normal authentication processes to the computer system.

- Trojan horse code carries out some malicious act such as data loss. It employs a form of social engineering, presenting itself as useful software in order to persuade the user to install the software on the computer system. (The term comes from the story of the wooden horse used to trick the defenders of Troy into taking concealed warriors into their city in Anatolia.)

- Worms are malware designed to replicate and spread to other computers.

- Adware is software which pops up advertisements when using browser software. The software may be more subtle and is designed to analyse which internet sites the user visits and present advertising of goods or services which match with the browser history.

- Spyware is a general term which includes malware software for system monitoring, a Trojan, adware or the tracking of cookies.

Some anti-virus software includes protection from other threats, such as infected and malicious URLs, spam, phishing attacks, online identity (privacy) and botnets.

Summary

☐ Terminology associated with encryption includes plain text, cipher text, encryption key and encryption algorithm and message digest.

☐ Symmetric encryption uses the same encryption algorithm and key for both the encryption and decryption process.

☐ Asymmetric encryption uses a private key and a public key.

☐ A digital signature is provided as part of the purchase of a digital certificate from a Certificate Authority.

☐ Digital signatures are used for proof of identity. They are calculated using a hashing algorithm provided with the certificate.

☐ The SSL and TLS protocols are used to provide secure communication between a client computer and a server.

☐ SSL/TLS will be used where the privacy of data is crucial, for example, for on-line card payments and authentication of logons.

☐ The range of malware includes viruses, worms, spam, phishing and pharming.

Exam-style questions

1   Raz and Tan wish to exchange some sensitive information via a message in an email. Initially, Raz wants to send the message to Tan in such a way that Tan can be assured that the message did come from Raz.

   a   The steps are as follows:

   1   Raz creates a **<answer 1>** using a **<answer 2>** function on the message.

   2   Raz encrypts the **<answer 1>** using his **<answer 3>** key. This is the digital **<answer 4>** for the message.

   3   Raz sends both the message and the digital **<answer 4>** to Tan.

   4   Tan decrypts the digital **<answer 4>** using Raz's **<answer 5>** key.

   5   Tan repeats what Raz did in Step 1 to the message.

   Select from the list of terms to complete the five statements.

   signature   hash   message-digest   encryption   private   public   email   [5]

   b   Tan finds that her results in Step 5 do not match her results in Step 4.

   Give **two** possible reasons for this.   [2]

   c   Even though Tan's results in Step 5 match the results in Step 4, she is still concerned that anybody receiving the message can actually read the contents.

   Explain what Raz and Tan need to do so that only Tan can read the message.   [3]

   Cambridge International AS and A Level Computer Science 9608 Specimen paper 3, Q6 2015

Monitoring and control systems

18.01 Overview of monitoring and control systems

Monitoring systems

A computerised **monitoring system** is what is says – a system designed to 'watch' or monitor some state external to the computer system. A house fitted with a burglar alarm system is a monitoring system. The inputs to the computer system are one or more sensors to detect the presence of an intruder. Movement will 'trigger' the sensor which will send a signal to the computer system. This signal would be interpreted by software and could trigger the sounding of an alarm or report on screen some warning message.

> **TERMS**
>
> **Monitoring system:** a system designed to 'watch' or monitor some state external to the computer system
>
> **Event-driven system:** the controller alters the state of the system in response to some event
>
> **Time-driven system:** the controller takes action at a specific point in time or after a certain time has lapsed

In this and other examples, the process is 'automatic monitoring' – meaning there is no human interaction in the monitoring process. The monitoring will be done with periodic sampling of inputs. The process will decide on the polling frequency, that is the time interval between samples.

Other monitoring systems include:

- a pollution or weather monitoring system, in which data readings from sensors are fed back to the computer system remotely and processed by software to produce graphs (of temperature and wind speed, for example).

- a car dashboard display showing the temperature outside the car.

Control systems

Control systems are either 'event-driven' or 'time-driven'. a computer which is acting as the control system is called a direct digital control (DDC) computer. DDC is the automated control of a condition or process by a digital device/computer.

In an **event-driven system**, the controller, in response to some event, alters the state of the system:

- A robot loads a part into a work area and the part is sensed as present.

- The level of liquid plastic in the hopper of an injection-moulding machine is monitored by a low-level switch. When the level reaches a critical low point, the control system opens a valve to start the flow of more plastic into the hopper.

- Parts moving along a conveyor past an optical sensor are counted.

Some control systems are **'time-driven'**. The controller takes action at a specific point in time or after a certain time has lapsed:

- The factory buzzer sounds a bell at specific times of the day to indicate the start of shift, start and end of the break period and end of the shift.

- Heat-treating or paint-spraying operations must be carried out for a certain length of time.

- In a washing machine, the agitation cycle is set to operate for a certain length of time, before the controller stops this phase of the wash cycle.

All process control systems have the following features in common:

- the continual measurement of input variables, such as temperature, pressure and flow rate.

- the execution by software of some optimising strategy and the implementation of safety procedures.

- the actuation of devices such as valves, switches and output warning lights.

- the generation of equipment performance data showing information about the state of the process in real time.

A typical petro-chemical plant may have as many as 2000 parameters which are sampled to control the process Measured parameters include temperature, pressure flow rates, liquid levels and chemical concentration of liquids. The time between samples will vary between under 1 second to, for example, every two minutes. The DDC computer may control hundreds of feedback loops. If process parameters exceed normal or safe limits then an alarm will be raised and require human intervention. The DDC computer may be one of a number each control a separate process, with each DDC connected to a central computer. The central computer will have authority to change the parameter settings for the various process control loops.

Feedback

All the above systems use feedback. Feedback from sensors are processed by software. Outputs from the system are then fed back as an input together with new data from the input sensors.

Hardware requirements

Transducers

A **transducer** is any device which converts one form of energy to another; examples include:

- A light bulb converts electrical energy to light by passing an electric current through a filament.

- An electric motor converts electricity into some form of mechanical energy to produce motion.

- A microphone converts sound wave energy into electrical signals.

- A loudspeaker converts electrical energy into sound.

Sensors

A **sensor** is a device which receives a signal and responds to it. The sensor must detect the presence of or change in some energy level. The signal is then converted to a form which can be understood and quantified by the connected computer system. The sensor is therefore performing two tasks:

- acting as a transducer to convert from one energy form to another

- quantifying the signal.

The signal is produced by some form of energy, such as pressure, heat, light or some chemical reaction. The sensor converts this energy into a quantified analogue or digital representation of the input signal. Think what happens when you touch a hot plate. The sensor is the skin on your fingers which then sends a signal to the brain. It is the brain which then decides 'that was hot' and causes the output – the pain!

> **TIP**
> A common misunderstanding is that a sensor is capable of some form of processing. This is not so – the sensor is only able to detect some analogue measurement, quantify the signal and send it, in a digital form, to the connected computer system.

Sensors can be classified as:

- thermal: a thermometer measures temperature; a thermocouple gauge measures temperature by its effect on two dissimilar metals; a calorimeter measures the heat produced from a chemical reaction

- mechanical: a pressure sensor measures pressure; an altimeter measures altitude from some fixed point; a liquid flow sensor measures flow rate; a gas flow sensor measures velocity and flow rate of a gas.

- electrical: an ohmmeter measures resistance; a voltmeter measures current; a galvanometer measures voltage.

- chemical: an oxygen sensor measures the percentage of oxygen in a gas and a carbon dioxide sensor detects the presence of CO_2

- optical: a light sensor detects light levels; a photocell is a variable resistor which responds to a change in light level; an infra-red sensor detects infra-red radiation waves.

Actuators

An **actuator** is a device which 'actuates' or moves something connected to it. An actuator uses some form of energy to produce the motion, and so an actuator is a specific example of a transducer.

Most actuators are 'electro-mechanical transducers':

- A strain gauge converts the deformation of an object into an electrical signal.

- A galvanometer produces an electric current in a coil. The current produces a magnetic field which is used to create movement.

- A generator converts some form of mechanical energy into an electric current.

- A motor converts an electric current into mechanical energy to create movement.

Another type of transducer is a 'thermo-electric transducer':

- A thermocouple converts heat entry into electrical energy.

- A thermistor is a variable resistor which is affected by temperature change. It converts heat energy to electrical energy.

Transducers, actuators and sensors are now produced on both the macroscopic (visible by the human eye) and microscopic scale. Nanotechnology is making possible devices on the nanoscale. Regardless of their scale, these devices operate using the same principles. If the device is produced on the microscopic scale then the software which communicates with the devices can similarly be contained on a small chip circuit.

Converters and multiplexers

Quantities in the physical world, such as temperature and pressure, are analogue by nature. Such sensed data will need to be passed through an analogue-to-digital converter to be sent to the DDC computer. A digital-to-analogue converter converts digital data to analogue quantities.

18.02 Bit manipulation to monitor and control devices

Bit manipulation operations

There are usually instructions in the processor's instruction set which use the logical operators: AND, OR, NOT and XOR.

We are familiar from programming with the use of these operators. In a high-level language, AND, OR and XOR operate on two conditions. At the machine-code level – and so, in assembly language – this group of instructions operate on two numbers on a 'bit by bit' basis, called a 'bitwise' operation.

In the following examples, we assume there is a bit pattern in the accumulator which is operated on by another bit pattern, NUM.

AND operator

The result for each bit position is obtained using the truth table for the AND operator.

ACC	0	0	0	1	0	1	0	1	
NUM	1	0	1	1	1	1	1	0	AND

ACC	0	0	0	1	0	1	0	0	

Input		Output
0	0	0
0	1	0
1	0	0
1	1	1

OR operator

The result for each bit position is obtained using the truth table for the OR operator.

ACC	0	0	0	1	1	1	0	1	
NUM	1	0	1	1	0	1	1	0	OR

ACC	1	0	1	1	1	1	1	1	

Input		Output
0	0	0
0	1	1
1	0	1
1	1	1

XOR operator

The result for each bit position is obtained using the truth table for the XOR operator.

ACC	0	0	0	1	0	1	0	1	
NUM	1	0	1	1	1	1	1	0	XOR

ACC	1	0	1	0	1	0	1	1	

Input		Output
0	0	0
0	1	1
1	0	1
1	1	1

Masking

The logical operators are particularly useful for the operation of 'masking out' certain bit positions. In these bit positions, we replace the original bit value with a zero bit.

For example, we want to 'mask out' bit positions 1, 3, 4 and 6 of the accumulator contents, shown in Figure 18.01.

	7	6	5	4	3	2	1	0
ACC	0	0	0	1	0	1	0	1

Figure 18.01 The accumulator value to mask

The method is that we form an 'AND mask' with:

- 0 in the positions to mask out

- 1 in the positions to retain the original content.

Figure 18.02 shows the masking operation.

	7	6	5	4	3	2	1	0	
ACC	0	0	0	1	0	1	0	1	
MASK	1	0	1	0	0	1	0	1	AND

	7	6	5	4	3	2	1	0
ACC	0	0	0	0	0	1	0	1

Figure 18.02 The masking operation

The result is that:

- the masked positions are set to zero.

- the retained positions are unchanged.

Matching

The instruction set will have several 'compare' instructions. A compare instruction sets the zero bit in the status register when a match occurs.

> **LOOK BACK «**
>
> Chapter 4, section 4.01 introduced the special-purpose register called the Status Register. Each of the eight bit positions is used to 'flag' or show the status of something.

For example, we want to compare the accumulator contents with value #79.

The simplest method does not involve a Boolean operator. We can simply subtract the number from the contents of the accumulator (see Figure 18.03). If the result is zero, then the values match.

	7	6	5	4	3	2	1	0
ACC	0	1	0	0	0	0	0	0
SUB #79	0	1	0	0	1	1	1	1

	7	6	5	4	3	2	1	0
ACC	0	0	0	0	0	0	0	0

Figure 18.03 Subtracting 79 from the accumulator

In practice, the assembly language will carry out a 'compare' instruction:

```
CMP ACC, #79
```

If the compare gives a TRUE result, the compare flag in the Status Register is set to 1.

Setting an individual bit position

Consider that the accumulator contains the ASCII code for upper case character 'K'. We want to change the code to lower case 'k'. The ASCII code for 'K' is 75 and for 'k' is 107; the difference is 32.

The bit patterns for the ASCII characters are shown in Figure 18.04.

	7	6	5	4	3	2	1	0
K	0	1	0	0	1	0	1	1

	7	6	5	4	3	2	1	0
k	0	1	1	0	1	0	1	1

Figure 18.04 The bit patterns for 'K' and 'k'

The task therefore is to change the bit in position 5 from 0 to 1. The OR operator does this, as shown in Figure 18.05, with a mask in which:

- 1 is in the position to 'set' (position 5)

- 0 is in all other positions (which are unchanged).

	7	6	5	4	3	2	1	0	
K	0	1	0	0	1	0	1	1	
	0	0	1	0	0	0	0	0	OR
k	0	1	1	0	1	0	1	1	

Figure 18.05 The bit patterns for 'K' and 'k' with an OR mask

Progress check 18.01

1 What would have been an alternative strategy for this which did not require the use of a Boolean operator?

2 Three of the bit positions in the Status Register are used as follows:

- Bit 0: Carry – flags to 1 when the previous compare was true

- Bit 1: Zero – flags to 1 when ACC contains zero

- Bit 2: Negative – flags to 1 when ACC contains a negative number (two's complement)

The other bits positions are unused. The Status Register currently contains:

	7	6	5	4	3	2	1	0
SR	0	0	0	0	0	0	0	1

Write the instruction to set the Negative flag to 1.

Testing one or more bits

The strategy for this combines 'masking' and 'matching'.

The contents of an accumulator is used to decide if a certain process can be started. The process can start if the pattern is as shown in Figure 18.06.

	7	6	5	4	3	2	1	0
ACC	0		0		1		1	1

Figure 18.06 The starting pattern for a process

The strategy is:

1 Mask the contents of X with a mask pattern (which has 0 in the 'mask out' positions and 1 in the 'retain' positions):

```
MASK = 10101001
```

2 Compare the result with the match pattern (which has 0 in the 'mask out' positions and the required values in the 'retain' positions):

```
MATCH = 00001001
```

Checking Pattern 1

Consider that the register contains `00011101` this is a match for the pattern in Figure 18.06. Figure 18.07 shows the process.

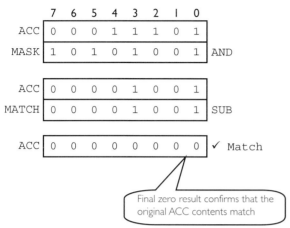

Figure 18.07 A matching pattern for starting a process

Checking Pattern 2

Consider that the register contains `11001010`; this is not a match for the pattern in Figure 18.06. Figure 18.08 shows the process.

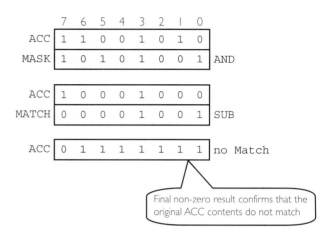

Figure 18.08 A non-matching pattern

Checking Pattern 2 using assembly language instructions

Table 18.01 lists the syllabus instructions for bitwise operations.

Instruction		Explanation
Opcode (mnemonic)	Operand	
AND	#n	Bitwise AND operation of the contents of ACC with n
AND	<address>	Bitwise AND operation of the contents of ACC with the contents of <address>
XOR	#n	Bitwise XOR operation of the contents of ACC with n
XOR	<address>	Bitwise XOR operation of the contents of ACC with the contents of <address>
OR	#n	Bitwise OR operation of the contents of ACC with n
OR	<address>	Bitwise OR operation of the contents of ACC with the contents of <address>

Table 18.01 Instructions for bitwise operations

Assume Pattern 2 is in location `NUMBER`. The following sequence of instructions describes the process used to check Pattern 2.

```
LDD NUMBER
AND #169      //#B1010 1001
SUB #9        //#B0000 1001
CMP #0
```

Using bit manipulation to monitor or control a device

There is nothing new here. A special register could have individual bit positions used as the setting to show the current state of some connected device. For example, bit 5 of the register could show whether or not an actuator which drives a motor is switched on or off.

Exam-style question number 1 has an example of the switching on and off of an actuator in a zoo reptile house.

Summary

- There is a fundamental difference between a monitoring system and a control system.

- Hardware needed to build a process control system includes sensors, actuators, D-to-A and A-to-D converters and multiplexers.

- Most control systems have several feedback loops to provide new input variables from the previous phase of outputs.

- Bitwise operations – AND, OR, XOR and NOT – can be used to manipulate a bit pattern.

- Various operations can be performed on a bit pattern:
  - masking out certain bit positions (with 0)
  - changing one or more bit positions (to 1).

- Single-bit positions can be used in a memory location or register to flag the status of some device.

Exam-style questions

1   A zoo reptile house has sixteen tanks which accommodate its reptiles. Each tank has to have its own microclimate where the appropriate levels of heat and humidity are crucial. The zoo implements a computer system which supplies the conditions in each of the tanks to a terminal in a central area. Warning messages are flashed up on the screen if any condition arises which requires the intervention of a zoo-keeper.

   a   State the name of the type of computing system described.   [1]

   b   State **two** items of hardware which need to be present in the tanks for this system to function correctly.   [2]

   c   This is the polling routine which is used to run the system indefinitely.

```
01 REPEAT
02    FOR i ← 1 TO .........
03       READ Condition1, Condition2 in tank(i)
04       IF Condition1 < Extreme[i,1] OR Condition1 > Extreme[i,2]
05          THEN
06             OUTPUT "Warning! Problem in Tank ", i
07       ENDIF
08       IF Condition2 < Extreme[i,3] OR Condition2 > Extreme[i,4]
09          THEN
10             OUTPUT "Warning! Problem in Tank ", i
11       ENDIF
12    ENDFOR
13
14    FOR i ← 1 TO 999999
15    ENDFOR
16 UNTIL ...............................
```

     i   Fill in the gaps in the pseudocode.   [2]

     ii   Explain what is stored in the array `Extreme`.   [2]

     iii   Explain what happens in lines 04 to 11.   [3]

     iv   Explain the purpose of the loop in lines 14 to 15.   [1]

d The zoo decides that the computer system needs to be updated. The computer system will now make use of actuators. These actuators will operate devices which adjust the microclimate.

Actuators can be in two states, on or off. Whether an actuator is on or off is determined by a single bit value (0 means off, 1 means on) in a specific 8-bit memory location.

The actuators to control the climate in Tank 4 use memory location 0804. Bit 5 of this memory location controls the heater.

7	6	5	4	3	2	1	0	Bit number
0	0	1	1	0	1	0	1	Value

Use some of the assembly language instructions to write the instructions that will ensure bit 5 of location 0804 is set to 1.

Instruction		Explanation
Opcode	**Operand**	
LDM	#n	Immediate addressing. Load the number n to ACC
LDD	<address>	Direct addressing. Load the contents of the given address to ACC
STO	<address>	Store the contents of ACC at the given address
OUT		Output to the screen the character whose ASCII value is stored in ACC
AND	#n	Bitwise AND operation of the contents of ACC with the operand
AND	<address>	Bitwise AND operation of the contents of ACC with the contents of <address>
XOR	#n	Bitwise XOR operation of the contents of ACC with the operand
OR	#n	Bitwise OR operation of the contents of ACC with the operand

[6]

Cambridge International AS and A Level Computer Science 9608 Specimen paper 3, Q3 2015

PART IV

FURTHER PROBLEM-SOLVING AND PROGRAMMING SKILLS

Computational thinking and problem solving

19.01 Abstraction

What makes computer science different? All the natural sciences deal with the world 'as it is'. The task of the physicist is to understand how the world works by applying the laws of physics – not to invent a world in which these laws apply.

The computer scientist must create **abstractions** of real-world problems which can – through an interface – be understood by computer users and can be represented – by a programmer – inside the computer.

TERMS

Abstraction: a representation of a real-world problem which extracts unnecessary detail

Abstract art is generally meant to be a work that represents something but has limited detail about the real-world object.

TIP

The paradox: Mere mention of the word 'abstract' tends to imply that something is more difficult to understand e.g. abstract algebra (sets and group theory) is more demanding than Form 7 algebra.

'Abstract' for the computer scientist is intended to hide unwanted detail and so to simplify our understanding.

Information hiding

An animal, such as a spaniel, is viewed differently by different users, who have some data or information hidden in their perception of the animal:

- The owner sees it as a loyal friend.
- The vet sees it as a mammal with a known bone structure, health issues and remedies.

In the real world, we take for granted that the detailed complexity of the internal working of some equipment is hidden from us in order for us to use the equipment.

For the design and implementation of computer systems are the same concepts relevant? The answer is 'yes' since,

for a programmer, some code may be useable without a detailed knowledge of its construction.

What has to be known is the interface to access and use the code. Abstraction is the result of **information hiding**.

TERMS

Information hiding: hiding design detail behind an interface

Functions and procedures with an interface

LOOK BACK ≪

Procedures and functions were introduced in Chapter 11.

An interface is a fundamental programming technique which is designed to make procedure and function code 'reusable' and hide the detail of the code (from other programmers, for example).

Progress check 19.01

Study the code in Figure 19.01. The function to search a string has an interface which only requires the programmer to know:

- the name of the string array to be searched
- the required value.

The novice programmer needs no understanding of the code inside the function `SearchStringArray`.

```
139     Private Sub btnDoSearch_Click
140         Dim SearchResult As Integer
141         Dim ThisString As String
142         ThisString = txtThisString.Text
143         If optName.Checked = True Then
144             SearchResult = SearchStringArray(myName, ThisString)
145         Else
146             SearchResult = SearchStringArray(myJob, ThisString)
147         End If
148
149         If SearchResult = 0 Then
150             txtOutput.Text = "NOT FOUND"
151         Else
152             txtOutput.Text = SearchResult
153         End If
154     End Sub
155
156
157     Function SearchStringArray(ByVal ThisStringArray() As String, _
158                               ByVal ThisString As String) As Integer
159         Dim Found As Boolean
160         Dim Posn As Integer
161         Dim FoundPosition As Integer
162
163         Posn = 1
164         Found = False
165         Do
166             If UCase(ThisString) = UCase(ThisStringArray(Posn)) Then
167                 Found = True
168                 FoundPosition = Posn
169             Else
170                 Posn = Posn + 1
171             End If
172
173         Loop Until Found = True Or Posn = UBound(ThisStringArray)
174         If Found = False Then
175             SearchStringArray = 0
176         Else
177             SearchStringArray = FoundPosition
178         End If
179     End Function
```

The SearchStringArray function searches any string array for the value stored in ThisString

Function interface

The programmer only needs to know that the function needs two parameters.

The user of the function doesn't need to know the detail of the code inside the body of the function.

Figure 19.01 Linear search code

The code can be 're-used' to search any string array. The form in Figure 19.02 allows the user to search either an array myJob() or myName(). For example, the user selects 'Search by job' and keys in the job description. The program outputs that the job is found at index position 43.

Figure 19.02 Program execution

Do you understand the code?

1 What is returned from the function?

2 What value is returned from the function when a requested name is not found?

3 What value is used as a loop counter inside the function code?

4 The code uses UBound(). Is UBound() a function, a user-defined function, a procedure or a method?

Object-oriented programming (OOP)

A basic feature of OOP is that much of the detail of how an object works is hidden from the user. Things we want the object to do are made possible by code called 'methods' which operate on an object.

LOOK FORWARD »

OOP gets extensive coverage in Chapter 21 when a number of different programming paradigms are covered.

Facts and rules

A complex system can be implemented with a knowledge base of facts and rules. Software – called the query processor – is available to the user to set goals or queries.

LOOK FORWARD »

This is the basis of the programming paradigm called 'declarative programming'. This is also studied in Chapter 21.

19.02 Algorithms

Binary search algorithm

LOOK BACK «

Chapter 10, section 10.02 introduced data stored in an array. The simplest search algorithm – a linear search – was covered in Chapter 11.

When can we use a binary search?

The data items must be stored in the array in order.

The method is essentially to repeat the following steps until the item is found:

1 Find the middle value and compare the required value with this middle value.

2 If not found then discard either the top half or bottom half of the list.

3 Calculate the new middle and go back to Step 1.

The structured English shows the algorithm in more detail:

```
INPUT the SearchValue
REPEAT
   Find the middle value in the list
   Compare with SearchValue
   IF found
      THEN
         OUTPUT "Found"
      ELSE
         IF SearchValue > current middle value
            THEN
               Discard the current top part of the list
            ELSE
```

```
                   Discard the current bottom part of the list
          ENDIF
     ENDIF
     // start a  new search with a list of half the size
UNTIL found OR there are no items in the list
```

Binary search pseudocode

The algorithm is also called a 'binary chop' as we are successively chopping the list in half before the next new middle value is calculated. The pseudocode algorithm searches the array `ThisArray`(upper bound N) for the value `ThisValue`. The identifiers are in Table 19.01.

Identifier	Data type	Description
ThisArray	ARRAY[1..N] OF STRING	The array of data items
N	INTEGER	Upper bound of `ThisArray`
ThisValue	STRING	The value to search for
Found	BOOLEAN	Flags to True When `ThisValue` is found
Top	INTEGER	Index to the current list
Bottom	INTEGER	Index to the current list
Middle	INTEGER	Index to the current list
NotInList	BOOLEAN	Flags to True when the list to consider is empty

Table 19.01 Identifiers for the binary search algorithm

The following pseudocode implements the algorithm:

```
Top ← N
Bottom  ← 1
REPEAT
    Middle ← Integer value of (Top + Bottom)/2
    IF ThisArray[Middle] = ThisValue
        THEN
            Found ← TRUE
            OUTPUT "Value is FOUND"
        ELSE
            IF Bottom > Top
                THEN
                    NotInList ← TRUE
                ELSE
                  IF ThisArray[Middle] < ThisItem
                    THEN
                        // Retain the top half of the list ...
                        Bottom ← Middle + 1
                    ELSE
                      // Retain the bottom half of the list ...
                      Top ← Middle - 1
                  ENDIF
            ENDIF
    ENDIF
UNTIL (Found = TRUE) OR (NotInList = TRUE)
IF NotInList = TRUE
    THEN
        OUTPUT "Requested item was NOT FOUND"
ENDIF
```

Progress check 19.02

Do you understand the binary search algorithm?

1 What is the condition which compares the requested value with the middle value of the current list?

2 When a new list is about to be set up, is the current middle value included?

3 What condition tests for a new list with no values?

4 When the top half of the current list is retained, which pointer value(s) are changed: `Top` or `Bottom` or both?

Progress check 19.03

Implement the above binary search algorithm with program code in your chosen language. Use a set of test data of 20 cities. Remember they must be stored in array `ThisArray` in order.

Binary search performance

The algorithm is a very efficient one for finding a particular value, since the size of the list is halved on every iteration. This means that for a list with 128 items, it would take at worst, seven comparisons – i.e. forming seven lists – in order to find a value. Compare this algorithm with a linear search where – on average – it would take 64 comparisons for a list with 128 data items.

> **TIP**
>
> The main control structure in the algorithm is a loop – every time a new list is considered, it is a new iteration. The algorithm is a said to have an iterative solution. When we introduce the topic of recursion later in this chapter we shall show a different solution – which does not uses a loop – which is recursive.

Sorting algorithms

Insertion sort

The insertion sort algorithm works as follows:

- Each item in the list is considered in sequence starting with the second.

- A sub-list of sorted items is formed on the left-hand side.

- The right-hand sub-list increases by one as each data value is considered.

The integers in the `MyList` array are to be sorted using the insertion sort algorithm. The original list is in Figure 19.03.

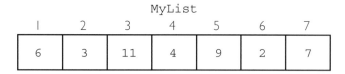

MyList

1	2	3	4	5	6	7
6	3	11	4	9	2	7

Figure 19.03 Unsorted list

The trace table in Figure 19.04 shows the changing position of the items. Row 1 shows the list after the second item (3) has been considered. The next item to be processed is 11.

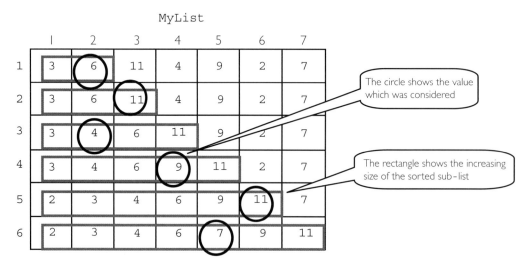

Figure 19.04 Insertion sort processing `MyList`

The identifiers are in Table 19.02.

Identifier	Data type	Description
MyArray	ARRAY[1..N] OF INTEGER	The array of data items
N	INTEGER	Upper bound of ThisArray
CurrentValue	INTEGER	The 'circled value' in the diagram
SortedListPosn	INTEGER	Loop counter for moving through the sub-list
InsertPosn	INTEGER	Index of the insert position in the sub-list
ShufflePosn	INTEGER	Loop counter for the sub-list when all values to the right have to be shuffled up one place
Index	INTEGER	Index of the current item considered
InsertPosnFound	BOOLEAN	Flags to True when position in the sub-list is found

Table 19.02 Identifiers for the insertion sort algorithm

The following pseudocode implements the insertion sort algorithm:

```
// consider all numbers starting with the second
FOR Index 2 TO N
    CurrentValue ← MyList[Index]
    // find the position in the sorted list to insert
    SortedListPosn ← 1
    InsertPosnFound ← FALSE
    REPEAT
        IF CurrentValue > MyList[SortedListPosn]
            THEN
                SortedListPosn ← SortedListPosn + 1
            ELSE
                InsertPosn ← SortedListPosn
                InsertPosnFound ← TRUE
            ENDIF
    UNTIL InsertPosnFound = TRUE
    // current value is to move to InsertPosn
    // and all others on the right shuffle to the right one place
    FOR ShufflePosn ← Index TO [InsertPosn + 1] STEP -1
        MyList[ShufflePosn] ← MyList[ShufflePosn - 1]
        MyList[InsertPosn] ← CurrentValue
    ENDFOR
```

Progress check 19.04

1 Write program code in your chosen language for the above insertion sort algorithm.

2 Draw up a trace table showing the changing contents of the array `MyAnimals` as the insertion sort is applied.

MyAnimals

1	2	3	4	5
DOG	CAT	RAT	EEL	BAT

Bubble sort

LOOK BACK «

This was covered in Chapter 11.

Performance criteria

Different sorting algorithms can be compared in terms of their efficiency. A full study of this would measure each algorithm's efficiency in terms of an 'order of complexity' measure (using the big-O notation) but this is outside the scope of our syllabus.

The number of items to be sorted will be a factor in the total sort time taken. Efficiency can be measured in terms of the total number of comparisons which have to be made in order to complete the sort.

A second criterion for judging algorithms is their space requirement: does the algorithm require memory space in addition to the memory containing the array elements? Study the quick sort and bubble sort algorithms:

- The bubble sort required temporary memory for only a single data item.
- The insertion sort used no additional memory.

Also, the efficiency should be discussed in terms of the worst case (a completely unsorted list), the best case (the original list is already in sorted order) or an average case.

Consider the 'best case' when the original list is already sorted:

- Bubble sort recognises that the list is completely sorted and will stop.
- Insertion sort requires that every item is considered.

Hence the conclusion is that, for a best-case scenario, the bubble sort will be more efficient than the insertion sort.

Stacks

A stack is a dynamic data structure which operates on the principle 'last item added will be the first to leave'. This is often abbreviated to 'last in – first out' or, turned the other way around, 'First in – last out'.

To implement a stack we shall assume an array with lower bound 1 and upper bound N stores the stack's data items. The stack is controlled by a single pointer which is the index position in the array of the item which is currently at the 'top of stack' position. The identifiers are in Table 19.03.

Identifier	Data type	Description
MyStack	ARRAY[1:20] OF INTEGER	Data values in MyStack
TOS	INTEGER	Index position of the MyStack array for the item currently at the top of the stack

Table 19.03 Identifiers for implementing a stack

Figure 19.05 shows the stack after the three items 106, 57 and 44 are added in that order. The first item to leave will be 44. If no items have left, the next new item will be stored at position 4.

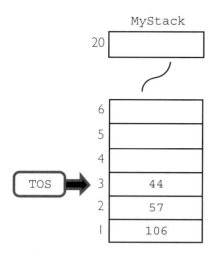

Figure 19.05 Items on a stack

Inserting an item

Inserting an item to a stack is called a 'push' to the stack. The algorithm is straightforward:

1 Check that the stack is not full

2 If space is available, then

3 Increment TOS

4 Input the new item

5 Add the new item at position TOS.

The extra identifier is in Table 19.04.

Identifier	Data type	Description
NewItem	INTEGER	New data item to be added

Table 19.04 New item identifier

The following pseudocode implements the algorithm for inserting into a stack:

```
IF TOS = 21
    THEN
        OUTPUT "Stack is full"
    ELSE
        TOS ← TOS + 1
        INPUT NewItem
        MyStack[TOS] ← NewItem
ENDIF
```

Deleting an item

Removing a item from the stack is called a 'pop' from the stack:

1 Check that the stack is not empty

2 If not, then

3 Output the item at position 'top of stack'

4 Decrement the stack pointer.

Progress check 19.05

Write the pseudocode for the 'delete from stack' algorithm.

Queues

A queue is a dynamic data structure which operates on the principle 'first item added will be the first to leave'. This is often abbreviated to 'first in – first out'.

To implement a queue we assume that an array with lower bound 1 and upper bound N stores the queue's data items. The queue is controlled by two pointers:

• A 'head' pointer points to the current head position of the queue.

• A 'tail' pointer points to the item which is currently at the rear of the queue.

Inserting an item

Consider the queue MyQueue which has 10 cells. The current state of the queue (in Figure 19.06) shows seven items have joined the queue and four have already left. The current queue occupies cells 5 to 7 (that is, its length is three items).

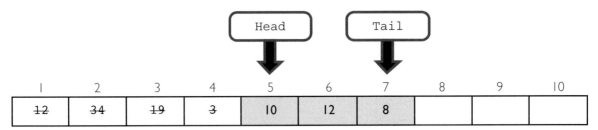

Figure 19.06 Items on a queue

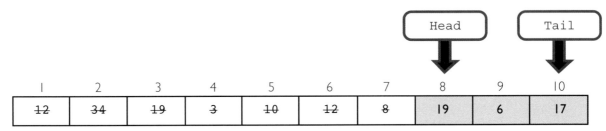

Figure 19.07 More queue changes

The stage will soon be reached where – once three more items have joined the queue – the queue will run out of space. The solution is to make a queue behave as a 'circular queue'. That is, once the `Tail` pointer reaches value 10 and a new value is to be added, `Tail` will be re-set to index 1.

Figure 19.07 shows the queue after more values have left and three new values have joined the queue. All the initial space is now used up.

Progress check 19.06

1 Draw the array and pointers for the initially empty queue.

2 In Figure 19.07, an item is about to leave the queue:

   a Which item is this?

   b What pointer change is required?

3 A new item is to join the queue. How will the algorithm know the position at which to store the value?

If a new value attempts to join the queue in Figure 19.07, we could store it at position 1. After three more items – 23, 89 and 41 – join, the state of the queue is as shown in Figure 19.08.

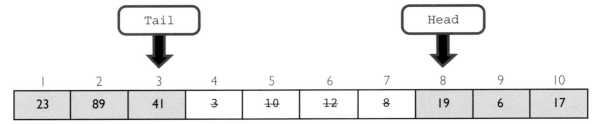

Figure 19.08 More changes – queue is now 'circular'

The queue is effectively the list of values: 19, 6, 17, 23, 89 and 41 (in that order).

We now have a situation where `Tail` < `Head`. This will indicate that the queue is currently in a circular state.

The following Visual Basic .NET code adds an item to a queue of size 6:

```
29 ⊟   Sub QueueJoin()
30         Dim NewItem As Integer
31         If (Head = 1 And Tail = 6) Or (Head = Tail + 1) Then
32           Console.WriteLine("Queue is already FULL - OVERFLOW")
33         Else
34           If Tail = 0 Then
35             Head = 1
36             Tail = 1
37           Else
38             If Tail = 6 Then
39               Tail = 1
40             Else
41               Tail = Tail + 1
42             End If
43           End If
44           Console.Write("New Item ... ") : NewItem = Console.ReadLine
45           Queue(Tail) = NewItem
46         End If
```

Deleting an item

The following Visual Basic .NET code removes an item from a queue of size 6:

```
51 ⊟   Sub QueueLeave()
52         If Head = 0 Then
53           Console.WriteLine("Queue is EMPTY")
54         Else
55           Console.WriteLine("Deleted was ..." + Str(Queue(Head)))
56           If Head = Tail Then
57             Head = 0
58             Tail = 0
59           Else
60             If Head = 6 Then
61               Head = 1
62             Else
63               Head = Head + 1
64             End If
65           End If
66         End If
```

Progress check 19.07

Do you understand the queue algorithms?

1 For the `QueueJoin()` procedure:

   a What line number tests for a full queue?

   b Describe the condition which tests for a full queue.

   c Which line number tests for the queue 'going circular'?

2 For the `QueueLeave()` procedure:

   a What condition tests for an empty queue?

   b At line 56, how many items are in the queue when the condition Head = Tail is True?

3 Write program code in your chosen language to Implement a queue simulation (size six). Drive the project from a main menu with options:

   1 Initialise queue

   2 Add item

   3 Remove Item.

Display the state of Head, Tail and the queue contents after each change, as in this screenshot:

```
Head:    1
Tail:    3
45  78  91   0   0   0

<1>    Initialise queue
<2>    Add item
<3>    Delete item
<4>    Exit
3
Deleted was ... 45

Head:    2
Tail:    3
45  78  91   0   0   0

<1>    Initialise queue
<2>    Add item
<3>    Delete item
<4>    Exit
```

Linked lists

A linked list is a data structure consisting of a set of nodes. Each node consists of the data value and a link pointer to one of the other nodes. The purpose of the linked-list structure is to link the nodes in some particular order – for example, alphabetical order of the data items.

We could implement a linked list where the data and link values are stored as two 1D arrays, as shown in Table 19.05.

Identifier	Data type	Description
Data	ARRAY[1..20] OF STRING	The data value for the nodes
Link	ARRAY[1..20] OF INTEGER	The link pointer value for the nodes
Start	INTEGER	The index of the node which is at the start of the linked list

Table 19.05 Identifiers for a linked list

LOOK BACK «

The various built-in data types were introduced and used extensively in Part 2.

To implement our linked list, we would like a type of data which consists of a string value (for the data value) and an integer value (for the link pointer).

This is possible. We can construct a new 'user-defined data type' made up of two or more of the built-in data types. The new data structure will be given an identifier name. The pseudocode is:

```
TYPE <identifer1>
    DECLARE <identifer2> : <data type>
    DECLARE <identifer3> : <data type>
    :
ENDTYPE
```

So for our linked list implementation, we can construct a Node data type:

```
TYPE Node
    DECLARE Data : STRING
    DECLARE Link : INTEGER
ENDTYPE
```

Note: We shall not use the data structures suggested in Table 19.05.

We shall have as many as 20 node values. We declare an array of data type `LinkedList` which uses our `Node` data type to implement the linked list, as shown in Table 19.06.

Identifier	Data type	Description
`LinkedList`	`ARRAY[1..20] OF Node`	The list of nodes

Table 19.06 Array identifier for a linked list

Figure 19.09 shows the data values stored in the arrays. Figure 19.10 shows the conceptual linked list which is created by the link pointers.

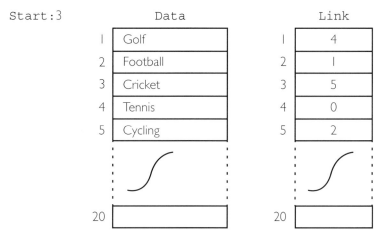

Figure 19.09 Items added to the linked list

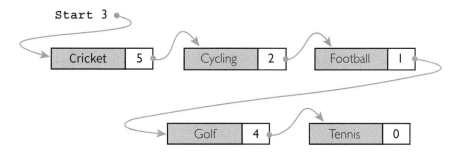

Figure 19.10 Conceptual linked list

There is some detail needed here. The program would need to know at this stage that the next available 'free' array position is 6. One strategy for this is to initialise the linked list as a linked set of nodes with the start point initially showing zero.

Progress check 19.08

The following values join a linked list data structure in the order shown:

> LONDON, AMSTERDAM, NEW DELHI, DHAKA, SINGAPORE and NEW YORK.

The data values are stored in array `City` with link pointers in array `Link` and a pointer `Start` to the first node in the list.

Show the contents of the two arrays and the current state of the linked list.

Finding an item

This algorithm is straightforward:

1 Input the required value

2 Look at the node pointed to by the start pointer

3 If found, output data value of this node

4 Else

5 Using the link pointer, move to the next node

6 Repeat moving up through the list until found, or we have reached the end of the list (Link = 0).

The extra identifiers required are in Table 19.07.

Identifier	Data type	Description
ThisItem	STRING	The item to search for
Found	BOOLEAN	Flags to TRUE when found
Current	INTEGER	Index of the current node considered

Table 19.07 Identifiers for finding an item in a linked list

The following pseudocode algorithm uses the array of nodes:

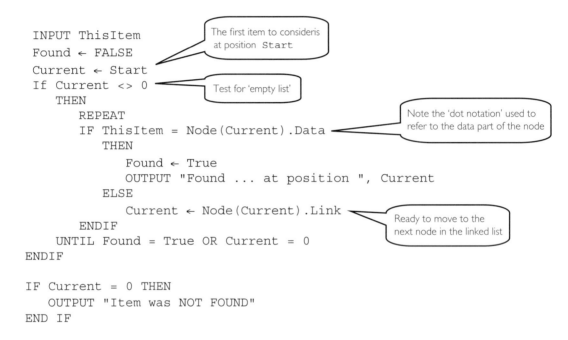

```
INPUT ThisItem
Found ← FALSE                    [The first item to consider is at position Start]
Current ← Start
If Current <> 0                  [Test for 'empty list']
    THEN
        REPEAT
        IF ThisItem = Node(Current).Data    [Note the 'dot notation' used to refer to the data part of the node]
            THEN
                Found ← True
                OUTPUT "Found ... at position ", Current
            ELSE
                Current ← Node(Current).Link    [Ready to move to the next node in the linked list]
        ENDIF
    UNTIL Found = True OR Current = 0
ENDIF

IF Current = 0 THEN
    OUTPUT "Item was NOT FOUND"
END IF
```

Inserting an item

Figure 19.11 shows an item being added to the linked list in Figure 19.10.

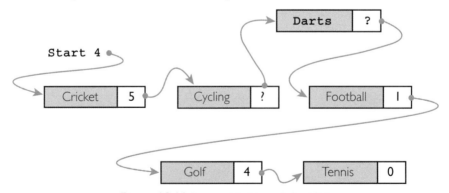

Figure 19.11 Item added to a linked list

The insert algorithm is:

1 Traverse the list until we find the first node which is greater than the insert item (i.e., Football). That establishes the new item is to be inserted between Cycling and Football.

2 Store the data value (Darts) at the next free location (6).

3 Adjust the link pointers:

- The pointer for Darts is the current Cycling pointer.

- The pointer for Cycling becomes 6.

There are special cases which must be considered:

- The linked list could be empty.

- The new node could become the new start of the list.

The following pseudocode implements the algorithm:

```
IF NextFree = 0
    THEN
        OUTPUT "REFUSED - list is full"          Is the linked list full?
    ELSE
        INPUT NewItem
        Node[NextFree].Data ← NewItem
    IF Start = 0
        THEN                                     Is the linked list empty?
            Start ← NextFree
            Temp ← Node[NextFree].Link           NextFree is the index
            Node[NextFree].Link ← 0              of the next available cell
            NextFree ← Temp
        ELSE
            // traverse the list - starting at Start to find
            // the position at which to insert the new item
            Temp ← Node[NextFree].Link
            IF NewItem < Node[Start).Data
                THEN
                    // new item will become the start of the list
                    NodeNext[Free].Link ← Start
                    Start ← NextFree
                    NextFree ← Temp
                ELSE
                    // the new item is not at the start of the list
                    Previous ← 0
                    Current ← Start
                    Found ← FALSE
                    REPEAT
                        IF NewItem <= Node[Current].Data
                            THEN
                                Node[Previous].Link ← NextFree
                                Node[NextFree].Link ← Current

                                Found ← TRUE
                            ELSE    NextFree ← Temp
                                // move to the next node
                                Previous ← Current
                                Current ← Node(Current].Link
                        ENDIF
                    UNTIL Found = True OR Current = 0
                    IF Current = 0                        New item is at the
                        THEN                              end of the linked list
                            Node[Previous].Link ← NextFree
                            Node[NextFree].Link ← 0
                            NextFree ← Temp
                    ENDIF
            ENDIF
    ENDIF
ENDIF
```

Deleting an item

Consider the original items (Figure 19.10). The task is to delete Golf from the linked list. A change will be made to the pointers, as shown in Figure 19.12.

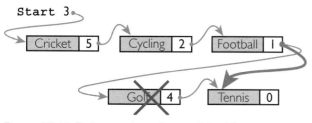

Figure 19.12 Delete an item from a linked list

The algorithm is:

1 Input the item to delete

2 Traverse the list until found

3 Make the pointer change: the pointer of the previous node (Football's pointer) now points to the node pointed to by the deleted item (Tennis).

A special case is when the item to delete is the first in the list.

Binary trees

A binary tree is a data structure – similar to a linked list – which links nodes together. A tree node consists of:

- the data value
- a left pointer to link to a descendant node
- a right pointer to link to a descendant node.

Tree terminology

Figure 19.13 shows a tree with five nodes; the values were inserted to the tree in the order: COURGETTE, SWEDE, PARSNIP, ARTICHOKE and TURNIP.

TERMS

Root: the first item to join the tree is the root value

Left sub-tree: all values to the left of the root form a sub-tree

Right sub-tree: all values to the right of the root form a sub-tree

Leaf node: a node value which has no descendants

The tree was formed as follows:

- COURGETTE is the first item, so becomes the **root**.

- Add SWEDE: compare SWEDE with COURGETTE and place to its right; link from COURGETTE.

- Add PARSNIP:
  o compare with COURGETTE and move right
  o then compare with SWEDE and place to the left
  o linvk from SWEDE.

- Add ARTICHOKE:
  o compare with the COURGETTE and place to the left
  o link from COURGETTE.

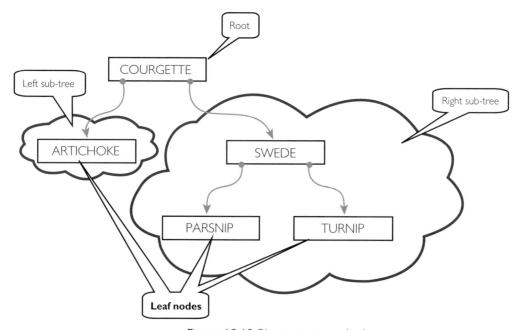

Figure 19.13 Binary tree terminology

- Add TURNIP:
  - o compare with COURGETTE and move right
  - o compare with SWEDE place to the right
  - o link from SWEDE.

Implementing the binary tree

The choice is either:

- three 1D arrays, for the data value, left pointers and right pointers

- a new data structure consisting of the three data items.

We shall use three 1D arrays as shown in Table 19.08.

Identifier	Data type	Description
TreeData	ARRAY [100] OF STRING	The data values
LeftPointer	ARRAY [100] OF INTEGER	The left pointer value for each node
RightPointer	ARRAY [100] OF INTEGER	The right pointer value for each node
Root	INTEGER	Index position of the root node

Table 19.08 Identifiers for a binary tree

For the tree in Figure 19.13, the data stored in the arrays and `Root` is shown in Figure 19.14.

Progress check 19.09

The following values join a binary tree data structure in the order shown: NEW YORK, ISTANBUL, SINGAPORE, LONDON, PARIS, CANBERRA, MOSCOW.

1 Draw the conceptual tree.

2 The tree data is stored in three 1D arrays: `Data`, `LeftP` and `RightP`. Show the contents of the three arrays and the root value.

Finding an item

The algorithm is straightforward:

1 Input the search item.

2 Current value is at Root. Repeat until found or there are no descendants to consider:

   a   If Current value = Search item then Found

   b   Else If search Item < Current value

   c   Then move left

   d   Else move right.

Root: 1

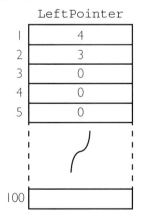
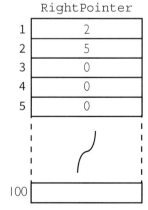

Figure 19.14 Binary tree data

Inserting an item

We shall need to check for the special cases:

• the tree is empty

• there is space available for a new item.

The algorithm will traverse the tree to locate the right or left position at which to insert the new value. The additional variables are shown in Table 19.09.

Identifier	Data type	Description
NewTreeItem	STRING	The item joining the binary tree
NextFree	INTEGER	Index of the next free array cell
Previous	INTEGER	Previous array position visited in the traversal
Current	INTEGER	Current value visited in the traversal
LastMove	CHAR	Indicates the last move in the traversal: • L – left • R – right • X – no previous move

Table 19.09 Identifiers for inserting into a binary tree

The following pseudocode implements the algorithm:

```
IF NextFreePosition > 100                    Test for binary tree full
    THEN
        OUTPUT "No more values can be added"
    ELSE
        INPUT NewTreeItem
        IF Root = 0                          Test for linked list is empty
            THEN
                Root ← NextFree
            ELSE
                // traverse the tree to find the position for the new value
                Current ← Root
                LastMove ← 'X'
                REPEAT
                    Previous ← Current
                    IF NewTreeItem < TreeData[Current]
                        THEN
                            // move left
                            LastMove ← 'L'
                            Current ← LeftPointer[Current]
                        ELSE
                            // move right
                            LastMove ← 'R'
                            Current ← RightPointer[Current]
                    ENDIF
                UNTIL Current = 0

                IF LastMove = 'R'
                    THEN
                        RightPointer[Previous] ← NextFree
                    ELSE
                        IF LastMove = 'L'
                            THEN
                                LeftPointer[Previous] ← NextFree
                        ENDIF
                ENDIF
                NextFree ← NextFree + 1
        ENDIF
ENDIF
```

Hash tables

A hash table is used to store data items in a table. The method for storing a data item (for example, a surname) is:

- A hashing function calculates from the surname – using a hashing function – a key number.

- This number acts as the index used in an associative array.

- The name is stored at this index position, together with the other data items for this name.

The hash table is a mechanism for 'looking up' a name from the hash table.

Inserting an item

A dataset of customer names and other data is to be stored in a hash table. The key for the hashing function is the customer name. There will be about 500 customers.

The hashing algorithm works as follows:

1 Look up the ASCII code for each character.

2 Calculate the total.

3 Divide the total by 503.

4 The remainder is the hash table index.

Figure 19.15 shows an example of inserting the name Piper into a hash table.

The choice of 503 was the first prime number which is greater than the anticipated number of entries in the hash table.

A possible problem is that two different surnames could 'hash' to the same key index. We need to have a strategy for dealing with this. The simplest would be to search the table for the first unoccupied position after an index that already has a dataset at this index position. This method is called 'linear probing' or 'open addressing'.

The hashing function can be given an identifier name. Then the hashing operation to generate a key is expressed as:

```
Index ← MyHashingFunction(<surname>)
```

> **TIP**
>
> The hash table data structure is essentially what the Python programming language implements as a data structure called a dictionary.
>
> Visual Basic has two variations on this: a data structure called an ArrayList and second data structure called a HashTable. Like the Python dictionary, the HashTable stores two values: a key which is used to access the data and the data value.
>
> The dictionary abstract data type is discussed later in this chapter.

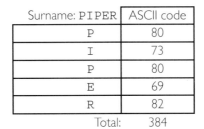

Surname: PIPER	ASCII code
P	80
I	73
P	80
E	69
R	82

Total: 384

Divide by 503... Remainder: 384

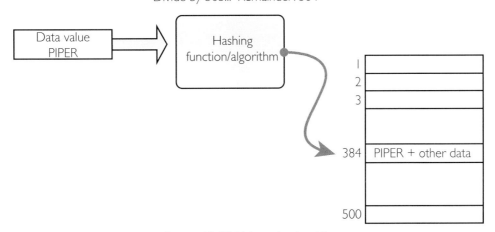

Figure 19.15 Using a hash table

Choice of hashing function

There are two issues:

- We need a function which will keep to a minimum the number of duplicate keys.

- The function should generate an appropriate range of keys.

In the example above, if we anticipate that there will be 500 hash table entries, then ideally the keys generated will be in the range of 1 to 500.

Finding an item

If the key is known, then it can directly access the correct entry in the hash table. In our example, the key was calculated from the data value and then the data can be accessed at this index position.

19.03 Abstract data types

What is an ADT?

An abstract data type is a collection of data items together with operations which act on that data. When we study object-oriented programming (OOP), we shall see that an abstract data type is implemented as a class. The data items are properties of the class and various methods are defined and available to act on an instance of the class.

A stack as an ADT

We create a class that knows how to initialise, pop from and push onto the stack:

```
CLASS StackOOP
    PRIVATE
        TopOfStack : INTEGER
        StackData  : ARRAY[1:20] OF STRING

    PUBLIC
        PROCEDURE InitialiseStack
            DECLARE i : INTEGER
            FOR i ← 1 TO 20
                StackData[i] ← 0
            ENDFOR
            TopOfStack ← 0
        ENDPROCEDURE

        PROCEDURE Push(NewItem : STRING)
            IF TopOfStack = 20
                THEN
                    OUTPUT "Stack is already FULL"
                ELSE
                    TopOfStack ← TopOfStack + 1
                    StackData[TopOfStack]← NewItem
            ENDIF
        ENDPROCEDURE

        PROCEDURE Pop
            // this is Progress check 19.05
        ENDPROCEDURE
ENDCLASS
```

Properties of the class:
- TopOfStack
- Stackdata array

Methods of the class:
- Initialise
- Push
- Pop

The programmer would create a stack object `MyStack` as an instance of `StackOOP`. A typical sequence would then be:

- Initialise the stack.

- Add (push) to the stack two values, for example, 376 followed by 208.

- Remove an item (pop) from the stack.

The programmer would write code as follows:

```
MyStack = StackOOP.Initialise
MyStack.Push(376)
MyStack.Push(208)
MyStack.Pop
```

The use of the class effectively hides the data (that the stack is implemented as a 1D array and is controlled by the `TopOfStack` pointer) and the methods from the programmer.

Other structures as ADTs

This 'data hiding' could similarly be implemented for other data structures we have studied.

Queue
An object, `MyQueue`, would require methods:

- `MyQueue.Initialise`

- `MyQueue.Add(<data item>)`

- `MyQueue.Remove`

Linked list
An object, `MyList`, would require methods:

- `MyList.Initialise`

- `MyList.Add(<data item>)`

- `MyList.Remove(<data item>)`

- `MyList.FindItem(<data item>)`

Binary tree
An object, `MyTree`, would require methods:

- `MyTree.Initialise`

- `MyTree.Add(<data item>)`

- `MyTree.Remove(<data item>)`

- `MyTree.FindItem(<data item>)`

Dictionary
An object, `MyDictionary`, would require methods:

- `MyDictionary.Initialise`

- `MyDictionary.Add(<data item>)`

- `MyDictionary.Remove(<data item>)`

- `MyDictionary.FindItem(<data item>)`

Progress check 19.10

Explain why the tree `Add` method has a parameter value, but the queue `Remove` method does not.

Alternative representation for a stack
The ADT could describe the operation with the data structure then passed as a parameter.

Consider the following ADT which operates on a stack data structure and has the following defined methods:

- `Create(ThisStack)` creates an empty stack with identifier `ThisStack`.

- `Insert(ThisStack, PushItem)` pushes new item `PushItem` onto the stack `ThisStack`.

- `Remove(ThisStack)` pops the next item from `ThisStack`.

- `Empty(ThisStack)` returns `TRUE` if `ThisStack` is empty.

Progress check 19.11

Describe the data structures after the following sequence of operations:

```
Create(Stack1)
Create(Stack2)
Insert(Stack1, "Football")
Insert(Stack2, "Cricket")
Insert(Stack1, "Boxing")
Insert(Stack2, "Netball")
Remove(Stack2)
IsEmpty(Stack1)
```

19.04 Recursion

A binary tree has the basic idea of recursion – we can think of the structure as a number of trees which are contained as part of a tree at a higher level. Consider the tree from Figure 19.13 in this way. The leaf nodes should be thought of a tree with no left or right sub-tree, as shown in Figure 19.16.

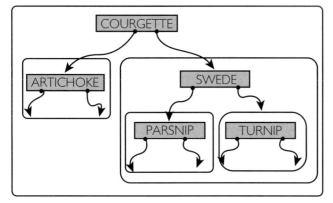

Figure 19.16 Binary trees and recursion

Recursion is not an easy concept to grasp. A recursive procedure is:

- one which is defined in terms of itself

- a procedure or function which calls itself.

Coded as a function, there must be a stopping condition to make the recursion terminate.

For example, in maths the 'factorial of number N' (written as N!) is defined as:

$$N! = N \times (N - 1) \times (N - 2) \times ... \times 3 \times 2 \times 1$$

$$\text{Factorial } 5 = 5 \times \text{Factorial } 4.$$

This fits with the definition 'defined in terms of itself'. Designed as a function `Factorial` would have a single parameter, i.e. the number, and is defined as follows:

```
FUNCTION Factorial(ThisNumber)
    IF ThisNumber = 1
        THEN
            RETURN 1
        ELSE
            RETURN ThisNumber *
                Factorial(ThisNumber - 1)
    ENDIF
ENDFUNCTION
```

LOOK BACK «

In the section on binary trees, we hinted that we could develop an entirely different algorithm which did not use a loop.

Binary search

This 'feels' like it could have a recursive solution since we are repeatedly forming a new (smaller) list to search from within the current list. The stopping condition is that the search item is found or the item is not in the list, as in this pseudocode:

```
PROCEDURE BinarySearch
   INPUT ThisValue
   Found  ← FALSE
   NotInList  ← FALSE
   // flags if the required value is not found
   Top   ← N
   Bottom  ← 1
   REPEAT
      Middle  ← Integer value of (Top + Bottom)/2
      IF ThisArray[Middle] = ThisValue
         THEN
            Found ← TRUE
            OUTPUT "Value is FOUND"
         ELSE
            IF Bottom > Top
               THEN
                  NotInList ← TRUE
               ELSE
                  IF ThisArray[Middle] < ThisItem
                     THEN
                        // retain the top half of the list
                        Bottom ← Middle + 1
                     ELSE
                        // retain the bottom half of the list
                        Top ← Middle – 1
                  ENDIF
            ENDIF
      ENDIF
   UNTIL (Found = TRUE) OR (NotInList = TRUE)
   IF NotInList = TRUE
      THEN
         OUTPUT "Requested item was NOT FOUND"
   ENDIF
ENDPROCEDURE
```

Tree traversal algorithms

To output the values in order from a binary tree required that we visit the nodes in some defined order.

Consider the tree in Figure 19.17.

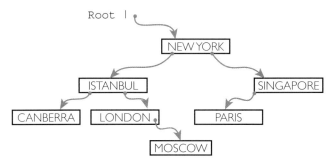

Figure 19.17 Binary tree data

The thinking would be as follows:

• Go to the root

• If there is a left node then move left

• Repeat moving left until the left pointer is Null

• OUTPUT the current value

• Move back to the Root – OUTPUT the root of this sub-tree

• If there is a right node – move right.

We can visualise this as moving through a sequence of sub-trees. Each sub-tree is dealt with in the order:

• Move left (if possible)

• OUTPUT the root

• Move right (if possible).

The algorithm is recursive as we are continually dealing with a sub-tree, and often have to leave the completion of the current tree (left – root – right) until later when we return to this tree.

The algorithm for the tree traversal follows. It assumes that the root of a tree or sub-tree is passed as parameter `Root`:

```
PROCEDURE InOrderTraversal(Root)
    IF Root.LeftPointer <> Null
        THEN
            // move left
            InOrderTraversal(Root.LeftPointer)
    ENDIF
    OUTPUT Root.Data
    IF Root.RightPointer <> Null
        THEN
            // move right
            InOrderTraversal(Root.RightPointer)
    ENDIF
ENDPROCEDURE
```

> This is a line which shows the procedure is recursive: it is calling itself.

> And again …

The algorithm is elegant requiring very few statements. Visiting the nodes in this order – which outputs the data values in order – is called an 'in-order' tree traversal. The order of the procedure calls is illustrated in Figure 19.18. The arrows show when a call is completed and the algorithm returns to a previous call. This process is called 'unwinding'.

```
Tree(NEW YORK)
    // Move left
    Tree(ISTANBUL)
        // Move left
        Tree(CANBERRA)
            // nothing to the left
            OUTPUT CANBERRA
            // nothing to the right
        ENDPROCEDURE
        OUTPUT ISTANBUL
        // Move right
        Tree(LONDON)
            // nothing to the left
            OUTPUT LONDON
            // Move right
            Tree(MOSCOW)
                // nothing to the left
                OUTPUT MOSCOW
                // nothing to the right
            ENDPROCEDURE
        ENDPROCEDURE
    ENDPROCEDURE
    OUTPUT NEW YORK
    // Move right
    Tree (SINGAPORE)
        // Move left
        Tree (PARIS)
            // nothing to the left
            OUTPUT PARIS
            // nothing to the right
        ENDPROCEDURE
        OUTPUT SINGAPORE
        // nothing to the right
    ENDPROCEDURE
ENDPROCEDURE
```

Figure 19.18 In-order traversal trace

Infix expressions

A binary tree can be used to represent an infix expression. Consider the following expression:

$$(x + y) / z^3$$

This can be expanded to include the 'to the power of' operator to read:

$(x + y) / z\hat{\ }3$

Figure 19.19 illustrates the infix expression as a binary tree.

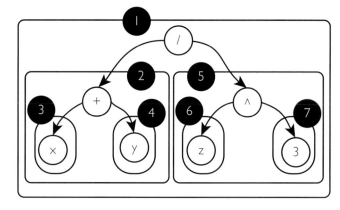

Figure 19.19 Infix expression as a binary tree

We can use the in-order traversal algorithm to trace the above tree. The output is shown in Table 19.10. The black cicles refer to the order in which the `Tree()` calls are made.

New Tree() call	Comment	Tree root	OUTPUT
1		/	
2		+	
3		×	×
	Unwind to tree 3	+	+
4		y	y
	Unwind to tree 1	/	/
5		^	
6		z	z
	Unwind to tree 5	^	^
7			3

Table 19.10 Trace table for expression as tree in Figure 19.19

Post-order traversal

The order can be changed. Consider a traversal of the tree doing:

- Move left (if possible)
- Move right (if possible)
- OUTPUT the root

This is called a 'post-order traversal'.

LOOK BACK «

There is a practical application of a post-order traversal when we studied reverse Polish notation in Chapter 16.

Progress check 19.12

Draw the binary tree for the expression:

a t × 1 2 / t 2 ^ × +

A compiler implementing recursion

Every time a new function/procedure call is made, the compiler must remember this return point in the current call. These return points and the arguments for the call must be stored and retrieved using 'last return point stored will be the first to be retrieved' (i.e. 'last in – first out'), so we need a stack.

Each time a new call is made the compiler transfers control to the procedure/function. When the method returns, it pops these values off the stack. The arguments then effectively disappear and the control returns to the return address.

There is the danger that after many calls that the stack space could be full and generate a 'stack overflow' error.

The general plus-point about recursive methods is that recursive solutions tend to require fewer steps for the algorithm and therefore less code.

Summary

- Abstraction is implemented with data hiding behind program interfaces.

- A binary search is an efficient search algorithm. A solution can be designed which is either iterative or recursive.

- Sorting is a key requirement for many applications. Two such algorithms are the insertion sort and the bubble sort.

- The performance of different sorting algorithms can be compared.

- Various abstract data types (ADT) include: stack, queue, linked list, binary tree, hash table.

- An ADT is a set of data items and operations which are performed on the data.

- A 'record' user-defined type can be constructed from the built-in data types of the language.

- A compiler will use recursion.

- Algorithms should be studied for the combinations of data structure and processing shown in Table 19.11.

Data structure	Find item	Insert item	Delete item
Stack		✓	✓
Queue		✓	✓
Linked list	✓	✓	✓
Binary tree	✓	✓	
Hash table	✓	✓	

Table 19.11 Summary of data structures and processing

Exam-style questions

1 A linked list Abstract Data Type (ADT) has these associated operations.

- Create linked list

- Add item to linked list

- Remove item from linked list

Each node in a linked list consists of data and a pointer to the next item in the linked list. Items in the linked list are maintained in order.

a A linked list is to be set up that stores names in alphabetical order. Show the final state of this linked list after the following operations are carried out.

```
CreateLinkedList

AddItem("Nushie")

AddItem("Kellie")

AddItem("Scarlett")

RemoveItem("Nushie")

AddItem("Jon")
```
[2]

b A programming language provides built-in array data structures. This linked list is to be implemented using these array data structures.

Define a record type, `ListNode`, for each node. [3]

c Write an array declaration to reserve space for 50 nodes in array `NameList`. [2]

d **i** The `CreateLinkedList` operation links all nodes to form the free list and initialises the `HeadPointer` and `FreePointer`.

Complete the diagram to show the value of all pointers.

HeadPointer

FreePointer

NameList

	Name	Pointer
[1]		
[2]		
[3]		
[4]		
:		
[49]		
[50]		

[4]

ii Write **pseudocode** to implement the `CreateLinkedList` operation. [2]

Cambridge International AS and A Level Computer Science 9608 Specimen Paper 4, Q3 a – d 2015

Algorithm design methods

20.01 Decision tables

A **decision table** is a tool for documenting complicated logic which is part of some business problem. The aim is to state all combinations of conditions and the outcomes which result.

TERMS

Decision table: a table used to express complicated logic

The decision table should be thought of as two parts:

- the conditions, which each have a True or False outcome.

- the possible outcomes.

The table then forms a grid where the outcomes can be shown for all possible combinations of conditions (see Figure 20.01).

If the problem was to be implemented as a computer program, the conditions would be the tests or questions asked by the code and implemented with IF–THEN–ELSE structures. The action entries would be procedures or operations which the program must perform.

For example, we need to monitor the progress of a software project. If the project is behind schedule, more programmers may be allocated (see Figure 20.02).

A credit customer places an order with a company. The company must decide whether or not to accept the order (see Figure 20.03).

This table is quite complex and we want to consider whether the table can be simplified.

TIP

The syllabus states that a table will have at most three conditions.

Condition(s)		
Are you hungry?	Y	N
Action(s)		
Get a meal	Y	

Decision table has one condition only

Figure 20.01 Simple decision table

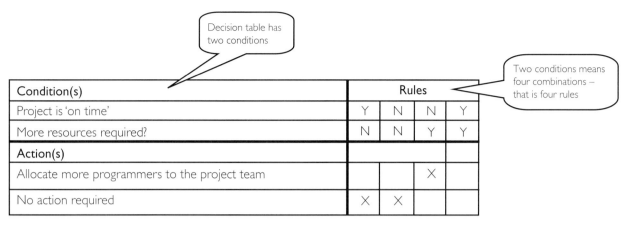

Figure 20.02 Decision table with four outcomes

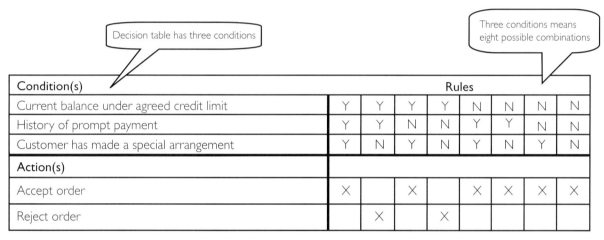

Figure 20.03 Decision table with eight outcomes

Simplification of the decision table

Figure 20.04 is similar to Figure 20.03. The rules have been numbered for easy reference.

Condition(s) Rules >	1	2	3	4	5	6	7	8
Current balance under agreed credit limit	Y	Y	Y	Y	N	N	N	N
History of prompt payment	Y	Y	N	N	Y	Y	N	N
Customer has made a special arrangement	Y	N	Y	N	Y	N	Y	N
Action(s)								
Accept order	X	–	X		X	X	X	X
Reject order	–	X	–	X	–	–	–	–

Figure 20.04 Can the table be simplified?

The simplification rule is 'look for two rules which have:

- the same action
- the same entry in all condition rows, except one
- this exception row has one Y and one N entry.

We can apply this rule to Figure 20.04 and combine rules as shown in Figure 20.05. Rules 1 and 2 cannot be simplified as they have a different action but we can simplify rules 7 and 8, rules 5 and 6, rules 1 and 3 and rules 2 and 4.

Condition(s) Rules >	1/3	2/4	5/6	7/8
Current balance under agreed credit limit	Y	Y	N	N
History of prompt payment	–	–	Y	N
Customer has made a special arrangement	Y	N	–	–
Action(s)				
Accept order	X	–	X	X
Reject order	–	X	–	–

Figure 20.05 Simplified table

However, consider the final two columns of Figure 20.05. A further simplification is possible: the final two columns consolidate as shown in Figure 20.06 (re-numbered rules).

Condition(s) Rules >	1	2	3
Current balance under agreed credit limit	Y	Y	N
History of prompt payment	–	–	–
Customer has made a special arrangement	Y	N	–
Action(s)			
Accept order	X	–	X
Reject order	–	X	–

Figure 20.06 Further simplification

Conclusion: since row 2 is all dashes, the condition 'history of prompt payment' is irrelevant and so this condition should be removed, as shown in Figure 20.07.

Condition(s) Rules >	1	2	3
Current balance under agreed credit limit	Y	Y	N
Customer has made a special arrangement	Y	N	–
Action(s)			
Accept order	X	–	X
Reject order	–	X	–

Figure 20.07 Final decision table

Progress check 20.01

Return to the decision table in Figure 20.02. Show the simplified table.

A completeness check

How do we know we have all the rules?

At the start this was clear: from the math, three conditions gives eight rules because $8 = 2^{\text{the number of conditions}}$.

For a table which has been simplified and contains dashes, the following calculation (applied to Figure 20.06 in Figure 20.08) allows you to check:

1 Count the number of dashes in each column.

2 Raise 2 to the power of the number of dashes in each column.

3 Total the values for the columns.

Applying this to Figure 20.06, we get a total of 8 (2^3, where three is the number of conditions).

Condition(s) Rules >	1	2	3
Current balance under agreed credit limit	Y	Y	N
History of prompt payment	–	–	–
Customer has made a special arrangement	Y	N	–
Number of dashes >	1	1	2

Figure 20.08 Checking for completeness

We can do the same calculation for the final table in Figure 20.07 (see Figure 20.09):

$$\text{Total} = 2^0 + 2^0 + 2^1 = 1 + 1 + 2 = 4 = 2^2 \text{ (where two is the number of conditions)}$$

Condition(s) Rules >	1	2	3
Current balance under agreed credit limit	Y	Y	N
Customer has made a special arrangement	Y	N	–
Number of dashes >	0	0	1

Figure 20.09 Final table

Progress check 20.02

1 A works uses chemicals requested by members of staff. Chemicals are sometimes unavailable. Some chemicals are hazardous and can only be given to staff who are trained to use them.

Complete and simplify the decision table.

Condition(s) Rules >	1	2	3	4	5	6	7	8
Chemical is available								
Chemical is hazardous								
Staff is trained								
Action(s)								
Issue chemicals								
Reject request								

2 A family books a holiday and may or may not have to pay for the one child who will be travelling.

- If the holiday price for the two adults is over $1000 the child goes free.

- If the child is aged 3 or under and the destination country is the USA they travel free.

a Construct the decision table.

b Simplify the decision table.

20.02 Jackson Structured Programming (JSP)

JSP is a formal methodology used for program design. However, the method focussed first on the data which is to be processed by the program – not the processing itself.

> **TERMS**
>
> **Jackson Structured Programming (JSP) diagram:** describes data to be processed by a program

> **TIP**
>
> The terms used will be the same as those used for program design – selection, sequence and iteration. However, you should be clear that these terms are describing the data. For example if a customer record will contain many transactions, we can describe this as the customer transaction data being iterated for each customer record.

Data items or components

The following symbol is used in a JSP data structure diagram to represent a data item or component.

Figure 20.10 shows a sequence of data items which can be presented in the order shown. It could show that a customer's data consists of the Customer name (A), followed by their address (B), followed by their credit rating (C).

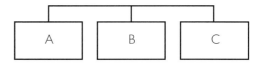

Figure 20.10 Sequence of components

If X represents the Customer, the JSP diagram becomes Figure 20.11.

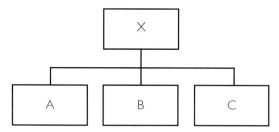

Figure 20.11 Customer data sequence

Progress check 20.03

A gym member, GYM-MEMBER, data record consists of:

- a membership number, MemberNo
- their name, MemName
- the membership type, MemType
- their renewal date, RenewDate.

Draw the JSP data structure diagram.

Selection

The following symbol is used in a JSP data structure diagram to represent 'selection'. Again, remember this is 'data selection' – not selection about what program code must be executed.

A record is kept of all gym classes available. The GYM-CLASS data consists of the leader, the activity and the level (B for beginner, I for intermediate and A for Advanced). Figure 20.12 shows the JSP data structure diagram.

Some gym classes also have recorded a final data value for a 'reserve leader'. Figure 20.13 shows the second level has a new component added with two alternatives:

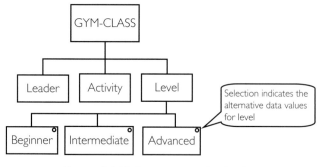

Figure 20.12 Sequence and selection

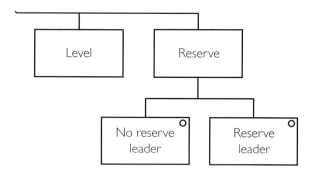

Figure 20.13 Selection with a null component

The 'No reserve leader' is a null component and can be omitted from the diagram as shown in Figure 20.14.

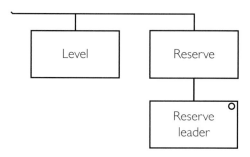

Figure 20.14 Omit the null component

Iteration

The following symbol is used in a JSP data structure diagram to represent 'iteration'. Again, remember this is 'data iteration' – not program code executed inside a loop.

A register (CLASS-REGISTER) is kept for each gym class. It contains the name of the activity, the date and the list of members attending (MEMBER-LIST) showing the membership number, as shown in Figure 20.15.

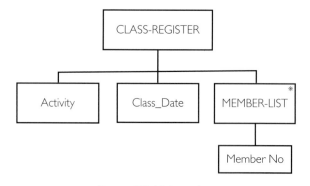

Figure 20.15 Iteration

Progress check 20.04

A driving test exam (DRIVE_TEST) consists of a front page of instructions (FRONT) followed by a number of questions (QUESTION). Each question consists of the question text and the number of marks for that question.

Draw the JSP data structure diagram.

The data for the gym classes and attendance is to be stored in a file CLASS-DATA. The file has a file header (FILE-HEADER) and file trailer (FILE-TRAILER).

LOOK BACK «

We have already met the concept of a file header when discussing bitmap files in Chapter 1.

Figure 20.16 has resulted in a sequence of 'mixed-type components' at the same level. This must always be avoided. The solution is in Figure 20.17. It introduces a component MEMBER-DATA which consists of an iteration of the members' data.

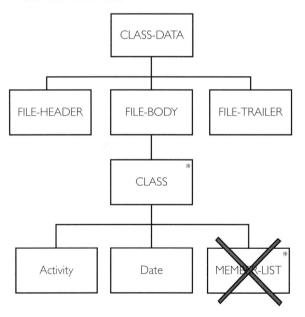

Figure 20.16 Incorrectly drawn JSP data diagram

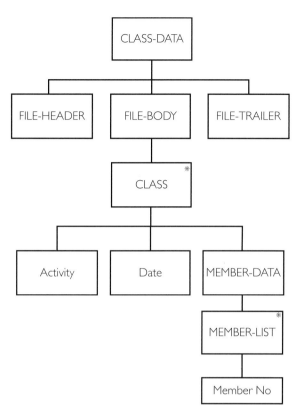

Figure 20.17 All components at each level of the same type

Progress check 20.05

A concert venue stores – in file MAILING-LIST – data for all customers who have previously purchased tickets. The data is:

- their email address.

- marketing permission given for use of their email address:

    o no permission

    o their concerts only

    o use by third-party partners.

The file stores data for all ticket purchases made by the customer. All concerts have 'premium' and 'economy' tickets available. Each purchase records:

- concert date

- artist

- ticket type

- number of tickets purchased.

Draw the JSP data diagram.

20.03 State-transition diagrams

A **state-transition diagram** is used to demonstrate the behaviour of an object. The object may be implemented as a class. Methods will be coded which transform the object from one state to another.

TERMS

state-transition diagram: documents the behaviour of a single object

State diagrams have only two elements:

- a circle (or rounded box) to represent each different possible state of the object.
- connecting arrows to indicate a transition from one state to another.

A label on each connecting arrow indicates the activity which causes the state transition. All state diagrams begin with an initial state of the object.

For example, consider a 'self-service' petrol pump which is to dispense petrol. Figure 20.18 shows three possible states:

1 Idle

2 Ready to dispense

3 Dispensing.

The arrows are labelled with the action which causes the change of state.

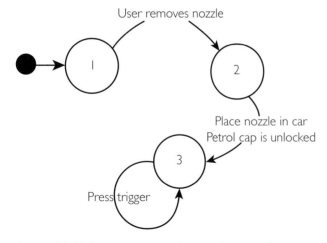

Figure 20.18 State-transition diagram for use of a petrol pump

The connecting line is labelled with:

- the event which acts as the trigger which causes the change of state.
- a guard, if the transition is conditional on some condition being met.
- the action which results from the event.

The minimum labelling of the connector is the event or trigger.

A state can have a self-transition that is a transition which returns to itself. In Figure 20.18, the user is continually pressing the nozzle of the pump and the petrol pump machine is remaining in the 'Dispensing' state.

The diagram may show a final state, indicated with the following symbol:

A state transition diagram can have more than one labelled end state.

Progress check 20.06

A connecting door between two rooms is always in one of three states:

- open
- closed
- locked.

Assume the door is initially locked.

Complete the diagram with the connecting transitions each labelled with the event which causes the transition. At the end of each day, the door is locked.

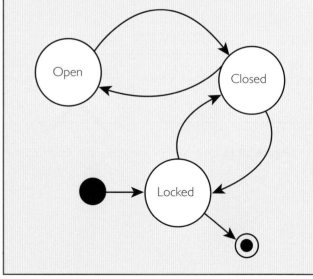

An ATM machine is used by bank customers. After the bank card is inserted by the user, the screen prompts for the PIN. After three incorrect PIN attempts, the card is retained. A correct PIN then displays the main menu:

1 Withdraw cash

2 Enquire about the account balance

3 Return card.

After a cash withdrawal or a balance enquiry, the main menu is again displayed. Figure 20.19 shows the state-transition diagram.

Progress check 20.07

A college plans to offer a course. The course is initially advertised, following which students enrol. The course can take a maximum of 10 students and is closed when 10 enrolments have been taken. There is a possibility that the course could be cancelled – both before or after any enrolments have been taken. If it is cancelled after there are enrolments, students are contacted to inform them.

Draw the state-transition diagram with the states:

• Advertised

• Enrolling

• Course cancelled

• Course closed.

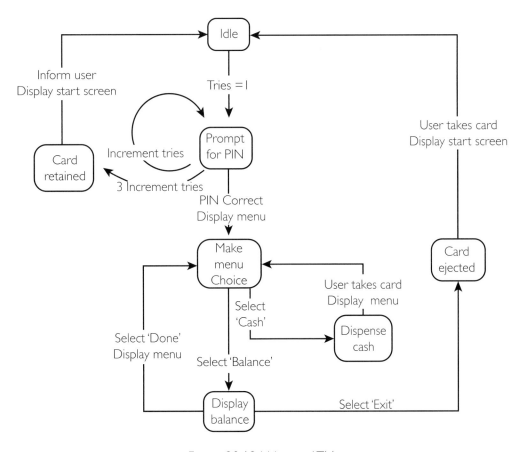

Figure 20.19 Using an ATM

Summary

■ A decision table is used to expressed complicated logic:

o It shows conditions, actions and the list of rules.

o Decision tables can often be simplified.

■ A Jackson Structured Programming diagram describes data to be processed by a program, using symbols data items, selection and iteration; a sequence of symbols at the same level should not contain mixed components.

■ A state-transition diagram is used to document the behaviour of a single 'machine'; it shows the various states and the transitions between states.

Exam-style questions

1 A manufacturer has an assembly line that produces a particular product. At the end of the assembly process, each product item is comprehensively tested to decide whether that item is acceptable or not.

The tests are split into three groups:

• Group 1: tests to check all dimensions are correct

• Group 2: tests to check strength at various points on the product item

• Group 3: tests to check paint colour and coverage.

Only if the item passes all three group tests is it accepted. If the Group 1 tests are passed, but exactly one of the other two group tests fails, the item is sent for repair. Otherwise the item is rejected.

a Complete the decision table showing all the possible outcomes and results.

[4]

Conditions	Group 1 tests								
	Group 2 tests								
	Group 3 tests								
Actions	Accepted								
	Repair								
	Rejected								

b Simplify your solution by removing redundancies.

[5]

Conditions	Group 1 tests								
	Group 2 tests								
	Group 3 tests								
Actions	Accepted								
	Repair								
	Rejected								

c The simplified table produced in **part b** is used to design program code.

Three functions are already available: G1Tests, G2Tests and G3Tests.

These functions return TRUE or FALSE, indicating the success or otherwise of the group tests.

Write **code** for a function Reject which will return TRUE if the product item is to be rejected, otherwise the function will return FALSE.

[3]

Cambridge International AS and A Level Computer Science 9608 Specimen Paper 4, Q2 2015

Chapter 21

Further programming

Revision objectives

By the end of the chapter you should be able to:

- ☐ show understanding of what is meant by a programming paradigm: low-level, imperative (procedural), object-oriented and declarative

- ☐ write low-level code that uses various address modes; immediate, direct, indirect, indexed and relative

- ☐ design appropriate classes and write code that demonstrates the use of classes, inheritance, polymorphism and containment (aggregation)

- ☐ write appropriate facts and rules based on supplied information and write code that can satisfy a goal using facts and rules

- ☐ write code to define a record structure, and to perform file processing operations for random file handling and on serial, sequential and random files

- ☐ show understanding of an exception and when it is appropriate to use exception handling and write exception-handling code

- ☐ describe features in editors that benefit programming

- ☐ know when to use compilers and interpreters

- ☐ describe facilities available in debuggers and how and when they should be deployed

21.01 Programming paradigms

A **paradigm** is a set of concepts, theories, methods, postulates, and standards for doing something. A paradigm is a 'school of thought'. A **programming paradigm** gives the way of building the structure and elements of computer programs. Certain types of problem will be better suited to the adoption of one paradigm than another.

> **TERMS**
>
> **Paradigm:** a set of concepts
>
> **Programming paradigm:** the way of building the structure and elements of computer programs
>
> **Low-level paradigm:** programming using the basic machine operations that the processor has been designed to carry out

Low-level programming

> **LOOK BACK «**
>
> Chapter 4 discussed the processor's instruction set and assembly language.

A **low-level paradigm** means programming using the basic machine operations that the processor has been designed to carry out. This has a major limitation in that a program developed by the programmer could only be executed on a computer which had the same processor, as the instruction set for different processors will be different.

Programming using machine code – even if the codes could be written in hexadecimal, not binary – would be extremely tedious. Hence we use assembly language, where mnemonics can be used for the different instructions. This approach could be appropriate for a program where there was a need to directly address the processor registers – for example, in the coding of a device driver.

> **LOOK BACK «**
>
> Chapter 4 covered various modes of addressing: immediate, direct, indirect, indexed and relative. The list here is the same.

> **TIP**
>
> Here, the requirement is to 'write low-level code that uses various addressing modes'.

Object-oriented programming

The **object-oriented paradigm** adopts a bottom-up approach and defines first the 'things' or objects which are at the core of the problem. The definition of a type of object is coded as a class definition.

The data values (properties) and methods (operations) an object can carry out are encapsulated in the class definition. Information hiding is used to protect the internal properties of an object. Objects interact by means of message passing using the methods defined for that object's class.

Classes can be organised in inheritance hierarchies. For example, a `CREDIT-CUSTOMER` class could inherit all the properties and methods of an earlier defined `CUSTOMER` class. This allows for class extension and specialisation.

Imperative programming

Imperative programming is also called **procedural programming** – which is a huge clue!

'First do this, next do that' describes the spirit of the imperative paradigm. The basic idea is that the commands produce a measurable effect on the program state. This phrase also conveys that the order of the commands is important. This paradigm therefore corresponds closely to the organisation of a standard (Von Neumann) computer.

The computational steps in an imperative language are called 'statements' or commands. Program statements/commands are executed in the order shown by control structures (loops and selection). This produces an incremental change of the program state as a function of time. Data is represented using variables and, as the program executes, the values stored by these variables can change. Typical commands offered by imperative languages include assignment, input/output and procedure calls.

Using the imperative programming paradigm, the natural abstraction is the procedure. A complete program can be designed in a modular way as a series of procedures. One or more actions is carried out by a procedure, which can be called as a single command (usually a 'call' statement).

Declarative programming

The **declarative paradigm** (also known as the 'logic paradigm' or 'rule-based paradigm') is dramatically different from other programming paradigms. The declarative paradigm fits extremely well when applied in problem domains that deal with the extraction of knowledge from basic facts and rules. The declarative paradigm seems less natural in the more general areas of computation.

Execution of the 'program' is to pose a question (or goal) with a query, with the program then searching for a solution. Execution is a systematic search of a set of facts making use of a given set of inference rules.

TIP

Don't confuse the declarative programming paradigm with the declaration of variables in a high-level language.

Low-level programming in practice

We illustrate each mode of addressing with a program.

LOOK BACK «

Familiarise yourself again with the assembly language instruction set given in Chapter 4.

Direct addressing

The operand address is the actual address to be used. The opcode for direct addressing is `LDD`.

Numbers 6 and 3 are stored in memory at locations N1 and N2. The following code multiplies 6 by 3 and stores the answer at location ANSWER:

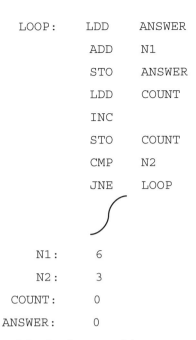

```
LOOP:     LDD     ANSWER
          ADD     N1
          STO     ANSWER
          LDD     COUNT
          INC
          STO     COUNT
          CMP     N2
          JNE     LOOP


     N1:      6
     N2:      3
  COUNT:      0
 ANSWER:      0
```

Consider the following features of the program:

- There is no 'multiply' instruction, so the calculation is done by adding 6 three times.

- The program illustrates setting up a loop in assembly language.

- The LDD and STO instructions both use direct addressing.

- The programmer has used symbolic addresses: N1 N2, COUNT and ANSWER.

Figure 21.01 shows a trace of the execution of the code.

ACC	Address			
---	N1	N2	COUNT	ANSWER
	6	3	0	0
0				
6				6
0				
1			1	
6				
12				12
1				
2			2	
12				
18				18
2				
3			3	

Figure 21.01 Trace of the program

The same program – without the use of symbolic address – is shown below. It assumes the program is loaded to main memory with the first instruction at address 100. Although all the addresses are shown as absolute addresses the instructions are still the same – they are using direct addressing.

```
100     LDD     112
101     ADD     109
102     STO     112
103     LDD     110
104     INC
105     STO     111
106     CMP     110
107     JNE     100
108
109        6
110        3
111        0
112        0
```

Immediate addressing

The address is not really an address at all – the operand is an actual value. The opcode for the load instruction is LDR.

In the following code, two of the instructions have 'hard coded' the number to be used. (It is not retrieved from a memory address, as in the two earlier programs.) The instructions have used the 'immediate' values: 6 and 3.

```
LOOP:     LDD     ANSWER
          ADD     #6
          STO     ANSWER
          LDD     COUNT
          INC
          STO     COUNT
          CMP     #3
          JNE     LOOP


   COUNT:     0
  ANSWER:     0
```

Relative addressing

Addresses are given the number relative to the start address of the program. For example if the first program instruction is at address 100, we would reference address 116 with an operand of +16.

100	LDD	+12
101	ADD	+9
102	STO	+12
103	LDD	+10
104	INC	
105	STO	+11
106	CMP	+10
107	JNE	100
108		
109	6	
110	3	
111	0	
112	0	

Indirect addressing

The address in the instruction will contain the address from which the data will be retrieved. The opcode for indirect addressing is LDI.

Figure 21.02 shows a trace of the program.

The following program displays four characters stored at location 120 onwards:

100	LDI	115
101	OUT	
102	LDD	115
103	INC	
104	STO	115
105	CMP	124
106	JNE	100
⋮		
115	120	
⋮		
120	72	
121	84	
122	77	
123	70	

ACC	Address 115	120	121	122	123	OUTPUT
72		72	84	77	70	ASCII 72 = H
120						
121	121					
84						ASCII 84 = T
121						
122	122					
77						ASCII 77 = M
122						
123	123					
70						ASCII 70 = L
123						
124	124					

Figure 21.02 Trace of the program

Indexed addressing

Indexed addressing uses the value found in the Index Register. The opcode for indexed addressing is `LDX`.

The following program displays four characters stored at location 120 onwards:

- This time the loop counter is being controlled by the value at address 114 (as before).
- The memory address from which to output the character is calculated as (120 plus the offset value stored in IX).

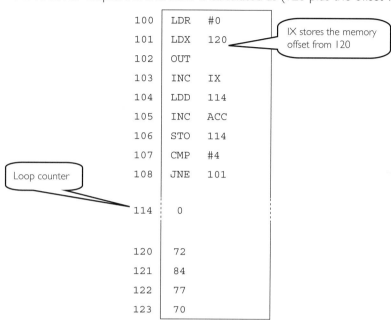

Figure 21.03 shows a trace of the program.

ACC	IX	114	OUTPUT
	0		
72			ASCII 72 = H
	1		
0			
1		1	
84			ASCII 84 = T
	2		
1			
2		2	
77			ASCII 77 = M
	3		
2			
3		3	
70			ASCII 70 = L
	4		
3			
4		4	

Figure 21.03 Trace of the program

Common constructs in assembly language

All the constructs we are familiar with in programming – selection with If statements and loops – have an implementation in assembly language.

Assignment: Add two numbers and store the answer at location RESULT.

Visual Basic: `Result = NUMB1 + NUMB2`

Simple selection: If the number is 100 output 'Y' otherwise output 'N'.

```
  7      If Numb = 100 Then            START:    LDD NUMB
  8        Console.WriteLine("Y")                CMP #100
  9      Else                                    JPE TRUE
 10        Console.WriteLine("N")      FALSE:    LDD N
 11      End If                                  OUT
                                                 JMP END

                                       TRUE:     LDD Y
                                                 OUT

                                       END:      END

                                       NUMB:     100
                                       Y:        89      // ASCII code for Y
                                       N:        78      // ASCII code for N

              (a)                                (b)
```

The JMP is needed to stop the control going into the 'false'

Figure 21.04 Equivalent selection code in (a) Visual Basic and (b) assembly language

Post-condition loop: The text CAT is to be output five times.

```
  7      Do                           START:    OUT CHAR1
  8        Counter = 5
  9        Console.WriteLine("CAT")             OUT CHAR2
 10        Counter = Counter - 1
 11      Loop Until Counter = 0                 OUT CHAR3

                                                OUT

                                                LDD COUNTER

                                                DEC ACC

                                                CMP #0

                                                JPN START
                                      END:      END


                                      COUNTER:  5

                                      CHAR1:    67       // ASCII code for C

                                      CHAR2:    65       // ASCII code for A

                                      CHAR3:    84       // ASCII code for T
              (a)                               (b)
```

Figure 21.05 Equivalent loop code in (a) Visual Basic and (b) assembly language

Object-oriented programming in practice

These terms – procedural, declarative and object-oriented – are not mutually exclusive. Many languages which are procedural also support the use of objects (e.g. Visual Basic .NET, C++ and many, many more).

An OOP language uses the data structure an 'object' to model a problem. Objects will have defined properties (like attributes in database design) and methods which act upon an object.

Classes

A class is the definition of what an object looks like – the object specification. The class acts as the template from which an instance of an object is created. The class defines the properties of the object and the methods used to control the object's behaviour. A class is given an identifier name e.g. `Customer`.

Properties

Think of properties as similar to the attributes in database modelling.

The member variables are private to the class and hence are effectively hidden from the programmer. In Visual Basic .NET values are assigned to an object and read using 'set' and 'get' property procedures.

Methods

Think of a method as something we can do with an object. ActiveX controls, such as a textbox, have events which are associated with that object type.

When we model real-world objects, such as a 'product' or 'customer', methods will be needed for every action required on that object.

The two most basic methods needed for each property of any class are:

- a 'set' method to assign a particular property (e.g. `Set_CustomerName`)
- a 'get' method to access and use the object's property (e.g. `Get_CustomerName`).

Class diagram

A formal diagram showing the class name, its properties and methods is called a class diagram.

TIP Don't confuse a 'class diagram' with an 'object diagram'. Object diagrams are no longer in the syllabus.

A garage stores data for all new vehicles (VEHICLE) it sells. Vehicles are classified as either cars (CAR) or commercial (COMMERCIAL) vehicles. A commercial vehicle is either a van (VAN) or a lorry (LORRY).

The class diagram in Figure 21.06 shows the object-oriented design. Things to note are that it has several instances of inheritance. The VAN and LORRY classes both inherit from COMMERCIAL.

There is a `DisplayData` method in the VEHICLE superclass. There is a method with the same name in both the VAN and LORRY classes.

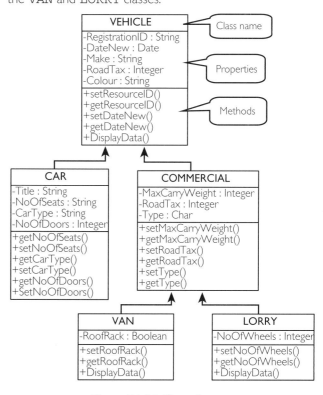

Figure 21.06 Class diagram

Inheritance

The class diagram in Figure 21.06 has already shown inheritance. The inheritance diagram in Figure 21.07 shows the parent and child classes.

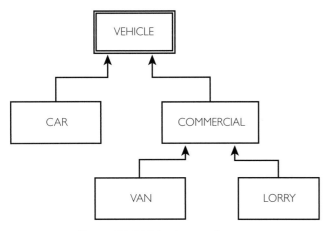

Figure 21.07 Inheritance diagram

VEHICLE is the superclass. The other classes inherit from this parent class or a subclass higher in the hierarchy. In practice this means that, for example, the **CAR** class will have properties and methods of its own, but it also inherits the properties and methods from the **VEHICLE** parent class.

Inheritance can be clarified by labelling each branch with the term 'is a':

- A car 'is a' vehicle.

- A van 'is a' commercial.

Inheritance involves defining a class and then using it to build a hierarchy of descendent classes. Each subclass inherits the properties and methods of its parent class.

> **TIP**
>
> The arrow always points to the parent class.

Progress check 21.02

A campsite has a number of numbered pitches. The pitches are of two types: for tents or for caravans.

Draw an inheritance diagram for the class design.

Class definitions

The Visual Basic .NET code in Figure 21.08 shows the class definition for the **VEHICLE** class.

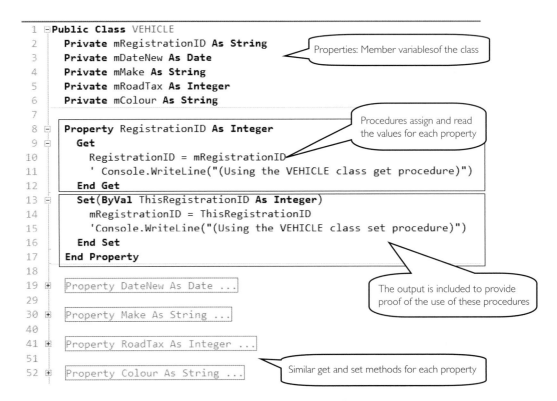

```
1  Public Class VEHICLE
2      Private mRegistrationID As String
3      Private mDateNew As Date
4      Private mMake As String
5      Private mRoadTax As Integer
6      Private mColour As String
7
8      Property RegistrationID As Integer
9        Get
10           RegistrationID = mRegistrationID
11           ' Console.WriteLine("(Using the VEHICLE class get procedure)")
12        End Get
13        Set(ByVal ThisRegistrationID As Integer)
14           mRegistrationID = ThisRegistrationID
15           'Console.WriteLine("(Using the VEHICLE class set procedure)")
16        End Set
17      End Property
18
19      Property DateNew As Date ...
29
30      Property Make As String ...
40
41      Property RoadTax As Integer ...
51
52      Property Colour As String ...
```

Properties: Member variables of the class

Procedures assign and read the values for each property

The output is included to provide proof of the use of these procedures

Similar get and set methods for each property

Figure 21.08 VEHICLE class definition

The code in Figure 21.09 shows the class definition for the CAR class, inheriting from VEHICLE.

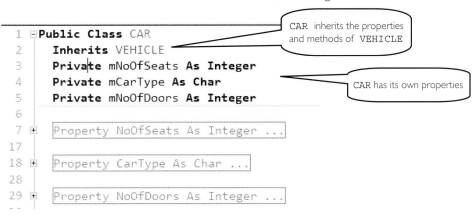

Figure 21.09 CAR class definition

Polymorphism

Polymorphism is the technique by which methods in the class hierarchy with the same name produce a different behaviour.

The VEHICLE and CAR classes both have a DisplayData method. The code in Figure 21.10 shows how those methods are related.

Figure 21.10 Overridable and overridden methods

Progress check 21.03

There is another example of polymorphism shown in Figure 21.06. What is it?

Objects

An object is an occurrence or 'instance' of the class definition. An instance is identified by an identifier name, such as MyCar. A program can create many objects of this type and store data about each object.

You should already have some idea about the use of objects if you have attempted to create a forms-based Windows application in Visual Basic .NET. The form will typically contain a number of ActiveX controls – such as a text box and a set of radio buttons – and these behave as 'objects'. Hence the .NET programming environment has a class definition of the properties and methods defined for each of these ActiveX controls.

A second type of object are those that take the form of abstract objects such as a 'connection' object or a 'recordset' object.

The third kind of objects are those which are used by the programmer to model some real-world problem. It is this third application of object-oriented programming we have focussed on with the vehicle application.

Figure 21.11 illustrates the creation of a car object and the get methods which are used to assign object's property values.

Sets up an identifier name for the object

Creates a new object

Assigns a value to the RegistrationID

These statements use the get methods from the VEHICLE class

These statements use the get methods from the VEHICLE

This statement uses the DisplayData method in the CAR

```
 3    Sub Main()
 4        Dim MyCar As CAR
 5        ' creating a car object
 6        MyCar = New CAR
 7        ' properties from the VEHICLE class
 8        Console.Write("Registration ID ..? ")
 9        MyCar.RegistrationID = Console.ReadLine
10        Console.Write("Date  when new ..? ")
11        MyCar.DateNew = Console.ReadLine
12        Console.Write("Make ..? ")
13        MyCar.Make = Console.ReadLine
14        Console.Write("RoadTax ..? ")
15        MyCar.RoadTax = Console.ReadLine
16        Console.Write("Colour ..? ")
17        MyCar.Colour = Console.ReadLine
18
19        ' properties from the CAR class ...
20        Console.Write("Number of seats ..? ")
21        MyCar.NoOfSeats = Console.ReadLine
22        Console.Write("Car type (S-saloon, E-estate, H-hatchback ..? ")
23        MyCar.CarType = Console.ReadLine
24        Console.Write("Number of doors ..? ")
25        MyCar.NoOfDoors = Console.ReadLine
26        MyCar.DisplayData(MyCar)
27
28        Console.ReadLine()
29    End Sub
```

Figure 21.11 Code for creating an object

Figure 21.12 shows the output when a car object is created.

```
Registration ID ..? 35647
Date  when new ..? 12/05/2016
Make ..? Toyota
RoadTax ..? 500
Colour ..? Red
Number of seats ..? 4
Car type (S-saloon, E-estate, H-hatchback ..? S
Number of doors ..? 4
Using the CAR class method
35647
12/05/2016 00:00:00
Toyota
500
Red
4
S
4
```

Figure 21.12 Creating an object

Encapsulation

Encapsulation is the combining of an object's properties and the methods which access that data. Encapsulation restricts the programmer's access to the object's data. The only code which allows the reading or writing of property data values are the get and set methods for each property. Study the code in FIG 21.12.

Data hiding is a very important concept of OOP and is a feature of data encapsulation. This provides a structure for the validation of data which can be hidden away from the programmer.

Containment

The basic idea here is that the properties of a class could be a set of properties which are already designed as a separate class.

For example, the vehicle data is to include data about the customer who first purchased the vehicle. The customer data already exists in class CUSTOMER. The test for containment is to use the words 'has a'.

In our application, VEHICLE 'has a' CUSTOMER.

Figure 21.13 shows code which adds a CUSTOMER to a VEHICLE.

```
1  Public Class CUSTOMER
2    Private mCustomerName As String
3
4    Property CustomerName As String          The CUSTOMER class is
5      Get                                     used in the VEHICLE class
6        CustomerName = mCustomerName
7        ' Console.WriteLine("(Using the VAN class get procedure)")
8      End Get
9      Set(ByVal ThisCustomerName As String)
10       mCustomerName = ThisCustomerName
11       'Console.WriteLine("(Using the CUSTOMER class set procedure)")
12     End Set
13   End Property
14 End Class
```

```
1  Public Class VEHICLE
2    Inherits CUSTOMER
3    Private mRegistrationID As String
4    Private mDateNew As Date                  Two lines are added
5    Private mMake As String                   to the VEHICLE class
6    Private mRoadTax As Integer
7    Private mColour As String
8    Private mCustomer As CUSTOMER
```

```
20       ' property from the contained class
21       Console.Write("Customer ..? ")
22       MyCar.CustomerName = Console.ReadLine
```

Figure 21.13 Classes using 'containment'

Unified Modelling Language

The syllabus has covered some of the fundamentals of the Unified Modelling Language (UML) which has become an industry standard for object-oriented design. The use of state transition diagrams and class diagrams are part of the UML methodology.

Figure 21.14 The UML logo

A full coverage of UML is outside the scope of this syllabus but is a topic a students would now expect to cover in any Higher Education Computer Science course.

Declarative programming in practice

Prolog is a declarative language. Prolog stands for 'programming in logic'. Given the necessary facts and rules, Prolog will use deductive reasoning to solve programming problems.

This is in contrast to traditional computer languages, such as Pascal or Visual Basic, which are procedural languages. In procedural languages, the programmer must provide step-by-step statements that tell the computer exactly how to solve a given problem. In other words, the programmer must know how to solve the problem before the computer can do it.

Compare this to the Prolog programmer, who only needs to supply a description of the problem and the ground rules for solving it. Prolog is then left to determine how to go about finding a solution.

A Prolog program for a given application will typically require only one tenth as many program lines as the corresponding high-level language program. Prolog is a very important tool in programming artificial intelligence applications and in the development of expert systems.

With Prolog you arrive at a solution by logically inferring one thing from something already known. Typically, a Prolog program is not a sequence of actions, it is:

- a collection of facts

- with rules for drawing conclusions from those facts.

Predicate logic

Prolog is based on a formal system called 'predicate logic'. Predicate logic is simply a way of making it clear how reasoning is done. Predicate logic was developed to convey logic-based ideas into a written form. In predicate logic, you first eliminate all unnecessary words from your sentences. You then transform the sentence, placing the relationship first and grouping the objects after the relationship. The objects then become arguments that the relationship acts upon.

Table 21.01 shows sentences transformed into predicate logic syntax.

Table 21.01 Predicate logic syntax

Natural language	Predicate logic
An open-top car is fun.	`fun(open_top_car).`
An orange is healthy food.	`healthy_food(orange).`

The two statements in Table 21.01 are facts. Rules enable you to infer one fact from other facts.

Here are some rules concerning a 'likes' relation:

Cindy likes everything that Bill likes.

Hilary likes everything that is green.

To encode these two rules in Prolog, you only need to change the syntax:

```
likes(cindy,Something) :-
likes(bill,Something).

likes(hilary,Something):-
green(Something).
```

The :- symbol is read as 'if' and it serves to connect the two parts of a rule.

You can think of a rule as a procedure. In other words, the rules above can be interpreted as:

To prove that Cindy likes something, prove that Bill likes that same thing.

To prove that Hilary likes something, prove that it is green.

The use of `Something` is like using a variable in a procedural high-level language.

Queries or setting goals

Once we give Prolog a set of facts, we can proceed to ask questions concerning these facts; this is known as querying the Prolog program or setting a 'goal'.

The Prolog environment will include an inference engine. This software provides a process for reasoning logically about information. The inference engine includes a pattern matcher, which retrieves stored (known) information by matching answers to questions. Prolog tries to infer that a goal is true (in other words, answer a question) by questioning the set of facts and rules.

In natural language we might ask: Does Bill like Cindy?

Prolog syntax: `likes(bill, cindy).`

Given this query, Prolog would answer 'Yes', because Prolog can find the fact that states this. Prolog knows:

`likes(bill,cindy).`

`likes(bill,dog).`

A little more complicated and general question: What does Bill like?

Prolog syntax: `likes(bill, What).`

In Prolog syntax, `What` is effectively a variable. Variables in Prolog always begin with an upper-case letter or an underscore. Prolog always looks for an answer to a query by starting at the top of the fact list. It looks at each fact until it reaches the bottom. Given the query about 'what bill likes', Prolog will return:

`What=cindy`

`What=dog`

`2 solutions`

Consider the question: What does Cindy like?

Prolog syntax: `likes(cindy, What).`

Prolog would answer:

`What=bill`

`What=cindy`

`What=dogs`

`3 solutions`

This is because Prolog knows that Cindy likes Bill, that Cindy likes what Bill likes and that Bill likes Cindy and dogs.

Consider a knowledge base designed to give advice on whether a person may legally drive a certain class of vehicle. The following partially completed knowledge base has some of these facts and rules. (They have been numbered for easy reference.)

```
01 age(edward,20).
02 age(robert,19).
03 age(flora,17).
04 age(emma,17).
05 age(andrew,16).
06 minimum_age(motor_cycle,16).
07 minimum_age(car,17).
08 minimum_age(heavy_goods_
      vehicle,20).
```

```
09 passed_test(edward,heavy_goods_
      vehicle).
10 passed_test(andrew,motor_cycle).
11 passed_test(emma,car).
12 hasprovisional_licence(andrew).
13 hasprovisional_licence(robert).
14 permitted_to_drive(X,V) If passed_
      test(X,V).
15 permitted_to_drive(X,V) If haspro
      visional_licence(X)
   And age(X,A)
      And minimum_age (V,L) And A >= L.
```

- Fact 1 means that Edward is 20 years old.

- Fact 6 means the minimum age for driving a motor-cycle is 16.

- Fact 10 means Andrew has passed the driving test for a motor-cycle.

- Fact 12 means that Andrew has a provisional driving licence.

- Rule 14 means that person X may drive a vehicle V if person X has passed the test for a vehicle of class V.

- Rule 15 means that person X may drive a vehicle V if person X has a provisional licence and is old enough to drive a vehicle of class V.

Consider the following query, which means, is Flora permitted to drive a car?:

   `? permitted_to_drive(flora, car).`

The inference engine would do the following:

1 Look at rule 14 and then scan the facts to see if Flora has passed the test for a car.

2 The answer is 'no', so rule 15 is examined.

3 The facts are scanned again to check if Flora has a provisional licence.

4 No relevant fact is found so the program returns 'no'.

Consider these queries:

```
? permitted_to_drive
   (robert, motor_cycle)
```
Returns the answer 'yes' using rule 15 and facts 2, 6 and 13.

```
? permitted_to_drive
   (emma, V)
```
Returns 'car' using rule 14 and fact 11

Progress check 21.04

1 Study the following knowledge base.

```
01 male(kai).
02 male(john).
03 male(ken).
04 female(tansy).
05 female(tadi).
06 female(natene).
07 female(yenene).
08 plays(yenene, tennis).
09 plays(tadi, tennis).
10 plays(tadi, golf).
11 plays(ken, rugby).
12 plays(natene, hockey).
13 plays(natene, golf).
14 plays(tansy, golf).
15 plays(ken, football).
16 plays(natene, tennis).
17 likes(yenene, X) :- female(X), plays(X, golf).
18 likes(natene, X) :- male(X), plays(X, rugby).
19 likes(tansy, X) :- male(X), plays(X, tennis).
```

> The comma is read as 'and'

a Explain in words line 16.

What is the output from the following goals?

b `plays(tansy, Y)`

c `likes(yenene, A)`

d Write a new rule which states: Ken likes all females and males who like golf.

2 Study the following knowledge base.

```
01 male(adan).
02 male(alano).
03 male(emidio).
04 male(gael).
05 female(celia).
06 female(chelo).
07 female(malona).
08 male(xavier)
09 male(angel)
10 female(sofia)
11 parents(chelo, celia, adan).
12 parents(emidio, celia, gael).
13 parents(alano, malona, angel).
14 parents(adan, malona, sofia).
15 parents(emidio, chelo, xavier).
16 sister_of(X,Y) :- female(Y), parents(Y,A,B), parents(X,A,B).
```

```
17 brother_of(X,Y) :- male(Y), parents(Y,A,B), parents(X,A,B).
18 sibling(X,Y) :- sister_of(Y,X) Or brother_of(Y,X).
```

a Explain fact 7.

b Explain fact 11.

c Is 17 a fact or a rule?

d Explain rule 18.

e What is the output for the following queries?

   i `parents(Who, malona, angel)`

   ii `parents(sofia, X, Y)`

21.02 File processing

The record data structure

LOOK BACK «

We studied this in Chapter 19, section 19.03.

An agency manages a number of bands who go on tour. The agency is storing data for each band – the start date of their next tour and the maximum number of concerts.

In Visual Basic the record structure uses the keyword `Structure`, as shown in Figure 21.15.

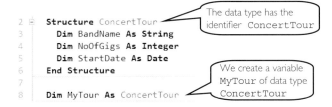

Figure 21.15 A Visual Basic .NET structure

Progress check 21.05

A program is to store the surname and initials (separately) for a number of employees who each have an employee code (typically D768). The program also stores the number of years of service and whether or not they are a full-time employee.

1 Write pseudocode for an employee record structure.

2 Write a declaration statement for a data structure to store data for 150 employees.

Random (direct access) files

Our work with files in Chapter 10 and Chapter 13 used text files consisting of several lines of text. We shall now use a direct access file. This means once we have a file of, for example, 30 records, it is possible to read any of the records directly (without reference to any others in the file). The term 'random' is somewhat misleading as records are written and read from the file in a systematic way.

Pseudocode

Remember when using text files the file was opened for either **READ** or **WRITE** It was not possible to read and write to the file in the same session. Using the **RANDOM** file mode, once the file has been opened we can read and write as many times as we would like, in the same session.

```
OPENFILE <filename> FOR RANDOM
```

In Figure 21.16, the file is opened at the very start of the program execution and only closed when the program terminates.

```
SEEK <filename>, <address>
```

Each record is given an 'address' at which it is to be written. For the programmer this will be some form of 'key number' or record key. In Figure 21.18, the key number is hashed from the band name.

The SEEK statement, only 'gets ready' to perform a following action. PUTRECORD writes a record to the file – it assumes the SEEK statement has already set the file pointer:

```
PUTRECORD <filename>, <identifier>
```

GETRECORD reads a record from the file – it assumes the SEEK statement has already set the file pointer:

```
GETRECORD <filename>, <identifier>
```

As before, when we used text, serial and sequential files, we need to close the file at the end.

```
CLOSE <filename>
```

Open and close the file: Program code

The Visual Basic .NET code in Figure 21.16 opens the file for random access at the very start of the program and closes it at the end.

```
10   Sub Main()
11       Dim Choice As Integer
12       FileOpen(1, "d:\ConcertsRandom", OpenMode.Random)
13       Do
14           Call DisplayMenu()
15           Console.Write("Choice? ") : Choice = Console.ReadLine
16           If Choice = 1 Then Call CreateDummyRecords()
17           If Choice = 2 Then Call EnterRecords()
18           If Choice = 3 Then Call RetrieveRecord()
19           If Choice = 4 Then Call DisplayRecords()
20       Loop Until Choice = 5
21       FileClose(1)
22       Console.ReadLine()
23   End Sub
```

Line 12: Opens the file

DisplayRecords() loops 30 times for procedure DisplayRecordData()

Line 21: Closes the file

Figure 21.16 Open and close a random access file

Creating a file of dummy records

The first task is to create a collection of 'dummy records' in the file. We anticipate there will be 26 band records, so we create a file with 30 records. In Figure 21.17, we use 'dot notation' to describe each data value which makes up the record:

- MyTour.BandName

- MyTour.NoOfGigs

- MyTour.StartDate

```
35   Sub CreateDummyRecords()
36       Dim i As Integer
37       For i = 1 To 30
38           MyTour.BandName = "******************************"
39           MyTour.NoOfGigs = 0
40           MyTour.StartDate = #1/1/2016 12:00:00 PM#
41           FilePut(1, MyTour, i)
42       Next
43       Console.WriteLine()
44       Console.WriteLine("Dummy file of band tours records created ...")
45   End Sub
```

Dummy values are inserted

The loop counter i is used for the record key for each record

Figure 21.17 –Write dummy records

LOOK BACK «

This dot notation is not new. We used it with user-defined data types in Chapter 19 to design a `LinkedList` data type.

Write a record to a file

In Figure 21.18, we write a real record to the file. The key is hashed from the band name (line 55) and the hashing algorithm generates a key number in the range 1 to 26.

```
47 ⊟   Sub EnterRecords()
48        Dim HashCode As Integer
49        Do
50          Console.Write("Band name (XXX to end)? ")
51          MyTour.BandName = Console.ReadLine
52          If MyTour.BandName <> "XXX" Then
53            Console.Write("No of gigs ? ") : MyTour.NoOfGigs = Console.ReadLine
54            Console.Write("Start date ? ") : MyTour.StartDate = Console.ReadLine
55            HashCode = Asc(Left(MyTour.BandName, 1)) - 64
56            ' range of hash codes 1 to 26
57            FilePut(1, MyTour, HashCode)
58          End If
59        Loop Until MyTour.BandName = "XXX"
60      End Sub
```

The hashing algorithm generates a record key in the range 1 to 26

`HashCode` is used as the record key

Figure 21.18 Write a record

Read a record

In Figure 21.19, we read a record from the file. The same key is hashed from the band name.

```
62 ⊟   Sub RetrieveRecord()
63        Dim HashCode As Integer
64        Console.Write("Band name ? ")
65        MyTour.BandName = Console.ReadLine
66        HashCode = Asc(Left(MyTour.BandName, 1)) - 64
67        FilePut(1, MyTour, HashCode)
68        Call DisplayRecordData(HashCode)
69      End Sub
70
71 ⊟   Sub DisplayRecordData(ThisHashCode As Integer)
72        Console.Write("record key: " + Str(ThisHashCode) + "  ")
73        Console.Write(MyTour.BandName + "  ")
74        Console.Write(Str(MyTour.NoOfGigs) + "   ")
75        Console.WriteLine(MyTour.StartDate)
76      End Sub
```

The same hashing function has to be used when calculating the record key for retrieval

Figure 21.19 Read a record

Operations on serial, sequential and random files

Files are needed to permanently store data. When data is stored by a variable or constant in a program the data will be lost as soon as the program terminates. The term 'file' is generally used to describe any type of data which needs to be permanently stored by the computer system and so a file could include: program files, image files, sound files or data files.

The discussion here is about data files only. The general use of files in a high-level programming language is called 'file handling'.

There are variations in the language keywords used by different programming languages so we start with pseudocode.

LOOK BACK «

A common file format when saving data records is to store one record per line in the file, with the data items separated with either a comma or some other separator character/formatting. This is called a 'comma-separated file'. Examples of this were used in Chapter 13.

Serial file organisation

Records are written into the file in no particular order. The file is said to have **serial organisation**. When the file is opened for reading, the records can only be read from the file in order.

Sequential file organisation

A possible improvement is to have the records ordered in some way, or example, stored in animal name order. The file is said to be a sequentially organised file, with animal name chosen as the key field.

LOOK BACK «

Serial and sequential files were studied in Chapter 13.

We always have the limitation for a serial or sequential file that records can only be read in sequence, starting with the first record in the file.

Pseudocode for file handling

The pseudocode we used for opening and closing files text files applies also to serial and sequential files:

```
OPENFILE <filename> FOR READ/WRITE

CLOSEFILE <filename>
```

A third file mode for opening the file is used to add a new record to the end of the file. This is called appending to the file.

```
OPENFILE <filename> FOR APPEND
```

We can write records to a file if it is opened in `WRITE` mode or `APPEND` mode:

```
FILEWRITE <filename>, <var1>, var2>
```

We can read records from a file opened in `READ` mode:

```
FILEREAD <filename>, <var1>, var2>
```

The programming language will have a number of functions available to test for certain conditions.

These would include:

- `EOF(<filename>)` to test whether we have reached the end of the file
- `EXISTS(<filename>)` to test for the existence of the file

Accessing serial and sequential files with Visual Basic

The following code shows a file-handling program. The original sequentially organised file was created with the text editor. The code illustrates:

- opening the file in the appropriate mode (Figure 21.20)
- appending a new animal record to the end of the file (Figure 21.21)
- displaying the file contents (Figure 21.22).

```
 2    Dim Choice As Integer
 3    Dim Animal As String
 4    Dim AnimalYoung As String
 5    Dim AnimalMummy As String
 6    Dim AnimalDaddy As String
 7
 8 ⊟  Sub Main()
 9      Do
10        DisplayMenu()
11        Choice = Console.ReadLine()
12        If Choice = 1 Then
13          FileOpen(1, "D:\Animal names.txt", OpenMode.Input)
14          DisplayFile()
15          FileClose(1)
16        End If
17
18        If Choice = 2 Then
19          FileOpen(1, "D:\Animal names.txt", OpenMode.Append)
20          AppendAnimal()
21          FileClose(1)
22        End If
23      Loop Until Choice = 3
24      Console.ReadLine()
25    End Sub
```

File mode: Input to read the data from the file

File mode – Append to add a new record to the file

Figure 21.20 Main menu code

```
34 ⊟  Sub AppendAnimal()
35      Console.Write("Animal ? ")
36      Animal = Console.ReadLine()
37      Console.Write("Young ? ")
38      AnimalYoung = Console.ReadLine()
39      Console.Write("Mummy ? ")
40      AnimalMummy = Console.ReadLine()
41      Console.Write("Daddy ? ")
42      AnimalDaddy = Console.ReadLine()
43
44      WriteLine(1, Animal, AnimalYoung, AnimalMummy, AnimalDaddy)
45    End Sub
```

Input from the keyboard the new animal data

Write the record to the end of the file

Figure 21.21 Append to file contents

```
46
47 ⊟  Sub DisplayFile()
48      Do While Not (EOF(1))
49        Input(1, Animal)
50        Input(1, AnimalYoung)
51        Input(1, AnimalDaddy)
52        Input(1, AnimalMummy)
53        Console.WriteLine(Animal + "  " + AnimalYoung + _
54                          "  " + AnimalMummy + "  " + AnimalDaddy)
55      Loop
56    End Sub
```

EOF function tests for end of file

Read the four data items from the file

Figure 21.22 Display file contents

File-processing operations for serial and sequential files

These operations are all concerned with 'access' to the data records in the file. We must always be clear if we are describing the 'file organisation' or 'file access'.

These algorithms for file-processing tasks all require 'access' to the file.

Display all records
File mode: READ

```
Loop
    Read a new record
    Output data
Until the end of the file is reached
```

Search for a record
File mode: READ

```
Input the name to find
Loop
    Read the next record
    IF matching record, then  Output data
Until 'Found' or the end of the file is reached
```
Special case: If the records in a sequential file are of a fixed length, a record can be retrieved using its relative position in the file. That is, the start position in the file could be calculated for the record with, for example, key number 15.

Add a new record: serial organisation
File mode: APPEND

```
Input the new data
Append the new record to the end of the file
```
See Figure 21.21 for a code example.

Add a new record: sequential organisation
This requires the use of two files: the original FileA and a new FileB.

```
Input the name to add
Search FileA
Loop
    Read record from FileA
    If current record > insert name
        Write new record to FileB
    Write current record to FileB
Until position to insert is found
Write all remaining records in FileA
    to FileB
Delete FileA
Rename FileB as FileA
```

Delete a record

This requires the use of two files: the original FileA and a new FileB.

```
Input the name to delete
Search FileA
Loop
    Read record from FileA
    If the current record is not the one to delete
        Write current record to FileB
Until EOF(FileA)
Delete FileA
Rename FileB as FileA
```

Amend an existing record

This is similar to the delete algorithm. It requires the use of two files: the original FileA and a new FileB.

```
Input the name to amend and the new data values
Search FileA
Loop
    Read record from FileA
    If the current record is not the one to amend
        Write this record to FileB
Until found
When the record is found write the new data to FileB
Write all remaining records from FileA to FileB
Delete FileA
Rename FileB as FileA
```

TIP

Some file-processing tasks require the use of two files. This is because a serial or sequential file can only be opened for either reading from or writing to in the same session.

Adding a record to a sequentially organised file: Example

This is an example of one of the algorithms that requires the use of two files. Records from the file are read until the position at which the new record to be inserted is found. As each existing record is read it is written to the new file. The new file will finally contain all the original records plus the new record at the correct position.

Assume the file has `AnimalName` as its key field.

```
OPEN existing file ANIMALS for READ
OPEN (a new empty) file NEW-ANIMALS for WRITE
INPUT NewAnimal
PositionFound ← FALSE
REPEAT
    FILEREAD next record from ANIMALS (including AnimalName)
    IF NewAnimal < AnimalName
        THEN
```

```
        PositionFound ← TRUE
        INPUT other new record data (AnimalYoung, etc.)
        FILEWRITE new record to NEW-ANIMALS
        FILEWRITE current record from ANIMALS to NEW-ANIMALS
    ELSE
        FILEWRITE current record to NEW-ANIMALS
    ENDIF
UNTIL PositionFound = TRUE
// now write all the remaining records from ANIMALS to New-ANIMALS
WHILE NOT EOF(ANIMALS)
    FILEREAD next ANIMAL record
    FILEWRITE this record to NEW-ANIMALS
ENDWHILE
// the latest version of the file must  be named ANIMALS so,
DELETE ANIMALS
RENAME NEW-ANIMALS AS ANIMALS
```

Progress check 21.06

1 Study the above algorithm for adding a record. Describe in structured English or pseudocode the steps needed to delete a record from the ANIMALS file.

Hint: The algorithm requires the existing ANIMALS file for reading and a new empty NEW-ANIMALS file for writing.

2 Describe in structured English or pseudocode the algorithm to amend a record in the ANIMALS file.

Hint: Again, the algorithm requires the existing ANIMALS file for reading and a new empty NEW-ANIMALS file for writing.

File-processing operations for random files

Display all records

File mode: RANDOM

```
Loop for every key number
    Read the record
    Output record data
```

Search for a record

File mode: RANDOM

Case 1 If the key number is known, read the data – SEEK then GETRECORD – and output the data.

Case 2 If the key number has been hashed from the data, then a hash of the required data will give the key number.

Case 3 The worst case is to loop through the records with each key number in turn, until it is found.

Add a new record

File mode: RANDOM

If the key number is hashed, generate the key number. Check this key number has not already been used before using SEEK then PUTRECORD to write the data.

If duplicate keys are possible there will need to be a strategy for dealing this this.

Delete a record

File mode: RANDOM

Strategy 1: SEEK to find the record and PUTRECORD to overwrite the data items with the dummy values. A following SEEK and GETRECORD will recognise this record no longer exists.

Strategy 2: Include an extra field in the original record structure to act as a Boolean flag. When a record is deleted, the flag value is changed to indicate 'deleted record'. We are effectively amending the record to mark it as deleted:

1 SEEK and GETRECORD to establish we have the correct record.

2 Change the flag value.

3 SEEK (with the same key number) then PUTRECORD to write the amended data.

Amend an existing record

File mode: RANDOM

1 SEEK and GETRECORD to establish we have the correct record.

2 Input the new data values.

3 SEEK (with the same key number) then PUTRECORD to write the amended data.

Processing random access files with Visual Basic

The following code implements the animals data as a random access file.

Not all the code is shown below. Many of the tasks are the same as those previously covered.

First, we define a record structure for each animal record (Figure 21.23).

```
1  Module Module1
2    Structure AnimalRecord
3      Dim Active As Char
4      Dim Animal As String
5      Dim AnimalYoung As String
6      Dim AnimalMum As String
7      Dim AnimalDad As String
8    End Structure
9
10   Dim MyAnimal As AnimalRecord
11   Dim KeyNumber As Integer
```

A 'flag field' indicates if the record is active (A) or has been deleted (N)

Global variables

Figure 21.23 Define a record structure

The file of dummy records is created using key number 1 to 30.

Figure 21.24 shows the code and screenshot for adding the 'camel' record with record key 5.

```
78  Sub AddRecord()
79    Console.Write("Key number ? ") : KeyNumber = Console.ReadLine
80    EnterRecordData()
81    FilePut(1, MyAnimal, KeyNumber)
82  End Sub
83
84  Sub EnterRecordData()
85    Console.Write("Animal ") : MyAnimal.Animal = Console.ReadLine
86    Console.Write("Young ? ") : MyAnimal.AnimalYoung = Console.ReadLine
87    Console.Write("Femaale ? ") : MyAnimal.AnimalMum = Console.ReadLine
88    Console.Write("Male ? ") : MyAnimal.AnimalDad = Console.ReadLine
89  End Sub
```

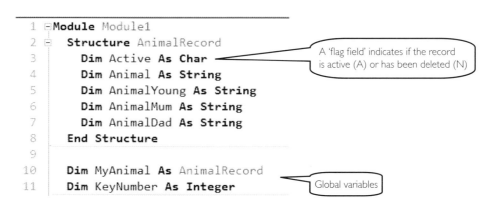

```
*****************************
Choice? 2
Key number ? 5
Animal camel
Young ? calf
Femaale ? bull
Male ? cow
*****************************
1. Create file of dummy records
2. Add new record
3. Delete new record
4. Amend record
5. Display one record
6. Display all records
7. End
*****************************
Choice? 5
Key number ? 5
Key: 1660945729 A camel calf bull cow
```

Record with key number 5 is entered

The male and female field values have been keyed in in the wrong

Figure 21.24 Add a record

Figure 21.25 shows the code for amending the incorrectly entered 'camel' record.

The programmer has used the same code for the 'amend record' and 'delete record' tasks. The menu choice number is the parameter to the `ChangeRecord` procedure. If the menu choice is 3, then the Active flag is set to 'N'; otherwise the new data is accepted.

```
30    Sub ChangeRecord(MyChoice As Integer)
31      Dim Confirmation As Char
32      Console.Write("Key number ? ") : KeyNumber = Console.ReadLine
33      FileGet(1, MyAnimal, KeyNumber)
34      Call DisplayRecordData(KeyNumber)
35      Console.Write("Confirm this is the record to change (Y.N) ? ")
36      Confirmation = Console.ReadLine
37      If Confirmation = "Y" Then
38        If MyChoice = 3 Then
39          MyAnimal.Active = "N"
40          FilePut(1, MyAnimal, KeyNumber)
41        Else
42          ' input new data for this record ....
43          EnterRecordData()
44          FilePut(1, MyAnimal, KeyNumber)
45        End If
46      Else
47        Console.WriteLine("Delete operation aborted ...")
48        Console.WriteLine()
49      End If
50    End Sub
```

Figure 21.25 Amend a record

Figure 21.26 shows a screenshot of running the code to amend the 'camel' record.

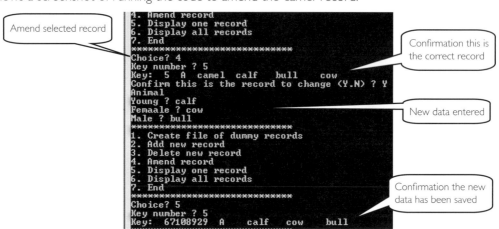

Figure 21.26 Amending a record

Figure 21.27 shows a screenshot of running the same code to delete the 'camel' record.

Figure 21.27 Delete a record

21.03 Exception handling

An 'exception' is a problem that arises during the execution of a program. An exception can occur for many different reasons, including:

- A user has entered invalid data which has caused the program execution to halt.

- A file that needs to be opened or a file directory that is referred to by code does not exist.

- A network connection has been lost.

- A virtual connection made to a database file has been lost.

Some of these exceptions are caused by user error, others by programmer error, and others by physical resources that have failed.

A **checked exception** is typically caused by a user error or a problem that cannot be foreseen by the programmer. For example, a 'file open' statement may have hard coded the name of a file or directory which does not exist. This type of error cannot be foreseen at compile time.

A **runtime exception** is an exception that probably could have been avoided by the programmer. An example would be an arithmetic calculation which 'attempts to divide by zero'. Again, runtime exceptions cannot be foreseen at compile time.

Code examples

Figures 21.28 to 21.30 show what happens when the system detects an exception that is not handled by the program. These are examples of 'checked exceptions'.

Figure 21.28 Device not ready

Figure 21.29 File not found

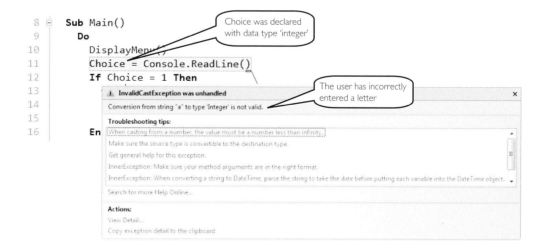

Figure 21.30 The user has input a letter

Figure 21.30 is an example of a runtime exception error.

Handling errors

In Visual Basic .NET, the basic structure which allows the programmer to 'catch' errors is illustrated with the following pseudocode:

```
Try
    // Statement which might cause an error
Catch
    // Handle exceptions that occur
    // within the Try block
Finally
    // Perform clean-up code
End Try
```

Figure 21.31 shows what happens when the system detects an exception that is handled by the program. The code after the error continues to execute and there is no indication of what caused the error.

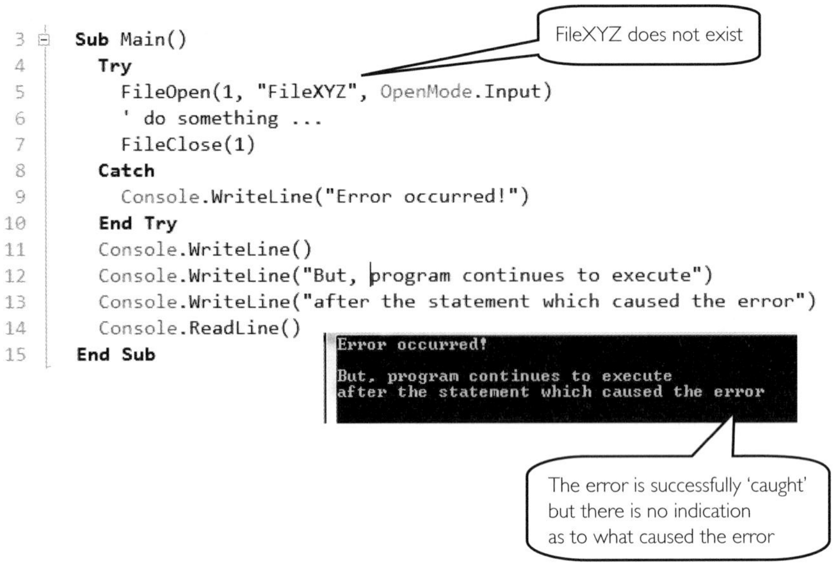

```
3      Sub Main()
4        Try
5          FileOpen(1, "FileXYZ", OpenMode.Input)
6          ' do something ...
7          FileClose(1)
8        Catch
9          Console.WriteLine("Error occurred!")
10       End Try
11       Console.WriteLine()
12       Console.WriteLine("But, program continues to execute")
13       Console.WriteLine("after the statement which caused the error")
14       Console.ReadLine()
15     End Sub
```

FileXYZ does not exist

```
Error occurred!
But, program continues to execute
after the statement which caused the error
```

The error is successfully 'caught' but there is no indication as to what caused the error

Figure 21.31 Exception is trapped

Visual Basic .NET has an **Exception** class, so the solution is to create a variable that is an instance of the Exception class. The basic code framework is as before but the **Catch** section mentions the error:

```
Dim e As Exception
Try
    // Code that might trigger an exception
Catch e
    // Handle the exception, using e
End Try
```

Figure 21.32 shows code using this format. Visual Basic .NET has several types of exception which are subclasses of the Exception class.

```
3    Sub Main()
4        Dim e As Exception
5        Try
6            FileOpen(1, "FileXYZ", OpenMode.Input)
7            ' do something ...
8            FileClose(1)
9        Catch e
10           Console.WriteLine(e.Message)
11       End Try
12       Console.WriteLine()
13       Console.WriteLine("But, program continues to execute")
14       Console.WriteLine("after the statement which caused the error")
15       Console.ReadLine()
16   End Sub
```

> The Exception class has a Message method

```
Could not find file 'C:\Users\Tony\AppData\Local\Temporary Projects\Exception
Divide by zero\bin\Debug\FileXYZ'.

But, program continues to execute
after the statement which caused the error
```

> The execution reports the Exception object's message

Figure 21.32 Using the exception object message property

21.04 Use of development tools and programming environments

Traditional program code was created using a text editor and then presented to the compiler for translation.

Modern software now wraps up all the features we need for the creating, translation, testing and execution of the program code with software called an integrated development environment (IDE).

LOOK BACK «

This was covered extensively in Chapter 20.

Features of an editor

A text editor is program that allows you to open, view, and edit plain text files. Unlike word-processing software, a text editor does not add formatting to text.

TIP

One of the more impressive pieces of software available (for free) for the editor stage is Notepad++.

In addition to all the expected text-editing features other facilities include:

- specification of the language used, in order that language keywords can be highlighted

- choice of font sizes and colour selection for various language components

- custom features including:

  o basic formatting

  o syntax highlighter

  o indentation styles

- search and replace across multiple open files

- bookmarks within a code listing

- collapse of code sections

- choice of character sets

- a number of plug-ins – for example to provide an FTP connection.

Compiler or interpreter?

LOOK BACK «

This was covered extensively in Chapter 20.

Facilities provided by a debugger

The features you should have used in your practical programming include:

- the ability to single step – one statement at a time – through the program code

- setting a breakpoint and then running the program up to that breakpoint, followed by inspection of the current value stored by one or more variables

- the display of the current value of all variables used in the code

- the setting up of an expression and displaying its current value.

LOOK BACK «

There were screenshots illustrating these IDE debugging features in Chapter 20.

Summary

- ☐ A programming paradigm is a 'way of doing things'. These include low-level, imperative, object-oriented and declarative.

- ☐ For OOP, instances of objects are created from a class definition. The class includes the properties and methods. A class can inherit from a parent class. A class design can include polymorphism and containment.

- ☐ Declarative programming uses a knowledge base of facts and rules. Information is obtained by setting a goal using a query.

- ☐ A data file can store data with a defined record structure.

- ☐ A random file allows direct access to individual records.

- ☐ File-processing operations can be performed on serial, sequential and random files.

- ☐ Robust program code includes code written for exception handling.

- ☐ A text editor is used for creating source code. The code is translated using a compiler or interpreter.

- ☐ Debugging facilities allow for program testing.

Exam-style questions

1 In a particular country to become a qualified driver you must:

- have a licence; there is a minimum age at which a person can be issued with a licence and it is different for cars and motorbikes

- pass a theory test; it is the same test for cars and motorbikes

- pass a driving test for that vehicle (car or motorbike)

A declarative programming language is to be used to represent the knowledge base shown below:

```
01 minimum_age(car, 18).
02 minimum_age(motorbike, 16).
03 age(yu, 16).
04 age(kong, 16).
05 age(ho, 15).
06 age(zhen, 21).
07 age(tain, 21).
08 age(shen, 21).
09 has_licence(yu).
10 has_licence(kong).
```

```
11 has_licence(ho).
12 has_licence(zhen).
13 has_licence(tain).
14 has_licence(shen).
15 able_to_drive(X, V) IF has_licence(X)
                          AND minimum_age(V, L)
                          AND age(X, A) AND A >= L.
16 passed_theory_test(kong).
17 passed_theory_test(yin).
18 passed_theory_test(zhen).
19 passed_theory_test(yu).
20 passed_driving_test(zhen, car).
21 passed_driving_test(yu, motorbike).
22 passed_driving_test(kong, car).
23 passed_driving_test(kong, motorbike).
24 passed_driving_test(shen, motorbike).
25 qualified_driver(X, V) IF able_to_drive(X, V)
                          AND passed_theory_test(X)
                          AND passed_driving_test(X, V).
```

These clauses have the following meaning:

Clause	Explanation
01	The minimum age for a car licence is 18
08	Shen is aged 21
13	Tain has a licence
15	Person X is able to drive vehicle V if person X has a licence, and the age A of person X is greater than or equal to the minimum age L to drive vehicle V

a List the clause numbers for the rules in this knowledge base. [1]

b Show the output produced from the clauses:

   i `passed_driving_test(Who, car)` [1]

   ii `able_to_drive(ho, motorbike)` [1]

   iii `NOT(has_licence(shen)).` [1]

c Write a clause to output:

   i all qualified motorbike drivers. [2]

   ii all drivers who have passed the theory test but not a driving test. [3]

d To produce the output from a clause, the inference engine uses a process called backtracking.

Consider the clause:

`able_to_drive(ho, motorbike)`

List the order in which clauses are used to produce the output. For each clause, describe the result that it returns. [3]

Cambridge International AS and A Level Computing 9691 Paper 33, Q4 Nov 2013

Software development

Revision objectives

By the end of the chapter you should be able to:

- [ ] show understanding of the possible role of program generators and program libraries in the development process

- [ ] show awareness of why errors occur and how testing can expose possible errors

- [ ] appreciate the significance of testing throughout software development

- [ ] show understanding of the methods of testing available

- [ ] show understanding of the need for a test strategy and test plan and their likely contents

- [ ] choose appropriate test data (normal, abnormal and extreme/boundary) for a test plan

- [ ] show understanding that large developments will involve teams

- [ ] show understanding of the need for project management

- [ ] show understanding of project-planning techniques

- [ ] describe the information that GANTT and PERT charts provide

- [ ] construct and edit GANTT and PERT charts

22.01 Program generators and program libraries

Program generators

A **program generator** is a program that generates other programs. The objective is that there will be less effort by increasing the automation of some programming task. The key question is what is generated. This could be as much as a fully-functioning app for a mobile device, where program code is never seen. One statement or descriptive line may generate a huge routine or an entire program.

With products such as PHPMaker, the generator is performing at a higher level than a high-level programming language. The software is a powerful automation tool that can generate a full set of PHP scripts which interact with a database. The generator software will create web sites that allow users to view, edit, search, add and delete records on the web. A criticism of program generators is that they generate excessive code which then executes slowly.

> **TERMS**
>
> **Program generator:** software designed to shorten the development time for program production

Other application areas are for:

- games creation with generators such as GameMaker

- the production of a graphical user interface using program wizards or templates which allow the programmer to design interactively while the compiler in the background generates the corresponding source code.

User interfaces is a popular application of a generator as all web-based applications will extensively use screen form designs.

Another strategy is that code may be generated from a diagrammatic representation of the data structures. Typically a set of class definitions could be generated from the class diagram (see Chapter 19).

Program libraries

> **LOOK BACK «**
>
> Program libraries were discussed extensively in Chapter 5, section 5.03.

22.02 Testing for errors

There are many examples of computer program errors which have hit the headlines and caused huge embarrassment. At worst, errors in a program have been responsible for loss of life.

- In the early 1960s, one of the USA Mariner space probes to Venus was lost forever due to an error in its flight control software.

- Families receive correspondence addressed to a family member who has been deceased for some months.

- At the turn of the century, it was feared that many computer systems would crash due to the 'millennium bug'. This was where software had been written using only two digits to encode the year part of a date field. It was feared that when the first two digits of the year field changed from 19 to 20, this would cause software to crash. In fact, it did not cause the widespread chaos that scaremongers had been predicting.

The aims of testing

The purpose of program testing is to discover errors that might be present in the software. Testing a program can never adequately prove or demonstrate the correctness of the program; testing can only reveal the existence of errors.

When is testing carried out?

- There will be discussion about testing before the development really begins (see the discussion of a walkthrough process, below).

- Tests are done at the development stage.

- Tests are done on the developed system.

The sequence in carrying out any test will be to:

- establish test objectives

- design test cases

- write test cases

- test the list of test cases

- execute each test

- evaluate test results.

Test documentation

All forms of testing should documented. Documentation will include:

- test plan: description of the system and plans for exercising all functions and characteristics

- test specification and evaluation: details of each test and criteria for their evaluation

- test description: test data and procedures for each test

- test analysis report: the results of each test.

Before some form of formal testing can take place all syntax errors will be removed. Modern IDEs are extremely helpful at identifying these errors. The compiler and interpreter software are both programmed to identify syntax errors, if they are not identified prior to translation. Syntax errors are not thought to be serious as they are generally easy to spot and correct.

Logic errors are those which result in the program not doing what is was intended to do. A simple example would be a loop which performs 99 iterations when the correct logic intended 100 iterations. Note, the program would probably still run and produce results. All of the following testing strategies are designed to identify and eliminate errors which could result either in the program crashing or the production of incorrect results.

Progress check 22.01

There is a logic error in the program below.

```
Sub Main()
    Dim i As Integer
    i = 1
    Do While i > 0
        i = i + 1000
        Console.WriteLine("i is ..." & i)
    Loop
End Sub
```

What fundamental error is there in this program code?

Types of testing

Dry run

A dry run is a mental run through of the computer program. The programmer examines the source code one statement at a time, following carefully the control structures to determine what the program will do when run. This could be taking place at the stage where the program code still has to be written and the dry run is done on pseudocode.

For a program which is based on a non-trivial algorithm, the dry run will be documented with pen and paper by completing a trace table.

LOOK BACK «

We introduced the use of a trace table in Chapter 12.

Progress check 22.02

A firm employees three sales staff and they are each given a target sales figure for the four quarters of the year. The data is stored in a 2D array `Target` of type BOOLEAN (illustrated below) and shows whether or not each target was met.

	1	2	3	4
1	TRUE	FALSE	TRUE	FALSE
2	FALSE	FALSE	TRUE	TRUE
3	FALSE	FALSE	FALSE	FALSE

The following code operates on the array:

```
FOR Quarter ← 1 TO 4
    NewArray[Quarter] ← 0
ENDFOR
FOR Person ← 1 TO 3
    FOR Quarter ← 1 TO 4
        IF Target[Person, Quarter] =
FALSE
            THEN
                NewArray[Quarter] ←
NewArray[Quarter] + 1
        ENDIF
    ENDFOR
ENDFOR
```

Complete this trace table:

Person	Quarter	Target [Person, Quarter]	NewArray [1]	[2]	[3]	[4]
	1		0			
	2			0		

What values is `NewArray` designed to store?

Walkthrough

A walkthrough is a process conducted by the development Team Leader, who takes the participants through the requirements specification to achieve a common understanding and to gather feedback. This is especially useful if individuals from outside the project team are involved. The client staff may have no prior knowledge of the software development process. The content of the development proposal is explained step by step by the Team Leader, to reach a consensus on changes or to gather information. A walkthrough is especially useful for higher-level documents, such as the requirements specification.

The aims of the walkthrough process are to:

- present the proposal to stakeholders both within and outside the project team

- explain and evaluate the contents of the requirements specification

- establish a common understanding of the likely involvement required by the client's staff

- examine and discuss the validity of proposed solutions and possible alternatives.

Black-box testing

Black-box testing is testing that is applied to a module, for example, a procedure or function. It checks that a module is functioning correctly by supplying the required inputs to the module and monitoring the outputs. There is effectively a 'black box' around the code and we are only concerned with what data goes in and what comes out of the procedure. Test cases are devised that provide a module with inputs.

Figure 22.01 shows some code and the output when the programmer runs it. The programmer has keyed in the job descriptions for:

- three jobs which exist in the array; the correct array index is returned each time

- a job which is not present in the array; the value −1 is returned.

```
3    Sub Main()
4      Dim Job(30) As String : Dim JobValue As String
5      Dim FoundIndex As Integer
6      Job(1) = "Teacher" : Job(2) = "Clerk" : Job(3) = "Gardener"
7      Job(4) = "Farmer" : Job(5) = "Manager" : Job(6) = "Cleaner"
8      Do
9        Console.Write("Which job ? ") : JobValue = Console.ReadLine
10       If JobValue <> "XX" Then
11         FoundIndex = Search(Job, 6, JobValue)
12         Console.WriteLine("Found return value is ..." & FoundIndex)
13         Console.ReadLine()
14       End If
15     Loop Until JobValue = "XX"
16
17    End Sub
18
19    Function Search(ThisArray() As String, UBound As Integer, ThisValue As String)
20      Dim Index As Integer
21      Dim Found As Boolean
22
23      Index = 1
24      Found = False
25      Do While Found = False And Index < UBound + 1
26        If ThisArray(Index) = ThisValue Then
27          Found = True
28          Return Index
29        Else
30          Index = Index + 1
31        End If
32      Loop
33
34      If Found = False Then Return -1
35    End Function
```

```
Which job ? Manager
Found return value is ...5

Which job ? Teacher
Found return value is ...1

Which job ? Cleaner
Found return value is ...6

Which job ? Pilot
Found return value is ...-1
```

Figure 22.01 Procedure code (with parameters)

The emphasis here is simply on inputting a value and checking the correct output is produced. This type of testing is effectively testing the procedure's interface. Sight of the actual source code may not be available to the tester.

White-box testing

This is again testing applied to a module, but this time the code inside the procedure is examined. Test cases are devised that exercise every possible route through the code.

In this way each logical path through the code is tested.

Integration testing

This will be the process which follows the white-box and black-box testing of individual modules.

> ## LOOK BACK «
>
> Chapter 20 discussed structure charts. The aim of a structure chart is to show how individual modules integrate with each other using parameter passing.

Alpha testing

Alpha testing is the initial stage where all the testing is done for the first time away from the development team, but still 'in-house'.

Beta testing

This follows completion of the alpha testing stage. An advance copy of software is released to selected customers and participants for trial purposes. A large company, such as Microsoft, might invite users to be beta testers for the next release of a software product.

Acceptance testing

This testing is effectively installation testing which takes place in the client's workplace. The customer checks that the supplied system meets the requirements as specified in the requirements specification document. The client may be asked by the developer to formally 'sign off' the system as proof of acceptance of the software. The key issues in the testing will include:

- volume tests – does the software deal with the volume of transactions?

- configuration tests – is the software working successfully with the operating system and are all input/output devices working correctly?

- compatibility tests – does the software function properly when it interacts with other existing software?

- quality tests – for example, is there an acceptable response time for interactive applications?

- recovery tests – are there clear procedures to recover data in the event of hardware or software failure?

Choosing test data

We are clear that for white-box testing we need to test every path through some particular code, and this may be dependent on a data value.

A CASE statement which has seven different pay grades would require that the developer carries out at least one test for each pay grade value. All of these values (which are valid and possible values) are 'normal' data. Thorough testing may require more than this. We should also test the code using extreme/boundary values.

For example, if the maximum credit balance allowed to a customer is $2000 we should test paths through the code which use this value.

Abnormal (or erroneous) data may be inadvertently entered by the user of the software. A menu choice which asks for a response of 1, 2, 3, 4 or 5 could crash the program if the user incorrectly keys some other character. Our discussion of exception handling is the program-coding technique to safeguard that this type of error will not cause the software to crash.

Entry of a new customer record with the credit limit as $3000 should be picked up as an error. The value is outside the range of permitted values.

> ### Progress check 22.03
>
> All players in a basketball team are awarded a match performance rating figure of 1 to 10. Suggest normal, borderline and invalid data values for the match performance data.

22.03 Project management

All business projects operate with staff organised into teams. For a software project, different members of the team have their own specialisms which they contribute: the analyst, the data designer, the programmer of language XYZ, the programmer who specialises in web applications with PHP code, the tester, the networking consultant, the technical author and many possible others.

Just as we highlighted some well-known failures due to inadequate program testing, there have been some even greater failures due to poor project management. There are many examples of projects costing millions of dollars which have either been abandoned completely or ended up costing several times the original budget.

The key issues for the management of any project are:

- effective leadership of a team of staff
- the financial budget
- time scales
- the resources requirement – staffing, hardware
- planning of all activities which make up the project, as many of the activities will be dependent on the prior completion of one or more earlier activities
- regular consultation with the client and other stakeholders to report on the development and invite feedback.

PERT charts

A **PERT** chart is a project-management tool. A PERT chart is a graphic representation of a project's schedule. It shows the sequence of tasks which tasks can be performed simultaneously and which tasks are dependent on the completion of others.

> **TERMS**
>
> PERT: Project Evaluation and Review Technique

The PERT chart can show detail such as:

- the critical path
- the earliest and latest start dates for each task
- the earliest and latest finish dates for each task
- slack time between tasks.

A PERT chart can document an entire project or a key phase of a project. The chart allows a team to avoid unrealistic timetables, to identify and shorten tasks that may be bottlenecks and to focus attention on the most critical tasks.

The critical path

The critical path is the sequence of tasks that must be completed. It shows the minimum time in which the project can be completed. If there is a delay in any of the activities on the critical path, it will cause a delay in the completion of the entire project.

Sample chart and terminology

Figure 22.02 shows a PERT chart with edges and nodes.

Edges are tasks or activities – the tasks in Figure 22.02 are labelled A, B, C, D, E and F. Events often simply represent the completion of tasks associated with arrows entering it. The duration of the task is shown on the edge line.

Nodes are time milestones – the nodes in Figure 22.02 are labelled 1 through to 6.

There is a fundamental error in the PERT chart in Figure 22.02. It would only be correct if the total time for tasks B and E was the same total time as for C, D and F.

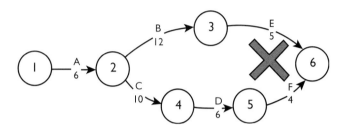

Figure 22.02 A PERT chart with error

Dummy activities

The solution is to add a dummy activity to the chart. A dummy activity shows the dependency between two events where no activity is performed. A dummy activity is shown with a dotted line, given a task identifier letter but with no duration time (see G in Figure 22.03).

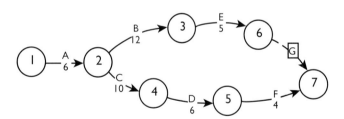

Figure 22.03 PERT chart with dummy activity

The PERT chart in Figure 22.03 is interpreted as:

- Tasks B and C can be done concurrently, but only after Task A has completed.
- The project will be completed when both task E and Task F have been completed.
- The sequence of tasks A, B, E takes total time 23 weeks.
- The sequence of tasks A, C, D and F takes total time 26 weeks.

Therefore the critical path time for the whole project is 26 weeks. The dummy activity indicates that Task E may be completed three weeks before the final completion date, or the starting of task E could be delayed by up to three weeks.

Slack time

This also means there is possible slack time for one or more of the tasks A, C or D. For example, once time point 2 is reached (after six weeks), one of B or E could be delayed by a maximum of three weeks or some combination of delayed start time which totals three weeks.

Early Start	Duration	Early Finish
	Task Name	
Late Start	Slack	Late Finish

Progress check 22.04

Is any slack time possible for Task B or Task E?

There are several variations on the symbol used for a node.

Task Name	
Scheduled Start	Scheduled Finish
Actual Start	Actual Finish

Figure 22.04 Alternative node symbols

Worked example

A software project is to be developed following the analysis stage.

The key tasks (in no specific order) are shown in Table 22.01.

Task	Description	Duration (weeks)
A	Produce the requirement specification	3
B	Detailed design	6
C	Code main program	6
D	Code module for database access	6
E	Code web forms	4
F	Carry out Integration testing	5
G	Write the user manual	3
H	Typeset and print user manual	6
I	Acceptance testing	3

Table 22.01 Project tasks

The PERT chart is shown in Figure 22.05.

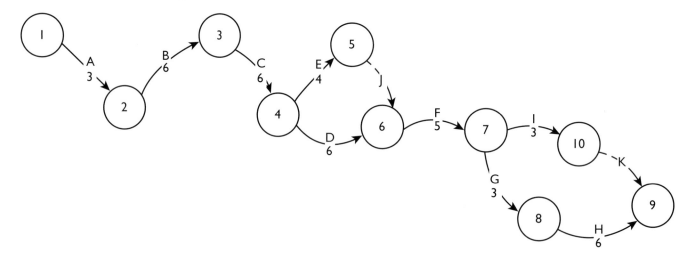

Figure 22.05 PERT chart

We can make the following conclusions from the chart:

- The critical path is A, B, C, D, J, F, G, H, K.
- The critical path time is 3 + 6 + 6 + 0 + 5 + 3 + 6 + 0 = 29 weeks.

GANTT chart

A GANTT chart conveys some of the same information as a PERT chart, but also shows new information. It allows us to record the progress of project, showing which tasks are falling behind and which tasks overlap.

The chart is constructed as follows:

1 Identify the tasks to be scheduled.

2 Determine the duration of each task.

3 List each task down the vertical axis of the chart; in general, tasks to be performed first are at the top.

4 Show dates on the horizontal axis.

5 Determine the start and finish dates for all activities.

6 Consider which tasks must be completed or partially completed before the next task.

The chart can be used to show the progress of each task which makes up the project. The task bar shading (or in Figure 22.06 the bold line) shows the percentage of the task completed; a blank bar indicates 'not yet started'; completely shaded shows 'Task completed'.

Figure 22.06 shows the current progress of the project as follows:

- Tasks A, B and C have been completed, which meant that both tasks D and E could commence.
- Task D is 50% completed.
- Task E is 20% completed.

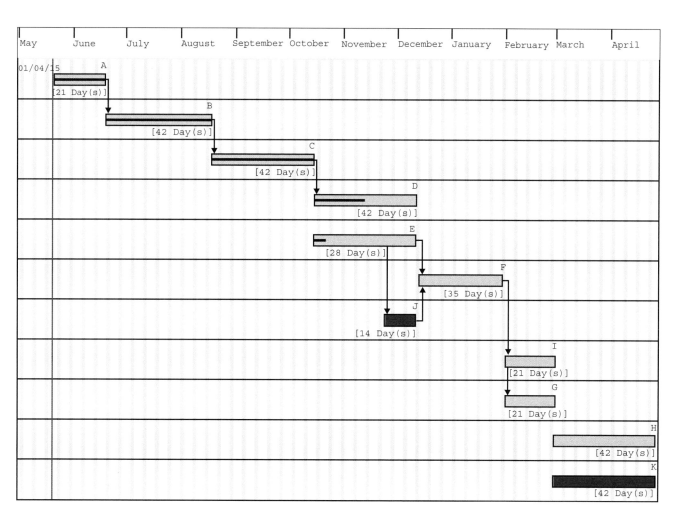

Figure 22.06 GANTT chart

Summary

- A program generator is software designed to shorten the development time for program production. Program coding may make use of existing libraries of program code.

- Programs contain errors, some of which may go undetected throughout the life of the software. Test strategies and a test plan are devised to identify errors through formal testing procedures. Methods of testing include a dry run using a trace table, a walkthrough, white-box and black-box testing, alpha and beta testing, integration testing and acceptance testing by the client.

- A test plan will be drawn up with carefully chosen test data which includes normal data, abnormal data and extreme or boundary data.

- Large software projects are done by teams. A large development project will require careful project management of resources and staff.

- Software tools which monitor project planning are GANTT and PERT charts.

Exam-style questions

1 A software development project consists, in part, of these activities.

		Weeks to complete
A	identify requirements	3
B	produce design	5
C	write code	9
D	black box testing	2
E	acceptance testing	3
F	prepare documentation	6

From this data, a Program Evaluation Review Technique (PERT) chart is constructed.

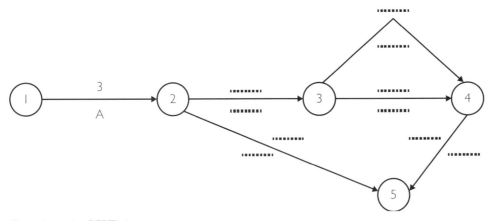

a Complete the PERT chart [4]

b i State the critical path. [1]

   ii State the minimum time for the completion of this development. [1]

c For activity D:

   i state the earliest start time. [1]

   ii state the latest start time. [1]

Cambridge International AS and A Level Computer Science 9608 Specimen Paper 4, Q4 2015

Answers

The sample answers and marks provided are for the progress checks and exam-style questions at the end of each chapter and have not been taken from real mark schemes.

PART 1

Chapter 1

Progress check 1.01

1   103
2   a   65
    b   170
    c   255
3   a   0000 0011
    b   0101 1001
    c   257 is too large to represent using only one byte
4   a   26
    b   267
5   a   0000 0111 1101
    b   0001 1001 0110
    c   1010 1110 1100

Progress check 1.02

Row 2: 4w5g5b8r8w

Row 3: 14w8r8w

Row 4: 30w

Exam-style questions

1   a   −90   (1 mark)
    b   −38   (1 mark)
    c   A6   (1 mark)
2   a   i   122   (1 mark)
        ii 5C   (1 mark)
        iii Fewer digits are used to represent any number;
            long strings of binary are difficult to interpret.   (1 mark)
            You are less likely to make a mistake when
            copying or converting a digit string.   (1 mark)
            It is easier to convert from binary to hex
            (or vice versa) than from binary to denary.   (1 mark)
    b   256   (1 mark)
3   a   i   1001 0110   (1 mark)
        ii 9C   (1 mark)
    b   height: 205 pixels;   (1 mark)
        width: 156 pixels   (1 mark)
    c   i   1 bit   (1 mark)
        ii Each colour is represented by a number.   (1 mark)
            1 byte makes possible 256 different numbers/
            colours   (1 mark)

iii   the header   (1 mark)
      the resolution   (1 mark)
iv   Four answers accepted from:
      A bitmap may contain the same sequence
      of pixels (i.e. a pattern) repeated many times   (1 mark)
      A bitmap may contain the same pixel in a
      long sequence.   (1 mark)
      A lossless technique is designed to lose none
      of the original detail   (1 mark)
      Lossless allows the original file to be re-created
      exactly   (1 mark)
      Lossy may result in a loss of detail   (1 mark)
      One lossless technique is 'run-length encoding'
      technique   (1 mark)
      store the colour and the number of consecutive
      pixels of that colour   (1 mark)
      JPEG and GIF file formats use RLE (i.e. a lossless
      technique).   (1 mark)
      Lossless techniques are founded on some form
      of replacement   (1 mark)
      Lossy techniques make a decision about what
      parts of the image are important and then
      discard certain information   (1 mark)
      Total: 4 marks

Chapter 2

Progress check 2.01

The Internet is the hardware infrastructure which makes global communication possible. It is a packet-switched network.

The WWW is the provision of 'content' and resources from various web servers.

Progress check 2.02

1   PSTN stands for Public Service Telephone Network.
2   Advantages to the company of using dedicated lines for all its digital communications include:
    o   Faster data transfer speeds
    o   Better support network

Progress check 2.03

*   The signals will be free of any interference.

*   Signals do not suffer from a loss of strength (attenuation).

*   The cabling – unlike copper wire – does not suffer from corrosion.

Progress check 2.04

1. 4 bytes = 32 bits
2. 255.168.4.13
3. The largest denary number possible for any of the bytes is 255.

Progress check 2.05

1. The client web browser application requests the page using the URI.
2. The DNS directs the request to the appropriate domain.
3. The server retrieves the page.
4. The server sends the page content, consisting of HTML tags and text content only, to the client.
5. The client web browser software 'renders' the page and displays it.

Progress check 2.06

1. The client web browser application requests the page using the URI.
2. The DNS directs the request to the appropriate domain.
3. The server retrieves the page.
4. The server sends the page content, consisting of HTML tags, text and a section of JavaScript code to the client.
5. The browser runs the JavaScript interpreter to process the code.
6. The client web browser software 'renders' the page and displays it.

Progress check 2.07

1. Line 15
2. First expression is the initial value for variable

   `loopCounter.`

   Second expression is the condition to test to end the loop.

   Third expression is the increment for

   `loopCounter.`
3. Line 27
4. A resit will be required
5. Line 13
6. `loopCounter, nextMark and totalMark`

Progress check 2.08

1. JavaScript is a 'client-side' programming language. The program code is processed by the client web browser. PHP as a 'server-side' scripting language. The code is processed by the server.
2. When a browser requests a page that contains PHP:
   a. The web browser requests the page.
   b. The web server is aware it contains code.
   c. The web server processes the code.
   d. The web server renders the page content (as HTML tags and text only).
   e. The web server delivers the page to the browser (as HTML tags and text only).
   f. The client browser displays the page.

Exam-style questions

1. a. Lines 10–35 (1 mark)
   b. i. `myWeight,myHeight or myBMI` (2 mark)
      ii. Lines 21–33
   c. i. One answer accepted from:
         prompts the user for input (1 mark)
         assigns the input to the given variable (1 mark)
      ii. One answer accepted from:
         displays the text shown (1 mark)
         in a dialogue box with the alert symbol (1 mark)
   d. router (1 mark)
   e. F – G – B – A – C (1 mark)
   f. The browser will have an interpreter to execute the JavaScript code. (1 mark)
   g. The browser loads the page from the local hard drive. (1 mark)
2. a. Uniform Resource Locator (1 mark)
   b. A – the protocol (1 mark)
      B – the domain (1 mark)
      C – directories on the web server (1 mark)
      D – The file (1 mark)

Chapter 3

Progress check 3.01

- Pressure – pressure pad in the road approaching a set of traffic control signals
- Temperature – computer-controlled oven that uses actuators to switch a heating circuit on or off
- Wind speed or flow– wind speed over some threshold value may trigger an actuator which closes the windows of a computer-controlled greenhouse
- Light intensity – when the intensity reaches a low threshold lights are switched on

Progress check 3.02

- Electric current – open/close doors on a train
- Hydraulic (fluid) pressure – power steering, braking system on a car
- Pneumatic (air) pressure – moving parts on heavy plant machinery such as a digger or fork-lift truck

Progress check 3.03

1 The logic circuit:

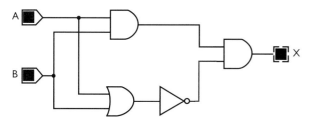

2 The truth table:

Input		Output
A	**B**	**X**
0	0	0
0	1	0
1	0	0
1	1	0

Progress check 3.04

1 It can be simplified using only two gates:

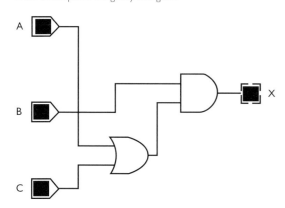

2 It can be simplified using one gate only: a NOR gate.

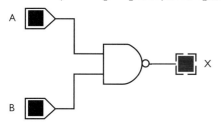

Exam-style questions

1 a

Input		Output	
A	**B**	**C**	**S**
0	0	0	0
0	1	0	1
1	0	0	1
1	1	1	0

1 mark for each correct row   Total: 4 marks

   b It adds together two single bits
(which is a 'half adder').   (1 mark)

2 Five answers accepted from:

a laser beam and a rotating mirror are used to draw
an image of the page on a photosensitive drum.   (1 mark)

This image is converted on the drum into an
electrostatic charge.   (1 mark)

the charge on the drum attracts and holds toner.   (1 mark)

the electro-statically charged paper is rolled against
the drum.   (1 mark)

the charge pulls the toner away from the drum and
onto the paper.   (1 mark)

heat is then applied to fuse the toner to the paper.   (1 mark)

Finally, the electrical charge is removed from the drum.   (1 mark)

the excess toner is collected.   (1 mark)

Total: 5 marks

Chapter 4

Progress check 4.01

IN, OUTCH and END

Progress check 4.02

1 Load 14 to ACC.

Copy the contents of ACC, that is, 14, to address 156.

2 Go to address 105 (value 102)

Copy the contents of address 102, that is, 56, to ACC.

3 Form the address 102 + 2 = 104

Copy the contents of address 104, that is, 165, to ACC.

Progress check 4.03

1   00000001 01100110
2   00000110 00011111
3   00001000
4   00001111 00101101

Exam-style questions

1   a   i   ACC = 77 (1 mark)
            Show contents of 203 copied to ACC (1 mark)
        ii Two answers accepted from:
            ACC = 65 (1 mark)
            Show 150 used as a forwarding address. (1 mark)
            Contents of 200 are copied to ACC. (1 mark)
    b   i   256 different instructions (1 mark)
        ii Store the ACC contents (1 mark)
            at address 65 (01000001) (1 mark)
        iii One answer from:
            fewer digits to write (1 mark)
            less chance of an error in writing the code (1 mark)
            easy conversion to/from a binary code (1 mark)
        iv 1041 hex (1 mark)
        v   LDI 150

0	0	0	0	0	1	1	0	1	0	0	1	0	1	1	0

            1 mark for each byte (2 marks)
        vi LDV 15

0	0	0	0	0	1	0	1	0	0	0	0	1	1	1	1

            1 mark for each byte (2 marks)
        vii True (1 mark)
            OUTCH or IN or END (1 mark)

c

ACC	Location 150	OUTPUT
65		A
200		
201	201	
76		L
201		
202	202	
65		A
202		
203	203	
77		M
203		
204	204	

1 mark for each group of trace table entries   Total: 5 marks

Chapter 5

Progress check 5.01

1 System software

2 Software which must be present to make the hardware usable. Software which provides a user interface between the user and the hardware.

Progress check 5.02

Processor; main memory; secondary storage; input/output devices; the user interface

Progress check 5.03

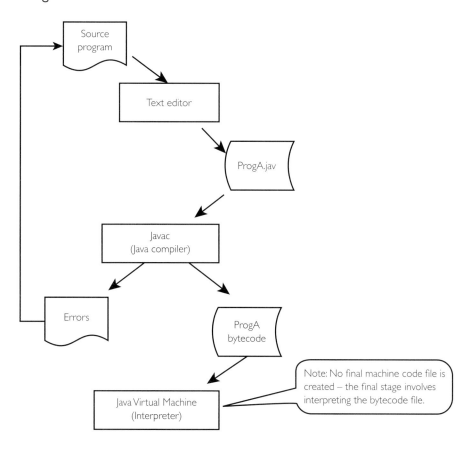

Exam-style questions

1	a	All the keywords which make up the syntax of the language	(1 mark)
		A token for each keyword	(1 mark)
	b	DECLARE, CONSTANT, CALL, REPEAT	(1 mark)
	c	A list of all the identifiers used by the program	(1 mark)
		A pointer to where their value is stored in memory	(1 mark)
	d	Three identifiers from:	
		i, Customer, Address, DiscountRate, InitialiseCustomerData	(1 mark)

Chapter 6

Progress check 6.01

Check digit is 9. The complete employee code should be 94379.

Progress check 6.02

Attribute	Verification / Validation check							
	Verify	From a list	Range	Format	Length	Presence	Uniqueness	Check digit
FamilyName	✓				✓	✓		
Forenames	✓				✓	✓		
DateOfBirth	✓	✓	✓	✓		✓		
Address					✓			
Email	✓			✓	✓		✓	
MemType		✓				✓		
NoOfVisits		✓	✓					
Before		✓						

Progress check 6.03

You should have checked that:

- for each row the total number of 1 bits is an odd number
- for each column the total number of 1 bits is odd.

Progress check 6.04

1 There is one error:

0	0	0	0	1	1	1	1
1	1	1	**0**	0	0	0	0
1	0	1	1	0	0	0	1
0	1	1	1	1	0	0	0
0	0	1	1	0	1	1	0

2 The error can be identified:

- The parity bit for byte 2 would be calculated as 1.
- The parity bit in column 4 would be calculated as zero.
- Therefore byte 2, column 4 contains the error – change the bit to a 1.

Progress check 6.05

- Security is the safeguarding of the data against accidental or malicious damage or loss.
- Privacy is preventing access to personal data by persons other than the subject or a third party who has permission to do so.
- integrity is the safeguarding of the validity and 'correctness' of the data.

Exam-style questions

1 a Three answers accepted from:

   Type of parity (odd or even) is agreed by both devices concerned with the communication. (1 mark)

   Transmitting device counts number of 1 bits in the byte (1 mark)

   One bit is reserved for parity bit. This parity bit is set to 1 or 0 in order to make the number of 1s in the byte an odd or even. (1 mark)

   The receiving device on receipt of byte counts number of 1s. If an odd number of 1s (if even parity used) gives an error. (1 mark)

   b Three answers accepted from:

   Odd parity is used (1 mark)

   Byte number 5 has an even number of 1s therefore an error (1 mark)

   Column 4 has an even number of 1s (1 mark)

   Therefore the 0 in row 5, column 4 needs to be changed to 1 (1 mark)

2 a The format is two upper case letter characters followed by four digit characters (1 mark)

   b The first two characters are selected from a list (1 mark)

   The length is exactly six characters (1 mark)

   The new product entered must be unique (1 mark)

   When the new product is entered the product code must be present (1 mark)

Chapter 7

Progress check 7.01

- Keep the client informed about progress and possible slippage.
- Keep Business B informed about when to interview staff, etc.
- Make Business B aware of any legislation they must comply with, for example, registration of application to comply with the Data Protection Act.
- Ensure the privacy and security of any personal data made available to Business A during the development of the software.

Progress check 7.02

1 Yes.
2 It's an offence under the Computer Misuse Act.

Progress check 7.03

- run the software
- copy the software
- distribute the software to other users
- study the code and change and improve the software

Exam-style questions

1 a product – 3 (1 mark)

management – 1 (1 mark)

self – 2 (1 mark)

   b i Management at fault need to keep whole project staff fully informed – i.e. a MANAGEMENT issue

This could impact on the whole project – i.e. a PRODUCT issue.

JUDGEMENT of the project leader is poor (1 mark)

      ii A SELF issue – staff should be expected to keep their skills up to date.

It could be the EMPLOYER is not able to move quickly into new areas of work (1 mark)

      iii This is a PUBLIC interest issue.

The employee has used good JUDGEMENT in bringing the issue into open discussion. (1 mark)

2

	Ethical	Unethical
To save tine Manjit often makes up the test results for her CODEIT programs		✓
Manjit has used many of the coding techniques she leant from other employees at CODEIT in her own spare-time programs	✓	
Manjit has twice recently turned down the opportunity to leave CODEIT and work for another company for more pay	✓	
Manjit organises training courses in the writing of software in her spare time.	✓	
Manjit has taken electronic copies of code from her CODEIT job and used it in her own programs		✓
Other employees at CODEIT often ask Manjit for help and she always refuses, saying she is too busy.		✓

1 mark for each correct row   Max. 6 marks

Chapter 8

Progress check 8.01

- The lists of attributes for all tables – YES
- The detail for all attributes – YES
- The customer data – NO
- The results of all queries – NO
- Query descriptions – YES

Progress check 8.02

1 Primary key – `PupilNumber`
2 Index the pupil name attribute – we shall frequently search the database for a pupil using their name

Progress check 8.03

If there is a tuple in the `ORDER` table which includes a `ProductID` value which is not present in the `PRODUCT` table.

Progress check 8.04

1 `CourseCode`

2 Integer (or, if you are using a program which supports it, Byte – a range of 0–255 will be OK)

3 Address and the course(s) on which they can teach (although this second suggestion presents a problem as some data may need to be stored in a new table)

4 `TrainerName` (as there will not be too many trainers and it is highly unlikely we shall have two trainers with the same name)

5 It cannot be `CourseDate` (as we have two different courses scheduled for the same date) so, it will be a composite key of `CourseDate` and `CourseCode`

6 One trainer will deliver many course-diary sessions; one course is offered many times in the course diary

7 `Trainer` to link back to the `TrainerName` attribute in table `TRAINER`

`CourseCode` to link back to `CourseCode` in the COURSE table.

8 ER diagram as shown.

Progress check 8.05

1

Foreign key	
Table.Attribute	Links to
STAFF.City	LOCATION.City
STAFF-RECORD.StaffID	STAFF.StaffID
STAFF-RECORD.CourseTitle	COURSE.CourseTitle
COURSE-SESSION.CourseTitle	COURSE.CourseTitle

2

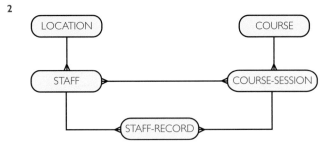

Progress check 8.06

1 a False – that statement is first normal form.

  b True

  c True

  d False – if it has a composite primary key we need to look carefully at the non-key attributes.

  e True

2 a True

  b True – if we know the tutor initials we automatically know the tutor name.

c True – if we know the tutor initials we automatically know the tutor room.

d False – 3NF is concerned with non-key attributes.

3 a `TutorInitials`

  b One tutor is responsible for many students,

Progress check 8.07

1

Table	Primary key	Foreign Key(s)
BAND	BandName	None
AGENT	AgentName	None
BAND-TOUR	TourName	BandName links to primary key BAND.BandName
BAND-TOUR-GIGS	TourName and GigDate Could also have been BandName and GigDate	TourName links to primary key BAND-TOUR.TourName VenueName links to primary key VENUE.VenueName BandName links to primary key BAND.BandName
VENUE	VenueName	None

2

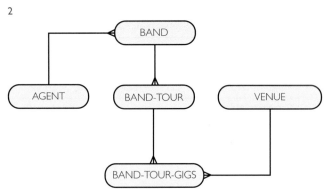

3 a
```
SELECT BandName
FROM BAND
WHERE AgentName = 'Maximum Exposure'
```
b
```
SELECT BandName
FROM BAND-TOUR
WHERE StartDate >= #01/01/2015#
```
c
```
SELECT TourName
FROM BAND-TOUR
WHERE StartDate > #01/06/2015#
  AND MaxNoOfGigs > 10
```
d
```
SELECT BAND-TOUR-GIGS.BandName, BAND-TOUR-GIGS.TourName,
    VENUE.VenueName
FROM BAND-TOUR-GIGS INNER JOIN VENUE
WHERE VENUE.Location = 'Paris'
```
e
```
SELECT GigDate, VenueName
FROM BAND-TOUR-GIGS
WHERE TourName = 'Back to the future'
ORDER BY GigDate
```

Exam-style questions

1	a	i	`RaceRunner(RaceDate, RunnerID)`	(2 marks)

ii

b	i	Not in 2 NF is table **RaceRunner**	(1 mark)
	ii	`RaceRunner(RaceDate, RunnerID FinishingPosition)`	(1 mark)
	iii	Not in 3NF is table **Race**	(1 mark)
	iv	`Race(RaceDate, RaceDistance, ClubName)`	(1 mark)
		New table **Club** …	
		`Club(ClubName, ClubTown, ClubSecretaryName)`	(1 mark)
c	i	`SELECT RunnerID`	(1 mark)
		`FROM RaceRunner`	(1 mark)
		`WHERE RaceDate = #26/11/2014#`	(1 mark)
	ii	`UPDATE RaceRunner`	(1 mark)
		`SET FinishingPosition = 2`	(1 mark)
		`WHERE RaceDate = #26/11/2014# AND RunnerID = 8816`	(1 mark)

PART 2

Chapter 9

Progress check 9.01

1 Assignment, selection, iteration, sequence

2 Stepwise refinement

Progress check 9.02

I

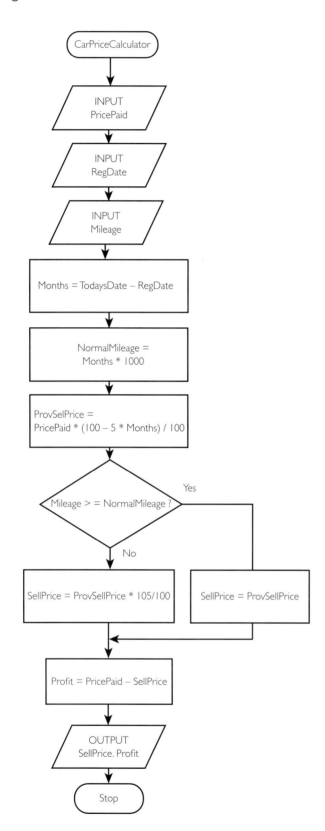

2

YearNumber	Amount	OUTPUT
1	100	
2	120	
3	144	
4	172.80	4

Progress check 9.03

The rates of tax will change.

The calculations for the amount of tax paid by an individual can change.

Exam-style questions

1
```
FUNCTION FindPassword(ThisUserID : STRING) RETURNS STRING
    DECLARE Found : BOOLEAN
    OPENFILE "PASSWORDS" FOR INPUT // for reading
    Found ← FALSE
    WHILE NOT EOF("PASSWORDS") AND Found = FALSE
        FILEREAD UserID
        FILEREAD EncryptedPassword
        IF UserID = ThisUserID
            THEN
                Found ← TRUE
        ENDIF
    ENDWHILE
    IF Found = TRUE
        THEN
            RETURN EncryptedPassword
        ELSE
            RETURN Error Code
    ENDIF
    CLOSEFILE "PASSWORDS"
ENDFUNCTION
```
(1 mark)

(3 mark)

(1 mark)

(1 mark)

(1 mark)

(1 mark)

1 mark for each table cell answer

Total: 8 marks

Chapter 10

Progress check 10.01

8 will be assumed to be an integer (data type `INTEGER`).

`"8"` is a string value consisting of a single character which is the digit 8 (data type `STRING`).

`'8'` is a character value (data type `CHAR`).

Progress check 10.02

1 4

2 `Sales[2,8]`

3 a Two ID arrays

b `DECLARE Surname[1:203] OF STRING`
`DECLARE DateJoined[1:203] OF STRING`

Progress check 10.03

1 The file `Products.txt` contains three lines of text:

Screwdriver

Hammer

Saw

2 The file contains the single line of text:

Saw

The earlier attempts at creating the file will have been overwritten.

Exam-style questions

1 a easier to follow logic of problem

can focus on one part at a time

produces reusable code

easier to maintain

can debug a small section at a time (2 marks)

b i courseworkID/other comparable identifier name

integer/other sensible (2 marks)

ii PASCAL solution

```
TYPE Assignment = RECORD
    CourseworkID : String[6];
    Subject      : String[10];
    Title        : String[10];
    DateSet      : TDateTime;
    HandInDate   : TDateTime;
    IsMarked     : Boolean;
    DateReturned : TDateTime;
    Mark         : Integer;
END;
```

```
VB.NET / VB 2005 solution
STRUCTURE Assignment
    DIM CourseworkID AS String
    DIM Subject AS String
    DIM Title AS String
    DIM DateSet AS Date
    DIM HandInDate AS Date
    DIM IsMarked AS Boolean
    DIM DateReturned AS Date
    DIM Mark AS Integer
END STRUCTURE
PYTHON solution
class Assignment :
    CourseworkID = "";
    Subject = ""
    Title = ""
    DateSet = datetime.date(1,1,1)
    HandInDate = datetime.date(1,1,1)
    IsMarked = False
    DateReturned = datetime.date(1,1,1)
    Mark = 0
```

Marking guidelines:

for correct record header   (1 mark)

correct definition terminator   (1 mark)

mark for all 3 dates declared correctly

• DateSet

• HandInDate

• DateReturned   (3 marks)

fields defined correctly for language

• Subject

• Title

• IsMarked

• Mark   (4 marks)

    iii I   (1 mark)

c uses/detect a marker written to the file …

    immediately after the last record

    when processing a variable length file

    records can be processed until the marker is reached

    returns a Boolean value   (2 marks)

d Found ← FALSE

```
WHILE NOT EOF(MyAssignments) AND NOT FOUND DO
    Read next record
    IF Assignment.Subject = "Physics"
        THEN
                Found ← TRUE
    ENDIF
ENDWHILE
```

set record found to false

while NOT EOF and record found is false

read next record

check subject field to see if it is the wanted one

if it is, set record found to true   (4 marks)

Chapter 11

Progress check 11.01

Identifier	Valid?	Explanation
1FaultTotal	✗	Starts with a digit character
NoOfFaults	✓	
Number Of Faults	✗	Contains spaces
NumberofFaults	✓	
Number_Of_Faults	✓	
Number-Of-Faults	✗	Dash character not allowed

Progress check 11.02

```
I  INPUT SearchName
   IsFound ← FALSE
   Index ← 1
   WHILE (IsFound = FALSE) AND (Index <> 21)
       IF Surname[Index] = SearchName
           THEN
               IsFound ← TRUE
               OUTPUT "Surname was FOUND - at position ", Index
           ELSE
               Index ← Index + 1
           ENDIF
   ENDWHILE
   IF IsFound = FALSE
       THEN
           OUTPUT "Surname was NOT FOUND"
   ENDIF
```

2 a

Identifier	Data type	Description
Registration	ARRAY[1:10] OF STRING	The array for the data items
i	INTEGER	Loop counter

b
```
FOR i ← 1 TO 10
    OUTPUT "Registration ? "
    INPUT Registration [i]
ENDFOR
```

The problem says 10 cars, so we use a For – EndFor loop

3 a
```
DECLARE i : INTEGER
DECLARE EMailAdress[1:1000] OF STRING
DECLARE NextEMail : STRING
```

b
```
i ← 1
REPEAT
    OUTPUT "EMail ...? "
    INPUT NextEmail
    IF NextEMail <> "XXX"
        THEN
            EMailAddress[i]← NextEMail
        ELSE
            i ← i - 1
    ENDIF
    i ← i + 1
UNTIL NextEMail = "XXX" !
```

The value 'XXX' use in this way is called a 'rogue value'

Progress check 11.03

1

Pass	i	UBound	Swapped	Animal 1	2	3	4	5
1		5	FALSE	CAT	ANT	COW	RAT	BEE
	1		TRUE	ANT	CAT			
	2							
	3							
	4		TRUE				BEE	RAT
2			FALSE	ANT	CAT	COW	BEE	RAT
	1							
	2							
	3		TRUE				BEE	COW
3			FALSE	ANT	CAT	BEE	COW	RAT
	1							
	2		TRUE			BEE	CAT	
			FALSE	ANT	BEE	CAT	COW	RAT
4	1			ANT	BEE	CAT	COW	RAT

2 The items were sorted on the third iteration of the loop.

295

Progress check 11.04

1 George Clooney

2 CrystalPalaceFC

3 Bin

4 12

5 a SUBSTR(MyString, 4, 7)

   b SUBSTR(MyString, 16, 20)

   c SUBSTR(MyString, 9, 10) & SUBSTR(MyString, 16, 20)

Progress check 11.05

1 17

2 1255

3 3

Progress check 11.06

1 a 80

   b 90−72 = 18

2 a HAPPY

   b 88

Progress check 11.07

Identifier	Data type	Description
PlayerAScore	INTEGER	Game total for Player A
PlayerBScore	INTEGER	Game total for Player B
Words	INTEGER	Loop counter
NextNum	REAL	A random number between 0 and 0.99999

Progress check 11.08

Pseudocode	Visual basic.Net	Python	Pascal
CHARACTERCOUNT	Len	Len	Length
ONECHAR	Mid	<Variable> [<index1>, <index1> + 1]	Copy
SUBSTR	Mid	<Variable> [<index1>, <index2>]	Copy
TONUM	Val	Int Float	Val
INT	Int	Int	Int
ASC	Asc	Ord	Ord
CHR	Chr	Chr	Chr
RND	Rnd	Random	Random

Progress check 11.09

1 Lines 18, 25 and 29

2 Line 04

3 We cannot determine that – the menu will continue to be displayed until the user enters 3.

Progress check 11.10

You would need to add a third parameter to the procedure header on line 10 of Figure 11.12:

```
PROCEDURE IncreasePrice(PriceArray : ARRAY OF REAL,
                        UBound : INTEGER,
            PercentageIncrease : INTEGER)
```

Line 13 of Figure 11.12 then becomes:

```
PriceArray[Item] ← PriceArray[Item] * (1 + PercentageIncrease/100)
```

You would call the procedure with:

```
CALL IncreasePrice(Electricals, 550, 20)
```

Progress check 11.11

```
OPEN "MyFile" FOR READ
// statement reads "while it's not the end of the file"
WHILE NOT(EOF("MyFile"))
   <statement(s)>
ENDWHILE

CLOSEFILE "MyFile"
```

Progress check 11.12

- declaration of variables: Pascal (keyword `Var`) and VB.Net (keyword `Dim`) must have variables declared before their use; in Python variables are not declared

- assignment of variables: common to all three languages – Pascal uses the := operator, VB.Net and Python use the = operator

- selection: the `IF–THEN–ELSE–ENDIF` construct has minor differences in exact syntax; Pascal and VB.Net have a `CASE` structure, Python does not

- loops: all three languages have a count-controlled loop structure and a pre-condition loop structure; Pascal (`Repeat–Until`) and VB.Net (`Do–Loop Until`) have a post-condition structure, Python does not.

Exam-style questions

1 a i 3 (1 mark)

   ii 2 (1 mark)

   b
```
FUNCTION CalculateNumberOfBoxes(NumberOfEggs : INTEGER)
                                RETURNS INTEGER
    DECLARE NumberOfBoxes : INTEGER
    NumberOfBoxes ← NumberOfEggs DIV 6  // how many full boxes?
    IF NumberOfEggs MOD 6 > 0 // need part of a box?
       THEN  // increment number of boxes
           NumberOfBoxes ← NumberOfBoxes + 1
    ENDIF
    RETURN NumberOfBoxes
ENDFUNCTION
```
1 mark for each emboldened answer Max 5 marks

   c A function always returns a value. (A procedure may or may not return one or more values.) (1 mark)

Chapter 12

Exam-style questions

1 a Single software program to allow... (1 mark)

      all aspects of the writing, testing and compilation process to take place. (1 mark)

   b Three answers accepted from:

      - syntax checking on entry (1 mark)
      - structure blocks (e.g. IF structure and loops begin/end highlighted) (1 mark)
      - general prettyprint features (1 mark)
      - highlights any undeclared variables / unassigned variables (1 mark)
      - commenting out/in of blocks of code (1 mark)
      - visual collapsing/highlighting of blocks of code (1 mark)

   c Two answers accepted from:

      - single stepping through the code (1 mark)
      - use of breakpoints (1 mark)
      - use of a variable/expression report window (1 mark)

PART 3

Chapter 13

Progress check 13.01

```
TYPE NurseData
    DECLARE NurseID                 : STRING
    DECLARE FamilyName              : STRING
    DECLARE FirstNames              : STRING
    DECLARE RegistrationDate        : DATE
    DECLARE HeathAndSafetyCourse    : CHAR
ENDTYPE
```

Stores value 'Y' or 'N' Could be defined as a BOOLEAN variable

Progress check 13.02

1 The enquiries staff will need direct access to particular records in the file.

2 The account number should be used as the record key, then the record can be directly accessed using the account number.

Progress check 13.03

1 01000111 00000101

2 01100110 00000010

3 10100100 00000100

Progress check 13.04

1 • The mantissa starts with digits 01.

• The mantissa starts with digits 10.

• The mantissa starts with digits 10.

2 • 01110000 01000001 – mantissa: 7/8; exponent: +1; denary number: 1.75

• 10001000 00000111 – mantissa: –15/16; exponent: +7; denary number: –120

• 10100000 10001001 – mantissa: –3/4; exponent: –119; denary number: -3×2^{-121}

Progress check 13.05

Mantissa: ½ + ¼ + 1/8 + 1/16 = +15/16

Exponent: 15

Number: $+15/16 \times 2^{15}$

$= +15 \times 2^{11}$

$= +15 \times 2048 = +3720$

Exam-style questions

1 a i +6.5 (1 mark)

  Exponent: +3 (1 mark)

  Mantissa: +13/16 (1 mark)

  ii (*Positive* …) The mantissa/byte 7 starts with a zero (1 mark)

 b i (*Normalised* …) The <u>mantissa/byte 7</u> starts with 01 and the first two bits are different (1 mark)

  ii

Mantissa								Exponent							
0	1	1	0	0	0	0	0	0	0	0	0	1	0	1	0

Mantissa								Exponent							
1	0	0	0	1	1	0	0	0	0	1	1	1	0	0	1

1 mark for each mantissa

1 mark for each exponent   Max. 4 marks

 c The precision/accuracy is increased but... (1 mark)

  The range of possible numbers is decreased (1 mark)

Chapter 14

Progress check 14.01

1 Transport Communication Protocol

2 Application layer, Transport layer, Network layer, Link layer

3 HTTP, FTP, POP3, SMTP

Progress check 14.02

1 • IP address (Internet Protocol address) is the source and destination address given to every data packet on a packet-switched network.

• A port number identifies a process; standard port numbers are allocated to server applications, e.g. port 80 for a web server; port numbers above 1046 are allocated dynamically for the client computer process.

• A socket is formed when a connection is made by the transport layer.

2 The socket is the IP address and the port number. The transport layer sends packets to and from a process using a socket number.

Progress check 14.03

• Tracker computer – the computer which keeps a mapping of all the swarm hosts and which pieces of the file they possess

• Seed – the computer which has the entire file contents

• Swarm – the collection of participating computers

Progress check 14.04

1 168.13

2 168.13.13

Progress check 14.05

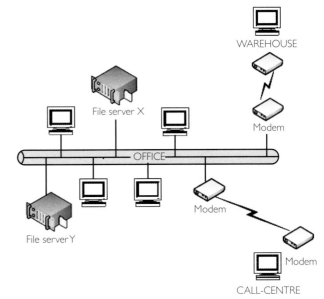

Exam-style questions

1 a Application Layer (1 mark)

  Transport Layer (1 mark)

  Internet Layer (1 mark)

 b Two answers accepted from:

  Ethernet (1 mark)

  token ring (1 mark)

  fibre optic (1 mark)

 c i network ID: the ID common to all computers on a network (1 mark)

   host ID: the unique ID of a particular computer on a network (1 mark)

  ii 205 = 11001101 (1 mark)

   It starts with 110, so it is a Class C address (1 mark)

  iii network ID: 205.123.4 (1 mark)

   host ID: 192 (1 mark)

Chapter 15

Progress check 15.01

Input		Output	
A	**B**	**Sum**	**Carry**
0	0	0	0
0	1	1	0
1	0	1	0
1	1	1	1

Progress check 15.02

1 $A.\overline{B}$

2 $\overline{C.D + \overline{D}}$

3 $\overline{P + Q + R.R}$

Progress check 15.03

1 $\overline{\overline{A+B}C}$

Progress check 15.04

1

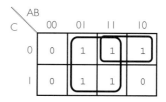

Input		Output
A	1	
1	1	1
0	1	1

2 $A + 1 = 1$

Progress check 15.05

1 A. B

2 A. B. D

3 A. C

4 P. Q

5 A

6 $A + B.\overline{C}$

Progress check 15.06

1

A	B	NOT A	NOT B	NOT (A OR B) = A NOR B	NOT A AND NOT B
0	0	1	1	1	1
0	1	1	0	0	0
1	0	0	1	0	0
1	1	0	0	0	0

2 This suggests a second form of De Morgan's law: $\overline{(A+B)} = \overline{A}.\overline{B}$

Progress check 15.07

1 $A.\overline{B}$

2 $\overline{A} + B$

3 A. B

Progress check 15.08

1 B + A. C

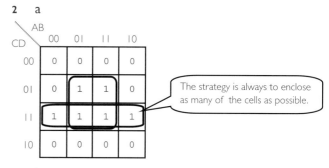

2 a

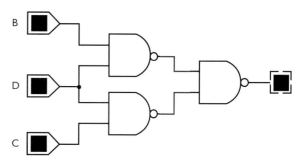

The strategy is always to enclose as many of the cells as possible.

b C.D + B. D

c This can be written as: $\overline{\overline{C.D}.\overline{B.D}}$ using De Morgan's law. The Boolean expression is then made up of NAND expressions.

Progress check 15.09

The second instruction needs the value in register R3. If instruction 1 has not completed, this value is not available to instruction 2.

Exam-style questions

1 a $X = A.(\overline{A} + \overline{B})$ (3 marks)

   b $X = A.A.\overline{B}$
   $X = A.\overline{A} + A.\overline{B}$
   $X = 0 + A.\overline{B}$
   $X = A.\overline{B}$ (3 marks)

   c The logic circuit has:
   - 1 AND gate and 1 NOT gate   (1 marks)
   - input to one NOT gate is B   (1 marks)
   - inputs to AND gate are A and output from NOT gate   (3 marks)

   d

A	B	X	Y
0	0	0	0
0	1	0	1
1	0	0	1
1	1	1	0

1 mark per correct row   Total 4 marks

   e half adder   (1 mark)

Chapter 16

Progress check 16.01

- Fixed partitions
- Dynamic partitions
- Paging

Progress check 16.02

1. A RUNNING process changes to RUNNABLE when it is interrupted.
2. A SUSPENDED process changes to RUNNABLE when it completes a sequence of disk read operations.
3. A RUNNABLE process changes to RUNNING when given use of the processor.
4. A RUNNING process changes to SUSPENDED when it has to wait for input.

Progress check 16.03

- User
- Estimated run-time
- Estimated run-time remaining
- Resources the process will require

Progress check 16.04

1.
   a. FALSE – an interpreter has better diagnostic features.
   b. FALSE – once compiled the compiler is not needed to execute the program.
   c. FALSE – no object file is produced using an interpreter.
   d. TRUE –both the source program and the interpreter must be in main memory.
   e. TRUE
   f. FALSE – an interpreter stops execution as soon as the first error is found.
   g. TRUE
   h. FALSE – compiler software is language specific; the compiler for a Pascal program is different from the compiler used for any other high-level language.

2.
   a.

Identifier	Data type	Memory address
Index	INTEGER	9873
Product	INTEGER	9875

   b. ■^9873=1■ ■ ^9875=^9873*^9873

Progress check 16.05

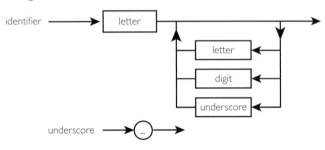

Progress check 16.06

1.
   a. Valid
   b. Invalid (there is no definition for digit 5)
   c. Valid
2.
   a. Valid
   b. Valid
   c. Invalid (a list cannot end with a comma)
   d. Invalid (no definition for the digits)

Progress check 16.07

Tracing the algorithm should give the values output in the order:

$$(3 \times p + 5) / (p - z)$$

Progress check 16.08

1.
   a. 25
   b. 3
   c. 64
   a. a b + 6 /
   b. 2 a * b + 3 ^

Progress check 16.09

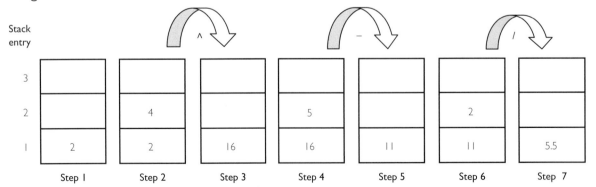

Exam-style questions

1 a Two from the following:

an object file (1 mark)

reports all errors (1 mark)

symbol table (1 mark)

b Two from the following:

The entire program does not have to be written before an attempt can be made to execute it (1 mark)

Program development likely to be faster (1 mark)

Better diagnostics (1 mark)

c Three from the following:

The compiler will make reference to meta-language statements (e.g. BNF) (1 mark)

The statements describe all possible forms of construction for each keyword (1 mark)

Similar meta-language rules exist for permitted identifier names (1 mark)

Errors is either the statement composition or identifier names are reported (1 mark)

d Two from the following:

Linker software ...

... links segments of code (1 mark)

... which have been compiled independently (1 mark)

... needed when the programmer has developed program libraries (that can be used by many applications) (1 mark)

Loader software ...

... loads object/executable code into main memory (1 mark)

... is often a relocatable loader (1 mark)

2 a Three from the following:

Main memory is divided into page frames. (1 mark)

The program is divided into pages. (1 mark)

Only some of the program pages are loaded to start execution of the program. (1 mark)

The operating system must manage the allocation of pages to page frames. (1 mark)

The page (map) table shows the mapping of pages to page frames. (1 mark)

Chapter 17

Progress check 17.01

1 Add 32 to the contents of ACC.

2 OR #B0000 0100

The 'hash' symbol makes it clear this is the number (not an address) and the 'B' clarifies that it's in binary.

The instruction could alternatively have been written with a decimal number: #4.

Exam-style questions

1 a 1 message digest (1 mark)

2 hash (1 mark)

3 private (1 mark)

4 signature (1 mark)

5 public (1 mark)

b The message did not come from Raz. (1 mark)

The message was altered on its journey. (1 mark)

c Three answers accepted from:

Raz encrypts the message ... (1 mark)

using Tan's public key. (1 mark)

Tan decrypts the message ... (1 mark)

using her private key. (1 mark)

Chapter 18

Progress check 18.01

1 Add 32 to the contents of ACC.

2 OR #B0000 0100

The 'hash' symbol makes it clear this is the number (not an address) and the 'B' clarifies that it's in binary.

The instruction could alternatively have been written with a decimal number: #4.

Exam-style questions

1 a monitoring system (1 mark)

b temperature (1 mark)

humidity sensors (1 mark)

c i line 02 - 16 (1 mark)

line 16 - FALSE (1 mark)

ii Array `Extreme` is a 2D array where each row corresponds to one of the particular tank. (1 mark)

Columns 1 and 3 contain the minimum values for heat and humidity and Columns 2 and 4 contain the maximum values for heat and humidity (1 mark)

iii For both heat and humidity: tests to see whether current reading is lower than set minimum value (1 mark)

test to see whether current reading is higher than set maximum value (1 mark)

If value outside range then warning message is output (1 mark)

iv The loop causes a delay so that the conditions are not monitored constantly. (1 mark)

d LDD 0804 (2 marks)

OR #B00100000 (or written as OR #32) (2 marks)

STO 0804 (2 marks)

PART 4

Chapter 19

Progress check 19.01

1   The index position of the requested item
2   (index value) zero
3   Posn
4   Function

Progress check 19.02

1   `ThisArray[Middle] = ThisValue`
2   No

3   `Bottom > Top`
4   Top only: `Top ← Middle - 1`

Progress check 19.03

Your program code should match exactly the insert algorithm given in the text.

Progress check 19.04

1   The following solution has been written as a procedure with the name of the array and its upper bound passed as parameters. A procedure, `DisplayList`, has parameters for the name of the array and its upper bound.

```
Sub SelectionSort(ByVal AnyList() As Integer, ByVal UpperBound As Integer)
  Dim SortedListPosn, InsertPosn As Integer
  Dim Index, ShufflePosn As Integer
  Dim CurrentValue As Integer
  Dim InsertPosnFound As Boolean

  For Index = 2 To UpperBound
    CurrentValue = AnyList(Index)

    SortedListPosn = 1
    InsertPosnFound = False
    Do
      If CurrentValue > AnyList(SortedListPosn) Then
        SortedListPosn = SortedListPosn + 1
      Else
        InsertPosn = SortedListPosn
        InsertPosnFound = True
      End If
    Loop Until InsertPosnFound = True

    For ShufflePosn = Index To (InsertPosn + 1) Step -1
      AnyList(ShufflePosn) = AnyList(ShufflePosn - 1)
    Next
    AnyList(InsertPosn) = CurrentValue
  Next

  Call DisplayList(AnyList, UpperBound)
```

2

MyAnimals

	1	2	3	4	5
	DOG	CAT	RAT	EEL	BAT
	CAT	DOG	RAT	EEL	BAT
	CAT	DOG	RAT	EEL	BAT
	CAT	DOG	EEL	RAT	BAT
	BAT	CAT	DOG	EEL	RAT

Progress check 19.05

```
IF TOS = 0
    THEN
        OUTPUT "Stack is empty"
    ELSE
        OUTPUT MyStack[TOS]
        TOS ← TOS - 1
ENDIF
```

Progress check 19.06

1

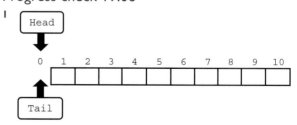

2 a 10

b `Head ← Head + 1`

3 It is stored at `MyQueue[Tail + 1]`

2 a Head = 0

b The queue has one item (note the queue is effectively 'reset' – Head=0 and Tail=0 – when it becomes empty)

3 You should have written program code in your chosen language for the `QueueJoin()` and `QueueLeave()` procedures.

Progress check 19.07

1 a 31

b If the queue is full for the first time, (Tail = 6 and Head=1), OR the queue has 'gone circular' and Head > Tail

c 38

Progress check 19.08

Start: 2

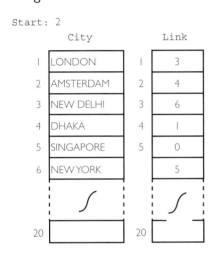

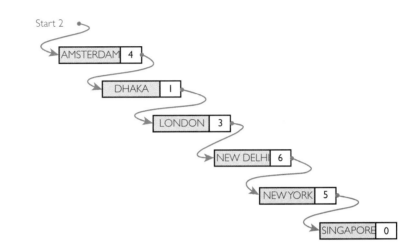

Progress check 19.09

1

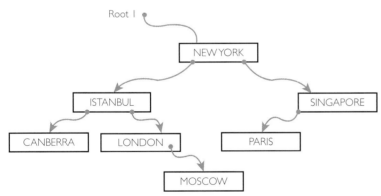

2

Root: 1

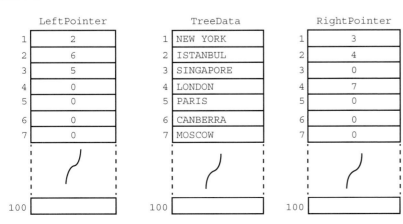

Progress check 19.10

The tree `Remove` needs to be told which item is to be removed from the tree. The value to be removed from a queue data structure is always the value at the head of the queue.

Progress check 19.11

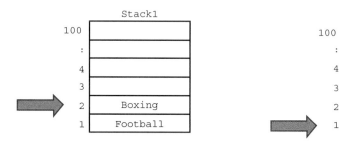

The arrow shows the 'top of stack' pointer for each stack.

Progress check 19.12

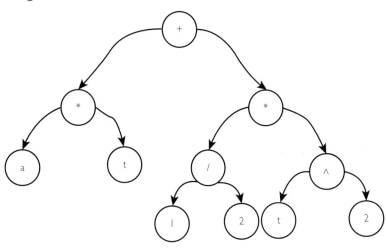

Exam-style questions

1 a
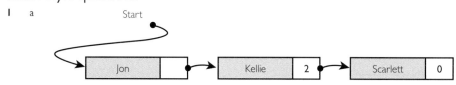

(2 marks)

b   TYPE ListNode
      Pointer   : INTEGER
      Name   : STRING
    ENDTYPE

(1 mark)
(1 mark)
(1 mark)

c   DECLARE NameList[1..50] OF ListNode

(2 marks)

d   i

HeadPointer
0

FreePointer
1

NameList

	Name	Pointer
[1]		2
[2]		3
[3]		4
[4]		5
:		
[49]		50
[50]		0

ii
```
FOR Index ← 1 TO 49
    NameList[Index].Pointer ← Index + 1
ENDFOR
NameList[50].Pointer ← 0
HeadPointer ← 0
FreePointer ← 1
```

Correct FOR loop

Correct setting of `Pointer[50]`, `HeadPointer` and `FreePointer`

(1 mark)

(1 mark)

2 a Class diagram needs:

noOfSeats declaration and associated show method in `PassengerVehicle`

inheritance arrows

constructor method in `Coach` class

seatBeltsFitted declaration and associated show method in `Coach` class

(1 mark)

(1 mark)

(1 mark)

(1 mark)

b Python

```python
class PassengerVehicle():
    def __init__(self, regNo, noOfSeats):
        # Sets all the initial values
        self.__regNo = regNo
        self.__noOfSeats = noOfSeats
    def showRegNo(self):
        print("Registration No: ",self.__regNo)
    def showNoOfSeats (self):
        print("No of seats: ",self.__noOfSeats)
```

Visual Basic

```vbnet
MustInherit Class PassengerVehicle
    Protected regNo As String
    Protected noOfSeats As Integer
    Public Sub showRegNo()
        Console.WriteLine(regNo)
    End Sub
    Public Sub showNoOfSeats()
        Console.WriteLine(noOfSeats)
    End Sub
End Class
```

Python

```python
class Bus(PassengerVehicle):
    def __init__(self, regNo, noOfSeats, maxStanding):
        super().__init__(regNo, noOfSeats)
        self.__maxStanding = maxStanding
    def showMaxStanding (self):
        print("No of standing passengers: ", self.__maxStanding)
```

Visual Basic

```vb
Class Bus
Inherits PassengerVehicle
    Private maxStanding As Integer
    Public Sub New(ByVal regNoValue As String,
                   ByVal noOfSeatsValue As Integer,
                   ByVal maxStandingValue As Integer)
        regNo = regNoValue
        noOfSeats = noOfSeatsValue
        maxStanding = maxStandingValue
    End Sub
    Public Sub ShowMaxStanding ()
        Console.WriteLine(maxStanding)
    End Sub
End Class
```

data declarations	(1 mark)
use of __ in identifiers to give "private" attribute	(1 mark)
use of 'self' parameter	(1 mark)
showRegNo function	(1 mark)
showNoOfSeats function	(1 mark)

Chapter 20

Progress check 20.01

Condition Rules >	1	2	3
Project is 'on time'	Y	N	N
More resources required?	–	N	Y
Action(s)			
Allocate more programmers to the project team			X
No action required	X	X	

Progress check 20.02

1

Condition(s) Rules >	1	2	4	5
Chemical is available	Y	Y	Y	N
Chemical is hazardous	–	Y	N	–
Staff is trained	Y	N	N	–
Action(s)				
Issue chemicals	X		X	–
Reject request		X		X

It might be clear that one or more of the original table entries can be a 'dash'. For example, if the chemical is not available, all four combinations can be consolidated to Rule 5 (the action is not influenced by the other two conditions).

2 a

Condition(s)　　　　Rules >	1	2	3	4	5	6	7	8
Cost > $ 1000	Y	Y	Y	Y	N	N	N	N
Destination USA	Y	Y	N	N	Y	Y	N	N
Child aged < = 3	Y	N	Y	N	Y	N	Y	N
Action(s)								
Pay for child						X	X	X
No charge	X	X	X	X	X			

b

Conditions(s)　　　Rules>	1	5	6	7
Cost > $1000	Y	N	N	N
Destination USA	–	Y	Y	N
Child aged < = 3	–	Y	N	–
Action(s)				
Pay for child			X	X
No charge	X	X		

Progress check 20.03

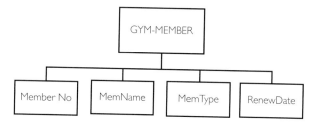

Progress check 20.04

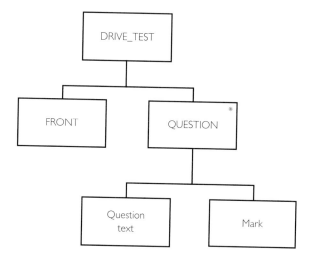

Progress check 20.05

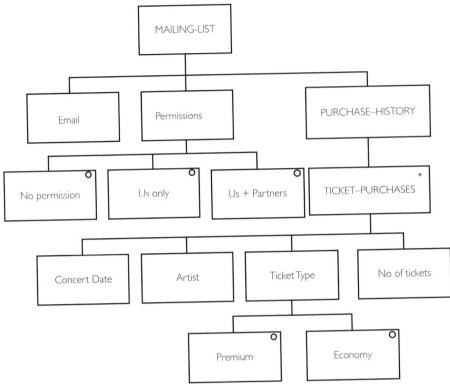

Progress check 20.06

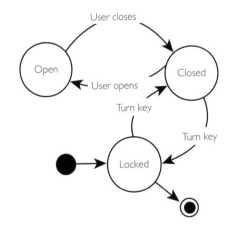

Progress check 20.07

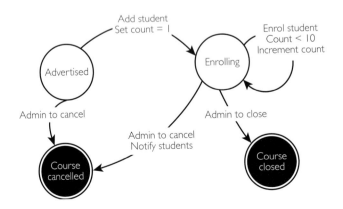

Exam-style questions

I a

Conditions		1	2	3	4	5	6	7	8
Conditions	Group 1 tests	Y	Y	Y	Y	N	N	N	N
	Group 2 tests	Y	Y	N	N	Y	Y	N	N
	Group 3 tests	Y	N	Y	N	Y	N	Y	N
Actions	Accepted	Y							
	Repair		Y	Y					
	Rejected				Y	Y	Y	Y	Y

correct column 1

correct columns 2 and 3

correct column 4

correct columns 5–8

(1 mark)
(1 mark)
(1 mark)
(1 mark)

b

Conditions		1	2	3	4	5
Conditions	Group 1 tests	Y	Y	Y	Y	N
	Group 2 tests	Y	Y	N	N	–
	Group 3 tests	Y	N	Y	N	–
Action	Accepted	Y				
	Repair		Y	Y		
	Rejected				Y	Y

correct column 1

correct column 2

correct column 3

correct column 4

correct column 5

(1 mark)
(1 mark)
(1 mark)
(1 mark)
(1 mark)

c Python

```
def Reject():
    If ((G1Tests() == True and G2Tests() == False
                        and G3Tests() == False)or G1Test() == False):
        return True
```

correct function header

correct if statement

correct return statement

(1 mark)
(1 mark)
(1 mark)

Chapter 21

Progress check 21.01

```
     WHILE: LDD COUNTER

            CMP #0

            JPE END

            OUT CHAR1

            OUT CHAR2

            OUT CHAR3

            LDD COUNTER

            DEC ACC

            JMP WHILE

  ENDWHILE: END


   COUNTER: 5

     CHAR1: 67              // ASCII code for C

     CHAR2: 65              // ASCII code for A

     CHAR3: 84              // ASCII code for T
```

Progress check 21.02

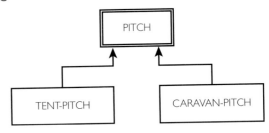

Progress check 21.03

The road tax is a property in the VEHICLE class and appears also in the COMMERCIAL subclass. This suggests that the road tax is calculated differently for some vehicles.

Progress check 21.04

1. a   Natene plays tennis (a 'fact').

    b   Y = golf

    c   A = natene; A = tadi

    d   `likes(ken, X) :- female(X)`
        `                 Or (male(X), plays(X, golf)).`

2. a   Malona is female.

    b   The parents of Chelo are Celia and Adan.

    c   Rule.

    d   X is a sibling of Y if Y is the sister of X or Y is the brother of X.

    e   i   Alano

        ii   X = Null; Y = Null (i.e. there is no fact which states the parents of Sofia)

Progress check 21.05

```
1  TYPE EmployeeData
       DECLARE Surname          : STRING
       DECLARE Initials         : STRING
       DECLARE EmployeeCode     : STRING
       DECLARE YearsService     : INTEGER
       DECLARE FullTimeEmployee : BOOLEAN
   ENDTYPE

2  DECLARE EmployeeArray : ARRAY[1:150] OF EmployeeData
```

Progress check 21.06

1 The algorithm assumes that the DeleteAnimalName record does exist in the original ANIMALS file.

```
OPEN the file for reading - ANIMALS
OPEN new file for writing - NEW-ANIMALS
INPUT DeleteAnimalName

REPEAT
   FILEREAD next record from ANIMALS (includes AnimalName)
   IF AnimalName = DeleteAnimalName
      THEN
          // do nothing
          Flag record is found
      ELSE
          Write this record to NEW-ANIMALS
   ENDIF
UNTIL record found

WHILE NOT EOF(Animals)
   FILEREAD next record
   FILEWRITE this record to NEW-ANIMALS
ENDWHILE

CLOSE both files

DELETE ANIMALS

RENAME NEW-ANIMALS as ANIMALS
```

2 This algorithm is very similar to the 'delete record' algorithm. It assumes that the AmendAnimalName record exists in the original ANIMALS file.

```
OPEN the file for reading - ANIMALS
OPEN new file for  writing - NEW-ANIMALS
INPUT AmendAnimalName
REPEAT
   FILEREAD next record from ANIMALS (includes AnimalName)
   IF AmendAnimalName = AnimalName
      THEN
       INPUT new data
       Flag record is found
         FILEWRITE the data to NEW-ANIMALS
    ELSE
         FILEWRITE the current record to NEWFILE
   ENDIF
UNTIL required record found

WHILE NOT EOF(ANIMALS)
   FILEREAD next record
   FILEWRITE this record to NEW-ANIMALS
ENDWHILE

CLOSE both files
DELETE ANIMALS
RENAME NEW-ANIMALS as ANIMALS
```

Exam-style questions

I a Rules are 15 and 25.   (1 mark)

  b i `Who = zhen`   (1 mark)

     `Who = kong`   (1 mark)

    ii `false`   (1 mark)

    iii `false`   (1 mark)

  c i `has_licence(X) AND passed_theory_Test(X) AND`
                          `passed_driving_test(X, motorbike)`

```
9 ?- passed_theory_test(Who), not(passed_driving_test(Who, car)),
 not(passed_driving_test(Who, motorbike)).
Who = yin ;
```

    ii OR *(using the anonymous variable)* ...

```
10 ?- passed_theory_test(Who), not(passed_driving_test(Who, _)).
Who = yin ;
```

Three answers accepted from: (3 marks)
each clause scores I   (1 mark)
use of two AND operators   Total: 4 marks

  d Three answers accepted from:

   `has_licence(ho)` returns TRUE or ... clause II   (1 mark)

   `age(ho, A)` returns 15 or ... A=15   (1 mark)

   `minimum_age(motorbike, L)` returns L=15 or ... clause 2   (1 mark)

   `A >= L` returns FALSE   (1 mark)

   `able_to_drive(ho, motorbike)` returns FALSE (I mark)

                                                                                     Total: 4 marks

Chapter 22

Progress check 22.01

It has an infinite loop.

Progress check 22.02

Person	Quarter	Target[Person, Quarter]	NewArray [1]	NewArray [1]	NewArray [1]	NewArray [1]
	I		0			
	2			0		
	3				0	
	4					0
I	I	TRUE				
	2	FALSE		I		
	3	TRUE				
	4	FALSE				I
2	I	FALSE	I			
	2	FALSE		2		
	3	TRUE				
	4	TRUE				
3	I	FALSE	2			
	2	FALSE		3		
	3	FALSE			I	
	4	FALSE				2

`NewArray` is storing, for each quarter, the number of sales staff (0, 1, 2 or 3) who did not meet their target for that quarter.

Progress check 22.03

Normal data: integers in the range 1 to 10 inclusive

Boundary data: values 1 and 10

Invalid data: 0, 11 and over, any 'non-integer' data value (e.g. a real number or string)

Progress check 22.04

No, because they are both tasks on the critical path.

Exam-style questions

1   a

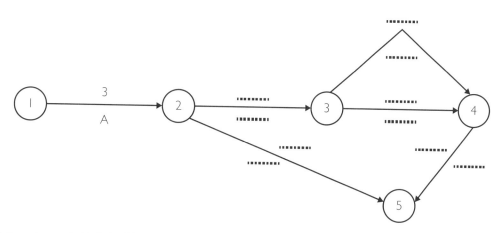

I mark for each correctly labelled activity   (Max. 4 marks)

b   i   1 – 2 – 3 – 7 – 6   (1 mark)

    ii   20 weeks   (1 mark)

c   i   8 weeks   (1 mark)

    ii   16 weeks   (1 mark)

Index